LIVES AND LETTERS

A series of diaries and letters, journals and

WILLIAM ALLINGHAM

A DIARY

William Allingham was born in Ballyshannon, Ireland, in 1824, into a Protestant family. After seven unhappy years in a bank he became a customs officer, working initially in Ireland and later in Lymington. But his first love was poetry and between 1850 and 1887 he produced twelve volumes of verse, gaining popular recognition in 1854 with the publication of *Day and Night Songs*. Allingham paid his first visit to London in 1847; four years later he started a lifelong friendship with Tennyson, the central figure in his diary. For a time he was a member of the Rossetti circle and he also wrote for Leigh Hunt's *London Journal*. He counted among his friends many distinguished men and women of the age, among them Thomas Carlyle, Yeats, and the photographer Mrs Cameron. In 1874 he married Helen Paterson, an illustrator, who bore him two children. William Allingham died in Hampstead in 1889.

John Julius Norwich was born in 1929. He was educated at Upper Canada College, Toronto, at Eton, at the University of Strasbourg and, after a spell of National Service in the Navy, at New College, Oxford, where he took a degree in French and Russian. In 1952 he joined the Foreign Office and remained in it for twelve years, serving at the Embassies in Belgrade and Beirut and with the British delegation to the Disarmament Conference at Geneva. In 1964 he resigned from the service in order to write.

He has published two books on the medieval Norman kingdom in Sicily, *The Normans in the South* and *The Kingdom in the Sun*; two travel-cum-history books, *Mount Athos* (with Reresby Sitwell) and *Sahara*; and an anthology of poetry and prose, *Christmas Crackers*. The first volume of his history of the Venetian Republic, *Venice, the Rise to Empire*, was published in 1977, and the second, *Venice, the Greatness and the Fall*, in 1981. In addition he writes and presents historical documentaries for BBC television.

Lord Norwich is chairman of the Venice in Peril Fund, a trustee of the Civic Trust, and a member of the Executive and Properties Committees of the National Trust. He is also a member of the Liberal Party in the House of Lords.

WILLIAM ALLINGHAM

A DIARY

EDITED BY

H. ALLINGHAM AND D. RADFORD

INTRODUCTION BY

JOHN JULIUS NORWICH

PENGUIN BOOKS

Penguin Books Ltd, Harmondsworth, Middlesex, England
Viking Penguin Inc., 40 West 23rd Street, New York, New York 10010, U.S.A.
Penguin Books Australia Ltd, Ringwood, Victoria, Australia
Penguin Books Canada Ltd, 2801 John Street, Markham, Ontario, Canada L3R 1B4
Penguin Books (N.Z.) Ltd, 182–190 Wairau Road, Auckland 10, New Zealand

First published 1907
Published with minor revisions by Centaur Press 1967
Published in Penguin Books 1985

Reproduced, printed and bound in Great Britain by
Hazell Watson & Viney Limited,
Member of the BPCC Group,
Aylesbury, Bucks

INTRODUCTION

It must be getting on for twenty years since I first discovered William Allingham's Diary. Before then, his name had been faintly familiar to me as the author of 'The Fairies' ('Up the airy mountain, Down the rushy glen'), surely the most embarrassing poem ever to have found its way into *The Oxford Book of English Verse*; but this scarcely seemed a recommendation and I had no particular desire for a closer acquaintance. The Diary, however—and I only wish I could remember how I came across it—was a revelation; within a quarter of an hour I knew that I had in my hands one of those books that would be a favourite for life, one that I should automatically buy whenever I chanced to see a copy in a second-hand shop, one that I would spend my life lending or giving away to all those friends whom I could trust to relish it as I did. Almost immediately, I copied the first extract into my commonplace book. It was the entry for Sunday, 28 June 1863: 'In the evening walked sadly along the shore of the Solent eastwards by Pylewell—returning, brought home a glow-worm and put it in a white lily, through which it shone.' Before I laid down the book, that passage had been joined by a dozen more. I know of no volume of comparable size that has yielded, to a compulsive commonplace-collector like myself, so rich and copious a harvest.

But diaries are the most personal form of literature, and if we are to enjoy them to the full we must first know something about their authors. William Allingham was a Protestant

v

Irishman of the middle class, born on 19 March 1824, in the little port of Ballyshannon, County Donegal. His father was a reasonably successful though chronically bad-tempered merchant, an importer of various commodities—chiefly timber—from Canada and the Baltic, his mother an invalid who died when he was nine; he readily admits at the beginning of the Diary that in his early childhood he felt no affection for either of them, 'or for anybody else'—a surprising confession for a man whose friendships were to afford some of the greatest pleasures of his life. He himself, after seven unhappy years in a bank, eventually managed to secure for himself a position in Her Majesty's Customs; and it was as a Customs Officer, first in Ireland and later at Lymington in Hampshire, that he spent the next quarter of a century, retiring only in 1870 to devote himself to literature. This was not a major change of direction. Poetry had always been his first love, and was to remain his consuming passion until he died. He had written verses since his childhood, and one often suspects as one reads the Diary that even during his years in the public service he was devoting at least as much time to his literary pursuits as he was to his professional duties.

How good was he as a poet? Despite the evidence of *The Oxford Book*, he seems to me to come about halfway up the second league. His *Day and Night Songs*, first published in 1854 when he was thirty, had considerable success and actually went into a second edition in the following year, revised and extended and boasting superb illustrations by his friends Dante Gabriel Rossetti, John Everett Millais and Arthur Hughes; while the work which he himself always considered to be his masterpiece—a long epic poem in heroic couplets entitled *Laurence Bloomfield in Ireland* describing the efforts of a young Irish landlord to raise local standards to a level comparable with those that he had known in England—had the distinction of being quoted by Mr Gladstone in the House of Commons within six weeks of its publication. It must be admitted that the couplet selected by the future Prime Minister—and transcribed in the Diary entry for 31 May 1864—is hardly likely to have impressed his audience with the power of its author's genius; but Gladstone went on to describe the work as 'extremely clever', later even inviting the poet to breakfast; and not long afterwards Allingham received (on the recommendation of Palmerston) a Civil List pension of £60 a year. Meanwhile no less a critic than Ivan Turgenev—who had tackled a roughly comparable theme in his own prose *Sportsman's Sketches*—had confessed after reading it: 'I never understood Ireland before.'

Few people plough through the five thousand-odd lines of *Laurence Bloomfield* for pleasure today, and fewer still would suggest that it had appreciably increased their comprehension of the Emerald Isle. Rather more, perhaps, turn from time to time to Allingham's shorter lyrics; but despite the assurance of his technique and the occasional memorable line ('Shoots the dark lightning of a swallow's wing', perhaps, or 'Like slumber on a mind still half-awake') the poet's ear seems all too often to betray him. Couplets such as

> O come hither! weeks together let us watch the big Atlantic,
> Blue or purple, green or gurly, dark or shining, smooth or frantic,

do little to increase his reputation; nor is it easy to take entirely seriously any poem beginning with the lines

> Ring-ting! I wish I were a Primrose
> A bright yellow Primrose blowing in the Spring!

Yet his friend Tennyson remarked that Allingham had 'a true spirit of song in him', while his poem *The Music Maker* was described by Rossetti as being 'just too noble' and by Coventry Patmore as 'the most touching poem I know'. Among his less distinguished contemporaries, too, he was generally admired and widely read. Clearly—comparing him only with his compatriots—he cannot hold a candle to Thomas Moore, born forty-five years before him, still less to W. B. Yeats, forty-one years his junior; but as a poet of Ireland—and his poetry, unlike much of his prose, is quintessentially Irish—he is not to be despised.

As a diarist, on the other hand, he is superb. He writes for himself only (he was, until his late marriage, a very lonely man) and often in note form—just a few words jotted down, vii one imagines, on the spur of the moment to catch a mood, an impression, even a fleeting thought. Take, for example, the entry for 9 January 1866: 'Ride to Brockenhurst—sudden snowstorm, careering between the trees and across the road like a charge of wild cavalry; wraps us in winter, clears off.' Or his visit to Winchester on 30 August: 'In the Chapel, bad glass in imitation of old. To Dining Hall by outside stairs, bread and butter on square slab of wood, beer *and tea* (a modern innovation) . . . Under gateway and out. Old walls, then clear brisk river, little houses with gardens, bridge, St Giles's with little red-tiled steeple-spire,—wide space. High Street, the downs rising beyond.'

And was anyone ever better at sketching a character in a few lines? On 16 September 1863 he heard Cardinal Wiseman lecture in Southampton: 'An Irish priest, he, in general appearance; face like a shrewish old woman in spectacles; voice tuneless, accent a little mincing. The substance of the lecture commonplace, the style tawdry and paltry.' His portrait of Rossetti, too, is unforgettable:

R. walks very characteristically, with a peculiar lounging gait, often trailing the point of his umbrella on the ground, but still obstinately pushing on and making way, he humming the while with closed teeth, in the intervals of talk, not a tune or anything like one but what sounds like a *sotto voce* note of defiance to the Universe. Then suddenly he will fling himself down somewhere and refuse to stir an inch further. His favourite attitude—on his back, one knee raised, hands behind head. On a sofa he often, too, curls himself up like a cat.

Best of all, for me, is this impression of the novelist Ouida (Louise de la Ramée): 'In green silk, sinister clever face, hair down, small hands and feet, voice like a carving knife.'

Yet the reason why William Allingham's Diary will live as one of the most enjoyable journals in all English literature is not so much for its sketches of character, brilliant as these frequently are; it is for the anecdotes. To any really inspired *raconteur*, two things are essential: an ear for dialogue and a sense of humour. In Allingham, both were faultless. Furthermore, he possessed the additional advantage of knowing— often extremely well—virtually all the leading writers and many of the most prominent painters of his day. Browning and Burne-Jones, George Eliot and Leigh Hunt, Swinburne and Ruskin and William Morris, even distinguished foreigners like Emerson and Hans Andersen when they pass through London, all throng his pages; one sometimes wonders whether he ever paid a social call (an activity which occupied a good deal of his life) without coming upon at least one such luminary. Two great names, however, stand out above all the rest: those of Thomas Carlyle and Alfred Tennyson.

Allingham had known Carlyle from the early 1850s — they seem to have been introduced by Leigh Hunt — and remained a close friend until the old man's death in 1881. They often went for walks together, despite the attendant dangers: 'We walk to Hyde Park, dodging the carriages sometimes, at risk. (He may catch his death thus, for he usually insists on crossing when he has made up his mind to it, carrying his stick so as to poke it into a horse's nose at need.)' Carlyle's conversation, too, is marvellously caught:

> After this we spoke of Historians. 'Ranke a diligent man, gave much about diplomacies useful in its way, no picture of men or things. He hangs up a kind of — well — a gray shadow, you might say, like an Ossian ghost, 'the stars dim twinkling through.' Macaulay like a Russian Steppe — green enough, but not a rock or tree to break the monotony.'
> I. — 'Macaulay tried to make an effect by style.'
> C. (smiling). — 'Then we can only say he did not succeed.'

But the figure that looms largest over the whole Diary is that of Allingham's hero, Tennyson. As early as 1846 we find the young Customs Officer in Belfast reciting *Locksley Hall* to the clerks, and on a visit to London five years later his friend Coventry Patmore arranges for him to go and call on the great man at Twickenham. Tennyson receives him warmly and delights him by reading aloud two of the poems from Allingham's first published volume. On his second visit in 1853 he met Edward Fitzgerald, but was otherwise less fortunate: 'I spilt some port on the cloth, and T., with his usual imperturbability spread salt on it, remarking as he did so, "I believe it never comes out!" Then we went upstairs to tea.'

Their friendship has a chance to ripen only after Allingham's appointment to Lymington in 1863, when he found himself only a few miles from Farringford, the Tennysons' house at Freshwater on the Isle of Wight. It continued, virtually unclouded, until Allingham's own death in 1889. This Diary provides the best account we have of Tennyson's manner and conversation; and Allingham, in recording it, never misses a trick. On 3 February 1867 they are walking together along the cliffs: 'I said (walking close behind him) "suppose I were to slip and catch hold of you, and we both rolled down together," on which T. stopped and said, "you'd better go on first." '

Most enjoyable of all is the poet's compulsive teasing of his neighbour, the pioneer photographer Mrs Julia Margaret Cameron:

Tea: enter Mrs Cameron (in a funny red open-work shawl) with two of her boys. T. reappears, and Mrs C. shows a small firework toy called 'Pharaoh's Serpents,' a kind of pastile, which, when lighted, twists about in a worm-like shape. Mrs C. said they were poisonous and forbade us all to touch. T. in defiance put out his hand.

'Don't touch 'em!' shrieked Mrs C. 'You sha'n't, Alfred!' But Alfred did. 'Wash your hands then!' But Alfred wouldn't, and rubbed his moustache instead, enjoying Mrs C.'s agonies. Then she said to him: 'Will you come to-morrow and be photographed?' He, very emphatically, 'No.'

The extracts quoted above form only a minute sample from a diary which—if we include Allingham's short memoir of his childhood and youth, plus the occasional interpolations to cover periods when he did not write which were added by his widow when she prepared the work for publication in 1907—extends over a whole lifetime; but they are, I hope, enough to give the flavour of the whole. What they do not show is the astonishing skill with which the writer selected his material. Most of us, if we attempt to chronicle our daily lives, painstakingly record our activities of morning, afternoon and evening; for Allingham, however, a scrap of conversation or a sudden visual impression ('the Moon rose like a surprise') was of infinitely greater importance than the humdrum events that filled his day. And how right he was! There are many published diaries that are more detailed, many that are more profound, and any number that are of greater value to historians. But there are few indeed that are livelier, or more consistently entertaining.

What was he like as a man? In recent years Allingham has been presented to us—when he has been written about at all—as a slightly pathetic figure: one who hovered on the fringes of the literary world of which he so longed to be a part, one who was content to be patronized and humiliated by the giants around him so long as he was allowed to remain within their shadow. Nothing, I believe, could be further from the truth. He was, admittedly, a cultural snob. He shamelessly sought out the great and famous writers of his day and cultivated their acquaintance. But if he was shameless it was because he saw no reason to be ashamed; his love of literature was deep and genuine—what could be more natural than to seek out those who shared that love, in whose company he could be happy and from whose experience he might learn?

He gave, moreover, as much as he received. He was amusing, well read, and utterly without pomposity. If he talked half as well as he wrote his diary, he must have been a delightful companion. Why then should we assume, as Mr Geoffrey Grigson has suggested, that he was a bore whose presence was to be endured rather than enjoyed? 'Mr Allingham is coming up the drive. Mr Allingham is in the house. I suppose we must ask Mr Allingham to dinner, or to stop the night.' Was it really so? As the Diary makes plain, his literary friends invited him again and again: whether it was the Tennysons at Farringford or the Carlyles in Cheyne Row, they would not have done so had they not been glad to see him. 'Here comes Mr Allingham, how very delightful. Let us by all means invite him to dinner, or indeed to stay as long as he chooses. Life is always more pleasant when Mr Allingham is of the company.' To me at least, that would seem a more probable scenario. A lion hunter he may have been, but his lions loved him.

John Julius Norwich

PREFACE TO THE 1907 EDITION

During the last ten years of his life at our quiet home in Surrey my Husband began, in the intervals of his literary work, to write his Autobiography.

I find in one of his note-books this memorandum: 'There are two tenable theories of Life, and consequently of Autobiography:

One: accept a set of conventional rules and abide by them.

Two—admit your limitations, attend to what interests you and try always to be sincere.'

Readers of this book will decide for themselves which of these lines my Husband followed—both in his life and in describing it.

Unfortunately, he wrote in detailed narrative only of the period dealing with his childhood, and some later portions—such as the accounts of his intercourse with Carlyle and Tennyson: nothing was left ready for publication

*   *   *

The different portions of the Autobiography are placed in chronological order, with the extracts from the diaries and note-books—the final selection of these from the large mass of material has been the subject of my anxious consideration for many years.

The responsibility of the publication rests with me alone

Helen Allingham

CONTENTS

PUBLISHER'S NOTE

THIS edition, edited by H. Allingham and D. Radford, was published in 1907. It is now reissued in its entirety, further editing being confined to literals and to the deletion of some notes that are now irrelevant.

CHAPTER I

1824–1846

THE little old Town where I was born has a Voice of its own, low, solemn, persistent, humming through the air day and night, summer and winter. Whenever I think of that Town I seem to hear the Voice. The River which makes it, rolls over rocky ledges into the tide ; before, spreads a great Ocean in sunshine or storm ; behind, stretches a many-islanded Lake. On the south runs a wavy line of blue Mountains ; and on the north, over green or rocky hills, rise peaks of a more distant range. The trees hide in glens, or cluster near the river ; gray rocks and boulders lie scattered about the windy pastures. The sky arches wide over all, giving room to multitudes of stars by night, and long processions of clouds blown from the sea ; but also, in the childish memory where these pictures live, to deeps of celestial blue in the endless days of summer.

An odd, out-of-the-way little Town, ours, on the extreme western verge of Europe ; our next neighbours, sunset way, being citizens of the great New Republic, which indeed, to our imagination, seemed little if at all further off than England in the opposite direction.

I was born in a little House, the most westerly of a row of three, in a street running down to the Harbour. Opposite was a garden wall, with rose-bushes hanging over. If I can remember anything of this first house, which perhaps I cannot, it is the top of the kitchen stairs at the end of the passage, and the dark unknown abyss below. My first appearance in this odd sort of world was in the blustery month of March, two days after the festival of Ireland's patron saint.

From the House that I was born in we moved to one somewhat larger, two doors eastward, when I was one year and four months old, and lived there a little more than two years. Of this second House I certainly retain many impressions. A picture of the Sitting Room, with its darkish carpet of geometric pattern, and its ruddy fire, its window, door, table, chairs, and sofa, in certain relative positions, is dimly revivable. The two or three steps at the front door, and the longer flight leading down into the kitchen, are indented, as it were, on my memory. Steps and stairs are very remarkable objects to most children, I should think, in their earlier stages in the art of walking. A sense of toil and danger is connected with them,—and of awe ; they are something like what Alpine precipices are to grown-up people.

And when this state of mind is gradually overcome, it blends with the triumphant feeling of power in mounting and descending these difficult heights, and penetrating at will new regions in the remotest recesses of the House.

An early expedition of mine down the kitchen stairs led me into a piece of ill-luck, the consequences of which, trivial as it seemed at the time, have woven themselves into the whole texture of my life, have sensibly lessened its whole share of pleasure and added to it daily and almost hourly vexations. I had crept down the back-stairs to the kitchen, and was pattering across the stone floor, unnoticed by a woman busily engaged in ' getting up ' some of the household linen. She snatched a ' flat-iron ' which had been standing in front of the fire, and, turning quickly round to carry it to the smoothing table, encountered Little Me unlucky !—nor was she able to check herself soon enough to keep the hot iron from touching my left eye. General agitation followed,

no doubt. I had to spend some days in a darkened
room, and compared myself (Aunt Bess told me afterwards) to old Isaac, whose eyes were dim, so that he
could not see.

The effect of this accident on my sight was not discovered for years afterwards ; its effects on my comfort
and character no one knows or even suspects but
myself.

While in this house, I received a small box of water-
colour paints (I have it still) from my god-mother,
Mrs. Jane Dixon. I was seated one day at the parlour
table in my little arm-chair, screwed on to the top of
its table to bring it to a proper height, and with paint-
box, brushes, and cup of water, was dabbing and daub-
ing away on various pieces of paper, to the envy of a
playfellow, who was at the same table, but had only
some bright coloured picture books for his share—a
tame amusement compared to painting one's own
pictures. My mother or nurse hinted that I might
share the use of the paint-box with my companion, but
the sense of property was too strong, and I refused.
When it appeared that the loan would be disagreeable
to me, no more was said : but then I began to turn the
matter over in my mind, and secretly bethought me—
' We shall all have to die in a few years ; it is not worth
while saving up these paints so carefully '—and I intimated my willingness to lend them. There was no sort
of moral notion in it ; and as to how I first got the
impression of death, I have no clue. It was very likely
by means of 'the dead-bell,' which tolled for funerals,
and whose every slow stroke, in the Church tower on
the hill, used to sound through the sleepy little Town,
and in later years of youth, to smite upon my heart.

It may easily have been among the first things to
awaken a child's curious questionings. The notion of
Death at this earlier time was not associated, as far as I
can recall, with the slightest dread or awe, or feeling of
any kind except that (which is perhaps one of the last

3

we should suspect in a child of three years old) of the transitory character of all human possessions.

Later, at the age perhaps of six or seven, I was for a time fully possessed with the conviction that *I should never die*—that I, for one, must in some way or other escape death. No reasoning led up to this idea, and no effort, voluntary or involuntary, was made to define the mode of exemption or the consequences. There was simply a perception of a fact which had become apparent—as of a mountain on the horizon on an exceptionally clear day, new, dim, but undeniable,—the fact that *I should not die*; nor did I take much notice of it,—there it was; and when the mental atmosphere gradually changed, it was invisible again.

In my fourth year (autumn of 1827) our family changed house again; father, mother, myself, and a sister a year and a half younger. The move was only across the street, but the new abode, known as The Cottage, had a character of its own. It was an irregularly built house of two stories, with the general shape of the letter L, standing among gardens and shrubberies. The front and the south gable were half-covered with clematis, which embowered the parlour windows in summer; and some wall-trained evergreen fringed the one window of the Nursery with dark sharply-cut leaves, in company with a yellow blossoming *Pyrus japonica*. Opposite the hall door, a good-sized Walnut Tree growing out of a small grassy knoll leaned its wrinkled stem towards the house, and brushed some of the second-story panes with its broad fragrant leaves. To sit at that little upper-floor window (it belonged to a lobby) when it was open to a summer twilight, and the great Tree rustled gently and sent one leafy spray so far that it even touched my face, was an enchantment beyond all telling. Killarney, Switzerland, Venice could not, in later life, come near it.

On three sides the Cottage looked on flowers and branches, which I count as one of the fortunate chances

4

of my childhood,—the sense of natural beauty thus receiving its due share of nourishment, and of a kind suitable to those early years. Grandeur of scenery is lost on a young child; I doubt if any landscape impresses him, however impressionable. Little things, close at hand, make his pleasures and troubles. I was enchanted with our flower-beds and little shrubberies; and in a grass-field to which we were sometimes brought, a quarter of a mile away, there was a particular charm in two or three gray rocks encrusted with patches of moss; but of the distant view of the Atlantic Ocean I took no notice at this time.

My Father was fond of flowers and we had a good show of all the old-fashioned kinds in their seasons. I loved the violet and lily of the valley, and above all the rose—all roses, and we had many sorts, damask, cabbage, 'Scotch,' moss, and white roses in multitude on a great shady bush that overhung the little street at our garden-foot. The profusion of these warm-scented white roses gave a great feeling of summer wealth and joy, but my constant favourite was the 'Monthly Rose,' in colour and fragrance the acme of sweetness and delicacy combined, and keeping up, even in winter time, its faithful affectionate companionship.

Before the front door grew my dear Walnut Tree out of its little mound, beyond which the narrow drive curved in something of a figure of S to the stable and byre, its little shrubbery on either side shady enough with lilacs and laburnums to yield forest haunts to the childish fancy. Two or three fig-trees there were also, whose fruit swelled but never ripened; and their crooked boughs were chiefly interesting as perches, from which strange altitudes one could look down on the household traffic, horse and foot. Near the north shrubbery's edge grew tufts of daffodil, and at one place it was overhung by a tall gable thickly clad with ancient ivy. This gable did not appertain to us; its one little window high up, nearly buried in dark leaves, belonged to an inscrutable and most mysterious interior. The Great Pyramid could not give me, in later life, so profound a sense of antiquity and awfulness as this old hay-barn gave to the little boy.

Our own more familiar outhouses were highly interesting, each in its own way; the stable for my father's one or two horses, where perpetual twilight reigned and characteristic odours, with its forks and curry-combs, slope-lidded corn-bin, and trap-door to the hay-loft above; next the stable, the harness-room, and over this an apple-loft, of most memorable fragrancy; a little higher up the yard, the byre with its two or three deliberate-stepping, sweet-breathed cows, and another loft; and close by in a corner the little stable, wood with thatched roof, of Sheltie, the brown-bear-like pony with long mane and tail, which I rode, and whose eccentricities gave birth to most exciting personal adventures. He was fond of standing nearly bolt upright on his hind legs, when I was fain to hug his thick mane. He often had views of his own as to the best road to take, and, suddenly refusing to move forward, would turn round and round like a wheel, then abruptly gallop off in the direction of his stable. One eventful day when I was riding Sheltie about our home limits one of the gates happened to be open, and we passed out unobserved into the street where the pony immediately quickened his pace and, taking the law into his own hands, carried me out of the town and along country roads into a wild unknown region. If I had any alarm or misgiving the joy of novelty overcame it, yet there was a sense of relief when my self-willed steed stopped before the field gate of a farm of my father's about two miles out, which I then recognised, having visited it in his gig once or twice before. The pony had been there at grass and recollected his good times. The cottagers ran out with many exclamations of wonder at sight of us, and one of them, holding Sheltie's bridle, brought me home again, full of a delightful sense of adventure and the importance of having been missed.

[1] My Father had this small farm on lease, and also a large field near the town, called 'The Big Meadow,' in which grazing was let to some neighbours' milch cows along with our own ; but he was not a farmer, and his agricultural produce went mainly to supply his own family and my grandmother's, the surplus being sold.

His business was that of a merchant — a wide designation, and in his case applicable enough ; he imported timber, slates, coal and iron, and owned at various times five or six ships, trading chiefly to Canada and the Baltic for timber. There were no exports, save now and again of human beings to Quebec. The emigration was small then to what it became in after years, but enough to make 'going to Ameriky' one of the most familiar phrases in daily life. My father went out every morning to his office, which was on the other side of the street from our house, and seldom returned till dinner time, half-past four. This and other household facts I became aware of by their recurrence, but took little or no note of them. Every child rates things for himself. Curiosity, mixed with imagination and the love of beauty, was naturally strong in me ; but even at this early age, unless I am mistaken, it sought its food in the interests and characteristics belonging to nature and life in general ; or rather say that, while rapidly and vividly receptive of all kinds of novel impressions, I strove unfailingly and quite unconsciously to group them according to some principle, refer them to some ideal—though it must be owned that, in the first decade of one's earthly career, principles and ideals are usually of an unsubstantial fantastic sort.

The persons moving around me were as *personæ* merely, and in and for themselves individually interested

---

[1] The Allinghams had migrated from England and settled at Ballyshannon, Co. Donegal, in the time of Elizabeth.

me little or nothing. I intend all through this record to avoid 'philosophising,' and give recollections and impressions as simply as may be. What it indicated (if anything special) I know not to this hour, but in these first years I do not remember to have felt any emotion of affection either for my parents or for anybody else. Caresses (if that is to be taken into account) I never had any share of from my parents; they were both undemonstrative in that way by nature, and my mother's constant invalidism and my father's hasty temper kept us children at a distance from both. Yet, coldness was never reckoned one of my faults, and later, say from twelve years old, my attachments to persons were warm and constant.

I dimly recollect my mother as thin, pale, delicate, gentle in voice and movement, with soft dark hair and an oval face slightly sun-freckled. She was kind, sweet, and friendly, and a great favourite with all who knew her; but her ill-health and early death left us, alas! to learn these her merits by hearsay and to love her shadowy memory when the mild presence had vanished for ever.

She was married in 1823, and bore the following children :—

William . . . born March 19, 1824.
Catherine . . „ March 25, 1826.
John . . . „ December 12, 1827.
Jane . . . „ August 25, 1829.
Edward . . . „ August 22, 1831
(who only lived a few months),

and a still-born son on May 27, 1833, at which time she was already far gone in 'a decline,' due rather to exhaustion than disease.

She died on Tuesday evening, July 2, 1833. She was perhaps not made for longevity, but with more wisdom in its atmosphere her dear and sweet life might have been preserved for many years.

I only recollect her as an invalid, and we children were not allowed to be much with her. But now and again she sung a little to the pianoforte, and two songs of that time have still for me a charm not their own— 'The Bonnie Breastknots,' and 'It wasn't for you that I heard the bells ringing.'

From my nurses and others I picked up a large number of tunes, for I had a decided 'ear for music,' and Ireland is, or used to be, a country with its air full of singing, whistling, and lilting. Fiddlers abounded, pipers were not scarce ; the fame of harpers lingered, but I never heard the Irish Harp till I went South.

My father (on the passage, in these years, between thirty and forty) was a short, active, black-haired man, with very light gray eyes, quick, impatient, curious as to the externals of objects, and easily amused, but disregardful of whatever did not immediately interest him. He had a turn for arithmetic, and was exact in the money part of all dealings ; punctual also as to set hours, and letter-writing.

In continuation of unbroken family custom, he was an unswerving adherent of the Established Church ; but in politics he had left the Radicalism of his early life for a kind of Toryism, which consisted mainly in reading a newspaper on that side, and giving a vote accordingly at the county election.

Honesty, prudence, industry, regularity, conformity, —few men will break down with these ; and my father had these, under fashions peculiar to himself. He had, moreover, though thrifty, a kind of open-handedness, or dislike and impatience of stint ; and, above all and best of all, an inherent aversion from every sort of double-dealing and deception, and a total incapacity to practise them. This sincerity, which was often naïve and sometimes impolite—he had in common with his brothers and sisters ; his mother was of the same nature, and it has descended to her grandchildren. I feel it is no merit in myself, but an inheritance, a something like the shape of my limbs, that I have always an uneasy longing to undeceive people in every case, trivial or important, whether connected with myself or others, where the slightest misconception seems to exist. This tendency (strangely associated with extreme shyness in admitting any personal intimacy) often runs into absurdity, and I am sure I have often left people puzzled by explaining to them more than enough, and setting them perhaps a'search for supposed motives. The tendency is native, and will work. This turn of mind also urges me to point out without delay all the faults I see in any person or thing, even when my admiration is very great, and although I am aware of the certainty of breeding misconceptions thereby.

Both mind and body were exceedingly active, and I was irresistibly drawn to pry into and examine all kinds of objects and places, climb up ladders, walls, gates, trees, sometimes no doubt committing breakage or causing alarm. But there was not the least tinge of malice in my nature, or capability of being pleased by the destruction of anything or the annoyance of anybody, and a wise and sympathetic senior could without special effort have done wonders for my education and happiness. I used often to wonder how it could have happened that I was so much wickeder than everybody else. I should have suffered much more hurt and harm by it but for certain compensations. My great curiosity and interest in outward things, and delight in their beauty and novelty, along with much activity of imagination, or rather fantasy, tended to save me ; and at my Grandmother's house—but a little way off, and to which I went as often as I could—I found something of that atmosphere of affection and confidence which is so suitable to the free growth of any tender young soul.

My Grandmother (my father's mother, Jane Hamilton her maiden name) managed to live by a very few simple rules (without even knowing these, as rules),

and managed to do it as well or better than most people.
She cared about her own household, first and last ;
maintained regular hours and a good larder ; was kind
to her servants, but kept them in their place ; petted
her grandchildren, and took a great deal of snuff. She
had a family Bible, with the births of her numerous sons
and daughters—eighteen in all, I think, but many of
these died in childhood—recorded in old-fashioned
writing on the fly-leaves, and a thick old cookery-book
bound in black leather ; and these I believe were all
her books. But she used to sit in the winter evenings,
with her cat on her knee, knitting stockings and
listening with apparent pleasure to Aunt Maryanne
reading the Waverley Novels, and would sometimes
make a remark on an extraordinary incident or character
—generally on some piece of villainy, and to this effect,
'They ought to have hanged him !' From this it may
be guessed that the modern scruples about capital
punishment had never intruded on her mind ; and
indeed, as far as I can recollect, she was in doubt about
nothing : if it was an old thing it had its label attached,
if a novelty she kept it at arm's length. Even the
rotation of our planet upon its axis (though not exactly
a new opinion) she never believed in. The bare notion
of such a turning and twirling would have been enough
to make her head light.

I now know that my Grandmother's was a small
house, but if I were to describe it from the impressions
of those years it would be spacious and many-roomed,
with a long, dim, lofty Entrance Hall, wide enough to
be the scene of many fancied adventures. The stairs
at its end mounted to a landing with flower-stands and
a window, and thence to a Drawing-room with what I
thought a large window to the street, a little room off
this, and two bedrooms looking to the back. Another
flight climbed to an upper lobby and the garrets. At
the end of the hall, between the foot of the staircase and
the kitchen door, was a door, generally locked, whence

a few descending stairs led to a curious back-room with hen-coops, a smell of live animals, an ancient wooden partition, and a window dim with old crusted dirt ; and from this a dark flight of stone steps descended to a truly mysterious and almost awful region, a dim back-kitchen paved with rude flags, with a well of living water of unknown depth in a recess of the wall.

Into the Hall (where an old fashioned lamp of elongated shape, which I never saw lighted, hung from the ceiling) opened the door of the Parlour, next the street, and my Grandmother's bedroom to the back of the house, both on the left hand as you came in ; and on the right, close to the head of the back-stairs, the Kitchen door. Another door on the right, belonging to a Store-room usually entered from the Kitchen, I never saw opened but twice or thrice, each opening an event and a revelation ; a press stood against it on the inner side, and a green hall-chair on the outer. Near the hall-door lay an oval mat, and at the stair-foot another, made of 'bent,' a coarse grass that grows on the sandhills by the sea ; these mats being finger-woven and carried round for sale by barefooted women and girls, one or more of whom called nearly every day to ask, ' D'ye want any mats ? '

The Kitchen was floored with square red tiles. Its one tall window, with thick window sashes, beside which was the washing-tub on its stand, looked out on a little back-yard. Opposite the door stood a long ' dresser ' with its rows of plates and dishes, tin porringers and strainers ; and under this, in the corner next the window, was the place of a large tub of fresh water which, with its clear olive depth and round wooden dipper swimming like a boat on its tremulous surface, used to give me great delight, judging (as I do in this and similar cases) by my distinct impressions of the forms and colours.

From my own experience I judge that a child's little *camera obscura*, however sensitive to the picturesque, cannot include it on a large scale. There were mountains in daily sight, where I lived, and a large cataract in the river close by ; I must also have seen the ocean sometimes, which was but three miles distant, yet it was none of these that impressed me with a sense of beauty and mystery, but the water-tub and the well, flowers and leaves, and, very particularly, a heap of gray rocks, touched with moss and in one part laced with briars, in a certain green field to which the nurse used often to bring us.

No doubt I was a troublesome youngster, superabundantly active, and there were two things which probably helped to make me unacceptable. I was a peculiar-looking, and, no doubt in the opinion of many, an ugly little chap, with an odd cast in his gray eyes ; secondly, I was never done asking questions, and hardly ever satisfied with the answers I received. I could read fluently at a very early age, and I remember nothing of being taught. But I do remember, before I could read, learning a sentence in the *Bible Story Book* by heart, and then making a pretence of reading it—out of vain-glory. The little woodcuts in that book—a duodecimo in two volumes—impressed me more than any pictures I have seen since. A wide lonely landscape of hills and water, with the sun looking down upon them, heading the chapter called ' The Last Day,' remains, in its effect on my mind, the grandest of all works of art. It was a woodcut about an inch long, and no doubt entirely commonplace in itself. I wonder whether something intrinsically great would have impressed me more. Probably not.

With my sisters I was always on good terms, but I cannot remember that they ever seemed to count much then in my life. Places had more reality than persons. My mind was busy with imaginations which gave mysterious importance to every nook of house and garden ; and when I began to catch glimpses of things in a wider range, and to overhear hints of a more wonderful world outside of this, magic pictures formed themselves within me of such heavenly beauty as no experience has matched. These had a consistency of their own, and recurred till they left impressions that resembled real memories, and have, I doubt not, made and do still make a large part of the scenery of my Dreams. Beautiful Dreams (I mean in sleep) have been no trivial part of the pleasures of my life. Certain Dreams show up again and again, like the opening of a familiar page. Sometimes there is an interval of years between two appearances of the same Dream. There are several Dreams, each distinct, of Lakes, of Rivers, of Mountains, of Woodlands, of Cities, of Great Buildings, of Strange Countries; a Dream of a Cave, and a Dream of a Gothic Ruin, a Dream of Flying, a Dream of Death, and many more. Dreamland has its own geography, of places wherein all strange adventures and experiences are possible.

My brother John and I had not much·in common; but one Sunday evening, I remember (this must have been in our second lustrum, perhaps well on in it), we were on the stairs of the Church gallery—a big boy quarrelled with me and suddenly made as though he would throw me over the railing. I was rescued quickly, but during the momentary struggle I saw John's face, who was some steps higher up, looking down with an expression of alarm and horror which I never afterwards forgot, and which gave me a new feeling towards him from that day. He never knew this; of such slight incidents and lasting effects life is full.

The said Church (of the United English and Irish Establishment) was an important object in my childish life. To me it was a spacious and awe-inspiring Edifice, with windows of peculiar shape, and a square Tower which was the measure of height,—'as high as the church steeple.' The broad path curved up to it from a tall old iron gate, through grassy hillocks and ancient tombstones, some of them quaintly carved. The Church stood on the highest ground, and commanded a wide prospect, from its tower-top a panoramic one. Eastward you saw the river rushing down its rocky dell, and behind this some of the hill tops that guard the unseen great Lake out of which it flows. To the south, at a distance of some ten miles, a long range of blue Mountains takes wonderful colours from the changing skies, and in their foldings run up shadowy valleys into a mystical inner region. Between this range and the little gray Town with its long stone bridge, at your feet, spreads the Moy (*math* = plain)—scene of many an ancient fight and foray, an expanse, sloping to the north, of rugged pasture, broken here and there with a rocky copse or farm-shading grove, and many low green rath-crowned hills. So one's gaze travelling round to the west, and over the sand-hills and foamy harbour-bar, gladly rests on the great line of the Atlantic Ocean, the nearest land out yonder being two thousand miles away. For north horn of the Bay rises the great rocky precipice called Slieve League, and round to the north and along the northen horizon peer up other blue mountain-peaks above a middle distance of gorsy slopes and wind-swept sheep-runs, sprinkled with gray rocks and boulders, and hinting to a familiar eye the green circle of a Rath on many a low hill. Mullinashee (Fairy Hill) this eminence is called on which the Church stands ; and not only from it but many another height extensive prospects are visible, with a wide sky overhead, and a pomp and change of cloud-pictures such as I have never seen elsewhere.

Even the streets of the Town afford many a glimpse of green fields, blue mountains, or flowing waters.

The Town and its horizon-circle belonged to each other (in my imagination at least) and gave me a sense of large space and infinite variety, very different no doubt from the image of Ballyshannon in the mind of some passing traveller who sees the poor dull little place, perhaps on one of those by no means unfrequent wet days, and wonders how any human being can willingly live there. But neither was I alone in my feeling. The people of Ballyshannon had, and I hope have, their full share of that warm attachment to familiar localities which is notable in the Irish.

'When a stranger stan's on the Bridge and luks up an' down, mustn't he be *delighted*!' said a native to me; and I never heard of any one going to live elsewhere who failed to 'think long for the ould place,' and, for a time at least, cherish the hope of returning.

Travelling at the time I am speaking of was a rare adventure to poor and even to middle-class people. The journey to Dublin was long and costly, and England a strange country which few even dreamt of seeing, except two or three shopkeepers who went once a year to Manchester and Leeds to buy goods, and the 'harvest-men,' who brought back home their wages, against the winter, and who like their neighbours invariably thought and spoke of 'the English' as of a foreign people, though never, that I heard, uncivilly, unless when some disputation arose. 'Ameriky,' far off as it was, was a more familiar name and idea; nearly all the letters received and dispatched by the poorer people were from or to that land of promise. The passage-money was but a few pounds, very often sent over by those already in the West, and the emigrants could in many cases embark in their own familiar harbour. I never heard any one express the least fear of the dangers and hardships of the long voyage in an often tightly-packed and ill-found sailing-ship; but great was the grief at leaving home and 'the ould counthry,' and vehemently, though not affectedly, demonstrative were the frequent parting scenes.

It has always been supposed that some countries have, so to speak, a peculiar magnetic attraction for the souls of their children, and I found plenty of reason, in the conduct of my neighbours as well as my own con-

sciousness, to count Ireland as one of these well-beloved
mother-lands. This home-love is strongest in the
dwellers in her wild and barren places, rock-strewn
mountain glens and windy sea-shores, notwithstanding
the chronic poverty in which so many of them live. In
these remote and wild parts Erin is the most characteristically herself, and the most unlike to Saxon England.
Her strange antiquities, visible in gray mouldering
fragments ; her ancient language, still spoken by some,
and everywhere present in place-names, as well as phrases
and turns of speech ; her native genius for music ; her
character—reckless, variable, pertinacious, enthusiastic ;
her manners—reconciling delicate respect with easy
familiarity ; her mental movements—quick, humorous,
imaginative, impassioned ; her habits of thought as to
property, social intercourse, happiness ; her religious
awe and reverence ; all these, surviving to the present
day, under whatever difficulties, have come down from
times long before any England existed, and cling to
their refuge on the extreme verge of the Old World,
among lonely green hills, purple mountains, and rocky
bays, bemurmured day and night by the Western Ocean.

I never came back to the Ballyshannon country after
an absence, without thinking that it looked to be the
oldest place I ever saw.

This impression was aided by the character of its
superabundant surface rocks—gray gneiss, gray mica-
schist masked with yellow lichens, dark gray limestone,
weather-stained, or knobbly with mysterious fossils ;
and the fields too are commonly intersected with rude
fences of loose gray stones picked from the soil. But
hints and tastes of a richer scenery were not wanting,
and all the more prized for their rareness. Productive
gardens and orchards there were about the Town, plenty
of flowers and fruit, few trees of any size (mostly
sycamores and ashes), but here and there a little grove
shaded the lawn and avenue of a modest country house,
and a mile or two up the rapid River thick copses

mingled with large trees embowered the water-side. A small well-wooded park in that region, called Camlin, seemed to me the very type of rich sylvan beauty, and my imagination no doubt soon caught rumours and formed pictures better than could ever be realised of the great Lake beyond, with its forested promontories and 'an island for every day in the year.' In the opposite quarter, that is on the west, our landscape reached the extreme of bareness, rough rocky pastures, miles of rabbit-warren and sea-strand, sward of Atlantic headlands shaven by the salt gale as by a scythe, with here and there a hawthorn bush or still rarer hedge, stretching wildly away to the eastward as though fain to flee altogether, almost the only arboreal things to be found far or near. The wild shore and boundless tossing sea, ebb and flow of the tide, ships, fishermen, wrecks, new lands beyond the sunset, these helped no little to feed and stimulate the childish imagination.

But of all the external things among which I found myself, nothing impressed me so peculiarly as the *Sound*, the Voice, which ceased not day or night ; the hum of the Waterfall, rolling continually over its rock ledge into the deep salt pool beneath. In some moods it sounded like ever-flowing Time itself made audible.

The pool below the cataract was one of the chief scenes of the salmon-fishing, so important to the town, and summer idlers had an untiring pleasure in lounging on the high green bank to watch the boats swiftly casting out and slowly hauling in their nets. Angling on the upper waters brought us every year, from April or May till August, a succession of visitors, often English, and we were further and more permanently enlivened by the presence of troops, Ballyshannon being an important military post, the gate between Connaught and Ulster. At the beginning of the century it had Infantry, Cavalry, and Artillery Barracks, fully occupied, I think, up to 1815. The Cavalry Barrack had been allowed to fall into ruin, and its black grass-grown walls had a strange and fascinating horror for the boyish mind ; but the Infantry Barrack was always more or less occupied, and the marching of the red-coats (especially to and from church), the playing of the bands, and the various bugle-calls at their regular times of the day, made a great impression. The Officers too were an interesting and frequently varying element in society. Officers arriving were sometimes billeted on private houses, and I remember the presence of mysterious military guests in our house more than once, on these terms. These, no doubt, were occasions of emergency, when it was suddenly found expedient to strengthen the garrison on rumour of an intended 'rising,' or in consequence of some unusual display of lawlessness. I came early to the consciousness that I was living in a discontented and disloyal country ; it seemed the natural state of things that the humbler class—which was almost synonymous with Roman Catholic, should hate those above them in the world, and lie in wait for a chance of despoiling them. Yet I never for a moment believed this of any of the *individuals* of this class amongst whom I lived. I used to fancy and sometimes dream frightfully of a swarm of fierce men seizing the town, bursting into the houses, etc. ; of soldiers drawn out in rank with levelled guns, of firing, bloodshed, and all horror.

Once there was something like an approach to realisation. It must have been at a time when our garrison was temporarily withdrawn or reduced to a detachment, that a rude army of ' Whiteboys ' actually marched through the town, armed with scythes, pikes, and I know not what. I was turned six years old then. I remember being at the corner of our lane, holding somebody's hand or lifted in somebody's arms, and have a most dim yet authentic memory-picture of a dark wild procession of men, crowded closely together, holding and brandishing things over their heads. It streamed past us up the long hill of the Main Street, and I daresay I was taken home before it had passed

by, for in the dim picture it is always seen passing on
and up interminably, a dark throng with pikes and
scythes held aloft. I looked with curiosity unmixed
with dread ; but it was probably after this that the
dread showed itself in dramatic forms in my dreams.
I have been told that my Aunt Bess on this day was
walking through the Purt (a long straggling street on
the south side of the river) when she met the mad
looking multitude with their pikes, etc. Some one said,
'That is Miss Allingham going to visit the poor,' and
they opened a way for her to pass through.

No outrage at all, I believe, was done by the
'Whiteboys,' or whatever they were ; and in fact I
have never, since I was born, known or heard of any
political or secret society offence in our Town or its
district. Ballyshannon was a sort of island of peace in
my day, as it had been for generations, and I hope is
carrying on the good tradition. We were far from
centres of excitement and agitation ; Dublin remote,
the nearest considerable towns some twenty-five and
thirty miles distant, and the scene of our county elections
to Parliament (very seldom contested) still further
away. We were a Borough (with two members) in
old College Green days, but had luckily lost that
privilege, which is a real curse to a small town. Newspapers were unknown to the humbler, and rare with
the middle classes. All the country gentry and nearly
all the well-to-do people were Protestants, having
the ascendency naturally belonging to money and
education, and their connection with a State-privileged
Church was, I imagine, less noticeable ; that is, there
was little if any political feeling on this head, though
plenty of theological aversion and contempt on both
sides ; and in any sort of public dispute or collision,
Catholics and Protestants (Orangemen, mostly of the
small farmer class, were those who were apt to show
up on such occasions) ranged themselves as by instinct,
or chemical affinity, on opposite sides.

Along with other helps to a comparatively tranquil existence, Ballyshannon had a most peace-loving and peace-making Parish Priest in Father John Cummins, whose big figure wrapt in voluminous coats, big stick, good-humoured big face crowned with reddish bob-wig and wide-brimmed hat, was one of the permanent institutions of our social existence throughout my boyhood and youth-hood, whatever curates might come and go. My father had no difficulty in exchanging many a neighbourly greeting and chat with Father Cummins, whose burly person standing on such occasions with legs apart, whose good-humoured brogue and hearty laugh that shook him all over,—'Upon me conshince, Misther Alligham!'—I well remember. He told one day with a big laugh how grateful another Protestant neighbour was on getting back some stolen goods by virtue of the Confessional, saying earnestly—'I protest, Mr. Cummins, this restitution of property is a gr-rand fayture in your religion!' and my Father too was sometimes advantaged by the same means. Father Cummins was nothing of a theologian, but he was duly proud of his great ancient Church, and used sometimes to ask an opponent with dignity the well-known question—'Where was *your* Church before Luther? Tell me that, sir!' He lived in a neat thatched cottage at the top of the town, with an elderly housekeeper, and a boy who drove him to distant parts of the parish in an old-fashioned jaunting-car, the pony, fat and sleek as a mole, being seldom allowed to go at faster pace than a quick walk. The good priest's great dread was of taking cold. He believed in fast-shut doors and windows, huge fires, heaps of bedclothes, and nobody but his housekeeper ever knew how many coats, waistcoats, and other integuments he was accustomed to wear. In diet I believe he was moderate, and he lived to old age without ever making an enemy. His successor, a tallish, dark, lean, shy man, was no less peaceable in life and teaching.

'The Rector,' as he was always called, but properly
the Vicar of Kilbarron, at the time when I appeared
upon the scene in a very small part, was the Reverend
Robert Packenham, brother to the wealthy lay rector,
who took the name of Conolly for his aunt's property
and was the chief landowner in our parts and long
M.P. for the county.

I was probably about four years old when they
began to take me to church on Sundays. The edifice
appeared to me spacious, lofty, and venerable. It was
cruciform, with round-topped windows, the ground floor
filled with high pews. There were three galleries,—
'the Singing Gallery' over the west door; 'the Soldiers'
Gallery' in the north transept; 'the Country Gallery'
in the south transept, used mostly by small farmers and
their families. The townsfolk and the country gentry
had pews in the body of the church; some very poor
people sat on benches in the aisle, and, at the other end of
the scale, two families had notably large and comfortable
pews, the Conollys in the right-hand corner as you came
in by the west door, the Tredennicks [1] of Camlin in the
left. The Tredennick pew was a place of mystic and
luxurious seclusion to my fancy, a sort of *imperium in
imperio*. Its woodwork completely partitioned it off from
the aisle, but chance peeps showed a snugly cushioned and
carpeted interior, and even a special little fireplace with
its special little bright fire on winter Sundays. In later
days I knew a high lady who deemed it proper to go
regularly to church once a week, but evaded part of
the tedium by taking with her a novel or other amusing
book, decently veiled in a dark cover. With such a
pew as this she could have made herself very comfortable; but if anything of the kind occurred there (which
probably never did) I had no suspicions of it.

Essentially, neither service nor sermon had the very
slightest interest or meaning for me, but the sense of a
solemn stringency of rule and order was deeply im-

[1] The Tredennicks, originally of a Cornish family.

pressed, and the smallest infraction, it was felt, might
have unimaginable consequences. A child's prayer-
book falling from the gallery astounded like an earth-
quake ; and once, I remember, when the congregation
suddenly started up in the midst of the service, pew
doors were thrown open, and people ran out into the
aisles (a lady had fainted)—it was really as if the Day
of Judgment had come. Connected with Church and
churchyard was a thought, vague, vast, unutterably
awful, of that Last Day, with Eternity behind it : yet
it was definitely localised too, and it seemed that not
only the Rising but the Judging of our particular dead
must be in our own Churchyard.

A terrible thought of Eternity sometimes came,
weighing upon me like a nightmare,—on and on and
on, always beginning and never ending, never ending
at all, for ever and ever and ever,—till the mind,
fatigued, fell into a doze as it were and forgot. I
suppose this was connected, though not definitely, with
the idea of a state of punishment. The suggestion of
eternal happiness took no hold upon my imagination ;
my earliest thought of Heaven pictured it as a Sunday
street in summer, with door-steps swept and the shutters
of the shops closed. Later, there was a vague flavour
of Church and psalmody.

Our Pew, painted like the rest a yellowish colour
supposed to imitate oak, was half-way up the Church,
on the right-hand side of the central aisle, and had the
distinction of a tall flat Monument of wood (or it
seemed tall), painted black in George the Second taste,
rising on the wall behind it. Atop was a black urn
with faded gold festoons ; at each side a pilaster with
faded gold flutings ; and there was a long inscription
in faded gold letters.

It seems to me very curious that, after sitting so
many an hour, so many a year, in that Pew, and
recollecting numberless little things around me there,
I cannot find in my memory one word of that

inscription, except 'SACRED' in a line by itself at the top, in Old English letters—not even the chief name, which was a lady's, (a remote and very slightly interesting relation or connection of ours, she must have been) nor the import of those Roman symbols which so ingeniously disguise a date to modern eyes. The wording no doubt was highly conventional, as nearly as possible meaningless, and felt by the child to be a sort of dull puzzle which after some attempts it was better to avoid. Had it been *verse*, of even moderate quality, it would have fixed itself in my memory ; with point, it would have stuck there for ever.

My usual place in the pew (habitude, or customariness, or whatever it may be called, being naturally strong in me) was the left-hand corner next the door, as you went in. Standing on the seat, I could look up and down the aisle, and sometimes rest my arms and head on a little triangular shelf that fitted into the corner. When I had, against the grain, to sit down, I kept looking at the faces of the people near to me in the Pew, and the countenance of a certain half-pay Army Lieutenant, ruddy, swarthy, with a longish nose somewhat bulbous at the end, holds a very disproportionate place in my memory, because he generally sat in full view. The tedium of the service was also mitigated by the interest which I acquired in watching for the regular recurrence of its various stages, with the attitudes—of sitting, standing, or kneeling—appropriate to each. Certain phrases were greeted as milestones upon the journey ; and at the end of the sermon (usually the most trying part of all, and of indefinite length) the words, ' Now to God the Father,' etc., caused an unfailing gush of inner satisfaction. There was something curious and amusing in the Litany with its responses, but it was mostly meaningless to me, as indeed was the Service as a whole (both at this time and later in life). The mystic phraseology had of course its effect, as any other such would have had, and the regular recurrence and solemn repetition of the performance. The gathering together, too, of neighbours, rich and poor, old and young, as in the presence of the Universal Father and Ruler, has an impressiveness different from anything else in daily life. If it could indeed be done simply and purely 'in spirit and in truth'! But here, in our small community, a section only of the neighbours drew together at the set solemn seasons; another section, though animated by the same motives, drew together in different place and manner, drew *apart* from the former gathering, many of whom came from the same households; and in the very act of worship both sections displayed and emphasised feelings of mutual suspicion, contempt and animosity.

Once or twice I was taken clandestinely to mass by a nurse, on some Saint's Day most likely, and stood or sat for a while just inside the Chapel door. It felt like a strange adventure, with some flavour of horror, but more of repulsiveness, from the poverty of the congregation and the intonation of the priests. I remember arguing with my nurse Kitty Murray, (who only died this year, 1883, at the supposed age of ninety-three—but I don't think it was she who took me to the chapel), for the superiority of Protestantism because 'the Catholics, you see, are poor people'; to which Kitty replied, 'It may be different in the next world.' A good answer, I felt, and attempted no retort; being indeed at no time of my life addicted to argue for argument's sake, or for triumph.

Although very brisk in body and mind, my health from the first was considered delicate. I was thin and pale, and for several years—between my fifth and eighth, perhaps—there was a swallowing of nauseous doses to be gone through several times a day. But this was nothing to the Surgeon's frequent visits with his horrible lancet, in consequence of a swelling on the middle finger of the right hand (which remains contracted), and even in memory the bitter pain of the repeated cuttings makes me wince. My Aunt Bess used to ' dress it,' a disagreeable operation for both of us. She was the Maiden Aunt of the family, at this time between forty and fifty, very charitable and helpful from an unwavering sense of duty, and inflexibly ' low-church ' in her religious opinions and practices. She did her duty by me, as by everybody, with firmness, regularity, and a general good sense; what was missing in her ministrations was that soothing personal atmosphere of love and sympathy which does everybody good without effort, and especially children. This blessing I should doubtless have enjoyed from my dear Mother, had her short married life been more fortunate. At my grandmother's, besides my Aunt Bess, lived two younger Aunts, Maryanne and Everina. Aunt Everina glides through my memory little more than a mild pale shadow, straight and slender, and low-voiced. She had by nature a pictorial gift, and painted in water-colour,—flowers, landscapes, portraits of friends and neighbours—as well as one might be expected to do who had no training and never saw any examples of good work. Aunt Everina's health was delicate, and she was perhaps about twenty-eight years old when she died.

Aunt Maryanne, the youngest, or youngest but one, of my Grandmother's large family was, both in person and temper, short and brisk with *nez retroussé* and lively gray eyes. She was quick and excitable, spoke fast, and a troublesome child would pretty soon feel her hands as well as her tongue. She was a Poetess, and wrote much on local and family subjects, but her simple ambition never even dreamed of actual print, and contented itself with sheets of note-paper, and little stitched books, neatly written out in something like printing letters, and given away to her friends. I have in my desk a ballad of hers on my father's approach-

ing wedding—'Will's to be married to Maggie,' etc.—
O Time!

Aunt Maryanne was a voracious novel-reader. The winter evenings come clearly before me; my Grandmother in her arm-chair by the fire, with close cap, knitting incessantly, her snuff-box on a little table, an old cat called 'Norway' snoozing on the hearthrug and sometimes jumping into her lap; Aunt Bess also knitting, grave and silent; Aunt Maryanne reading aloud a Waverley Novel. I used to sit with paper and pencil, 'drawing' and also listening to the story. At any thrilling crisis ejaculations of interest or excitement were heard, and the end of a chapter often gave rise to comments, always on the incidents and characters, just as though they were real, never on the literary merits of the work or the abilities of the author. Criticism of the latter kind was all but unknown in our circle, and surely its estate was the more gracious.

When I acquired, no one knew how, the art of reading rapidly, and at once applied it to every readable thing that came my way, I used sometimes to find my Aunt's novel in the daytime and take a run into the story in advance of the evening reading. On one or perhaps two occasions when I afterwards sat listening, I was unable to resist the temptation to give a hint of what was coming, whereupon Aunt Maryanne, starting up from her chair, clutched me firmly with both hands and bundled me out of the room—a very justifiable assault. Scott of course furnished the staple of the winter evenings' entertainment; but some minor story-tellers contributed to the amusement. I remember Galt's *Laurie Todd*, and Horace Smith's *Brambletye House*, with the catchword, 'Think of that, young man!'

I think the Waverley Novels that most impressed me in those early days were *Guy Mannering*, *The Antiquary*, *Ivanhoe*, *Kenilworth*, *The Talisman*, but there were scenes in *Waverley*, *The Fortunes of Nigel*, *Quentin Durward*, *The Fair Maid of Perth*, *The*

Pirate, *The Monastery*, vivid as any real experience. In Poetry Scott again was first favourite, and the verse-novels of *The Lady of the Lake* and *Marmion*.

[Here William Allingham's account of his childhood ends.

The following reminiscences of his schooldays are given from two letters, the first written by his brother John in 1904, the second by an old schoolfellow, Mr. Robert Crawford, the Engineer :—]

'I can recall Willy since the thirties of last century, *i.e.* since he was seven or eight years old. In 1837 or 1838 he and I occupied the same bedroom in the old Bank House on the Mall. It had one window looking west—a gable window—and off the room was a closet containing a number of books and pamphlets in the Norwegian and English languages. I remember the great storm of January 1839, and the window of our room being blown in, notwithstanding a feather bed being placed against it. Willy, I think, used sometimes to walk in his sleep at that time. He was very agile and expert at all juvenile games. He was then attending Wray's School in Church Lane, then the only school in Ballyshannon—indifferently attended by Catholics and Protestants. Wray taught Latin—nothing else. Willy left this school in the Spring of 1837 to go to a boarding-school at Killeshandra, Co. Cavan, kept by one Robert Allen, a commonplace person of the cocksure evangelical type. After a short time there my father got him into the Provincial Bank at Ballyshannon (of which he was Manager). This was in 1838, when Willy was fourteen years old : in December 1839 was moved to the Armagh branch of the Bank—and later to the Strabane and Enniskillen branches in succession.'

'He was a particularly bright and clever boy, and conquered the most difficult lessons with a facility that made him an object of envy to his less brilliant comrades. He devoted just sufficient time to his prescribed lessons to enable him to hold his own with class-work, while he diligently pursued investiga-tions on his own account in a far wider field of learning. As a result he frequently caused surprise to his seniors, by the fixed opinions he held upon many subjects usually supposed to be suited only to the comprehension of intellects of maturity, and by the clear manner in which he expressed his convictions concerning them. He was a great lover of Nature in all her phases, and particularly humane towards dumb animals, of which, however, so far as I know, he never made pets. Sports he abstained from, on principle, considering them cruel.'

[Allingham's recollections of boarding-school were by no means happy.

He was still delicate in health, and an accident at this time to his sore finger produced severe inflammation of the arm, and necessitated surgical treatment. He was at Killeshandra for a year only ; at the age of fourteen his school education was brought abruptly to an end.

His father, now married again, had been out of health for some time, and told by a doctor that he could not live very much longer : he determined, therefore, to put William, at once, in the way of earning his own living, and found him a place in the Bank at Ballyshannon.

Here the lad began a seven years' service to his uncongenial work. The sudden end to the possibility of all further organised study and education was, to him, a deep disappointment and lasting regret.

In December 1839 he was moved to the Armagh branch of the Bank, and here he was, at first, often very lonely and homesick.

From Strabane Allingham wrote on May 11, 1841, asking his father to send him 'Elia, first series, and Shelley poems. I shall return Elia second part and Lamb's Tales. Johnson's Poets are very welcome and a great treat.'

In the summer of 1843, at the age of nineteen, he paid his first visit to London.

29

The following was written to his father at this time.]

NORFOLK HOTEL, SURREY ST.,
STRAND, *July 22,* 1843.

MY DEAR FATHER—Here I am in a very quiet place, within twenty yards of the busiest street in London.

I slept in Oxford, the night before last, and saw most of the city, the Bodleian Library, etc. I have seen no place equal to it, to please my taste. Old churches, colleges and halls at every step, and plenty of old houses with gables to the street and latticed windows.

I can find my way here capitally. I walked this morning, before breakfast, to St. Paul's, round by Newgate St., Holborn, and Drury Lane. A matter of between two and three miles, I should think.

I write to let you know where I am. Of my journey I will tell you no more at present, except the following facts, which I thought rather droll—

1st, then,—at Stafford, in the neighbourhood of the great potteries, we had a *horn* vessel to drink from.

2ndly, at Birmingham (the World's Toyshop) a large shop had no 'Chinese Tumblers.'

3rdly, at the Angel Hotel, Oxford, the bedroom was supplied with a *Cambridge* Bible—and lastly, the first tune I heard in London was the 'Sprig of Shillelagh.'—Yours, my dear father, truly, W. ALLINGHAM, Junior.

[After seven years in the Bank, Allingham obtained, at the age of twenty-two, a post in the Customs. An account of this is given, as follows, in the few remaining pages of this first part of his autobiography.]

CHAPTER II

1846-1848

HEARTSICK of more than seven years of bank-clerking, I found a door suddenly opened, not into an ideal region or anything like one, but at least into a roadway of life somewhat less narrow and tedious than that in which I was plodding. My father was offered a place in the Customs for my brother; John was too young for the post; it could not be kept vacant and was offered to me. In the spring or summer of 1846 I gladly took leave for ever of discount ledgers and current accounts, and went to Belfast for two months' instruction in the duties of Principal Coast Officer of Customs, a tolerably well-sounding title, but which carried with it a salary of but £80 a year. I put up at a Temperance Hotel in Waring Street, slept soundly (O Youth!) in a small front room in that narrow noisy thoroughfare, trudged daily about the docks and timber yards learning to measure logs, piles of planks, and, more troublesome, ships for tonnage: indoors part of time practised Customs book-keeping, and talked to the clerks about literature and poetry in a way that excited some astonishment, but, on the whole, as I found at parting, a certain degree of curiosity and respect.

I preached Tennyson to them, hitherto an unknown name, and recited bits from *Locksley Hall*, meeting at first a cold reception, but afterwards better acknowledgment. One of the head-clerks came up to me one morning with the greeting, 'Well, I've read *Locksley Hall*, and it's a very fine poem!'

I don't recollect being at a theatre in Belfast. I went a few times to a music hall, but my spare time was mostly spent in reading and haunting book-sellers' shops, where I venture to say I laid out a good deal more than most people in proportion to my income, and managed to catch glimpses of many books which I could not afford or did not care to buy. From Belfast I repaired to the little town of Donegal, and entered on my office of Principal Coast Officer of the district, a very large one extending over many miles of coast, the greater part of it wild and rocky and lying exposed to the full violence of Atlantic gales and waves. Visiting wrecks was part of my duty, which sometimes demanded long journeys in stormy weather over rugged hilly roads, on an outside car, with various attendant discomforts which would now seem appalling. But these expeditions on the whole were pleasures, and have left pleasurable memories. They were part of the freer physical life upon which I entered in passing from the Bank to the Customs. Her Majesty's Customs at Donegal occupied a narrow little first-floor room in Dillon's Hotel, a good-sized and comfortably kept house, where I also boarded and lodged at moderate annual rate, having a back room where my meals were served to me separately, by particular favour, and the chairs, tables, and sometimes the floor, were piled and littered with books of all sizes, old and new. Here I could sit reading for hours every day with little interruption, stepping across the passage when wanted at my office to receive notice of the arrival of a vessel, or sign her papers when outward-bound, or make out a Light-Bill (so much for each Lighthouse passed on the voyage), or witness the engagement or paying-off of seamen. Outdoors, there came the occasional visiting of vessels, measurement of logs and deals, and 'bread-stuffs' (chiefly maize) and — by far the most troublesome business, but the most interesting—the examination of the fittings and provisions of Emigrant ships, and the calling over, when ready for sea, of the lists of Passengers, who came forward one by one, men, women, and children, to pass the doctor and myself. There were also visits to coastguard stations, to navy and other Pensioners, and now and again, as I have said, to a Wreck, usually at some distant part of the coast.

I was the only Customs Officer in the district, which suited my mood perfectly, but no doubt helped to foster the feeling of *isolation* which is so strong in me. My district was officially 'in the Port of Sligo,' to which I sent monthly accounts, and the collector visited me once a quarter, and I was also in some respects under the sub-collector of Ballyshannon ; but there was seldom any interference. My family name was a guarantee in itself ; I discharged my functions intelligently and con-scientiously, as well as with popularity, and the nature of them and of the *locus in quo*, gave me a scope and freedom of action, and a personal respect everywhere, not usually associated with so humble an official position as mine. I enjoyed my new position on the whole, without analysis, as a great improvement on the Bank ; and, for the rest, my inner mind was brimful of love and poetry, and usually, all external things appeared trivial save in their relations to it.

Yet I am reminded by old memoranda that there were sometimes over-clouding anxieties, sometimes, but not very frequently, from lack of money, more often from longing for culture, conversation, and opportunity ; oftenest from fear of a sudden development of some form of lung disease, the seeds of which I supposed to be sown in my bodily constitution. I can recall few details of my first year at Donegal.

I used to go over often to Ballyshannon in the evening and return in the morning, or from Saturday to Monday, sleeping at my Father's ; generally travelling by the

Derry and Sligo mail-coach, and kept up all my old intimacies with the places and people by the Erne.

I had for literary correspondents Leigh Hunt, George Gilfillan, and Samuel Ferguson ; and for love-correspondent, F., whose hand-writing always sent a thrill through me at the first glance and the fiftieth perusal. What a day it was when one of those letters reached me !—all the more prized for the difficulties that beset their transmission. I loved an Ideal, angelically fine, impossible to hurt or destroy as a dream of Heaven ; but it had a very sweet little human core, which (I am thankful) keeps its spring-flower-like tenderness in my memory. Appropinquity can breed love, it can sometimes sully or kill it. Fate kept us mostly separated in space even while we were one in spirit ; our rare meetings were, to me at least, mystically sacred occasions.

[The story of William Allingham's life, in strict auto-biographic form, ends at this point. He wrote out, from his note-books, conversations he had had with interesting men, evidently with the intention of incorporating them in his account, but beyond this date nothing was completed.

The story is continued in diary form, the first entry being in June of the following year.]

1847.—In June this year I took my holiday and went to London, and on the evening of my arrival went to the Princess's Theatre to see Macready in *Macbeth*. He disappointed me ; his elocution grated ; but I was struck by the way he delivered one phrase—' There's no such thing ! '

Next night to *Norma* at Her Majesty's Theatre—a ' command ' night and a great squeeze, but I got a good seat in the pit. Jenny Lind is not physically well-fitted for the part of Norma, and her girlishness was made more noticeable by the stoutness of her Adalgisa (Barroni). She had also against her the fixed notions of

the public as to the character and person of Norma (a
kind of Medea) being very different from every one
who had represented it before her, A punster might
say she was ab-Normal. Grisi too had appeared in
it (*her* best character perhaps) only three days before.
Yet Jenny Lind's personation was not only very fine
(her singing, of course, most beautiful), but carried her
audience with her throughout. Her bitter disappointment was very sad, her shame and agony in the last
scene truly affecting. Her pity for Adalgisa was most
tenderly expressed :—

> Ah sventurata ! del tuo premier mattino
> Già turbato è il sereno !

And in the subsequent scene, when Adalgisa says,
' How pale thou art ! ' the tone of Norma's reply—
' Pallor di morte,'—sank into one's heart. Jenny Lind
is the only actress I ever saw that I could imagine
myself in love with. She is too good for the stage.

Thursday, June 17.—Covent Garden Opera. Grisi
in *Norma*. She looks the part better than Jenny does,
and had a specially grand moment when she rushed up
the altar-steps and smote the sacred shield. But she
never touched my heart like the Swedish lady.

Wednesday, June 23.—Found Edwardes Square,
Kensington, and Leigh Hunt's house, No. 32, left card.

Thursday, June 24.—Note from Leigh Hunt.

Friday, June 25.—To Edwardes Square, saw cab
with white horse driving away from No. 32, knocked,
and found that it was Leigh Hunt, who had just gone
off ' to the rehearsal of his play.' This was the Play to
be acted for his benefit by Dickens and others. If I
had been one minute sooner he might have taken me
with him—perhaps even into the theatre ! wild thought !

Sunday Evening, June 27.—32 Edwardes Square,
and find Leigh Hunt at last. I was shown into the
Study, and had some minutes to look round at the
Book-cases, Busts, old framed engravings, and to glance

at some of the books on the table, diligently marked and noted in the well-known neatest of hand-writings. Outside the window climbed a hop on its trellis. The door opened and in came the Genius Loci, a tallish young old man, in dark dressing-gown and wide turned-down shirt-collar, his copious iron-gray hair falling almost to his shoulders. The friendly brown eyes, simple yet fine-toned voice, easy hand-pressure, gave me greeting as to one already well-known to him. Our talk fell first on reason and instinct; he maintained (for argument's sake, I thought) that beasts may be equal or superior to men. He has a light earnestness of manner, and toleration for almost every possible different view from his own. Of freewill he said, 'I would much rather be without it. I should like to feel myself taken care of in the arms of beneficent power. —Paganini incomparable; when he came forward and struck the first chord, my neighbour in the Opera pit (an Italian) exclaimed in a low voice, "O Dio!" Violin, or better violino, is the name for his instrument. Common English players *fiddle*, it is a good word for their playing. Macready is not a genius, he is our best actor now because there is no other. He keeps a fine house, but is not in what is called the best society.'

I ask him about certain highly interesting men. 'Dickens—a pleasant fellow, very busy now, lives in an old house in Devonshire Terrace, Marylebone.

'Carlyle—I know him well.

'Browning—lives at Peckham, because no one else does! a born poet, but loves contradictions. Shakespeare and Milton write plainly, the Sun and Moon write plainly, and why can't Browning?' I suggested he was the Turner of poetry, to which Leigh Hunt replied, 'Now, you've said it! He's a pleasant fellow, has few readers, and will be glad to find you admire him.' (! !)

'I shall now be able to see my friends oftener, and will take an opportunity of asking Dickens, Carlyle,

and Browning to meet you.' (Gracious Powers ! ! !)
'I would do so for few.'

'Moxon is not a publisher but a *secreter* of books.

'Browning says, "People *may* find my publisher after a careful search, but myself scarcely at all."

'If I see Dickens at Mr. Talfourd's on Tuesday, I'll mention you to him.'

Jenny Lind—I said I admired and loved her so much that I wished she would leave the stage, to which Leigh Hunt replied : 'Would not that be a pity, when the public sympathises with her sweet genius ? '

W. A.—'I doubt that : the public is a bad judge of the finest things.' L. H. agreed.

W. A.—'It is pleasant to walk home from the theatre on a fine night, perhaps the best part of the amusement.'

L. H.—'And one is going to rest.'

Speaking of his poem, 'The Glove and the Lions,' I objected to the knight's flinging the glove in the lady's face, but Leigh Hunt argued for it : 'He treated her as no woman. Every one admits the justice of it—except *you*, now—Browning? Oh, he is sure to take the opposite view from everybody else !' I said it would make me suspect the knight of having been frightened, 'cowardice is passionate.' 'That's true,' said Leigh Hunt.

Walked back, under a lovely moon, to Surrey Street, Strand.

Friday, July 2, *Evening.*—Leigh Hunt's. He was tired, but asked me to stay.

L. H.—'I hate Dante : in reading him I first found that a great Poet can be an unamiable man. Wordsworth was personally very disagreeable. I am asked to meet Hans Christian Andersen, now in London. Can't understand why people want to see *me*—I am used to myself. O yes, I like to see some men of letters. Dislike mountains, can't bear height, my legs shudder at the thought of it.—London is the best place for you ; why don't you try and live in it ? ' Walk back.

Monday, July 5.—A short interview with Hans Andersen. He had not English enough to allow of our conversing, asked me to write to him ; but I have nothing to say save that I love him, and many people tell him that. He is tall and lanky, with queer long face, but friendliness and intelligence shining through. Feels out-of-sorts in London.

Wednesday, July 7.—Evening at Leigh Hunt's. I give him Heywood's *Hierarchy of Blessed Angels.* ' A nice book to have ! ' he remarks. ' I see you are of a giving turn.' Religion, ' Painful to see any assemblage of fellow-creatures we cannot join. Ask a man why he does not worship Brahma, and he will begin to give you *reasons.* Believers in any form of religion don't like to be reminded of the possibility of doubt.' I met Andersen the other day at dinner and we were mutually unintelligible. I had the pleasure of feeling his arm, his arm in mine, on the way to dinner ; it was the thinnest arm I ever felt. He looks like a man in the last stage of consumption ; but, observe, I don't know that he is in the last stage of consumption. He looks like a large child, a sort of half-angel. There were many people of rank present, yet no one in the room looked more *distingué* than Andersen, the shoe-maker's son.'

Sunday, July 11.—At Leigh Hunt's. He looks wonderfully different in the street from in the house. There, a spare old man in a frock-coat and black stock, with weak eyes and rather careworn look ; here, a *young* man (though of sixty), with luxuriant if gray locks, open shirt collar and flowing dressing-gown, bright face, and the easiest way of talking in the world. He is fond of droll paradox, full of delicate appreciation, gay, gentle, good-humoured, with a natural gift, well cultivated, of finding out the ' soul of goodness in things evil.'

Monday, July 12.—Having received a civil little note signed ' S.R.' giving me leave, I went to Mr. Rogers's house in St. James's Place, and was shown

through three rooms hung with good pictures. In the
parlour Raphael's 'Christ in the Garden,' Guercino
(Mr. Rogers's favourite, the servant says), Landscape
by Rubens, Guido's 'Crown of Thorns,' Rembrandt,
etc.

Tuesday, July 13.—Liverpool. Coach to George's
Dock, *Maiden City* steamer. Walk, dull narrow lanes
between huge warehouses, numbers of Irish. Breakfast
in small hotel. Steamer—Cumberland mountains. Isle
of Man—gentleman on deck remarked that was 'a fine
island to be out in the sea.' Drunken sailor-passengers
at horseplay on deck, afterwards fell asleep in a heap.

Wednesday, July 14.—Came on deck at Moville,
beautiful morning ; the Foyle looked spacious and fine
as we glided up to Derry.

Friday, July 16. — Coach, fine day ; Strabane,
Stranorlar, and through Barnesmore Gap to Donegal.
Old James greets me with his kind old smile and says,
'Sure, you've seen all sorts of elegance.'

July 17.—To Ballyshannon. My father in the
garden.

Monday, July 19.—Coach to Donegal. Then car to
Killybegs on Customs duty : horse falls.

Tuesday, July 20.—Killybegs. Walked over Carn-
tullagh to Bruckless to my good friends the Barretts.
I prefer the rocky grandeur of this prospect to the
luscious richness seen from Richmond Hill. Woman
gathering wild heartsease 'for tea' : they use many
herbs thus. Dine at Bruckless ; go up river in boat.

July 21.—Bruckless ; boat to Killybegs, passing
rocks with caverns.—Visit three vessels, *Andromeda,
South Durham* and another Brig. Land and visit Roman
Catholic Church, where is a good copy of a Murillo for
altarpiece. Boat again, heavy rain.

'Sowing wide the fruitless main,'—good line: whose ?
why, Leigh Hunt's. He has many happy lines and
phrases. I feel in succession clammy, damp, wet, then
rivulets running down the backs of my legs. Bruckless.

Barrett lends me a suit of his clothes, a world too wide, including a monstrous dress coat with brass buttons. Dinner, Dr. M. and ladies, Sam Cassidy, etc. Songs, loo, supper, hot lobster—bed 2.30.

Thursday, October 28.—Donegal. Set out for Lochrus on Customs duty. Outside car, moors and bare mountains to Ardara, when the groves of Woodhill give a softening. The sun set into a jagged cloud breathing flame from its openings, rested on the dark mountains, disappeared, leaving a gloomy memory which soon faded too. Then the wind blew colder, the road became indistinct, the moors blended into a dim waste. Dine at Ardara, snug little room, adorned with pictures of Christ entering Jerusalem, Mary Queen of Scots, and Byron in a very large turn-down collar, with his arm round the waist of a lady with dark eyes and ringlets. A young naval officer in another room, who smokes cigars. Biddy says with pride, 'O, Ardara's never without a stranger!' Driving back—in calm cold air, the stars shone in intense points of light all over the sky, the Heavenly Plough at rest in the unfurrowed air, the Pleiades glittering in the east, and we travelling straight south from the Polar Star. Then the moon-dawn spread up the sky, and above a low black outline of hills was lifted the bright snow-cold Presence, showing the solitary road and ghostly brown moorland stretching away on either side.

November 1.—Donegal—dry, but gloomy and blowing. Order Miss Barrett's poems and Hood's poems—receive first number of *Howitt's Journal.*

Friday, November 5.—The poor crazy man who likes to be called *Mister* Gallagher says he 'finds his head rather hypothetical to day'; attributes it 'to the familiarity of the atmosphere.' *Howitt's Journal* has my 'Hallow Eve Chant' inaccurately printed. Play on the fiddle.

November 9.—Emerson is in Manchester. I wrote to him to-day.

Friday, November 12.—Donegal Fair. Went to
Ballyshannon, a fine clear cold day. Heard saying,
' Like Manus, I may go where I like,' and asked origin
of it. One Manus died and came before St. Peter,
who was sending Catholics off in one direction and
Protestants in another. ' What are you '? says St.
Peter. ' Nothing at all,' says Manus. ' Then go where
you like.'

Saturday, November 13, 1847.—*Mendelssohn dead !*
Wrote lines, ' By the shore, a plot of ground.'

Wednesday, November 24.—Letter from Emerson.

November 30.—Visit Poorhouse, Tom Read, crazy
man with small sharp black eyes ; sometimes keeps a
piece of iron on his head to do his brain good ; plays
on a fiddle, the first and second strings only packthread,
' Ain kind Dearie,' ' Pandun o' Rafferty,' grunting and
groaning all the while, and groaning fiercely when he
struck a note out of tune. I promise him strings.
' Does your Honour live far away ? '

December 3. — Irish Idylls. Read *Blot in the
'Scutcheon.* Bravo, Browning !

December 5.—Dream—dine with the Queen, who
asks me to ' try her custard pudding.' I ask if Her
Majesty knows the song of ' Miss Baily,' and recite it to
her. Cobbett's *Year in America* good. Cobbett was
a Man.

December 21.—Carlyle on Johnson : unfair cut at
poor Keats—' If a man *can* be killed by a review, let it
be done.' If Carlyle is a sturdy big-boned man, let him
be thankful and considerate.

[In the following year nothing is recorded in the
diary at any length until September.]

Saturday, September 16, 1848.—Donegal. To Inver.
Cranny by field-path. The MacMunn family friendly
and cheerful, both old and young, a pleasure to see.
The freshness and innocence of the country on everything in such a household.

Drive back to Donegal ; slanting sunrays and shadows on the blue hills. Pastoral vale of Killymard, some barley still green, some in stooks, oats mostly ripe, little wheat. I like to think of the Cranny family. Great the boon of a sweet face ! Immense the benefit of a good matron—doing, helping, encouraging, checking, soothing, suggesting, guiding everything and everywhere, without fuss, almost unnoticed. Watching every wheel and pivot, every movement of the little commonwealth's mechanism, and with a soft feather and light touch applying the oil of gentleness wherever needed, so that the whole runs smoothly, without grate or jar, and with only the soft hum of happy employment, as of bees among blossoms. O the beauty of a household rich in innocence, industry, and mutual love !

Ultonians, in whom Scotch and English order and decency are blended with Irish heartiness, are a good kind of people, and the peculiar wild fun and tender fancy belonging to the Kelts are, not seldom, transfused among those who have lived so long in the midst of Irish customs, traditions, music, and scenery,—not to speak of intermarriages. MacMunn is doubtless a Scotch name, in spite of the saying, ' Per O atque Mac veros cognoscis Hibernos.' Perhaps Hiberni stands for Kelts. A question : if Scotch Kelts be taken as descended from Irish (Scotic) ancestors, how comes there to be such a crowd of Macs among the Lowlanders, and many of them with emphatically Lowland characteristics ?

Glimpse of happy domestic life at Cranny to-day delightful. Delightful also to drive back at evening to the certainty of rest, retirement, books, and perhaps something good from the Post Office—which may this moment be on our table waiting to greet us.

Sunday, September 17.—Fine morning, but a smell of winter in the sunny air ; night frosts. On Martin's car to Ballyshannon. Dull wide sky. Thoughts on things in general. Are there not moods when earth life seems long enough, and to fall asleep for ever nothing to repine at ? Yes, but these are not the best moods. Between the third and fourth mile-stone my mind brightens, without any traceable cause. Perhaps God will leave the human race on the Earth planet until, in the aggregate, they shall have ransacked and learned everything possible to them about its nature and laws.

Tuesday, September 19.—Ballyshannon—fine. Practise violin with Hagarty, 12 to 2. Wet evening. Violin again, *Haydn* and *Mozart*.

September 26.—Dine at Peter Kelly's, nine priests at table—much song-singing afterwards.

Sunday, October 8.—Dublin. Conviction of O'Brien. Church. Anthem, fine voices. Mere harmony soon cloys.

As to the Religious Service, who came here for that ? Ah, if there were one sufficient faith and worship for all—how happy, peaceful, perfect a privilege it were to come together, how noble to be a Minister, and how noble it would behove a Minister to be !

Tuesday, October 10. — Dublin ; to Hawkins St. Theatre to see Jenny Lind in *Sonnambula*, her opening night here. An hour at door, crowd thickening, rush and crush upstairs to lower gallery. Curtain rises, the charming Jenny has to wait till the reiterated greetings subside. ' Three cheers for Jenny Lind ! ' (from the gallery). ' Wan cheer more ! ' ' A cheer for her Mother ! ' at which Amina smiled. Then we had *Come per me sereno*, etc., all to perfection, but sung as I fancied more floridly than when I heard her in London. She looks thinner. Flower-scene most exquisite and touching ! *O fiore—Ah non credea*, the flowers falling through her hands as she sings. *Ah ! non giunge* not very good, I thought ; encored, on account of its difficulty. Half a dozen to a dozen bouquets were thrown, no extraordinary excitement. When curtain fell I rushed down and made my way into the pit in the hope of getting one of Amina's flowers which had fallen near the footlights, but it was gone. Cold air outside, crowd, Jenny's carriage, police.

The Theatre *at best* a hollow, unwholesome, unsatisfying excitement.

October 14.—Opera again. *La Figlia del Reggimmento*. Jenny's camp manner, dashing shake of the hand, etc., but no way bold or impudent.

December 29.—Chateaubriand. He is not entirely free from some of the particular sins of French writing. He affects Byronism.

To Session Court : girl convicted of stealing a purse and sentenced to seven years' transportation ; she is removed shrieking violently. It seems a severe sentence.

Wrote to Henry Sutton.

CHAPTER III

1849-1850

Monday, January 1, Donegal, 1849.—Write on slavery. Black *v.* White (is writing for pay advisable?) Walk to mill. Hungry—dinner—violin, Tennyson's poems. Reverend Jos. Welsh and English land-agent Wilson, after attending investigation into the Wray explosion, came to a snack in my room. Wilson looked into my Tennyson, and saying, 'Now this is what I call *stuff!*' began to read out part of Ænone. I said, 'Let me look at it,' and put the book in my pocket without another word. He appeared rather stunned. How Tennyson gives the effect of everything,—enriched with a peculiar glow! Violin again.

Friday, January 5.—Frost. Customs accounts. To Killybegs by Mail-Car, walk up the long hills, slip on skates and skate a little by the road-side, then run after the car, warm. Denis laughing.

Inver. Sun sinking, deep red globe with a stroke of black cloud in the centre; now an arch, as it were the open gate of Heaven revealing glory within; now a ruby moon; now the last look from a deep eye of radiance, and—all's gone.

Wrote 'Crucible.' Read aloud.

January 8.—At Killybegs. Read Tennyson and Wittick's *Norway*. *Fairy Song* : 'Wee folk, good folk,' etc. Violin.

Thursday, March 15.—Ballyshannon. Plant ivy 45

round the Old Barrack ruins, accompanied by three pairs of slate castanets. Walk through fields at Coolcolly, with sycamores, green mounds, and rillet hid within a hedge, a place of mysterious beauty to me in old old days of childhood ; and so across the Abbey river, round Legaltion Lough, and home. Mem.: the word ' brook' not used here : they say ' river ' or ' water ' ; and ' water ' is also applied to large streams. After dinner down the Mall ; boys with hoops leaping wall. Aboard *Kent*. Sailors on boat, a coarse and reckless set.

People catching young eels (*lifogues*) no thicker than twine, in bags ; they are cooked into the shape of cakes or small cheeses. But this catching of the fry is not allowed. Tea. French.

Mr. Heagney (the Collector) remarks on hearing of the death of a retired Customs officer whom he knew, 'It's a queer world this ! There's a man gone that had eleven and eightpence a day—eleven and eightpence ! I wonder where Moses and Aaron are now, and David and Goliath, and all these. They were certainly here—they certainly were. And Nero and Caligula too—bad, bad men, tyrants—tye-ranny—tye-rrannous !—not a chirp in them ! ' Some ships were waiting in the bay for a chance of crossing the bar. I asked, ' Will they get in to-day ? ' Mr. H. (ironically), ' Ay !—there's a line of breakers as white as Ananias's wall at Jerusalem, and the Alps and Apennines out beyond them. Get in ! '

Sunday, June 24.—Ballyshannon. Have been appointed Controller of Customs at Ramsey, Isle of Man, at £120 a year. Letter to-day ordering me to go. Last Sunday here—for how long ?

Thursday, June 28.—Walk along river by Upper Fall to Stonewold. Then Jane, Clarissa, sister Jane and I by riverside, grassy headlands, leafy gulfs, rushing white steam (described in *Music Master*) to Camlin.

Saturday 30.—Coach to Dublin. Dawn purple and

gold, plains of Meath, the round sun rises. Very like the first morning I ever entered Dublin.

Dine at Professor MacGauley's, Marlboro' St. Smell of machine oil. Scientific Bachelor's *ménage*—viands, roast beef, and boiled mutton. Scampish looking young woman waited. At dinner, Bishop Denvir (Catholic), Dr. O'Connell, D.D., Priest Laffan, Dr. Stapleton, M.D., Uncles John and James, John-James and Edward, W.A., and the host. Priest Laffan has red cheeks and black eyes, big calves and rich voice,— sure to be a singer. After dinner much talking and laughing, but the bishop silent.

Shakespeare's morality, and that of the other Elizabethan Dramatists. Catholicity. Uncle John (tho' his wife is devoted to the Church) is well known to be thoroughly heterodox. Dr. O'Connell fell to bantering him. 'You would make as good a clergyman as any of us, sir! You'd only have to speak dogmatically and correctly' (*i.e.* no matter what you believed). Uncle John shook his head. Presently O'Connell exclaimed (he was very talkative), 'O my God!—I saw some children in the street to-day fighting about a marble, and I longed to be like them, all their happiness centred in that!'

Uncle John.—'I shouldn't care for such happiness.'

Dr. Stapleton.—'To mortify the flesh, that's the whole thing; the flesh; to mortify the flesh.'

Then O'Connell told us how he answered 'Old Whately' on some logical point and got the better of him. After this came a discussion on hypocrisy, MacGauley arguing that it was better for public morals when a man concealed his vices. Dr. S. exclaimed, 'Give me the rock that shows its head above the billows.' Then they came back to religion, and Uncle John said some plain things about the incredibility of much that is taught under that name, backed by his brother-in-law, Dan Brett, a shrewd and gentlemanly old Dubliner. Dr. O'Connell turned on Brett, seeking to pose him,—'Do you believe in a God?' to which Dan quietly replied, 'I decline answering that question, because I consider it offensive.' On which the professor proposed that we should go to the workshop. The silent bishop had already gone thither, and we found him mending an engine-band.

The Church of Rome, entrenched within elaborate logical lines, fears no assault made according to logical rule. She knows that the existence of the Deity can neither be proved nor disproved by argument, and that the opponent who says 'Yes' or 'No' to this question may be made to look foolish.

We looked at furnace, etc., and passed into the lecture-theatre and workshop. A large bottle labelled *Liq. Ammon. Fortiss.* stood on a shelf. Dr. Stapleton remarking knowingly, 'Mac never has this good,' pulled out the stopper and put his nose over the bottle, but immediately jerked his head aside as if he had received a blow—as in fact he had. We all felt the violent smell, and there was laughter; but in the course of a few minutes all one side of the doctor's face grew red and swollen, tho' he was in too jovial a mood to notice it much. We saw models of various engines, microscopes, electric machine, air-pumps, and what not. Then we returned to the parlour again and more liquid applications, internal this time, and not ammonia. The D.D. and M.D. showed the effects plainly in both the manner and substance of their speech. They proposed 'changing professions.'

Dr. S.—'I'll teach you how to manage the ladies,—and I know that you could do it well. I could make the ladies cry at my sermons and give lots of money; they'd say, "what a fine man he is!"'

Our host had discovered something that wanted setting right in the workshop and stayed behind. Dr. O'C.: 'Poor Mac! he'll be so annoyed. Go down for him, tell him to come up till we have a game of cards.'

After an argument between MacGauley and John-

James on valves, our party took leave and mounted a back outside-car in Gloucester Street, which was driven with erratic speed. Uncle John remarked in his usual placid way, ' I look on myself as in some danger now,' and my cousin gave anecdotes of upsets but. we got safe home.

Sunday, *July* 1.—Dine at Seafield. Uncle John tells of sturdy beggar who accosted him with a menacing look, ' If I'm not fed, I'll ate a man!' to which Uncle J. answered quietly, ' Don't spare him on my account.'

July 2.—North Wall. Isle of Man steamer.

Douglas, *Isle of Man*, *July* 3.—Custom-House : walk about narrow streets. Sign declaration. Collector Baldwin gentlemanly and clever, says of Isle of Man : ' It's a queer place—a very queer place!' Doesn't like it. Coach for Ramsey. Hilly road : horses crawl up and dash down alarmingly. Driver and guard both boys, the first of Lancashire parentage, the other, ' Joe,' of Irish. Manx language. Green hills and valleys with the level sea behind, just like Ireland. Cloven stones : Irish Joe shows the superior 'cuteness of his breed, and looseness of statement as well. Hill into Laxey—I walk up hill beyond ; talk to a girl singing by the roadside and to a boy herding cows, and find them frank and civil. We see King Orry's grave on the hill. Joe sings ' His courting coat on,' and some Manx songs. I sing. View of Ramsey, Albert Tower, etc. To Albert Hotel ; pay six shillings for carriage of trunks, etc. Tea and bed.

Ramsey, *Wednesday*, *July* 4.—Ask if I can go to the Tynwald to-morrow.

Ramsey, *Thursday*, *July* 5.—6 o'clock—fine market-place ; coach. Crowds on the road. Coach passengers hearty and conversational. Dumpling-faced woman in black satin, with black eyes and hair to match. Pretty wooded road takes us past Bishop's Court, lying low, with neat pastures, the palace of ' Sodor and Man,' a Bishop who has several other ecclesiastics to help him

in supervising the church affairs of an island of 50,000 souls, mostly Methodists. 'Sodor,' whatever it was, *non est inventus* : Bishop should go and look for it. Coach ; crowds on the road. Kirkmichael (Kirmickle) ; into a barer country with peep of the sea, and so to St. John's, where we see booths and people, and the tent upon ancient Tynwald Hill itself, a little grassy mound about twelve feet high, cut into three terraces and a flight of steps. I go into the empty tent, no one questioning. Take a sketch. Soldiers march in, playing Fulla-la-la-lu. Coach arrives with band. Crowd moves slowly about as at a small country fair. In the church, the more fashionable folk : the portly deemster and the dapper deemster, both bowing and smirking among their numerous acquaintances. The building new and showy, with painted windows and confectionery chandeliers. Enter Governor Hope, a tall red-haired, light-complexioned Scot, in green uniform, high-plumed cocked hat resting on his arm. A stout butcher-like parson then goes through the service. Then out, the procession is formed and moves to the hill, which is now thronged. A functionary stands at the door of the tent and reads something which few can hear, but which is understood to be the Laws recently passed by the House of Keys. A small man next me is in extreme anxiety to hear and see—calls out 'Silence there !'— 'Down with that parasol !' then to me, 'Can you hear what they're saying ? Is it Manx ? Has he a wig on ?' 'No, but he has a pair of spectacles.' All over here. They return to church, some huzza, Hope enchanted, smiles and waves his golden hair ; when his hat and feathers are on he looks at least ten feet high. Then the booths are full of countryfolk, male and female, with mugs of ale, etc. Fiddlers—soldiers— band. Drovers with horses. Fishermen—drunken men and boys. Wearisome. 6 o'clock, coach at last, driver drunk, galloping down hills, swaying and
shaking, a dangerous journey; one woman-passenger

frightened;—dumpling-faced woman doesn't mind, 'has
enjoyed herself *so* much ! '—eats ginger-bread. Another
stout young woman only says, 'Eh, law !' when the
coach lurches. The driver grows benevolent, says often,
'Bless you, sir—bless you—bless you !' We get safe
back to Ramsey after all. The Manx horses seem used
to this sort of travelling, and I suppose they manage
their drivers.

July 6.—A man at *table d'hôte* to-day, dark, long-
haired, notable looking ; as he sat after dinner with
wine and cigar a thought flashed—*Could* it be Alfred
Tennyson ! Talked a little with him, and Tennyson
quickly vanished.

Sunday, *July* 22.—Talk metaphysics with Schiller
(' relation of the poet '). He calls himself a Progression-
ist. We spoke of Swedenborg. Performance of *Faust*
at Frankfort—Richter, Goethe, Carlyle, etc.

Monday, *July* 23. — Leave come — preparations.
Steamer.

Wednesday, *July* 25.—London—Norfolk Hotel,
Surrey Street. *Cholera bad.* Never thought about it !
Out to visit Vernon Gallery. Drury Lane pit, found
The Beggar's Opera very dull, and Sims Reeves, in spite
of his voice, a vulgar singer.

July 26.—To Cheyne Row, Chelsea. Mr. Carlyle
not returned, and may not for another month. Edwardes
Square—Leigh Hunt not in.

Saturday, *July* 28.—Fine. Royal Academy. Turner's
'Wreck Buoy '—Webster's 'Slide,' Mulready's 'Women
Bathing,' Martin's blue ' Happy Valley.' Stanfield's
water looks like beer after Turner's prismatic crystal.
Landseer's 'Dying Lion,' Leslie's ' Don Quixote and the
Chaplain.' Water Colour Exhibition.

August 3.—Lincoln's Inn. St. Mary Axe, Duke's
Place, Synagogue. There remains a higher feeling than
curiosity in witnessing the religious ceremonies of this
ancient Race in the heart of a great alien City, and in
the 1849th year of a rival Era.

Sunday, August 5.—To Kentish Town and walk to Highgate Cemetery, terrace, catacombs, yews, view of London. Out to churchyard to find Coleridge's grave, locked ; inquire for sexton's house, he is 'at church' ; so I have to peep through gate at what a man tells me is the railing round C.'s grave, under an ivied wall. Look then at the house where he lived with Dr. Gilman (now Surgeon Brendon's), plain corner house of last century with dormer windows and large window in gable, shaded by a mimosa. Some fine elms and beeches are ranged in front, and tall trees rise behind. Out of one window looks a black cat, perhaps belonging to the Witch of Christabel. Splendid evening, sun-lighted road, down Highgate Hill on omnibus. Fleet Street. Chop at 'The Cock.' Curious old mantelpiece, which I sketched on fly-leaf of Poe's Poems, bought at a book-stall. Had the waiter ever heard of a Mr. Tennyson ?—'Mr. Tennyson, sir ?—No, sir.' Tried the other waiter : he *had* heard of him, but had never seen him.

I.—'You're not "the plump head-waiter"?'—'Oh, you mean William, sir. He's here every day but Sunday.'

Thursday, August 9.—Chop at 'Cock' with half a pint of port to drink the Poet's health. The veritable William waited on me.

'Are you Mr. Tennyson's friend'?

William.—'He says so, sir.'

This answer puzzled me. (Does William think it was a liberty to put him in rhyme?) 'Has he been often here?'

W.—'I don't know his appearance at all, sir. A gen'elman might be coming 'ere for twenty years without my knowing his name. Thousands 'ave asked me the same question, and some won't believe but that I know all about it. But I don't. I should like to see him,—very much. I'm told he's *breaking*, sir. I should like to see him.' William evidently felt sorrowful, and in a manner aggrieved, at never having identified the man who spoke of *him* so familiarly.

August 11.—To Colchester. Find Henry Sutton's lodging. Talk, then out to walk. Visit the castle by twilight, the time for all ruins. Sutton gives me a letter to Mr. Patmore.

August 15.—Letter from Mr. Coventry Patmore, very kind, and made me happy : ticket for Museum Library enclosed.

August 16.—To British Museum. I ask for Mr. Patmore, and am shown in to him—a tall, thin, mild-faced young man, very kind. We talk about Blake. We walk through the rooms.

Friday, August 17.—To Slater, publisher, and talked to him about a new edition of Blake's poems : civil, and seems inclined to publish.

Saturday, August 18.—British Museum Library : Mr. Patmore. He helps me to look up Blake, but without success ; they seem to have nothing of his. We look at books of Middle Age Art ; saints and demons. P. tells me he has written a book or article on architecture, with a quite new theory,—'You will be surprised it has not been hit upon before. Can you walk up with me this evening ? '—' Yes.'

On the way to Camden Town he told me about his new poem.

Neat small house on left-hand side of road, near a railway bridge. Mrs. Patmore—'Emily.' Tea and cake. Two small sitting-rooms with folding door between : front room has engraved portraits of Words-worth and Faraday over the mantelpiece ('the two greatest men of our time '), a round table with ten or a dozen books, and plaster cast of a statuette of Puck— just alighted on a mushroom and about to push with his toe a bewildered frog which a snake is on the point of snapping up. You can see that he saves the frog out of fun mostly, and to tease the snake. He is a sturdy elf, plainly, yet not humanly, masculine. A very original bit of work, by 'a young artist named Woolner.' In the back room P.'s writing-table at the window, with a few bookshelves beside it. I noticed Coleridge's *Table Talk* and *Aids to Reflection*, and Keats's *Remains*. Then we started on a walk northward. Patmore thoroughly agrees with me that artistic form is necessary to poetry. 'Tennyson perhaps likes the "Vision of Sin" best of his own poems. He said it was suggested to him by a line rejected from another poem.' (This line is, I afterwards learned, 'A little grain of conscience made him sour.')

We came to Hampstead Heath, and looked past a foreground of fir-trees over a wide undulating prospect tufted with trees, and richly cultivated, a lake shining in the distance under the evening sky. On the other side huge London lying sombre and silent. We were just in time to see the effect of the lighting of the lamps. The dusky mass awoke, and here and there, and soon all over, glowed with multitudinous sparks,— 'like,' said Patmore, 'the volcanic crust of the earth not yet cooled'—or like the advancing judgment of the Last Day : no ark avails against that fiery deluge. The evening was growing cold as we returned to Highgate and descended the hill, P. showing me on the way the house, in a sort of crescent with trees before it, where he formerly lived, and where Emerson and Tennyson sat at his table and liked each other.

Incidentally a poem was mentioned, 'The Pilot's Daughter,' which it seems Emerson showed to Patmore. 'It was mine,' I said ; 'I sent it to Emerson in a letter' (Patmore surprised). 'Are *you* the writer of that ? I must take care what I say!' Then he went on to ask me how much poetry I had written : had I as many verses as would fill seventy pages ? 'Seventy pages like that would be something uncommon!' (this is mighty encouraging!) After some supper Patmore showed me in MS. his poem of 'The Storm,' or 'The Two

Journeys.' Tennyson's mark is on the margin in various

places : ' + *T*.' Patmore said : 'When Tennyson finds
anything in poetry that touches him—not pathos, but
a happy line or epithet—the tears come into his eyes.'
He went on to tell me : 'I have in this room perhaps
the greatest literary treasure in England—the manu-
script of Tennyson's *next poem*.   It is written in a thing
like a butcher's account-book.   He left it behind him
in his lodging when he was up in London and wrote to
me to go and look for it.   He had no other copy, and
he never remembers his verses.   I found it by chance,
in a drawer ; if I had been a little later it would probably have been sold to a butter-shop.'   Before I went
away Patmore took out this MS. book from a cabinet
and turned over the leaves before my longing eyes, but
Tennyson had told him not to show it to anybody.
Mrs. Patmore had copied it out for the press, and T.
gave her the original.

I was not even told the title at this time.   It was *In
Memoriam*.

'It is the best thing he has ever done,' said
Patmore.

Sunday, *August* 19.—Dinner at Mr. Patmore's.   Discussion on writing poetry—he for consciousness, I for
unconsciousness : he thinks a poet ought to know
exactly what he wants to do and how to set about it ;
I am for knowing all one can, but also for poetising
without conscious reference to rules and precedents.   I
produce my verses—'Pilot's Daughter,' 'By the
Shore,' 'Fairies,' etc.   P. praises, and proposes a joint
publication.

Tuesday, *August* 21.—Eugene P. calls and we walk
westward and into Hyde Park.   In Piccadilly we meet
Leigh Hunt and I greet him.   As we say good-bye
Eugene Patmore says, 'I am very glad to have seen
Leigh Hunt—he's much pleasanter-looking than I
expected,—an excellent face.'   Leigh Hunt is now
sixty-five.   If I ever have any doubts about him, they
vanish at one glance of his eye.

September 4.—Unexpected letter : appointed Sub-Controller at Ballyshannon. £120 a year.

Ramsey, October 10.—Walk on shore—into coffee-room : characteristic island scene : Mr. G. at table, a plate of sandwiches before him, nodding stiffly off his chair with half-closed eyes : T. asleep on the sofa. I waken G. for half a minute, when he goes to sofa and lies down, half on T., half on a chair. I sketch them. Landlord comes in. ' When you've done with them I want to get 'em off.' Sketch done, I waken them with a tune on the poker and fire shovel : G. puts a bed-chamber candlestick twice on his head before he is convinced it is not his hat ; they get away somehow. Island of Trinculos and Calibans, no Prospero, alas no Miranda.

Monday, October 15.—' Steamer coming ! seen cross-ing the bay,' hurry to boat, with Manx kitten in a basket (G. declares it was stolen from him). Men pull fast, one swinging a lantern for signal—' She mayn't wait for you ! '—' She's brought to ! ' Alongside, I tumble up, boxes ditto ; one of the men—' You were very near being left behind.'

Saloon, chat. On deck, Ramsey light in the distance, Point of Ayr brilliant. Good-bye !

Manx kitten escapes and is recovered after an excit-ing hunt. Close to Mull of Galloway. Talk with Captain C. Below, all turned in but Mr. L. Mr. F. shows his jolly red John Browdie face over the edge of his berth. Next to him a drunken gentleman trying hard to repeat—

> She walks the water like a-a-a thingolife,
> As if t'dare (stage whisper) th' el'ments, t'strife.

I turn in, drest. In the morning some one asks, ' Steward, where are we now ? '

Steward (aggrieved, with an Ulster accent) : ' Ah, it's a shame for you to be always asking me questions ! You haven't given me a bit a' pace the whole night.'

' I only asked you once.'

'You've been askin' me all night.'

It was human, and not a bit insolent. Can an Englishman of the serving class assert himself without insolence ?

Five in the morning, off Portrush, Mr. F. up and others. Drunken gentleman lowered over the side into a boat. I turn to sleep again, till I hear, 'within four miles of Derry,' when up and on deck to a cold fine morning and beautiful broad river. Land at wharf, car to inn, walk up town and back to breakfast. Then railway, and with my cousin Sam Watt to Strabane. Sims's Hotel, greet and am greeted by various—all seems as if it had happened already.

Wednesday, October 17.—Up about 7. Wet and windy. O for a coach, not an outside-car ! Tom the waiter (blackish, bilious, middle-aged little man) in a chronic rage with nobody in particular, just as formerly. A coach *is* to go. Cup of tea. Inside seat 9s. 9d.— Donegal. Letter from Arthur Clough, which I read in coach. Home. Custom-House.

I forgot to record that on my day of leaving the Bibulous Island, while waiting for the steamer I ordered and drank a glass of whisky toddy, thereby making a sensation in the hotel, for up till then I had never drunk a drop of alcohol in Mona, partly from economy, but more to keep at arm's length the continual incitement to liquid excess. If one considers the case as a moralist, I don't know whether I was right or wrong to take this toddy *in extremis*. It put me, at all events, in the true light as a voluntary abstainer not a vowed teetotaller, and I am as unwilling to be thought better than I am—as worse.

Ballyshannon, March 25, 1850.—Read announcement of new poem by Browning, 'Christmas Eve and Easter Day '—what will he do with it ?

Saturday, April 6.—Abbey River, Washpool : sit under shadow of ruined house with back to a rock, reading Emerson on Plato, to the tune of running water,—a good accompaniment to study.

Sunday, *April* 7.—A guinea from *Household Words* for 'Lady Alice,' with a compliment from Dickens. Walk, Rockfields, the valley edge ; Hanagan's steps. After tea wrote 'The Touchstone.' Bed late.

Friday, *April* 12.—Busy at Office. Goethe's Autobiography. Riverside, lie on grass, hat off, scribbling down poems ; an ant or spider sometimes crossing the sunny page ; bee bustling in my ear. For some days I have written a poem every evening ; am beginning to know how to write poetry.

Monday, 22.—Bundoran, walk on shore towards the caves. Read Emerson on Swedenborg, high and pleasant thoughts ; look over the Atlantic to America and to Emerson. Thought of a tragedy. Evening— 'Flowers and Poets.'

Thursday, *April* 25.—Letter from Patmore, returning 'The Music Master' ; is going to show my lyrics to Tennyson. Copy twelve new ones and send them with letter.

Saturday, *April* 27.—Fine—Stonewold—rode brown mare. Home and find Wordsworth is gone ! Rode back to Stonewold, chanting an improvised psalm to the departed spirit. Do not tell of the death : nobody to care. Sunset beautiful.

Sunday, *April* 28.—Lines on Wordsworth's death. Evening—revise 'The Music Master.'

Tuesday, *May* 2.—Very fine. Fair Day. Women trying to sell cow, 'As honest a little cow as stands in the fair.'

Down the Mall with Thoreau's book, *Week on the Concord and Merrimac Rivers*, green slope near the Coves. Boat, floating. Thoreau's nature and freshness, mixed with impatience. Back to town and sit on wall to watch the Fair.

London, *Friday*, *July* 19.—With Woolner, two

Rossettis, and Buchanan Reid in omnibus to Chelsea, to Holman Hunt's lodging, large first-floor room looking on river, near the old church. Deverell—much talk on pictures, etc. ; we have coffee and fruit ; some lie on the floor smoking.

Elegiac poem—' To N. P. Rogers, Esq., in Heaven.' Painter proposing to call his picture ' Gil Blas about to endeavour to assume an air of unconcern while waiting on the robbers in their cave '—a very subtle shade of expression. ' Bring some milk from the pantry.'—Tipsy man in reply : ' Is it done up in paper or lying about loose ? '

Hunt's picture of ' Claudio and Isabella '; he has to be at the Royal Academy every morning now at seven, copying for somebody. As it was now late, and his guests showed no wish to depart, Hunt lay down on three chairs for a nap ; but they only made merry of his drowsiness, proposed to sit on him, etc., and so the time lounged on till dawn was broad upon the river and its trailing barges, and D. G. Rossetti (usual Captain on such occasions and notorious night-bird) uprooted himself at last from some cushion or easy-chair, and all departed, after three o'clock, save myself, to whom Hunt kindly offered a spare bed.

July 21.—To Mrs. Howitt's, tea, Miss Meteyard and others.

September 7.—Letter from T. Carlyle, Ecclefechan, recommends me to study general history and German.

September 17.—Letter and portrait from Leigh Hunt.

CHAPTER IV

1851–1853

I ventured to send my first volume of verse (1850) to Tennyson from Ballyshannon. I don't think he wrote to me, but I heard indirectly that he thought well of it; and during a visit to London in the summer of 1851 Coventry Patmore, to my boundless joy, let me know that I might call on the great Poet, then not long married, and living at Twickenham.

Saturday, June 28, was the appointed day, and in the warm afternoon I walked from Twickenham Railway Station to Montpelier Row, quite away from the village. It proved to be a single row of about a dozen moderate-sized houses, that seemed dropped by accident among quiet fields and large trees, 'Chapel House' where T. lived (so called I know not why) being the last at the south end of the terrace, where I think the byroad ended.

I was admitted, shown upstairs into a room with books lying about, and soon came in a tall, broad-shouldered swarthy man, slightly stooping, with loose dark hair and beard. He wore spectacles, and was obviously very near-sighted. Hollow cheeks and the dark pallor of his skin gave him an unhealthy appearance. He was a strange and almost spectral figure. The Great Man peered close at me, and then shook hands cordially, yet with a profound quietude of manner. He was then about forty-one, but looked

60

much older, from his bulk, his short-sight, stooping
shoulders, and loose careless dress. He looked tired,
and said he had been asleep and was suffering from hay-
fever. Mrs. Tennyson came in, very sweet and
courteous, with low soft voice, and by and by when I
rose to take leave she said, ' Won't you stay for dinner ? '
which I was too happy to do. Mr. Tennyson went
out, and returning took me upstairs to his study—a
small room looking out to the back over gardens and
trees. He took up my volume of poems, saying, ' You
can see it is a good deal dirtier than most of the
books.' Then turning the pages, he made critical
remarks, mostly laudatory. Of ' Cross Examination ' he
said, ' I looked sharp at it to see if any of the rhymes
were forced.' He objected to ' rose ' and ' clothes ' in
' The Touchstone ' (since corrected). Then he asked,
' Do you dislike to hear your own things read ? ' and
receiving a respectfully encouraging reply, read two of
the ' Æolian Harps,' first, ' Is it all in vain ? ' then,
' What saith the River ? ' The rich, slow solemn chant
of his voice glorified the little poems. In reading the
last line of the second—' For ever, ever, ever fled
away ! ' he paused after the two ' evers ' and gave the
third as by an afterthought, thus adding greatly to the
impressiveness. He especially admired—

> Night with her cold fingers
> Sprinkles moonbeams on the dim sea-waste.

I said, ' That was Donegal Bay.' T. replied, ' I
knew you took it direct from nature.' The pieces never
seemed to me so good before or since.

At dinner there was talk of Wordsworth, etc.
T. spoke of George Meredith's poems, lately sent to
him, author only twenty-three ; ' I thanked him for it
and praised it—" Love in the Valley " best.' I said I
also knew the book, and had bought it. T. gets enough
poetry without buying : ' They send me nothing but
poetry ! '—' As if you lived on jam,' I said.

T.—'And *such* jam! Yes, I did lately receive a prose book, *Critical Strictures on Great Authors*, "a first hastily scribbled effusion," the writer said. There was this in it, "We exhort Tennyson to abandon the weeping willow with its fragile and earthward-tending twigs, and adopt the poplar, with its one Heaven-pointing finger." ' 'A pop'lar poet,' says I.

After Mrs. Tennyson had gone upstairs, Patmore was announced. T. said, 'You didn't know Allingham was here,' and it rejoiced me to hear the familiar mention of my name. Over our port we talked of grave matters. T. said his belief rested on two things, a 'Chief Intelligence and Immortality.'——'I could not eat my dinner without a belief in immortality. If I didn't believe in that, I'd go down immediately and jump off Richmond Bridge.' Then to me, rather shortly, 'Why do you laugh?' I murmured that there was something ludicrous in the image of his jumping off Richmond Bridge. 'Well,' he rejoined, 'in such a case I'd as soon make a comic end as a tragic.' I went out to the garden, where were Mrs. Tennyson with Mrs. Patmore and her sister. Returning to the house there was tea, to which Tennyson came in, muttering as he entered the room 'we exhort Tennyson.'—— I smiled. He said, 'What are you laughing at? You don't know what I'm saying.' I said 'O yes, I do.'

After tea he went upstairs and smoked, Patmore and I sitting with him : English and Irish characteristics ; the English an ill-mannered people. Edgar Poe : T. did not know 'The Raven,' and I recited some lines of it, to which T. listened attentively. New Forest : Tom Taylor's story of artist painting in the Forest suddenly seeing a little brown man, who had crept up unseen and clutched his bottle : 'Gin?' says he ; 'Water,' says the painter, and the little brown man immediately disappeared. When we took leave T. came out to the gate and again shook hands with me.

I said, 'Ask me to find a lodge for you on the West

coast of Ireland'; he, 'I should like it very much.'
We walked to Richmond railway station, I feeling that
a longing of my life had been fulfilled, and as if I had
been familiar for years with this great and simple
man.

In 1853, being in London, from Ireland, for a short
holiday, I wrote to Twickenham and had a kind reply
under the Poet's hand asking me to come, and adding
——'As my wife is not very well you must "tread
softly and speak low."' So on Thursday the first of
November I went from Waterloo Station to Richmond
by rail, walked over Richmond Bridge—a fine day,
autumnal woodlands mirrored in the river, struck a field-
path on the left, and passing after a bit under some tall
trees emerged through a little gate upon the grass-plot
fronting Montpelier Terrace. As I came forward to
Chapel House two other men approached the door, one
of them something like T., and went in, not without a
suspicious glance or two at me.

I was soon in the Poet's much-longed-for presence,
who shook hands in the most delightful, simple, friendly
way, and asked me to stay and dine ; then said he had
to go away for a little and handed me a book for my
amusement. When he returned he was carrying in his
arms his baby son, called 'Hallam' ; the child had a
ball to amuse him, which he liked to drop on the floor
exclaiming, 'Tha ! ' or 'Da ! ' as it fell. Then T. took
me up to wash my hands in the dressing-room, its
window looking across several gardens, and a sunset
sky shining through the trees. Returning to the
drawing-room I found Mrs. Tennyson—sweet, pale,
and kind ; Mr. Frederick Tennyson the eldest of the
brothers, and Mr. Edward Fitzgerald (*Omar Khayyám*),
the two gentlemen whom I had encountered at the front
door. Mr. Fitzgerald ('Fitz '), an old and intimate
friend, told droll stories with a quaint gravity, much
amusing Mrs. Tennyson in particular. One was about

old Miss Edgeworth, whom he knew, and her turban. She used to take it off for coolness and resume it when visitors were announced. One day by some mischance a strange gentleman came into the room and found her writing with her almost bald pate plainly visible. Miss E. started up with the greatest agility seized her turban which lay close by and darted through an opposite door, whence she quickly reappeared with the decoration upon her head, but unluckily turned wrong side foremost. He also told us of Mr. Edgeworth's tombs of his three wives in the park at Edgeworthstown.

After dinner, poetry was the subject. Mr. Fitzgerald stood up for 'Pope's 'Homer,' and tried in vain to get T.'s approval.

'You think it very wonderful surely?'

T.—'I don't think I do.'

'O yes, you do, Alfred!'

T.—'No, I do not.'

Frederick T. set Schiller above Goethe, to which I strongly objected. A. T. said : 'If one of you is for Goethe and the other for Schiller, you'll never agree on poetry.' Moore was mentioned ; his skilful versification in fitting words to music. T. objected to the line—

She is far from the land where her young hero sleeps.

I did not find much the matter with it, but T. would not allow 'young hero' to pass, the metre requiring a dactyl there : 'I wonder you don't see,' he said. 'Subaltern' I suggested. 'Yes, that would do, as far as sound goes.' We turned to Campbell's 'Soldier's Dream,' and T. objected to 'Our bugles sang truce,' both for the two *ss* and the accentuation. Of the two lines—

And thousands had sunk on the ground overpowered,
The weary to sleep and the wounded to die—

he said, 'Those are perfect.' Then we spoke of
Shelley's accents, and I quoted—

> Of the snake's adamantine voluminousness,

but without effect. I called Browning a *vivid* man,
to which T. assented, adding, 'How he did flourish
about when he was here!'

Then came on Dickens' cockney *History of England*,
Professor Aytoun (not praised), Thackeray's *Book of
Snobs*, and Mr. Martin Tupper.

I spilt some port on the cloth, and T., with his
usual imperturbability spread salt on it, remarking as
he did so, 'I believe it never comes out!' Then we
went upstairs to tea. I praised the view from the
windows at the back. He said nothing would grow in
his own garden but stones: 'I believe *they* grow. I
pick up all I can see, and the next time I come there
are just as many.' Then T., Frederick T., Edward F.
and I to the study, where smoking and stories, some of
an ammoniacal saltness. When I took leave, Mr.
Frederick T. shook hands kindly, spite of our differences
of opinion, and T. came with me to the front garden
gate.

When I got to station the last train was gone, and
I walked into London by Kew and Turnham Green,
followed all along Kew Garden wall by a possible
footpad, whom I outstept.

CHAPTER IV (*continued*)

1850–1863

[FROM 1850 until 1853 Allingham held the post of
Custom-House Officer in his native town, Ballyshannon.
Under these dates the entries in his diaries were, for
the most part, in the form of memoranda. No fuller
record is forthcoming, the only account which he
wrote out in detail being that of his two visits to
Tennyson at Twickenham. The whole would doubtless
have served as material for the autobiography which he
began in later life. Wherever possible, extracts have
been made.

These quiet studious years were interrupted only by
visits to London, and by shorter visits, from time to
time, to Dublin and other places nearer home. Allingham's reading was wide and incessant. Besides keeping
abreast of current literature—in close touch with the
output of his many contemporaries — he worked
diligently at history, at Latin, at Greek ; and with
these studies found time also to practise his violin.
After the day's work and the evening's study he played
it, not infrequently, into the next morning's hours.
His quick appreciation of nature filled his note-book
with almost daily impressions. No effect of sea or sky,
mountain or lake, field or road, escaped him ; and to
the record of these larger impressions was added that
of a careful observation of the growth of leaves, of
flowers, and of the doings of the birds. Now it was

the sight of 'a beautiful greyhound,' the 'running of a rabbit,' or the flight of a bird that arrested him, and found a place among the memoranda he so faithfully kept.

For comradeship, for experience of people and of character, he was always ready. He never failed to perceive the human incidents by the way : in the routine of his daily life, or in the more varied opportunities of travel—in the train, on the coach, by the roadside.

He was keenly alive to the happenings in his own town, and his sympathy was for the difficulties and sufferings of the unfortunate no less than for the interests and pleasures of the well-to-do. Those in trouble were sure of his attention. He had that gift of thoughtfulness which means so much to the sufferer. In his heart the flower of kindness bloomed day by day for those who needed sympathy.

He was often in the infirmary, to sit with a sick neighbour, and in the National School to see how it fared there with the children. To festive gatherings he often contributed by singing, and he never failed to attend the Ballyshannon Fairs. At one of these he records how he went into a 'show' where there was a gaming-table, and 'put on once,'—to see what it was like, as, later, he 'once' attended high mass.

His physical energy was as great as his mental activity : Allingham was a rider, a skater, a swimmer, and a great walker. Whenever he came upon young people playing games, jumping or running, he joined their sport, and was, as a rule, the winner. Even his scanty notes at this time show what pleasure it gave him to 'climb the rocks,' or row, or 'wade out bare-legged to the fishing boats.'

To children his kindness was unfailing, and there are many entries, through these peaceful years, of his talks and games with the little ones about him.

In 1850 Allingham published his volume of *Poems*. In the June of this year he was in London, for a few days, the guest of Mr. and Mrs. Arthur Clough at University Hall, and went to Willis's Rooms to hear one of Thackeray's Lectures on the English Humorists. There he met Dickens, Forster, and Mrs. Carlyle, and a few days later he dined with Thackeray and Father Prout. Under this date he wrote, 'Thackeray hoaxes us by describing the night as lovely, bright moon, stars, etc.—is in fact raining, and cabs are sent for.'

He was also at a performance given at the Hanover Square Rooms, in which Dickens played Boots, and Mrs. Gamp 'in brown bonnet and corkscrew curls.'

During this time in London he saw a good deal of William and Mary Howitt, then living in St. John's Wood, but his chief companions were Dante Gabriel Rossetti and Woolner, and their party frequently included William Rossetti, F. G. Stephens, Blanchard, and Hannay.

He was often at the opera, and much of his time was given to the study of the pictures of the Pre-Raphaelite Brotherhood.

In August he was at home again, attending to the Customs, and making constant notes of the beautiful aspects of Ballyshannon, especially of the sea. The following was written on October 21 of this year :—

'Shaded avenue of vaulted foliage, pillared with slender stems. The trees, moved by the night-wind, mingled their rustling with the rustling of the unseen rivulet. In the foreground drooped, like a green mist, the long pale leafage of a large sallow. Risen behind the fluctuating shade there quivered through it, in threads and sparks of fire, the loveliness of the young golden moon ; and high above the highest dim tree-tops came out one star, trembling.'

Through these years his reading included Homer, Plato, Plutarch, Meredith's Poems, Coleridge, Emerson, Gibbon, Dante, Swedenborg, Byron, Barnes, Bacon's *Essays*—he read and walked every evening. But in spite of this rich company of minds he was sometimes 'unhappy and discontented,' and regretted his want of 'a regular system of education.'

In September 1853 he left Ballyshannon, exchanging his post for the Customs Office at Coleraine ; but he found little to do in that town, and speaks of his work there as 'morose duty.' His daily interest was in reading, correspondence, and the writing of his poems. He made several friends during his short stay, and it was there the children (for whom he seems to have always had sweets in his pocket) used to sing, 'here comes the lozenge man,' when they saw him coming. In October he went to Belfast to inquire about some literary post with a publisher ; it evidently came to nothing, for later in the same month he was in London, on leave, once more among his old friends, and constantly with Rossetti.

Early in 1854 Allingham gave up the Customs, determined to try literary life in London. The following letters, to his father and sister, were written at this time.]

COLERAINE, Feb. 12, 1854.

MY DEAR FATHER—I have really and truly given up the Customs—as I mentioned yesterday in a letter to Catherine—and am to leave this on Thursday next for London viâ Belfast. Having decided on the step, it would have been useless to delay, especially as the opening of the London season is the very best time for entering on my new occupation. How precisely I am to be employed and what immediate income I may expect out of it I think it better to defer speaking of till I have made a beginning, but I will write you after my arrival in London, and regularly afterwards, and I hope to pay you a long visit in the latter part of the summer, and to see you enjoying plenty of the open air. The Premier and the Home Secretary are your seniors by half a dozen years each, and their posts are no idle ones.

It is natural that my resolve should appear to you and others to be a rash one—an unusual one I know it is, but the circumstances are unusual, and after giving the thing long consideration

I feel that I am right—whether I shall succeed or not to the extent of my hopes.

I neither expect, nor desire much, to make more money, for a year or two, than will support me respectably; and meanwhile I shall endeavour to make what use I can of the means afforded me by London to compensate for the defectiveness of my education.

I know London pretty well—shall live regularly and quietly —have many and good friends there, and hope to strengthen and extend my acquaintance—and shall have opportunities, of various kinds, quite unattainable elsewhere. If I have good health, I see little risk in the enterprise, and incalculable advantages. At all events, I could not be satisfied without making the trial, and the step is irrevocably taken, so pray don't throw cold water on it, which could only serve to make me uncomfortable, without doing any good : and do not be uneasy about it. As I shall probably make some calls on the road I may not reach London before Monday or Tuesday next. I do not yet know the address of my lodgings, but letters sent, meanwhile, to the care of C. Patmore, Esq., 8 [The] Grove, Kentish Town, London, will reach me.

Give my best regards to all at home, and believe me, my dear Father, yours most sincerely,   W. A., Jr.

DERBY,
Wednesday, Feb. 22, 1854.

MY DEAR CATHERINE—I wrote to my father from Liverpool, and also sent him a *Daily News* with a long Ode of mine called ' Peace and War,' which I hope has arrived.

I came here yesterday to spend a day or two with my friend Mr. Gurney (*not* Coventry) Patmore, who is editor of the *Derby Mercury*, and may not reach London before Friday. . . . I dined with Mr. John Miller, a rich and well-known merchant, who is a great picture buyer, and an admirer of Millais, Hunt, etc. He has a fine family and is an agreeable acquaintance.

But I also met a man of greater interest—Nathaniel Hawthorne. I called on him at his Consul's office, a dirty little busy place on the line of docks, and was very kindly received. He happened to have heard my name. He is about forty-six years old, middle sized, hair dark, forehead bald, features elegant though American, cheeks shaved, eyes dark. He is very bashful in manner, and speaks little and in a low tone.

He has not yet had time to visit London, but intends to do
so some time in Spring, when I hope to see more of him.
He looked oddly out of place in Liverpool. I will write again
from London when I arrive, and meanwhile remain, my dear
Catherine, ever yours,   W. A., Jr.

LONDON, 50 SOUTHAMPTON ROW,
RUSSELL SQR., *March* 8, 1854.

MY DEAR FATHER—I was very glad to receive your kind
letters—also one, a day or two ago, from Catherine. I have
got into lodgings down in London, in a central situation. I
have at 17/- a week (which is thought low) a sitting-room and
bedroom which are comfortable enough, and the street is a
wide and good one,—but I am not sure that I am settled yet.
As to my employment, it will be writing for newspapers and
periodicals—of which more by and by ; but the subjects in
general would not be of much interest in Ballyshannon.

Whenever I do anything that I think you would like to see,
I will take care to send it to you. There was a little Nursery
Song of mine called ' Wishing ' in *Household Words* some weeks
ago. Mr. Dickens is going to write a story called ' Hard
Times,' as long as five monthly numbers, in *Household Words*.
He lives within two streets of me, but I have not yet seen
him. I hear he writes all day and in the evening takes a long
walk in the direction of Hampstead or Highgate.

At first I cannot expect to do more than support myself,
and must feel some degree of anxiety as to my prospects, but
if my hopes of using properly the advantages of London be
not disappointed I shall in time make a good position. This
evening I bought 2 packets of flower seeds in Covent Garden
Market and sent them by post, one to you and the other to
Mr. Stubbs. As the packets are different, you can, if you like,
exchange some of the seeds with each other. I hope to see
some of them blowing in flowers in July.

I have had a note from Mr. Hawthorne, which I send you,
as you may like to see it. Pray return it at your leisure. . . .
Whenever you want anything done in London, let me know,
and I shall be most happy to attend to it, and with kindest
regards to all at home I remain my dear Father, always
affectionately yours,   W. A., Jr.

[Immediately upon coming to London he was at
work for *Household Words*, *The Athenæum*, and various
reviews.

He walked and dined almost daily with Rossetti, and gave him, certainly, one sitting for his portrait; but this was probably never finished—there is no further record of it in the diaries.

During these months, also, he saw a great deal of Clough, of old Mr. and Mrs. Rossetti, and of Christina Rossetti.

Everything promised success along the lines of professional journalism, but this profession was not congenial to Allingham, and the following letter to his sister, in June of the same year, gives very definitely his reasons for preferring his former way of life.]

LONDON, 1 QUEEN SQR., BLOOMSBURY,
June 3, 1854.

MY DEAR CATHERINE—After many delays I began this note, as above, three days ago, and was interrupted by somebody coming in. I would have written to you long ago, but for the way I was circumstanced. I still like London, and find I could make quite as large an income by writing as I expected. I had yesterday a letter from an editor who heard of my intention of going away, offering me £100 a year certain for doing something for him once a fortnight, and this is the 3*rd regular* engagement that has been offered to me, with others in prospect; so that if I would 'take off my coat to it' (which is what Thackeray advised), I could make at the very outset £300 or £400 a year. But to do this I must give myself up entirely to desultory and ephemeral writing, truckle to editors and people, and undergo countless anxieties and annoyances, which would not at all suit me; and therefore I think it much better, all things considered, to return into quiet exile and make the best of that. . . . I believe all my friends here are sorry I am going—though some, Carlyle in particular, think it a blessed escape for me out of the profession of literature. . . .

On the 1st of June I was at the Annual Meeting of Charity Children in St. Paul's—very pretty to see. Countless rows of boys and girls, each school with its own uniform, banners, beadles, etc., ranged under the dome, all rising and sitting down and singing together. After the service, it took them perhaps half an hour to march out, by two doors, all in their new clothes for the year. All the girls wear white mob caps and

white aprons, but the gowns and ribbons of the different schools
vary in colour,—the prettiest dresses, I think, were buff frocks,
blue ribbons, and long yellow gloves. The beadles, in gold
laced gowns and cocked hats of immense size, walked in front
of each division, and were received with expressions of admiration (sometimes ironical) by the crowd outside—but the
children seemed to make a pleasant impression on everybody.
I felt proud to recognise the regiment of 'Queen Sqr., Bloomsbury,' among this army of infantry. I have come to like
my lodgings very much and they are admired by all my
visitors ; being both quiet and lively—for though there is no
thoroughfare for carriages at the upper end of the Square, it has
a great many foot passengers and is full of children, having a
fine plane tree, several poplars and hawthorns, and a grass plot
in front of my three windows. I can go into the garden when
I like, and have the gardener to touch his gold-laced hat to
me, under the shadow of Queen Anne, whose statue and title
adorn the Square. Part of one of the lines of street leading
down from it to Holborn, and that thro' which I usually pass,
is Kingsgate Street,—in which there is an Easy Shaving shop ;
but Mr. Sweedlepipe seems to have given way to a successor,
and I have not ventured to inquire if Mrs. Gamp were
within. . . .

Tell Edward[1] his fish is admirable, and admired by artists.
Of course it is from a book ? Let him try some simple
thing from nature.—Best regards to all, from yours my dear
Catherine ever affectionately   W. A., Jr.

[Allingham's friends, on the whole, thought his
decision to leave London wise. Carlyle, in particular,
declared himself 'very glad to hear it,' and added
characteristically, when saying good-bye, ' you'd have
gone from bad to worse ; now you can do your day's
work, and if you have anything to say or write, do so ;
and if no man will have it, you can say, " well, thank
God, I can do without selling it." '

Allingham obtained another appointment in the
Customs at New Ross ; and on the eve of his departure
thence he was busy with a last sitting to Munro for his
bust (a cast of which is now in the possession of Mrs.
Allingham), and going over his *Day and Night Songs*

---

[1] Allingham's half-brother.

with Leigh Hunt, Rossetti 'doing ivy leaves on *Day and Night Songs.*' [1]

A remark of Kingsley's, which evidently pleased Allingham, was recorded on one of these farewell days : it was the description of the Atlantic wave as 'a wall of water a mile long walking in and dashing itself into ten thousand shivers against the cliffs.'

On July 5, he was at his new post, working at the *Music Master*, and in the autumn of this year he wrote, among other poems, his well-known, 'Robin Redbreast.'

He quickly made himself acquainted with the walks and excursions around Ross, and there are many little pen-and-ink sketches in his diary of the places which specially interested him. There is a pretty entry, this spring, of an accidental meeting with three little children in the rain, and of how they had to shelter together under the laurels, and saw the horse-chestnut buds bursting into leaf ; and of how they went home together under an umbrella, and a pair of clear eyes 'came peeping from under a little blue cloak.'

In July this year he went to the Lakes for his holiday, and in November he was back in his old place at Ballyshannon, having effected another exchange with the Customs. Here reading went on as steadily as ever : he added astronomy to his other studies, and his notes show that he was often 'out late at night—to see stars.'

Early in 1856 Allingham received the first number of the *Oxford and Cambridge Magazine*, praising *The Germ*, and writing of Rossetti's illustration to Allingham's poem, 'The Maids of Elfin Mere,' as 'the best drawing that has ever appeared in illustration of a book.' His annual visit to London, this year, took place in May, and one of his first calls was with Arthur Hughes upon Rossetti, who, however, was not at home, but

---

[1] This refers to the design which Rossetti made for a cover to Allingham's *Day and Night Songs*; it was not used.

whose picture of Dante's Dream was discovered somewhere in the room. It was put on the easel, and
Allingham made a little note in his diary of the 'two
lovely figures' and 'rainbow of angels.'[1] The visitors
also came upon his picture called 'Found,' in one of
the many stages of its progress,—'The calf in cart and
bit of wall,' Allingham writes—that calf which grew so
many times into a cow during the thirty years in which
the picture was being painted.

He made many excursions, this month, with Rossetti
and Miss Siddal, and he was always of the 'assemblage'
which gathered so frequently at Rossetti's rooms.

One specially pleasant evening he recorded, when he
dined at Mr. and Mrs. Tom Taylor's with Tennyson
and Holman Hunt, and they sat under a walnut tree,
while Mrs. Tom Taylor sang 'The Brook,' and Hunt
and Tennyson talked about Jerusalem.

In March 1857 Allingham seems to have been in
Dublin, at a reception at the Castle, and at this time he
mentions a visit in Belfast to Mr. McCracken, one of
the first patrons of the Pre-Raphaelite Brotherhood.

In July of this year he was in London, seeing a
good deal of William Morris, at the Burne-Joneses, and
also at Morris's own rooms in Red Lion Square, when
the talk was of 'mediævalism,' of 'beauty of form and
colour,' and of the subjects in which Morris was the
great master.

During this holiday there were many delightful
breakfast parties, which included Hughes, Whitley
Stokes, Stephens, Boyce, Hannay, Patmore, Rossetti,
Morris, and Burne-Jones.

Carlyle he saw many times during this visit, and he
records at length a characteristic answer to a suggestion
of his that Carlyle should write his autobiography :—

'I would,' said Carlyle, 'as soon think of cutting

[1] Rossetti gave Allingham a pencil study for this picture, in which
Allingham stood, for a few minutes, as model for profile and hand.

my throat with my penknife when I get back home !—
the biographers, too ; if those gentlemen would let me
alone I should be much obliged to them. I would say,
as Shakespeare would say to Peter Cunningham, " Sweet
friend, for Jesus' sake forbear ! " '

This holiday was finished by Allingham at the Lakes,
where he visited the Tennysons at Coniston. In the
autumn there is, in his diary, mention of a letter in
connection with the Professorship of English at Cork,
which called forth a note of discontent : ' If I had [but]
entered Queen's College four years ago,' he says—' dissatisfied and weary, twisted and deranged.' But the
mood does not last long : quite soon again he writes,
' I lie on the grass in the sun, the bay and green hills
before me, and read Benvenuto Cellini's Autobiography.'

The following is an extract from a note-book, of
August 1858, of a meeting with Thackeray] :—

Returning to Paris, after a short tour in Switzerland and North Italy, I found Thackeray in the Hotel
Bristol with his two daughters. He not well—often in
bed till mid-day or later—struggling with (*Pendennis*),
but in the evening usually recovering himself.

I told him I had been with the Brownings (who were
then in Paris, staying in the Rue Castiglioni, No. 6).

' Browning was here this morning,' Thackeray said,
' what spirits he has—almost too much for me in my
weak state. He almost blew me out of bed ! '

' A wonderful fellow, indeed ! '

' Yes, and he doesn't drink wine.'

' He's already screwed up to concert pitch.'

' Far above it. But I can't manage his poetry.
What do you say ? '

(I spoke highly of it).

' Well, you see, I want poetry to be musical, to run
sweetly.'

' So do I '——

' Then that *does for* your friend B. ! '

I spoke of Browning's other qualities as so splendid
as to make him, as it were, a law in himself. But
Thackeray only smiled and declined further discussion.

'He has a good belief, in himself, at all events. I
suppose he doesn't care whether people praise him
or not.'

'I think he does, very much.'

'O does he? Then I'll say something about him
in a number.'

Thackeray took me to dine with him in the Palais
Royal. He noticed with quiet enjoyment every little
incident—beginning with the flourish with which our
waiter set down the dishes of Ostend oysters. After
tasting his wine Thackeray said, looking at me solemnly
through his large spectacles, 'One's first glass of wine
in the day is a great event.'

That dinner was delightful. He talked to me with
as much ease and familiarity as if I had been a favourite
nephew.

After dinner Thackeray proposed that we should go
to the Palais Royal Theatre, but on issuing forth he
changed his mind, and said we would call up Father
Prout. 'His quarters are close by. You know him,
don't you?'

'Yes, I know that singing priest a little.'

He was then Paris Correspondent of the *Globe*, and
his letters were much admired. It was said that the
Globe had been obliged to buy a fount of Greek type
by reason of Mahony's fondness for classical quotations.

In a narrow street at the back of the Palais Royal,
in a large lowish room on the ground floor, we found
the learned and witty Padre, loosely arrayed, reclining in
front of a book and a bottle of Burgundy. He greeted
us well, but in a low voice and said, 'Evening boys,
there's a young chap asleep there in the corner.' And
in a kind of recess we noted something like bed-clothes.
Thackeray was anxious to know who this might be, and
Prout explained that it was a young Paddy from Cork

or thereabouts, who had been on a lark in Paris and spent his money. Prout found him 'hard up,' and knowing something of his friends in Ireland had taken him in to board and lodge, pending the arrival of succour.

This piece of humanity was much to Thackeray's taste, as you may suppose. Thackeray said the Burgundy was 'too strong,' and had brandy and water instead.

We talked among other things of Dickens. I said how much a story of Dickens might be improved by a man of good taste with a pencil in his hand, by merely scoring out this and that.

Says Thackeray (with an Irish brogue), ' Young man, you're threadin' on the tail o' me coat ! '

I did not understand at first.

' What you've just said applies very much to your humble servant's things.'

I disclaimed this, and Prout said emphatically, ' Not a word too much in them ! '

[In 1859 Allingham was in London in September— ' Three hours in D. G. R.'s rooms as of old '—and the month following he was travelling in Holland and Germany.

He spent three days at Weimar, and on October 22 he writes in his diary]—

To *Goethe's House*, with Schuchardt, who was his copyist for some years.

The hall.

The stairs (bronzed casts—one, a boy).

The lobby.

The reception rooms with glass cases, busts, drawers of medals, etc. Torso (of a boy ?) at end.

The working room, etc., low and plain.

First, clothes-room, old boots of the anklejack sort, flannel shirts, dress coat, old hat (very big). Writing-room, desks, little glass Napoleon, memoranda of annual events : pasteboard pyramid ' for judging works of art,' on the sides, each a different colour, the words, Verstandt, Vernunft, Sinnlichkeit, Phantasie. Cushion for leaning arms on.

Bedroom, green arm-chair wherein he died, medicine-bottle. Lumber-room beyond. I open shutter of bedroom.

Book-room, narrow and dark, row of shelves in the centre. Carlyle's *German Romances* (uncut), with C.'s writing descriptive of sketches of his house in Scotland.

Dine with Mr. Marshall at the summer Club House on the Hill, and have genial talk, then to his house ; he shows his poems in the *Republic of Letters*, gives me Goethe's *Letters of F. von Stein*.

[On November 8 he writes : 'at home in this old Ballyshannon,' and soon his 'Nightingale Valley' appears, and he mentions letters of thanks, for copies, from Rossetti, Patmore, Woolner, and Stokes.

On December 28 is entered : 'My father's birth-day—seventy years.'

Allingham remained in Ballyshannon through 1860, 1861, 1862, but during the two earlier years he made very few entries in his diaries.

In May 1860 he was in London, and writes: 'In Carlyle's garden, some twenty yards by six ; ivy at the end. Three or four lilac bushes; an ash stands on your left ; a little copper beech on your right gives just an umbrella to sit under when the sun is hot ; a vine or two on one wall, neighboured by a jasmine—one pear tree.'

In September 1862 Allingham exchanged his post at Ballyshannon for one in the London Customs : but work at the docks was not congenial, and this second attempt to settle in London was again unsuccessful. He seems to have been ill and depressed during this time, and in October he was away on sick leave.

The great pleasure of the year was his intimacy with the Burne-Joneses; much of his time was spent with them.

This autumn, also, he often saw William Morris, in Red Lion Square, and went down several times with him to the Red House. He writes of Mrs. Morris—'tall, wonderful.'

There are many pleasant pictures of the Burne-Joneses—'Edward drawing, Mrs. Edward cutting out shoes for Pip'; or again, 'Mrs. Edward sings old ballads and Rossetti's songs.' With them he also frequently met Swinburne, Webb, and Faulkner. One day he records, more fully, an evening with Rossetti, 'lying on the grass in Lincoln's Inn Fields, and talking with him of Christina's poems;' and an account of a visit to the Carlyles on August 10 of this year, is given here at length:—]

Being up from Ballyshannon for a holiday, I was at Cheyne Row to-day. Mrs. Carlyle received me with great kindness. I had a new hat of some shape that amused her; she tried it on. Spoke of Thackeray's new house, his dinners, Poodle Byng, T.'s daughters. Carlyle has grayer hair than when I last saw him, and patches of white in whisker. He spoke of competitive examinations.

National Portrait Gallery—Lord Brougham. The Committee wanted to put in Brougham's portrait, the man still living, contrary to rule. C. opposed, and added that when Brougham did die he would speedily be forgotten. Lord Stanhope, Chairman, said with polite surprise, 'Oh, a very remarkable man, surely—great statesman, great orator!' 'No' (C. persisted), 'Brougham had done nothing worth remembering particularly; and at all events the rules of the Gallery, etc.,' and gained his point.

It was on this occasion that C. noticed Dizzy, who was present as a member of the Committee, looking at him in a noticeable way. 'He took no part in the discussion,' C. said, 'but I could see that he was looking at me with a face of brotherly recognition—a wholly sympathetic expression.' C. used often to refer to this brotherly look of Dizzy (which, however, may not have meant very much!) 'I found this look in his face— although I had more than once or twice said hard things of him publicly. I saw he entirely agreed with me as to Brougham.'

It gave C. a little leaning to Dizzy when he thought of it, tho' it did not change his opinion that D.'s success was a scandal and shame for England.

[Allingham was back in Ballyshannon in December, but there are no entries in his diary until March 1863, when he was again in London arranging for another exchange in the Customs. He was advised to take Lymington, in Hampshire; and when established there his diaries are once more carefully kept.

The story continues in his own words.]

CHAPTER V

1863

EARLY in 1863 fortune not choice fixed my abode at Lymington in Hampshire. 'You will be near Tennyson,' said Carlyle, when I was taking leave of him. 'I doubt if I shall see him,' I replied, disheartened by a second failure to settle in London, and disinclined for even the best company. 'Yes, yes,' said C., 'you are sure to come together.'

I went to Lymington on Friday the 8th of May, pleasant little old Town on its green hill, looking across to the Isle of Wight some five miles away, to which a steam-boat plied three or four times daily. I was Lymington's Custom-House Officer, the only one, my office being a small first-floor room over the Coastguard Station, looking upon the little Harbour, (muddy at low water, occupied chiefly by pleasure-yachts) and the woods of Walhampton beyond. A little higher up a Ferry-Boat rowed by a big man in a jersey, a Blue Giant, kept crossing to and fro, and higher still was a Toll-Bridge, to which the Boldre Water or Lymington River ran down in its green valley, a quiet rural stream, from the oaks, beeches, and brackens of the New Forest.

Depressed tho' I was, I felt a great deliciousness in the quiet green lanes and hedges, thickets, woods and distances ; and the evening after my arrival, standing at the field gate close to the Town, I heard four nightingales.

On Wednesday I crossed the Solent in our Steam-boat
for the first time, and stood in Yarmouth, a quaint
little old place, with its little waterside castle, Governor's
House (now the George Inn), and the arms of Henry
the Eighth carved in stone on a weedy wall, returning by the last boat. I talked with the 'Engineer' of
the Steam-boat, a pleasant and intelligent young man.
We spoke a little of Tennyson, whom he knew well
by sight. I asked had he read any of the Bard's
writings ? and he replied quite simply and modestly
that he could not understand Mr. Tennyson's poetry,
he saw it was intended for people of higher education
than himself. Mr. T., he said, had smoked a pipe
with George (the steward) in crossing.

The young man, native of Lymington, who is
going to London by exchange with me, with money
advantage in his favour, seems well fitted for town life.
When I praised the landscape he remarked that he
was 'No judge of beauty,' and to my question as we
walked towards his house—'Do the nightingales sing
down this way ?' he answered quietly, 'Very likely
they do, I shouldn't know a nightingale if I heard it.'
He was not in the least contemptuous, but absolutely
obtuse on such matters, and wished, no doubt, to let
me know that it was useless to bring them forward in
his company. One sees the practical advantage of
variety of character. This young man won't mind
Thames Street and the barrel organs.

May 12-13.—Lymington Pleasure Fair. Booths in
the streets with toys and sweets, noise and clatter. Shows
—some monkeys and a wild boar, a ' Zulu Caffir ' ; fat
woman (leaving her baby behind the scenes) does
conjuring tricks—Dancing-booth—Shooting-galleries.
Gypsies—black-eyed girls in tawdry bright attire, brown
old witches, gypsy young man lithe and tall, wonderfully handsome animal, a black panther—and about
as trustworthy ? How Oriental these people keep !
The English rustic, getting drunk, bellows discordant

songs, tumbles down and snores, the Irishman quarrels and strikes. Perhaps the kind of drink has something to do with it. Pothouse beer is bad, but raw public-house whisky is a frightful potation. What a country is Ireland! her chief manufacture is *Calamity Water*, a name too of her own devisal.

Saturday, May 23.—Hear of the death of my half-brother Thomas at Raphoe Royal School, where he was assistant-master—honest and diligent, with a tenacious memory. He was successful at Dublin University—showed no original faculty.

Wednesday, June 24—Heard Spurgeon preach in a tent in a field beside the town. ' If any man thirst, etc,' anecdotes—prayer—good lungs. Rain—Spurgeon put on his hat, many opened umbrellas. After the service, people came to shake hands with him, and I drew near. He said, ' I must be gone. I trust God has given us some souls this evening.' I walked behind him ; he has a big body, short legs, flat feet : Anglo-Saxon?—large brain, no doubt. His mind a mystery to me, but not interesting.

Sunday, June 28.—In the evening walked sadly along the shore of the Solent eastwards by Pylewell—returning, brought home a glow-worm and put it in a white lily, through which it shone.

It was not till Friday the 3rd of July that I first saw Freshwater. I crossed by the evening boat, walked over the bridge, and after two or three miles of beautiful green-sided roads, spoilt here and there by Forts, reached the enchanted realm of Farringford, but coasting outside could not see the house and would not of course enter any gate. In the dusk I saw the ' noble Down' rising up, its Beacon against the sky, then got to the shore and the sea and white cliffs. I was thinking all the while of Tennyson, and felt very doleful. Yet I had not the faintest thought of presenting myself to him or wish, even, to meet him by chance on his return (he was from home at this time).

I have lost the faith I used to have in people's wishing to
see me—perhaps it is merely one of the signs that youth
has passed away. But I feel a natural bond to him (I
say it in humility) and to a very few others, and only
in their company am better contented than to be with
nature . and books. With these persons I feel truly
humble, yet at the same time easy. I understand and
am understood, with words or without words. It is not
fame that attracts me, it disgusts me rather. Fame
has cooled many friendships for me, never made or
increased one. Fame is a thing of the 'World,' and
the 'World' is a dreadful separator.

In the late summer dusk I returned through charming narrow leafy roads—the Moon rose like a surprise.

At Lymington in these first months I was busy
doing *Laurence Bloomfield*, the last five chapters,
which were coming out month by month in *Fraser's
Magazine*. After this 'The Ballad Book' for Macmillan occupied the best part of my leisure time—
much reading, comparing, selecting and copying of
Ballads, to perhaps little result.

Monday, *July* 6.—At Southampton Dock Station
my eye was caught by a middle-sized but singularly
well-knit figure of a man, strong, light, easy of movement, almost Greek in his poses but altogether natural
and unconscious. He turned his head and who was it
but Tom Sayers in a white hat, with a bunch of charms
to his watch-chain. The high-shouldered pugilist such
as Leech draws is not the genuine article. Sayers has
rather falling shoulders though wide and muscular, so
has Heenan, and Tom King. Ease and freedom of
movement characterises them all, especially Sayers.
They doubtless much enjoy life in their way, so long
as they keep within tolerable bounds, and the fighting
itself is a great animal pleasure.

Tuesday, *Wednesday*, 7-8.—Wandered in the New
Forest—view of the wide woodland from Emery Down.
Slept at the Crown, Lyndhurst—Church, window de-

signed by Jones ; Fresco, half done, of the 'Foolish Virgins' by Leighton. Lymington—a travelling circus in the cricket-field, where I see Tom Sayers spar with 'Young Brooks': noticeable, how slight the movements Tom made to avoid a blow, moving his head sometimes so little, that his antagonist's glove rippled up Tom's short hair—then Tom's hand went in like a flash of lightning.

Saturday, July 11.—Copy and send off *Laurence Bloomfield*, Chapter X., to Froude. Train to Southampton, young Parson with pleasant voice arguing with old working man, who said he cared no more for a clergyman than for a chimney sweep, and scolded bishops.

Tuesday, August 4.—Mrs. Arthur Clough, the poet's widow, who had written to let me know, reached Lymington Terminus with her three children, also her sister Mrs. Coltman and her children, where I met them, and we crossed over to Yarmouth together, a roughish passage. They went on to Freshwater to a house they had taken there ; I returned to Lymington.

August 10.—A very kind letter from Charles Kingsley, quite unsought for, offering me introductions to 'Sam St. Barbe,' (the banker here) and Captain Mildmay. Next day a letter from Rossetti, complaining of being 'restless,' and asking if he shall come and pay me a visit. I reply 'Yes,' but he finds it mighty hard to make the start, and puts off time after time, coming at last.

August 16.—Stick at *L. Bloomfield*, Chapter XI., all day, and *finish*.

Saturday, August 29.—Came to Freshwater and walked with Mrs. Clough and Mrs. Coltman on Afton Down ; slept at the Albion Hotel, amid a noise of waves. The Landlady a big dreadful woman with fiery face. Next morning breakfasted at Mrs. Clough's. They all went to Church. I was left at home with Clough's letters and American diary, which or a selection from them Mrs. C. thinks of publishing.

After an early dinner, we walked to Farringford and found that the family were expected in about ten days. Mr. Tennyson was ill (the woman said), and coming to London from Harrogate. Mrs. Clough being an intimate, we were admitted to the living rooms, and saw plenty of books on shelves and tables, including numerous presentation volumes of poetry, and the new magazines—among which I noted with some satisfaction *Fraser* with the new chapter of *Laurence Bloomfield* (so lately teasing me in MS.).

Monday, September 14.—Note from Mrs. Clough, from Bournemouth—'Mrs. Cameron will be glad to see you at lunch, to meet Mr. Henry Taylor.' Mrs. Clough was returning to the island to-day, and I joined her with Mr. and Mrs. Coltman on the 3 o'clock steamer. The Tennysons on board. T. and I just spoke a few words, and then I went forward with Mrs. Clough and kept out of his way. Returned to Lymington.

Wednesday, September 16.—Southampton : Heard Cardinal Wiseman lecture on 'Self-culture' at the Hartley Institute. An Irish priest, he, in general appearance ; face like a shrewish old woman in spectacles ; voice tuneless, accent a little mincing. The substance of the lecture commonplace, the style tawdry and paltry.

Saturday, October 3.—Cross by 3 o'clock Boat, invited to spend Sunday at Mrs. Clough's. Rainy and roughish. The Coltmans are gone. Mrs. Clough tells me I am invited to go to the Tennysons with her to-night. (Hurrah!) We drove to Farringford, picking up on the way Mr. Pollock (afterwards Sir F. P.) and his son, a youth in spectacles. Drawing-room, tea, Mrs. Tennyson in white, I can some-times scarcely hear her low tones. Mrs. Cameron, dark, short, sharp-eyed, one hears very distinctly. I wandered to the book-table, where Tennyson joined me. He praised Worsley's *Odyssey*. In a book of

Latin versions from his own poetry he found some slips in Lord Lyttleton's Latin—'Cytherea Venus,' etc. 'Did I find Lymington very dull?' I told him that since coming there I had heard Cardinal Wiseman lecture (on 'Self-culture'), Spurgeon preach, and seen Tom Sayers spar. 'More than I have,' he remarked. In taking leave he said, 'Come to-morrow!'

Sunday, October 4.—In the forenoon I walk over alone to Farringford ; find first Mrs. T., the two boys, and their tutor, Mr. Butterfield, fair-haired, modest-mannered. T. at luncheon : 'John Wilson's *Life*—leave such things alone ! they're done for money.'—'Entozoa—germs were mingled in a convict's food, for experiment ; after his death the parasites were found stuck all over him inside. Fancy one feeding on your brain!'—'What do we know of the feelings of insects? nothing. They may feel more pain than we.' I think *not*.

T. takes me upstairs to his 'den' on the top-story, and higher, up a ladder, to the leads. He often comes up here a-night to look at the heavens. One night he was watching shooting-stars and tumbled through the hatchway, falling on the floor below, a height of at least ten feet I should say. The ladder probably broke his fall and he was not hurt. I quoted 'A certain star shot madly from his sphere.'

T.—'I've never heard any Sea-Maid's music in Freshwater Bay, but I saw an old lady swimming one day.'

The view of sea and land is delectable, stretching northward across the Solent up into the New Forest. Then we went down and walked about the grounds, looking at a cedar, a huge fern, an Irish yew. The dark yew in *Maud* 'sighing for Lebanon' he got at Swainston,—Sir John Simeon's. In one place are some little arches half-covered with ivy, which I pretend to believe are meant for mock ruins. This T. repudiates. He paused at a weed of goatsbeard, saying, 'It shuts up at three.' Then we went down the garden, past a

large tangled fig-tree growing in the open—'It's like
a breaking wave,' says I. 'Not in the least,' says he.
Such contradictions, *from him*, are noway disagreeable :
and so to the farmyard.

'Have you a particular feeling about a farmyard ?'
he asked, 'a special delight in it ? I have. The first
time I read Shakespeare was in a haystack.—*Othello*—
I said, "This man's overrated." Boys can't understand
Shakespeare, nor women.' We spoke a little of the
Shakespeare 'Ter-Centenary' next year.

'Most people pronounce "Arbŭtus" wrong, with
the second syllable long. Clematis, too, which should
be Clē-mătis.'

In the porch, or somewhere near it, I noticed a dusty
phial hanging with some dried brown stuff in it. 'It's
a Lar,' he said, with a twinkle in his eyes. 'And what
else is it ?' I asked. 'An old bottle of Ipecacuanha.'
I thought the woodwork of the windows a rather crude
green : 'I don't know why you shouldn't like it,' he
said. We looked at the great magnolia stretching up
to the roof, then into the hall and saw some fossils.
'Man is so small !' he said, 'but a fly on the wheel.'
Mrs. Clough was in the house and she and I now
departed, T. coming with us as far as the little south
postern opening on to the lane, afraid to go further.
He said he was one day pursued full cry along the road
by two fat women and sixteen children ! Another day
he saw a man's face, who had climbed on the outside
fence and was looking over into the garden : 'I said to
him, "It isn't at all pretty of you to be peeping
there ! . You'd better come down"—and he did.'
'Was he like an educated man ?' 'Yes—or half-
educated.' In parting he said to me, 'We shall see
you sometimes ?'—which gladdened me.

Mrs. Clough and I dined at Mrs. Cameron's.

Sunday, October 11.—Walk, Boldre, Hayward Mill,
Common. Gypsies—old woman asks me to look at
her son who is very ill in waggon. I see him, lying

pale with heavy black eyes and tangled hair, speechless, has 'lumps in his throat' she says—quinsy? I promise to send some one to him if I can. Call on Marshall, the relieving officer,—'at church,' leave a letter for him about the sick gypsy.

Monday, October 12.—Finish twelfth and last chapter of *Bloomfield* and post it.

Saturday, October 17.—Fine evening. New Forest. Holmsley, Wilverly Post, heath and woods in front, russet gold; rest by a rivulet, thick beech woods, cottage—the woman says it is unhealthy and very lonesome—

> Under the shade of melancholy boughs.

Two woodpeckers, green as parroquets. The setting sun, the fiery ferns, the gold beechen-leaves. Lyndhurst, bed at Crown.

Sunday, October 18.—To Rufus's Stone, moorlands under heavy sky, thick embossment of russet golden beech-woods filling the vales, blue distance—showers.

How many days of my life I pass without a word of conversation. But am I not as well off as I deserve to be?

> O days of youthful gladness!
> When I, a happy fool,
> Thought failure, sickness, sadness,
> Th' exception, not the rule.

Monday, October 19.—News of the gypsy. 'Getting better; lump broke.' Write to Southampton paper against cutting down trees in 'the Ditches' (old moat).

Thursday, October 22.—I receive proof from *Fraser's Mag.* of the twelfth and last chapter of *L. Bloomfield*. Eight of the chapters I have written month by month (missing one month) for the magazine. So fate would have it. It's not properly compacted as to plan, and never will be now. But with indefinite time at command I should most probably, as so often before, have tried a dozen different shapes and ended by throwing the thing aside. It has good work in it here and there.

A story in 5000 lines,
Where Homer's epic fervour shines,
   Philosophy like Plato's—
Alas, I sing of Paddies, Priests,
And Pigs, those unromantic beasts,
   Policemen and Potatoes!

Friday, October 23.—Very fine; in the New Forest. Holmsley—path to Burley, field-lane fern-banked, delightful. Hamlet on its gorsey common, a big oak among the hollies. Sat down and read Woolner's *Beautiful Lady* which the post brought me to-day from the author. Tender and sweet. Well tastes poetry thus on a solitary ramble. I remember distinctly every breathing of the verses which were in the first number of *The Germ*, nearly fourteen years ago. Real love of nature and delicate truth of touch; with the quaint guild-mark, so to speak, of the P. R. B. (I can't bear to be verbally quaint myself, yet often like it in another).

   I recollect my lady in a wood,
Keeping her breath and peering—(firm she stood
     Her slim shape balanced on tip-toe—)
   Into a nest which lay below,
   Leaves shadowing her brow.

   . . . the breeze
   Lifts gold from leaf to leaf, as these
   Ash-saplings move at ease.

Thackeray, I recollect, was much touched by Woolner's poem, and by Hunt's etching to it of the Lover pressing his face down upon the new-made grave-mound. But hopeless grief is too sad a subject for Art, save to the Young.

   Passing a Keeper's lodge, came to the 'Twelve Apostles,' old oaks, most of them rugged hollow pillars with a few living branches. Sunset light, lonely road running through great beech-woods; double-dyed with sunset gold: I picture myself attacked by ruffians, with various dénouments. Such things never do happen in the Forest. The gypsies only beg, and perhaps filch. Pass Alum Green, the moon rising over the hamlet, and strike a dampish forest-path to Brockenhurst road, where I enter a wayside inn, and sit comfortably by a great peat-fire, two antlers above the chimney, drinking beer and reading in Woolner's book. Home by rail about 8.

I go on studying Old Ballads—(no original lyrics coming now, alas!) Custom-house daily. Yachts, steamers, pensioners, accounts, coastguard. Periodical visits to Pitt's Deep, Buckler's Hard, Keyhaven, and Hurst Castle, walking or riding. Boat and punt—sailing, etc. Measuring vessels is the most troublesome duty, boarding yachts and examining their stores the most disagreeable.

Sunday, December 13.—Walk from Lymington to Christchurch, by cliffs and beach,—mean, straggling little Town among flat watery fields, by a broad muddy estuary. It has a huge and striking old gray Church, part Norman, much decayed, and full of coughs and rheumatisms for the worshippers, being very unfit for the Protestant service. At evening service with a regulation sermon. After which I found, at the east end under a great window, the cenotaph to Shelley and Mary, at which I stood looking while the Choir practised their Christmas anthem in the empty dim-lighted building.

The monument is of white marble, a woman supporting a dead man, life size, very like a Pieta :—odd jumble of ideas. Bed at Newlyn's Hotel. Stars, humming wind, frost?

Next morning, pretty view from a bridge of the great old Church, ivied ruin and large willow beside it—everything else very ugly. By train through flooded meadows to Ringwood, and on to Lymington. 'Goodman Dodd,' etc.—wrote to my Father.

This man spreads himself out, gives ear to the foolish public,
That man shuts himself in, gives ear to a foolish clique ;
Foolish the public, the cliques, the ignorant ones and the knowing,
Wise the soul of a man who lets all go quietly by.

Sunday, December 20.—I lunched at Farringford.
We all helped in wheeling Mrs. Tennyson to the top
of High Down. Then A. T., the Tutor and myself
walked to Totland's Bay, the talk all upon Classic
Metres, of which he is full at present. I am invited
for Christmas.

Tuesday, December 22.—Feel out of sorts and as it
were stupefied ; write to Mrs. Tennyson declining the
Christmas invitation, which I was so glad to have ! On
the second day after, came a very kind note from
Mrs. T. renewing the invitation, and on the 26th I
went to Farringford. The post brought me a gift of
a purse from Mrs. Clough.

Saturday, December 26.—At Yarmouth I find Mrs.
Cameron shopping, who gives me a seat in her carriage,
and tells me she has a copy of Henry Taylor's
Works for me as a Christmas Box. In a subsequent
examination which she put me through as to my
opinion of H. T.'s poetry I fear my answering fell
decidedly below her expectation, for the Christmas Box
was never given, nor did either of us mention it
afterwards.

At Farringford I find F. T. Palgrave. Tennyson,
he, and I walk up High Down.

Dinner at six, the usual immediate move (with the
wine) to Drawing-room, and talk all about Classic
Metres, to which I naturally have little to contribute,
nor can I see that the discussion throws much if any
light on English metrical effects.

Farringford, Sunday, December 27.—A. T. comes
in to breakfast without greeting, which is sometimes his
way. I play at football with the two Boys. (Hallam
is about eleven, Lionel about nine.) Then walk with
A. T., Palgrave, H. and L. along High Down to the
Needles. Lionel talks to me ; he is odd, shy, sweet,
and, as his mother says, *daimonisch.* Hallam has
something of a shrewd satirical turn, but with great
good nature. To the cliff edge, then returning we

creep up long slopes of down and rest at the Beacon. Thistles and other growths crouch into the sward from the fierce sea-winds. I quote 'a wrinkle of the monstrous hill.' We talk of 'Christabel.' Race down, I get first to the stile. After dinner more talk of 'Classic Metres'; in the drawing-room, T. standing on the hearth-rug repeated with emphasis (perhaps apropos of metres) the following lines, in the following way :—

> Higgledy—piggledy, silver and gold,
> There's—(*it's nothing very dreadful!*)
> There's a louse on my back
> Seven years old.
> He inches, he pinches,
> In every part,
> And if I could catch him
> I'd *tearr* out his *hearrt*!

The last line he gave with tragic fury. Prose often runs into rhyme. T. imitated the waiter in some old-fashioned tavern calling down to the kitchen— 'Three gravies, two mocks, and a *pea*'! (soup under-stood). On 'pea' he raised the tone and prolonged it very comically.

Farringford, December 28.—A. T., Palgrave and I walk to Alum Bay and look at the coloured cliffs, smeary in effect, like something spilt. A. T. reproves P. for talking so fast and saying 'of—of—of—of,' etc. He also corrects me for my pronunciation (or so he asserts) of 'dew.' 'There's no *Jew* on the grass!' says he—'there may be *dew*, but that's quite another thing.' He quotes Tom Moore's 'delicious night,' etc. (four lines), with a little grunt of disapprobation at the end. Home at four. T. goes to have his hot bath. I revise *Laurence Bloomfield* (which Macmillan is printing) in the boys' room.

At dinner : Mr. and Mrs. Bradley of Marlborough, Mr. and Mrs. Butler of Harrow.

In the drawing-room A. T., P., and the two Bs. all on 'Classic Metres.' T. setting the schoolmasters right

more than once, I noticed. I asked Mr. Bradley afterwards, when he called on me at Lymington, did he
think he could read one—any one—of Horace's Odes
as it was intended to be read? He said he was sure he
could *not*. He has brought into use at Marlborough
the 'new' pronunciation (Italian vowel sounds K for
C, etc.), which, he says, puzzles himself much more than
the boys. I like him much, and wish he were not a
Parson or that Parsonism were a different kind of thing.
I had the ladies all to myself, and we discoursed profoundly on 'poets and practical people,' 'benevolence
true and false,' 'the gulf between certain people and
others,' etc. Mrs. T. confessed herself tired of hearing
about 'Classic Metres.' The company gone, T., P. and
I went to Palgrave's room, where the poet read to us the
'Vision of Sin,' the 'Sea Fairies,' and part of the 'Lotos
Eaters,'—a rich and solemn music, but not at all heavy.
He will not admit that any one save himself can read
aloud his poems properly. He suffered me to try a
passage in the 'Lotos Eaters' and said 'You do it better
than most people,' then read it himself and went on
some way further. Thus I got from him *viva voce*
part of a poem which has always seemed to me among
his most characteristic works.

December 29.—After breakfast I took leave of
Mrs. Tennyson and the boys. P. civilly invites me to
his house at York Gate. When I went to T.'s room he
said, 'Come whenever you like,' and as I went out
by the garden he came after me and saw me through
the gate. Truly friendly—a delightful visit! I walked
to Yarmouth in happy mood and crossed to Lymington
on the steam-boat.

Wednesday, December 30.—Walked to Pitt's Deep
and visited the Coastguard Station; returned at dusk,
dirty roads, starry sky. Be content: what folly in a
poor man to wish for an easy life and at the same time
for much that he could only get by hard work.

CHAPTER VI

1864

I HAVE been an 'Official' all my life, without the least turn for it. I never could attain a true *official manner*, which is highly artificial and handles trifles with ludicrously disproportionate gravity. True that ordinary men are thus kept in order and the dull work of the world got through : but for my own part I always get back to the question, is it really necessary that men should consume so much of their bodily and mental energies in the machinery of civilised life ? The world seems to me to do much of its toil for that which is not in any sense bread. Again, does not the latent feeling that much of their striving is to no purpose tend to infuse large quantities of *sham* into men's work ? In the Government offices, of which I know something by experience, I believe the clerks could do all they really do in half the allotted time, and, moreover, that much of their work when done is itself useless.

January 16, 1864.—Letter from Mrs. Tennyson, asks me if I know of a house near Lymington that would suit her Father and Sister (Mrs. Weld). I go to the house-agents. Aubrey House might do.

January 17.—At Southampton. Arrival of the *Poonah* P. & O. steam-ship. People returning from India, greetings. Ayah on deck. A single one of these brown slender women with black eyes and undulatory movements (they must have soft bones),

in muslin and gold ornaments, makes all Hindustan
real. How cold she must find this weather. Mail-bags
landed, 340 in number.

February 27.—Wrote to the Papers proposing to
name the new bridge at Blackfriars 'Shakespeare
Bridge,'—with statues if they like. The Blackfriars and
the Globe Theatres stood near this place. A bridge is
the best place in London for statues. In vain. The
Times said it was not an English custom to give the
names of writers to our streets or public places.
Excellent argument. Ballad : 'The Abbot of Inis-
falen.'

March 1.—Going on with Ballad Book. 'Grunsey
and Dodd' appears in *Macmillan's Magazine* this month.

Tuesday, March 22.—Dry haze, groaning east wind,
headache. I now believe the atmosphere with its
changes has much more to do with health and spirits
than I used to think possible. As we go on we find
that many 'old-fashioned notions' have a good deal in
them. But we had not much east wind at Ballyshannon. Poem : 'Emily.'

24 *to* 28.—At Farringford, for an Easter holiday.
Professor Jowett was staying at a neighbouring house
with two Oxford pupils, and came in to Tennyson's
every day. One day T., J., and myself on the shore,
throwing pebbles into the sea. Alas, I fear I have not
set down anything of the conversations. This is
usually the way when there is too much.

> A man who keeps a diary pays
> Due toll to many tedious days ;
> But life becomes eventful—then
> His busy hand forgets the pen.
> Most books, indeed, are records less
> Of fulness than of emptiness.

I recall an interesting talk with Professor Jowett at
Freshwater, one night that I walked with him from
Tennyson's to his lodging at the Terrace. The con-
versation turned to the subject of *conventionalities*, and

I urged how lamentable it was to see men, and, especially, distinguished men, accepting in public, or even actively supporting ideas which they abjured in their own minds. This was my hobby and I rode it at a pace that the Professor was probably little accustomed to, yet he listened and answered not only with patience but apparent interest, and when we arrived at his door invited me, somewhat to my surprise, to come in and continue the conversation, I remember, in a room dimly lighted with one candle. He seemed to agree with me in the main, but argued to the effect that by an open and unguarded non-conformity a man might ruin his career and lose all influence and authority. I said in my usual impulsive style—' Oh, he would find the apparent obstacles to be only shadows on his road.' To which J. replied gently, but with a tone of conviction, ' I fear he would find them very real.'

He is a soft smooth round man, with fat soft hands, and a very gentle voice and manner, but with no weakness of will or lack of perseverance. He is extremely cautious, but not in the least cowardly,—can quietly make his way, doubtless, into very hard substances, as some very soft creatures do (speaking without disparagement). J. indeed has publicly shown great frankness, *for an Oxford don*, and will be a reformer *ab intra*.

I know full well how too impatient I always am, how too-too lacking in *savoir faire*. Yet I don't think I was wrong to speak freely to him, for once. Nay, I don't see how any thinking man can be at perfect peace with himself while his public conduct and private belief are not in agreement. I do not know one English Writer now living who is consistent. Emerson is : but supposing he were an Englishman ? an absurd supposition, for Emerson is entirely an American product.

Saturday, April 2.—To Embley Park, Romsey [the home of Florence Nightingale's parents], invited from Saturday to Monday. Mrs. Clough is there (she is niece

of Mrs. N. and cousin of Miss Florence Nightingale).
Large house in a rich park : a rhododendron avenue.
Immense drawing-room. Mr. Nightingale—tall, thin,
courtly, white-haired, with blue swallow-tailed coat
always buttoned ; in manner very quiet and sad.   By his
desire I read from *In Memoriam* one evening, and the
poem seemed to impress him deeply.   He and his wife
live alone at the end of their days in this great house.
Florence they never see and rarely, I think, hear from.
She secludes herself in London on the ground of
health and needing all her strength for public interests.
There is a statuette of her in the hall.

April 10.—Walked over to Brooke, Mr. Seely's,
with one of the Camerons, and saw Garibaldi in the
drawing-room, who, understanding me to be a poet,
called me 'mio caro,' and shook hands heartily.   He
stood leaning sideways on a stick and looked of shorter
stature than I expected : his face exactly like the
portraits, the image of bravery, sincerity, and goodwill.
I took my leave quickly, as there were numerous
visitors to see the great General.

April 22.—*Laurence Bloomfield* published.   Many
letters and notices of it came to me, mostly favour-
able.   The *Irishman* newspaper calls me 'a mitigated
Whig,' but praises my pictures of the peasantry.

May 16.—Tennyson praises *L. Bloomfield*, and says
it was a very difficult thing to do.

May 23-25.—Visiting Rev. W. Barnes at Came,
Dorchester.

Tuesday, May 31.— Mr. Gladstone quoted *L.
Bloomfield* last night in the House of Commons,
describing it, according to the *Times* report, as an 'extremely clever work.'   The two lines he gave, apropos
of some proposed alteration of the spirit duties, were
these :—

> Poor Paddy of all Christian men I think
> On basest food pours down the vilest drink.

(Chap. xii. ll. 296-297.)   99

I opened the *Times* in a news-shop and felt a thrill at seeing my own words so unexpectedly.

Monday, June 6.—Very fine. Tennyson and the Boys come across the Solent to me and we make an excursion to Beaulieu Abbey. I take them through Walhampton by the Fir-walk.

Tuesday, June 7.—Lord Palmerston has recommended me for a Civil List Pension of £60 a year— 'on account of the merit of his poetical writings.' Serviceable : but do I like it ? How *much* rather would I do without it ! But I have no turn at all for making money, that's certain, and perhaps I may give some equivalent.

Saturday, June 25.—To London. Parker's Hotel— Surrey St. Georgie Jones and Philip—Lyceum, *Hamlet.*

Sunday, June 26.— To Warwick Crescent ; Pen Browning, then enter the great Robert, who greets me warmly and gives me 'Dramatis Personæ.' He commended *Bloomfield* with reservation—'Not so poetical as some of your things—but O so clever.' We talk of Tennyson, etc.

Down to Chelsea and find D. G. Rossetti painting a very large young woman, almost a giantess, as 'Venus Verticordia.' I stay for dinner and we talk about the old P. R. Bs. Enter Fanny, who says something of W. B. Scott which amuses us. Scott was a dark hairy man, but after an illness has reappeared quite bald. Fanny exclaimed, 'O my, Mr. Scott *is* changed ! He ain't got a hye-brow or a hye-lash—not a 'air on his 'ead ! ' Rossetti laughed immoderately at this, so that poor Fanny, good-humoured as she is, pouted at last— 'Well, I know I don't say it right,' and I hushed him up.

Monday, June 27.—Got down to Chelsea by half-past eight to D. G. R.'s. Breakfasted in a small lofty room on first floor with window looking on the garden. Fanny in white. Then we went into the garden and

lay on the grass, eating strawberries and looking at the

peacock. F. went to look at the 'chicking,' her plural of chicken. Then Swinburne came in, and soon began to recite—a parody on Browning was one thing; and after him Whistler, who talked about his own pictures— Royal Academy—the Chinese painter-girl, Millais, etc. I went off to Ned Jones's, found Mrs. Ned and Pip, and F. Burton; talked of Christianity, Dante, Tennyson and Browning, etc. Enter Miss Hill and another lady, and Val Prinsep.

Wednesday, June 29.—Dine at Bertolini's. Haymarket, pit, Sothern in 'David Garrick' and 'Dundreary Married.'

Thursday, June 30.—To Warwick Crescent to lunch with Browning by invitation. Pen plays 'Chopin.' I say to R. B., 'Did you ever play as well as that?' to which he replied, 'A thousand times as well!' We spoke of Tennyson. T. told B. he thought 'Sludge' too long. B. answered, 'I hope *he* thought it too long!' —that is, Sludge, when the confession was forced from him. Sludge is Home, the Medium, of whom Browning told me to-day a great deal that was very amusing. Having witnessed a séance of Home's, at the house of a friend of B.'s, Browning was openly called upon to give his frank opinion on what had passed, in presence of Home and the company, upon which he declared with emphasis that so impudent a piece of imposture he never saw before in all his life, and so took his leave. Next day Browning's servant came into his room with a visitor's card, and close behind followed the visitor himself—no other than Mr. Home, who advanced with a cordial smile and right hand outstretched in amity. He bore no ill-will—not he! Browning looked sternly at him (as he is very capable of doing) and pointing to the open door, not far from which is rather a steep staircase, said—'If you are not out of that door in half a minute I'll fling you down the stairs.' Home attempted some expostulation, but B. moved towards him, and the Medium disappeared with as much grace as he could manage. 'And now comes the best of it all,' said B.—'What do you suppose he says of me? —You'd never guess. He says to everybody, "How Browning hates me!—and how I love him!"' He further explains B.'s animosity as arising out of a séance at Florence, where a 'spirit-wreath' was placed on Mrs. Browning's head, and none on her husband's.

B. spoke of London, parties, theatres, Sullivan, Gounod, etc. : 'If I could do exactly as I liked I should often go to an Opera or Play instead of to a party. I could amuse myself a good deal better. I should always treat myself to a good place.'

He spoke of his own poems—would rather write music—longs also to be a sculptor ; 'If one could only live six hundred years, or have two lives even.' We went to the Underground Railway, Bishop's Road, together. 'I am going' (he said) 'to a house where the eldest son is dead.'

I walked through the Park to Woolner's in Welbeck Street, and found not only Woolner, but Tennyson there (up for some days), and also F. Palgrave. Woolner is engaged to dine with Novello, and I very gladly agree to stay and keep Tennyson company. T., P., and I walk in the Regent's Park, P. goes home. T. and I dine together. He has the proof sheets of a new book with him—some flitting notion of calling it 'Idyls of the Hearth'? 'Gladstone dined here on Monday'—Swinburne—Milnes—De Sade—Naked model—'the chastest thing I ever saw.' T. said he must begin to correct his proofs, and with the word came the sound of a barrel-organ, bringing dismay! I took my leave, promising to quash the music, in which attempt I succeeded, seeing the grinding man well out of the street, then walked off to 5 Blandford Square, where I found Barbara L. S. B. and the Doctor,[1] and also Mrs. Clough and Bessie Parkes.

Plenty of friends and talks to-day.

---

[1] Dr. and Madame Bodichon.

Woolner lifts to the skies a German animal sculptor,
Julius Haenel (43 Pyraneesche Strasse, Dresden), two
or three small bronzes by whom he shows me, and
admirable they are. H. finds it difficult to get money.
Woolner says, 'If Haenel had done the lions in Trafalgar Square people would have come from distant
countries to look at them.'

July 1.—At the British Museum—Patmore ; he
tells me of his conversion to the Church of Rome and
intended marriage with Miss Byles. We talk of the
Rossettis, etc. (but our intimacy is a thing of the past).
I look at Ballad Books. Dine with Ned Jones and
Georgie (Gt. Russell St.). Little Philip. Picture of Circe.

Saturday, July 2.—Tom Taylor, friendly as usual,
carries me to luncheon at Lavender Sweep, where are
Mrs. Taylor, her Father, Mr. Cipriani Potter, Miss
Beales. Thence to Macmillan's, for a family dinner,
large house at Balham, 'The Elms.' Boys at seasaw in
the garden. Return to the T. T.'s, and with them in
a fly to a musical party at Charles Hallé's, Cavendish
Square. Madame H., a French-American, is a pleasant
hostess. Kate Terry, Val Prinsep, Browning, Lady
Annabella King, Sir John Simeon, Miss Cushman,
Madame Parepa, etc. etc.

July 6.—Breakfast at Lord Houghton's, sixteen
guests. He introduces me to Captain Hamilton Aïdé,
who lives at Lyndhurst. Bishop Wilberforce, Swinburne, Vambery the Hungarian traveller, Hon. Mr.
Stanley (of Alderley), supposed Mohammedan. Vambery speaks, in beautiful English with a slight foreign
accent, of his travels in Central Asia disguised as a
Dervish. If discovered he would have been tortured
to death. A Dervish, he said, must observe the ceremonies and fasts more strictly than an ordinary
Mohammedan, but he sometimes procures a relaxation
in this way : the Holy Man announces one morning
that he has had a *dream*, in which permission has been
given to him to eat, drink, sleep, amuse himself as he

likes, for a certain number of days; and he does so accordingly, and is considered to be more holy than ever. The Bishop of Oxford inquired, in his exquisitely bland tones, 'Is it permitted to an ordinary Mussulman to have a dream of this nature?' To which Vambery replied, with the grave politeness which characterises him, 'He might dream, my lord, but no one would pay attention to it: one must be a Holy Man to have this privilege,'—at which there was a good deal of laughter.

Vambery's account of his strange experiences was made the more interesting by frequent interruptions from Mr. S., who put questions, sometimes in a tone of no very good breeding, with the view of making him appear inaccurate, but Vambery always answered with good temper as well as perfect success. He is going back to Central Asia. 'I hope' (Lord H. said to me after breakfast) 'S. won't get him murdered.' I thought this breakfast very amusing; Swinburne found it dreadfully dull.

Thursday, July 7.—Lunch with Browning: tell him of the pseudo-Dervish and the English Mohammedan, which amuses him. He wishes he had been at the breakfast; it seems he had an invitation, but too late. Mr. Robert Lytton comes in—'Joachim; Tennyson; Browning's new poem in blank verse.' Out with B.

Friday, July 8.—To Gabriel's, where are Madox Brown and Webb.

Saturday, July 9.—D. G. Rossetti and I dine at Hotel de Provence, Leicester Square, then to Opera, where Taylor has promised us places for 'Mirella.' Gabriel, who detests music, soon went away; I remained.

Sunday, July 10.—E. B. Jones and I to Woolwich by rail, return by river. Evening, Highgate: The Howitts, friendly, walk back.

Wednesday, July 13.—Dined at Tom Taylor's; Mr. Story (American Sculptor, who lives in Italy), wife and daughter, Mr. E. M. Ward; I next Miss Story, who is chatty. Joke about the Bishop of Oxford, who told a lady he had had himself weighed, just as he came out of his bath, and was exactly——naming the weight. 'With or without *soap*, Bishop?' asked the lady. Mrs. Taylor plays. Miss S. sings. Mrs. Story asks me to call on them at 61 South Audley St.

Friday, July 15.—Dine and sleep at Macmillan's, Balham. M. says he and his brother Daniel and his sister used to have better conversations together on literature than he ever heard since 'from Tennyson and all the rest of them.' He gave his opinion of Goethe, which was not high. A pleasant German lady played the piano well ; we talked of Freiligrath, etc.

Sunday, July 17.—Hot. Browning having written a note about me to Arthur Sullivan the composer, I visited the latter to-day. He lives at 27 Claverton Terrace, Pimlico, and is organist at some church— perhaps in that neighbourhood. A. S. is short and tight, with dark complexion and thick curly black hair parted in the middle. Perhaps partly Jew?—a suspicion confirmed by his Mother's appearance, who is stout and dark. His Father, a South of Ireland man, is, I believe, dead.

We talked of Operas and Songs : some notion floating among us that I might furnish him with words to set. He thinks *Faust* the best possible subject for an Opera, and wishes it had fallen to his lot to set it. Asks me if I can come to Covent Garden Theatre on Tuesday evening : he plays the organ in the Cathedral scene in *Faust.* I tell the traditionary story of the origin of the name Sullivan, which seems to interest him. An Irish Chieftain, famous for generosity, had one day at his board a Stranger-Guest —no unusual thing there. After the banquet this man, who was in truth a bitter enemy, cried aloud, 'A boon, O Chief!' 'Ask for what thou wilt,' said the Chief, 'it shall be given thee.'

'Give me thy right eye,' said the other.

And sooner than break his word the Chief plucked

out his eye and ordered it to be given to that evil guest. Henceforward the generous man was called *Suil aon*, the One Eyed.

By steamer to London Bridge and rail to Plumstead ; after some wandering, find the Red House at last in its rose-garden, and William Morris, and his queenly wife crowned with her own black hair.

Monday, July 18.— The Red House. $7\frac{1}{2}$ A.M. Rose-trellis.   Jenny and May, bright-eyed, curly-pated. We hurry to the train.   W. M. brusque, careless, with big shoon.   Daldy the Publisher in train, 'Nightingale Valley.'   I call on Samuel Laurence in Wells Street and see portrait of Leigh Hunt, etc.   Then to E. B. J.'s, Gt. Russell St., where Swinburne comes in later.

Tuesday, July 19.—To S. Laurence's Studio and up with him to Islington and have tea with his family. To Covent Garden Theatre and behind the scenes to Sullivan, watch him playing the organ ; Mr. Gye comes, and afterwards I have a Stall-chair.   *Faust*—Artot, etc.   Patti in box.   (S. has no ideas outside of music.)

July 21.—Back to Lymington.   The country looks delightful, yellow corn, bending orchard boughs.

Monday, August 29.—To Aubrey House, where Mr. and Mrs. Weld are now settled.   It is near Keyhaven, on the way to Hurst Castle, and has the cliffs of the Island in full view.   Walk back through the marsh under bright stars.

October 8.—Crossed to Yarmouth in the steamer. Mrs. Cameron on board and Anthony Trollope and wife.   I sat next Anthony outside the coach to Freshwater ; he asked a great many practical questions about the houses and lands which we drove past—did not seem interested about Tennyson.   Told me he had been in every *parish* in Ireland.   He put up at Lambert's Hotel.   I to Tennyson's, where a friendly reception. Macmillan here, also Mr. and Mrs. Pollock, the latter literary in her talk.   Macmillan read aloud 'Boadicea,' Tennyson at one point interjected, 'What a fine line !'

(I forget what line it was). He also said, ' " Maud " is
wonderful ! '

Monday, *October* 10.—Farringford. Cricket with
the two boys. Mrs. Tennyson's Alma Song : ' Frenchman, a hand in thine ! ' Poem : ' Dream of a Gate.'

October. — Mrs. Clough being at Bournemouth
invited me to visit her there, and I went over on Friday
the 28th.

Friday, *October* 28. — Up at 7 — fog. Drive to
Christchurch, the sun breaking through fog. Enter
the great Priory Church and look at the Shelley
Monument. Call at the gate of Boscombe in passing
and leave Lord Houghton's note of introduction with
my card. After luncheon I walked out to Boscombe
and found Lady Shelley at home—a small lively pleasant
woman, who invited us to dinner for to-morrow.
Dinner-tea at Mrs. Clough's, and then I was left alone
to examine Clough's letters, and MS. lectures on English
Poetry. Mrs. C. wants advice as to what to publish.

Saturday, *October* 29.—Boscombe. Sir Percy and
Lady Shelley and *two sisters of Percy Bysshe Shelley*. I
sat between them at dinner, having taken in Shelley's
favourite sister, whose name is spelt ' Hellen.' She was
lively and chatty, and I looked at and listened to her
with great interest. She is tall, very slender, and must
have been graceful and handsome in her youth. I saw,
or fancied, a likeness to Shelley. She was sumptuous
in light purple silk, which became her. She looked
about fifty-six, but must be much more. Her sister,
who seemed rather younger, was much less lively.
Tennyson's name occurring in conversation, Miss
Hellen Shelley let it plainly appear that neither he nor
any modern poet was of the least interest in her
eyes.

' After Shelley, Byron, and Scott, you know,' she said
to me, ' one cannot care about other poets.'

Somebody had once read to her a poem of Tennyson's, which she liked, but she could not remember

what it was. It seemed doubtful that she had ever heard of Browning.

Mr. Grantley Berkeley at dinner—a tall strong man over sixty, like a militaire. He lives in this neighbourhood on small means, is a great sportsman, and his talk worth listening to on the habits of animals, etc. He doubts whether there is such a disease as hydrophobia—thinks most or all of the deaths may be due to the effects of a punctured wound or diseased blood, *helped by fright*. Says he can't walk as he used to do—' My feet stick to the ground.' Describes a quarrel with a game-keeper, in which he threw the man, who was insolent, into the river. He is off-hand and pleasant to talk to, enjoys society and private theatricals. In the drawing-room we found Miss Hellen Shelley stretched on a sofa, with two dainty white satin shoes with rosettes peeping beyond the purple robe, and looking really elegant. Her recollections of Leigh Hunt were not of a friendly sort, so I did not pursue the subject. She always speaks of her brother as ' Bysshe.' A young lady sung an Italian song. I came away about 10. Sir Percy Florence Shelley is a rather short, fair and fattish man of forty-five. The nose, which is like his mother's, projects when seen in profile, but the front face is roundish and smooth, with small eyes, and a bald forehead over which the pale light-brown hair is partly drawn. His voice is very quiet but in a high key (the only point reminding one of his father), his words few, and whole manner placid, and even apathetic. He likes yachting and private theatricals, cares little or nothing for poetry or literature. He has a thinly-humorous, lounging, self-possessed, quietly contemptuous manner of comment and narration. When I mentioned Tennyson's poetry, Sir Percy said fellows had bored him a good deal with it at one time. He never read any of it of his own accord—saw no sense in it.

Sunday, October 30.—A good while to-day over

Clough's letters : strange feeling, reading the private
letters of a man whom you knew. Walked alone at
twilight up the valley and through groves, then back
to dinner-tea.

Monday, October 31.—Fine, chilly. Return from
Bournemouth to Lymington. Walk with George
St. Barbe to Boldre Church. He knows Grantley
Berkeley, and has gone otter-hunting with him.

Tuesday, November 1.—Rev. Wm. Barnes comes on
my invitation to give a lecture at the Literary Institution.
He duly arrives by train at 3, and I gladly welcome
the good old poet. We walk about the Town and
he shows much interest in the Furniture Brokers' shops,
old china, pictures, etc.—and bargains for a little oil-
painting. Aïdé arrives, whom I have invited to meet
Barnes. I take them for a walk to Buckland Rings,
supposed ancient British Camp ; then dinner at my
lodging (which I hope went off tolerably), and we
moved to the Lecture Room. Mr. Barnes lectured on
' West of England Speech,' and read some of his own
poems. What the audience liked best was ' A Bit o'
Sly Coortin',' which he gave at my particular request.
It was evident that on the whole he seemed to them
flat, in comparison with the paid Entertainers who
occasionally come round. Aïdé came back to sup with
us at my rooms, and then drove off to Lyndhurst,
Barnes promising to visit him there. B. and I chatted
till near 1.

Wednesday, November 2.—Wm. Barnes ; he praised
my Stratford-on-Avon dialogue, suggested some points
of dialect, but does not understand the Warwickshire.
I saw him into the train at 1.40. A man of simple
manners and virtuous life, and a true poet. Though he
is so much my elder, I was one of the first to make a
stir about him, in talk and by the Press. The Brownings,
Tennysor, Clough, Rossetti, etc. etc.—it was I who
introduced Barnes's Dorset Poems to each and all of
them.

I met in the street old 'Lawyer M.,' who said he had been at the lecture last night, and 'thought it the damnedest stuff he ever heard,' to which I made brief reply.

Dined at Captain Mildmay's. Lord Eversley (bland and courtly), Miss Shaw Lefevre, Mr. and Mrs. De la Tour, Mr. Cornwallis West (heavy swell), etc., fine dinner, powdered lacqueys. Mrs. Mildmay plays *well* on the concertina ; Mrs. De la Tour sings ; Chat to her and Miss Mildmay—Show them Astrologer's Bill, etc. etc. The only bit of conversation I gleaned from the late Speaker (Lord E.) was this : helping himself to a lump of ice after dinner, he turned to me smiling and said, with great grace of manner—' Ice, I think, is agreeable at all seasons.'

Saturday, November 5.—To Aubrey House, where is now settled old Mr. Sellwood (father of Mrs. Tennyson, Mrs. Weld, and Mrs. Tennyson-Turner). He is tallish, very thin, with white hair and beard. He was a confidential Family-Solicitor of the old school, at Horncastle in Lincolnshire. Weld (once Secretary to the Royal Society) is a bit of a sportsman, is away from his family a good deal, and writes slight books of travel—a Summer here, a Winter there.

December 7.—To Forest Bank, to meet Barnes. Aïdé sends carriage to Brockenhurst. At dinner Mrs. Craufurd, Miss Burrard. Mr. Weld mentioned : I describe him as ' geographically restless,' which amuses them.

CHAPTER VII

1865

Monday, January 2.—Proofs of my book, *Fifty Modern Poems*, from Bell and Daldy.

Wednesday, January 3.—Newman's *Apologia* and his portrait ; the narrow refined bookish man. Does all this about Oxford and the Fathers, etc. etc., really matter ?

Thursday, January 5.—'The Dial' American Magazine. I don't like mock-Emersonianism. Balzac's *Ursula* ; is he an honest writer ? Droll correspondence with E. B. Jones, who wrote me a letter from a sham 'Mary Jane,' admirer of my poetry, enclosing her photograph. I replied to Mary Jane, and enclosed it to the care of E. B. J. His rejoinder. Carlyle's *Fredk.*, Vol. IV.—Swedenborg.

Monday, January 23.—At Farringford. Breakfast. A. T. says my poems are 'cleaner cut' than most.

'Are you going away ?'

'Yes.'

'You'd think it graceful of me to stay with you now ?'

I assured him I wished him to do exactly as he liked.

'Stay till three' ; but I could not, so bade him Good-bye. He asked me about E. B. Jones and said he should like to know him better.

Mrs. T. tells me that her father likes Aubrey House.

January 28.—I accept invitation to lecture in Dublin, in May, on Poetry.

February 20.—Weld calls; tells me that Woolner is at Farringford.

Wednesday, March 8.—Woolner comes across from Island in the 1.30 steamer. I meet him and go on to Brockenhurst Church and show him the Old Yew and Oak, with which he is well pleased and promises to come down and visit me. I walk into the Forest by Ladycross, get into swamp and have to try back. Shower of sleet. Ruined cottage with two yews beside it; meet Under-Gamekeeper, who tells me he lived in that old place twenty-one years; has seven children; is now in a new cottage.

'Which do you like best?'

'I'd sooner be hanged at the Old Cottage than die a natural death at the other!'—an odd way of expressing his feeling.

Heathy Dilton, farmyard, wood and ferns, Royden Bridge, Boldre and Lymington. Dine at G. St. B.'s, afterwards play Pope Joan and win 1s. Found it dull. Conversation in the country always purely local.

Buckle, Vol. I. Madox Brown sends ticket and catalogue for his Exhibition.

Thursday, April 6.—To Farringford—luncheon; I praise the beauty of some trees, and A. T. comes out to look at them; ventures round the corner, and we call at the Camerons'. I walk back to Yarmouth, and when near the bridge meet the two Miss Thackerays, who have just landed on the Island and are walking to Freshwater. I tell them the way, which is rather puzzling.

Saturday, April 8.—To Freshwater: a colony: the Miss Thackerays, the Prinseps, G. F. Watts, Miss Stephen, Mrs. Baine, etc.

Thursday, April 13.—To Salisbury; 14th, Stonehenge; 15th, Wilton, etc.; 16th, Salisbury, Romsey. I have described this tour in a 'Ramble.'

Friday, May 12.—Leave from the Customs. Train

to London. Talk with a fellow-passenger, who is much
in rich men's houses—Lord Ashley's, Lord Palmerston's,
etc., now going to Windsor Castle ; a House Decorator.
He says Tradesmen's Bills for the Royal Family are
always very closely looked into—a good example.
Euston Hotel, Princess's Theatre, *Arrah-na-Pogue* ;
the Irishism of it melts me, and especially Boucicault's
singing of 'The Wearing of the Green,' which I hear
was prohibited by the authorities in Dublin on account
of the wild excitement it caused in the theatre. The
Irish dancers good.

Saturday, May 13.—Euston to Chester, carriage
all to myself, read. At Chester came in a family
of foreigners, puzzling people. French ? No. They
were highly conversable, and proved to be Signor
Quaglieni, an Italian, proprietor of a large circus now
about to open for the season in Dublin, and part of his
company, viz. his wife and several children, married
daughter with baby, and his son-in-law, whom he introduced to me as 'a great man—*enorme* !' He is the
chief equestrian, I understood. They have been at
Brescia and other Italian towns, Vienna, Constantinople.
We had a good crossing to Kingston, steamer very
steady. We stayed on deck. Like most show-folk,
the circus people seemed happy enough, and on good
terms among themselves. One of the little girls, taking
slight hold of a man's hand, sprang on a post with
professional agility.

I am to be guest of my good friends Mr. and Mrs.
Samuel Ferguson. They are both out on my arrival,
and on their return give me a most warm and hospitable reception.

Friday, May 19.—Dublin. Car with S. F. to
Stephen's Green—' Chemical Preparation Room ' (jokes
about that). Introduced to chairman, Dr. E. Kennedy,
and committee, then march through door and find
myself in lecture-room, as depicted by S. F. Look
over audience and see people I know, but take no

special note of any. After the chairman's introduction, I read my lecture on Poetry for an hour, but often departing from the written text into more colloquial forms. I made no stumbles and felt no sensations of fear, depression, elation, or any other sort. This I find satisfactory to remember, and put along with some other personal experiences as indicating character—such as, the falling of a firework into a straw-yard and my immediately climbing the wall and putting it out ; the defending myself against two dogs, one a bloodhound, in a solitary warren ; the recovery from a sudden qualm on the scaffolding of a tower. The quality of coolness, presence of mind, when face to face with occasion, can only be discovered by trial, and it is agreeable to know or believe that one possesses it. As long as a question is open for decision I can be as vacillating as any one alive.

Monday, May 22.—Call at Ferguson's—invitation from Petrie. I dine at the Ship Tavern, Abbey St., and go with my cousin David and two young ladies to Quaglieni's Circus, first to promenade then to reserved seats. A handsome circus and good performance. I have the honour of a personal greeting from the Signor and some of the ladies of the company. His son-in-law is clown. David and I drive out to Seafield and have supper.

Tuesday 23.—Clontarf—Capel St., etc. Dine at Petrie's : [1] his four daughters, Miss Green, Samuel Ferguson.

Petrie says, 'College men are not those who do fine original things.' Irish music; violin, G. P., pianoforte, Miss Petrie, delightfully expressive playing. S. F., strange to say, has no feeling whatever for music. I write my name in *Bloomfield* and *Fifty Modern Poems*. Walk with Samuel Ferguson to Earl Street, and take a car to Seafield : its driver happens to be one Murphy,

[1] George Petrie, antiquarian and musician, for whom Allingham had a great affection and admiration.

formerly in the Revenue Police at Ballyshannon. He
told me he drove 'Brown of Killybegs' lately, and
how rejoiced Brown was to meet him. Brown was an
illicit distiller, and on one occasion Murphy fired a
musket ball through his hat.

Wednesday, May 24.—Move from Clontarf to the
Verdon Hotel. Call at Capel St. and see Mr. Dan
Brett, his legs swollen, sad,—novel reading his only
pleasure. Boys read stories, old people read novels,
the first curious about life, the second weary of it.

To Miss Allen's, West Row, and am photographed ;
Miss A. talkative, tallish, good-looking. Call at
Wilde's, and drive with him as far as Hospital, where
a patient is waiting for him—'to have his eyelids
chopped off.' There is no doubt but surgeons enjoy
operating, and were it otherwise what tortures would
not surgeons suffer, and would they be able to do the
needful work so well ?

N.B.—They are sometimes accused or suspected of
doing things which are not needful. Wilde was lately
in London ; praised the doctors there for ability—
adding, ' but we have plenty of fun and *blagardin*'
among us here '—are not so stiff and stuck up, he
meant.

At Verdon Hotel, Catholic Bishop, McGettigan—
greets me warmly and asks me to dine with him, which
I have to decline. Compliments about *Bloomfield*
(which contains, by the by, a sketch of him). The
hotel people are impressed by the Bishop's attentions
to me. He is a tall, very comely man, with a pleasant
brogue and simple manners—speaks and preaches in
Irish *ad lib*. A good man—if he were only not a
Bishop !

Friday, May 26.—Dublin. Started by rail for
Enniskillen at half-past eight. In my carriage a man
going to Canada ; we talk about Darcy M'Gee, etc.
He had only just time to catch the Canadian Steamer
in Lough Foyle, but at Dundalk Junction the Derry

train went off without him, for which the railway people's stupidity was chiefly blamable. I gave him my card and promised to testify in writing to that effect.

To Enniskillen by Steamer down the lake to Belleek, about 25 miles, then by 'Bus to Ballyshannon, and find myself ' at home ' once more—among old faces and places ; my Father appearing tolerably well for him, and cheerful, though now over seventy. He drank my health after dinner. Countless greetings from friends.

Saturday, *May* 27. — Ballyshannon — rainy — my Father poorly. I sit with him and write letters. Little Stewart Johnston, Jane's son. Dr. Sheil, Wm. Lipsett, etc. Walk to the Abbey graveyard—is the ivy which I planted growing ? My bedroom is out in the yard, a stable-loft adapted, ladder at one end, window, without glass, at the other, with rustic back-gardens beneath, and the blue head of Slieve League visible many miles away. A long room, uncarpeted, with slanting roof. I like it : no noises or bothers.

May 30.—Dinner, trout. Down the Mall, pool filled, beautiful, tide in, salmon-boat hauling in the Pool, always interesting. Chat with numerous friends of all classes.

May 31.—Walk in the garden at midnight and hear corncrake.

June 1.—My old nurse, Madge McNulty, to whom I am always ' Master Willy,' and indeed to most people here. Jack McN. (who *partly* sat for ' Jack Doran ').[1]

Friday, *June* 2.—To Bundoran. Uncle Edward's. Visit Mrs. Tomes.

June 12.—Left old Ballyshannon for Dublin, taking kindly leave of everybody. I don't think I have any enemies hereabouts. My Father and I have been on affectionate terms all the time.

Thursday, *June* 15.—Dublin to London.

[1] One of the characters in *Laurence Bloomfield*.

Monday, *June* 19.—London to Lymington. Lymington looks very pretty, and the view from my
windows in Prospect Place is delightful. I send 'Home-
ward Bound' to Dalziel for his book.

June 23.—Very fine. Walk to Aubrey House,
Mrs. Weld, Agnes; boat to Hurst Castle, the Jersey
steamer passes; fortifications, shingle poppies. Dinner-
tea. Mr. Selwood—pleasant day—walk home by
field-paths under the stars.

Saturday, *June* 24.—After Custom-House, steamer
to Island. Farringford, hid my bag—find some people
in the hay-field and Mrs. Cameron photographing
everybody like mad.

Went to house: A. T. says, 'Are you come to
stay?' I confess the bag and we go to fetch it. Mrs.
Cameron focuses me, but it proves a failure and I
decline further operations. She thinks it a great
honour to be done by her. Dress for dinner. Mr.
King, the publisher, at dinner and Mrs. King. Talk
of Ireland,—Petrie and other men, of whom A. T.
hardly knows the existence. The cholera. T.'s den
at top of house; smoking,—Public Schools, Charterhouse, etc., effect of a few bad boys on the rest—
Tupper—Swinburne. The Kings take leave, are at
the Albion Hotel. I sit reading and A. T. comes
down to me.

Farringford, *Sunday*, *June* 25.—Fine—at breakfast
A. T. with his letters, one from D. of Argyll. Swinburne—Venables. Out and meet the Kings—Mrs.
Cameron. Return to Farringford. Dinner (which is
at 6.30 always). Sitting at claret in the drawing-room
we see the evening sunlight on the landscape. I go to
the top of the house alone; have a strong sense of
being in Tennyson's; green summer, ruddy light in
the sky. When I came down to drawing-room found
A. T. with a book in his hand; the Kings expectant.
He accosted me, 'Allingham, would it disgust you if
I read "Maud"? Would you expire?'

I gave a satisfactory reply and he accordingly read 'Maud' all through, with some additions recently made. His interpolated comments very amusing.

'This is what was called namby-pamby!'—'That's wonderfully fine!'—'That was very hard to read; could you have read it? I don't think so.'

What strikes me most in 'Maud' this time, as always, is the section beginning, 'O that 'twere possible after long grief and pain.' It contains the *germ of the whole*, and was written many years ago.

Upstairs, talk of Poe. I praise Emerson, to which T. rather demurs but says little. By and by he asks me to lend him Emerson's books, which I will gladly do. I feel his naturalness much.

Monday, June 26.—Cloudy. Farringford. A. T. last night intended to come across with me and let me show him some places. Now, at breakfast time, he can't make up his mind.

The Queen is liberal minded, she thinks Churchmen are in the way to ruin the Church by bigotry—likes droll stories—story of great fire and little fire to burn doll—When T. visited her she curtseyed very low in receiving him—was there anything particular in this?

Another Majesty, Dowager Queen Emma of the Sandwich Islands, is expected soon on a visit to Farringford.

Saturday, July 29.—To Farringford. After dinner T. spoke of boys catching butterflies.

'Why cut short their lives?—What are we? We are the merest moths. Look at that hill' (pointing to the one before the large window), 'it's four hundred millions of years old;—think of that! Let the moths have their little lives.'

Speaking of the Colonies, he said, 'England ought to keep her colonies and draw them closer. She ought to have their representatives sitting in London, either in or in connection with the Imperial Parliament.'

Tennyson is always well at sea. 'To own a ship, a

large steam-yacht,' he said, 'and go round the world—
that's my notion of glory.'

Of the Norwegian waterfalls he said, 'I never was
satisfied with water before. On the voyage out, standing at the door of the deck cabin, I saw a moving hill
of water pass the side of the ship. I got on the top of
the cabin, and saw the sea like a mountainous country,
all hill and valley, with foam for snow on the summits ;
—the finest thing I ever saw.'

Tennyson loathed the necessity, which he fancied
himself under, of writing for money. 'The fine thing
would be to have a good hereditary estate and a love
of literature.' Of the expenses of land-owning he said,
'it costs £100 an acre, and brings in nothing yet.'

T. said he had read part of Carlyle's *Frederick* till
he came to, '*they* did not strive to build the lofty
rhyme,' and then flung the book into a corner.

He read some extracts in the *Spectator* about poetry,
and referred to Carlyle's contemptuous way of speaking
of poets, saying, 'We are all tadpoles in a pool, one a
little larger or smaller than others!' How differently
Goethe would have spoken of this minor poet : 'he
was useful in his own time and degree.'—See MS. in
'Minor Poets.'

'I was at an hotel in Covent Garden, and went out
one morning for a walk in the Piazza. A man met
me, tolerably well - dressed but battered - looking. I
never saw him before that I know of. He pulled off
his hat and said, "Beg pardon, Mr. Tennyson, might I
say a word to you?" I stopped. "I've been drunk
for three days and I want to make a solemn promise to
you, Mr. Tennyson, that I won't do so any more." I
said that was a good resolve, and I hoped he would keep
it. He said, "I promise you I will, Mr. Tennyson," and
added, "Might I shake your hand?" I shook hands
with him, and he thanked me and went on his way.'

Thursday, August 10.—Steamer to Ryde, Spithead,
ships of war. Ryde pier, rich idlers, white shoes,

yachts' boats. Steep streets, photographers, libraries, fruiterers, hotels. Old town, country road, man mowing barley. Sun Inn, old fashioned, cold meat and ale. Portrait of Ellen Terry on the wall ; I say to girl who waits (the landlady's daughter), 'I know who that is.' Says she to me, 'Yes, it's Mrs. Watts—she's staying here' ; which much surprised me.

It seems she used to put up here in old times, when playing at the Ryde Theatre, and now, being married —and separated—she goes about by herself from place to place, and has come for a while to her friendly old quarters. She gave them this likeness on some former visit. I was in hope of seeing her fair face again, but she was gone to Sandown for the day.

Mem.—The privileges granted to Pleasure Yachts appear to me utterly absurd and unjust. They pay no lighthouse dues, no Port or Harbour Dues, no fees on engaging or discharging men, all of which must be paid by every merchant vessel. They are allowed to have their 'stores' of dutiable goods, wine, tobacco, etc., free of duty. So are merchant vessels, but on over-sea voyages only, and in restricted measure. Why should the rich owners of Pleasure Yachts be thus favoured? The only reason I have heard given is that yachting is a 'nursery for the Navy.' Is it?

There are at least 7000 men and boys, all picked, engaged in Yachts. From all I have observed and heard here on the Solent, the most Yachtish piece of water in the world, nobody that can possibly help it ever goes from the idler and better paid Yachting into either the Navy or the Merchant Service. The gentlemen in livery who abound in Rotten Row and elsewhere might almost as well be supposed a nursery for the Army as yachting a nursery for the Navy.

Sunday, August 6.—Lonely. Walk, field-path, Pennington Farm, standing corn. Ditch crowded with wild-flowers. Would I had a companion!

August 14.—Sunny. Yacht *Pilgrim*—the monkey

—am shown the young Millionaire's sea-journal and observe such spelling as, 'addopt,' 'to or three,' 'oceant,'—but of course *he* may spell as he likes.

Wednesday, August 16. — Headache, depressed. Walk to Aubrey House, meet Captain Barton, pleasant friendly man ; he has a turn for languages ; has lived near Buda, and knows Hungarian. Charles Tennyson Turner, like Alfred, though of shorter stature. Manner peculiar to the family, at once dignified, odd, very easy and natural ! Way of speaking odd but distinct, and the phraseology always original. Enter C. R. Weld with fishing tackle and one trout,—talk on Natural History—terrible to be attacked by an Eagle, 'like a flying bulldog,' I say : 'Couldn't be anything much worse than that,' says C. T. T. I like him much, and we seem to take to each other.

Thursday, August 31.—Steamer *Solent* to Portsmouth to see the French Fleet now at Spithead, *Solferino* and other iron-clads, black brutal hulks. We carry a tricolour and cheer the French ships in passing.

Friday, September 1.—Very fine. C. House, pay pensioners, then hurry off to Gosport to see more of the French invasion ! High Street. A pleasant boatman rows me past the old *Victory* to *La Reine Hortense* (curious juxtaposition !) moored in the middle of Portsmouth Harbour, and I board and look through the Imperial ship, bedrooms and all, shown round by a polite young Frenchman, of what rank I know not. When I thanked him at parting he replied, 'Pour rien, M'sieur' !—exact equivalent of the Irish phrase in similar case, 'I'm much obliged to you, Pat'— 'Nothing, sir.'

Portsmouth Hard—Queen St., etc., crowds, taverns, French and English sailors drunk together, some arm-in-arm, mutually friendly and unintelligible. The French turn up their straw hats all round. I said to old boatman, 'They look pretty much like English sailors.' He : 'Ah ! they tries to come as near us as they can !'

Illuminations, crowds, noise. Queer bedroom atop of a house—sleep I don't know how. (The world-wide miracle of Sleep.)

Monday, September 11.—Cloudy but warm—Institution—take the chair at 'Penny Reading': any use? The people prefer rubbish. Linden arcade, *brown* half-moon low in the east—mind ill at ease.

> From thirty-five to forty-five
> 'Tis sometimes hard to keep alive,
> Hopes are dying—when they're dead,
> Joys are flying—when they're fled,
> Perhaps we can be comforted.

Thursday, September 14.—Fine, warm, windy. Trip in steamer. On board a blind man singing to a harmonium played by a woman: 'Became blind at fifteen.' 'Those feel it less who are born blind,' I suggested. 'Perhaps,' he answered, '*but I am glad to have seen the world.*' We ran past the Needles, touched at Bournemouth Pier and took in new passengers, then came the cliffs of Swanage Bay, the Old Harry rock, with tossing and sea-sickness. Landed at Swanage, an out-of-the-world place, houses roofed with large gray stones, narrow crooked street. Many stone-masons here. Beyond, a valley with trees and brook. Lunched at 'The Ship,' kept by Mrs. Diddlecomb, and back to steamer—more tossing and discomfort, of which I had a little.

On deck made friends with a quick bright Boy of seven, whose father sat grave and silent reading letters in a female hand. Boy and I talked oceans of nonsense. Passengers got out at Bournemouth and Yarmouth; then we ran for Lymington by starlight, missed the channel, and stuck in the mud. We had to land by boat, some of the women frightened; one, a smooth fair woman, 'going to Leicester to-morrow,' threw her arms round me, which was some compensation. The oars sparkled as they dipped. Landed at the Bath, with wet feet; to Custom-House, and home to dinner.

September 20.—Walked to Aubrey. Met a poor
looking woman who asked, ' How far to Lymington ? '
I answered, ' half a mile,' saw she looked very tired and
questioned her. Says she has walked twenty-two miles
to-day, on her way from Portland, where she has been
to see her son, who is in the Convict Prison (for theft).

' My poor boy ! it wasn't altogether his fault,—he
fell into bad company—he has got three years. He got
the Governor's order for me to see him—he wouldn't
have asked for it if he had known how bad-off I was.
I walked down from London to see him, and now I'm
walking back. I saw him for about half an hour, in a
cage as you might say.'

I fully believed her and gave her something, for
which she was very grateful.

' God return it to you ! '

What women suffer from husbands, and from
children !

September 23.—Warm and bright—walk in Forest,
but without enjoyment—my thoughts astray.

September 27.—Old Mr. Rice's death-bed—asks to
see me and takes leave of me—the feeble white face of
a once strong man. The Reverend Mr. W. comes
and, he gone, I return for a moment. ' Have you
anything to say to me, Mr. Rice ? '—' No.'

A quiet silent man (employed in Portsmouth
Harbour in youth—afterwards rope-spinner by trade),
who has gone steadily and I believe honestly along his
humble track in life. He is over threescore and ten,
his old wife is gone before him, his family are grown
up (three of his sons are masters of yachts, one keeps
a tavern), almost all his bodily powers have ebbed away,
tho' his mind seems unaltered.

'What should the Old Man do but die ? ' He is
entirely content it should be so, and has nothing to say
about it.

September 30.—Cross to Island. Mrs. Cameron on
board, with heaps of photographs. To Farringford after

5 o'clock, come in at the tail of a 'drawing-room' in honour of Queen Emma of the Sandwich Islands, to whom I am presented—middle sized or rather less, pleasant face, with black hair and dusky complexion. (Her grandfather an English or American sailor?) Several parsons and parsonesses present. A few words with Tennyson, who asks me if I will come for a walk to-morrow. Drive with Lionel in ponychaise down to the shore, then good-bye, and walk away, lonely. Rasher at Inn. Out by moonlight, little bay, chalk cliffs, moonshine on the sea.

Thursday, October 5.—Walked up and down Lymington High Street and examined the forms of the separate houses—some seventeenth—most eighteenth century? One may live long in a town and never do this. Old bricken chimneys are often beautiful,—new, in the same class of buildings, never.

Where did the good taste, or instructive rightness, in former days come from?—and whither has it fled?

Saturday, October 7.—Decline St. B.'s dinner—walk to Buckland, new green sprays,—short second Spring, on Winter's edge.

Has anybody walked habitually alone as much as I? Many, doubtless,—but none that I know. And who fonder of congenial company?

October 13.—To Lyndhurst and visit Miss Dickson at her new house 'The Bird's Nest.' Miss D., quick and pleasant in talk—writes music (as 'Dolores') and sings her own songs very sweetly in a small voice. Her setting of Tennyson's 'Brook' is enormously popular and has brought hundreds of pounds to the publishers : she has got about £10 by it altogether. But (they would argue) it was a speculation, and the success has helped her name.

Thursday, 19.—Death of Lord Palmerston (he did me a good turn). G. St. Barbe has told me about P. riding over sometimes from Broadlands to the New Forest Hunt, never wore an outside coat in any weather, at most turned up his collar. Generally liked, I should guess, and a good deal trusted—without exciting any enthusiasm.

To Farringford. Tennyson has been visiting Weimar, which he declares to be 'the most interesting place in Europe.'

He saw there (as I did) kind James Marshall, the Grand Duchess's private secretary, and through him Goethe's House, etc.

'I touched Goethe's coffin,' said Tennyson, 'and I thought of *you* then' (looking at me).

I felt this as a very great compliment. Miss Simeon asked, 'Why did you think of Mr. Allingham?' T.—'You ignorant maid! don't you know his beautiful little poem about Weimar?'

Friday, October 27.—To London. At E. B. J.'s, 41 Kensington Square. Rain. In driving from Waterloo past Westminster Abbey saw crowd of people with umbrellas—Lord Palmerston's funeral.

Saturday, October 28.—41 Kensington Square— two studios. 'Zephyr carrying Psyche'—delightful —precipice, green valley, Love's curly little castle below. Designs of 'St. George and Dragon.' Drawings of Heads. Circe (a-doing), she stretching her arm across.

Go to see Chang the Chinese Giant, and meet Lord Houghton there, always friendly, invites me to come with him on Sunday to Westminster Abbey to hear funeral sermon on Palmerston—to call for him at the Athenæum Club. Mrs. Chang. The Dwarf, queer little toad. Dine at Bertolini's.

Sunday, October 29.—With Lord Houghton to Westminster Abbey.

He took me to the Deanery and introduced me to Dean Stanley and Lady Augusta ; three or four others were present. After a few minutes we moved to the Abbey, entering by a special door ; the Dean went his own way, and our party was taken in charge by a special verger, who marched before us with his silver staff and ushered us to seats in front of the pulpit. I imagined myself for the time Marquis of Ballyshannon. Dean S., looking in his skull-cap a hundred years old, preached his funeral sermon on Lord Palmerston. He made no pretence of giving any religious colour to it, praised P.'s honour, courage, cheerful good sense, ' In trying circumstances he never took fright,' said the Dean, ' never was flurried, never desponded,' and so on.

We went out by one of the public doors, like ordinary minor Christians.

Tuesday, October 31.—Lymington, showers. Rev. William Barnes comes to me by invitation. I go up from the Custom-House and find him sitting by my fire in Prospect Place. We dine at 6.30 : to the Literary Institution, where B. lectures on *House and House-Life* —caves, huts, tents, etc., Wives (laughter), Praise of the good wife,—Odd lecture, rather puzzled everybody. Had Dr. Adams and Doman to meet Barnes at supper.

Wednesday, November 1.—Breakfast—Barnes. Showed him the *Ancient Laws of Ireland*, and read him some of *Gammer Gurton's Needle*, which he did not know before. Both books interested him. Custom-House, pay pensioners. Barnes has been invited to go with me to Farringford, and we cross to Yarmouth, nearly fouling a collier on the way.

B.'s old-fashioned ways, his gaiters, his long knitted purse which he ties up in a knot, broad brimmed hat, homely speech.

We drive in a fly to Farringford, where T., Mrs. T., Miss T. meet us in the hall. T. and B. at once on easy terms, having simple poetic minds and mutual goodwill. Talk of Ancient Britons, barrows, roads, etc. I to upper room and dress, T. comes in to me and we go down together. Dinner : stories of ghosts and dreams. To drawing-room as usual, where T. has his port, B. no wine. T. says : ' modern fame is nothing : I'd rather have an acre of land. I shall go

down, down! I am up now.' T. went upstairs by
himself.

Tea: enter Mrs. Cameron (in a funny red open-work shawl) with two of her boys. T. reappears, and Mrs. C. shows a small firework toy called 'Pharaoh's Serpents,' a kind of pastile, which, when lighted, twists about in a worm-like shape. Mrs. C. said they were poisonous and forbade us all to touch. T. in defiance put out his hand.

'Don't touch 'em!' shrieked Mrs. C. 'You sha'n't, Alfred!' But Alfred did. 'Wash your hands then!' But Alfred wouldn't, and rubbed his moustache instead, enjoying Mrs. C.'s agonies. Then she said to him: 'Will you come to-morrow and be photographed?' He, very emphatically, 'No.'

She turned to me—'You left a Great Poet out of your *Nightingale Valley*, and have been repenting ever since in sackcloth and ashes—eh?' She meant Henry Taylor.

I tried to say that the volume was not a collection of specimens of Poets, but she did not listen. Then she said graciously, 'Come to-morrow and you shall be taken.'

T. and I went out to the porch with Mrs. C., where her donkey-chaise was waiting in the moonlight.

Tennyson now took Barnes and me to his top room. Darwinism—'Man from ape—would that really make any difference?' Huxley, Tyndall.

'Time is nothing,' said T., 'are we not all part of Deity?' 'Pantheism?' hinted Barnes, who was not at ease in this sort of speculation. 'Well!' says T., 'I think I believe in Pantheism, of a sort.' Barnes to bed, T. and I up ladder to the roof to look at Orion. Then to my room, where more talk. He likes Barnes, he says, 'but he is not accustomed to strong views theologic.'

We talk of Browning, for whom T. has a very strong personal regard. 'Browning must think himself the greatest man living. I can't understand how he should care for my poetry. His new poem has 15,000 lines—there's copiousness! I can't venture to put out a thing without care. Good-night.' Bed about one, sleep middling.

November 4.—Lymington. Fine—Measured the Yacht *Stella* by girting, then rowed round by ferry and bridge in the sunshine, and felt as if it were shining out of old times. I seldom care to row in this shallow muddy river. Homer. Letter from Phil Jones beginning, ' Please, Mr. Allicum—'

Wednesday, November 8.—*Fraser* has a contemptuous notice of my *Fifty Modern Poems*, which takes me unpleasantly by surprise. What can Froude mean, after all his private cream and sugar?

Saturday, November 18.—Fine. I meet Woolner at the train and take him to my lodging. We cross to Yarmouth together, and by fly to Farringford.

Sunday, November 19.—To breakfast at Farringford —read Gladstone on Homer (not much use?) Stroll with A. T. and Woolner before luncheon. Walk after on the Downs, A. T., Woolner, Weld and I ; rain, and shelter in an empty cottage. Woolner tells of Coventry Patmore's new wealth from his second marriage, his magnificent wines, etc.—has bought an estate in Sussex. Catholic now. We climb to the edge of the Downs and looked over the gray sea.

Woolner said, ' This is better than Welbeck St.!' T., ' But it's lonesome. Sunday touches Sunday.' (He meant that the weeks ran away without incident.)

Monday, November 27.—Studying Max Müller these days ; suppose he is a great authority on Language. Walk, Pennington Common, moonlight—plan a set of *Japanese* Poems (quasi-Japanese). Longing for *freedom*.

Solentisms.— The folk who live by the Solent say *mash* for marsh, '*ood* for wood, *waps* for wasp, *year* for here, *postes* for posts, *haps* for hasp, *porching* for poaching! *acker* is to stammer ; *butt* a beehive ; *I'll*

twist 'en ! ' means I'll do it—*i.e.* some troublesome feat.
They say *sha'n't us* for sha'n't we, *to he* for to him, and
make many or most neuter objects masculine ; it being
a jocular saying among themselves, ' In 'Am'sheer everything's 'e but a tom-cat — see one, and, *There she
goes* ! '

November—— Heavy blasts shake the house.

Clough's Letters.   Sorting old letters with kind
thoughts of old friends.

CHAPTER VIII

1866

January 9.—Ride to Brockenhurst—sudden snow-storm, careering between the trees and across the road like a charge of wild cavalry ; wraps us in winter, clears off. Froude writes apologetically about the review in *Fraser*. (*N.B.*—The article was by a Scotch lawyer named Skelton, at whose house near Edinburgh Froude is in the habit of putting up.) Lewes's Goethe—don't like it. L.'s opinions on Goethe's works occupy much space, and might be almost wholly spared.

January 22.—Death of dear good *George Petrie* (in Dublin, on the 18th).

Tuesday, *January* 23.—Fine and spring-like, but I not well—thinking of George Petrie all day—sad and sweet recollections. In the mild sunshine of his company I never had a vexed moment. His presence like one of those tender old Irish airs which flowed so lovingly from his violin.

Thursday, *February* 1.—From Custom-House window see Tennyson on board the steamer as she passes, and hurry to station. Mrs. Tennyson and Lionel go off in a fly to Aubrey. T. and I walk, by Pennington, Everton, etc. Dark and moist day, some showers. Talk of Plato and Greek manners. In Lymer Lane we come to a Spring by the wayside. ' I'd give any-thing,' T. said, ' to have such a one at Farringford.' Crossed a brook which ' broadened on the road,' and

this also delighted him. ' Whenever I come to see
you,' he said, ' bring me to a Brook. I'd sooner have
it than a hundred ruined Castles.'

Saturday, February 3.—To Brockenhurst by train,
where Aïdé meets me and we walk to Lyndhurst.

Forest Bank, dinner—Aïdé and his sweet courtly
old Lady Mother, ' Gussy' Gore (son of Mrs. Gore
the novelist), and his wife, Paul Graham, etc.

Sunday, February 4.—Forest Bank. A. and Paul
Graham to church. I at home, look at A.'s sketch-
books (1847, etc.), chiefly of foreign scenes. Find Vol.
of my own poems, marked here and there. After
lunch, A. and I call at the Gore's—a curious place. The
house was a brewery, and an odd delightful room was
made of a storehouse and loft thrown together.

Mrs. Sartoris, who thought of taking the place before
the Gores, said it would be ' the romance of rheumatism.'

Dinner at 7. Drawing-room, fashionable chat of
Mrs. Aïdé and Paul Graham (who is just of age).

Thursday, February 15.—To Buckland Road, six
elms and a fir tree uprooted, top of fir carried across
road and plunged into the ground. Fiddle—try songs.
Lonelyish—supper, milk.

> Whence or when I know not,
> She will come at last,
> And with one look will pay me
> For all the lonely past.

March 20.—Showery, chilly. De Musset, essentially
trash ? Meditations : what is life worth without love,
without faith ?

Friday, May 18. — Farringford. Walked with
Tennyson among the trees and lawns. T. said, ' White
lilac used to be my favourite flower.'

A.—' It is something like a white peacock.'

Then I told him what Browning said to me about
a passage in the ' Princess '—' Tennyson's taken to
white peacocks ! I always intended to use them. The
Pope has a number of white peacocks.'

We went through the gate and down to Wisley Green. T. remarked, 'I have not been outside my own grounds before for ever so long.'

We spoke of Byron. T. greatly admired him in boyhood, but does not now.

'When I heard of his death (it was at Somersby, my Father's rectory) I went out to the back of the house and cut on a wall with my knife, " Lord Byron is dead." '

'Parts of *Don Juan* are good, but other parts badly done. I like some of his small things.'

A.—'Any of his Tales, or Mysteries, or Plays?'

T.—'No.'

A.—'He was the one English writer who disparaged Shakespeare. He was a Lord, and talked about, and he wrote vulgarly, therefore he was popular.'

T.—'Why am I popular? I don't write very vulgarly.'

A.—'I have often wondered that you are, and Browning wonders.'

T.—'I believe it's because I'm Poet-Laureate. It's something like being a lord.'

The true poetic crown, he said, was not made of what we call laurel ; he showed me a specimen of the classic laurel growing at Farringford (sent him, I think, by Mr. Edward Lear), a small bush with pointed twinkling leaves.

May 25.—A little excursion from Friday till Monday. Wimbourne, Blandford, Salisbury, Fording-bridge, Ringwood, etc.

Wednesday, June 13.—Breakfast at Farringford. Letter from an Irishman, Belfast, addressed—

'To the Laureate of England'—

asking the meaning of something in *In Memoriam*. T. in the lawn and meadow running about bareheaded (for exercise), 'like a madman,' his sister says.

Friday, June 22.—Very fine. Train to Lyndhurst

Road and walk into Forest—beeches cut down—warm—

pretty country towards Dibden and Southampton. Tents, with folk like Gypsies (but they say *no*), peeling rushes for rushlights : you leave a strip of green on the pith for backbone. Beaulieu, the Duke's park, old church and ruins. Village, tide in. Cottage hung with roses, man in front garden tells me he has lived there fifty-three years. I praise the beauty and quiet, but he often thinks he 'ought to a'pushed out into the world—gone to London or some large place.' Boys fishing for bass. The miller's, a piano going inside ('it is the miller's daughter,' no doubt). Rasher and ale at the inn. The young lady at the bar with short curls and towny air finds it 'very dull here.' I walk away at 20 to 9, sunset light over heath and forest, long road. The night-jar whirring.

Saturday, July 14.—Returning to lodgings from office find that a telegram has come and the servant has gone out with it to find me, taking wrong way. Frightened—my Father? Turns out to be very pleasant, 'Crown Hotel, Lyndhurst. A. Tennyson to W. Allingham. Will you come to us here?' Dine hastily and rush to train.

Sunday, July 15.—Breakfast at Crown 9.30. A. T., Mrs. T., Hallam and Lionel. A. T. and I out at 12. Swan Green, forest path, Halliday's Hill, we *swim* through tall bracken. T. pauses midway, turns to me, and says solemnly, 'I believe *this* place is quite full of vipers!' After going a little further, he stopped again and said, 'I am told that a viper-bite may make a woman silly for life, or deprive a man of his virility.'

We entered Mark Ash, a wood of huge solemn Beech trees, the floor thick-matted with dead leaves ; a few trees were broken or fallen ; some towered to a great height before branching. We sat on the roots of a mighty Beech. T. smoked. We shared in sandwiches and brandy. Then he produced a little pocket *As You Like It*, and read some parts aloud.

Returned by Holm Hill—View to Isle of Wight, with six or seven distances one behind another. T. limps, his boots pinch him—paid £2 : 12 : 6 for them ; his Bootmaker in the Burlington Arcade, highly fashionable. ' Writes to me, " *Mr*. Alfred Tennyson." '

I suggested, ' he feels he is doing you an honour, being plain *Mr*., in consenting to make your boots.'

T.—' One day while he was measuring me, I called his attention to my corns, and said, " Have *you* any corns ? "—From that moment he threw off all respect!'

We agreed that with the French, or Italians, or Irish you can be familiar without breeding contempt.

We strike again into the woods and reach the hill over Swan Green at 4. The donkey-chair with Mrs. T. and the boys appears, and a stupid little donkey-driver. It jolts down the rough wood-path. Huge flies draw blood.

H., L., and I go in search of the great Knightwood Oak and find it, looking fresh and healthy, but one limb lost. ' Kelt and Saxon.' Dine 7.30. T. on sofa at window, pleasant chat.

' I hate publishing ! have published much for booksellers' reasons. A grain of originality is a great thing.'

' True knowledge of people very hard to get at : physiognomy is misleading.'

I argue against this and think that, if you can read them, faces will tell you the truth.

T.—' You may think you have insight when you haven't.'

I out, and take a dark walk to corner of Fox Leas and back. Owls shouting. Corncrakes.

Monday, *July* 16.—' The Crown.' Breakfast—rough waitress, poorly managed Inn. I pack up and go down the Brockenhurst Road, A. T. having started before me. At Fox Leas corner find him sitting under a tree. Talk of a trip to Ireland. Good-bye, walk to station, train to Lymington.

Wednesday, July 18.—Considering about T. and
Ireland. Brockenhurst. Walk to Lyndhurst by
Holland's Wood and Pondhead. Inquire at two
places for lodgings,—'taken.' Crown, all out, engage
a bedroom.

Dinner, A. T., Mrs. T., H. and L. The sherry
here, T. says, a compound of spirits of wine—a bottle
of it 'stunned me.'

We talk of plans and routes for a trip. T. has
decided against Connemara. T. and I out in starlight,
down street, lower road. He is surprised to find I
have a habit of taking a walk after dinner.

'What is that star?'

'Arcturus.'

T.—'I see it shuddering and tearing away!—my
eyes are so bad. In the Plough each star is a wide
blot of misty light.

'The old mail-coach travelling sometimes delightful.

'I remember going from London to Bath in
spring outside the coach—all very fresh and bright, a
delicious day! No words can express the heavenly
feeling I had.'

Dogs—T., 'When I lived in Epping Forest I had
a big mastiff; he once ate up a little dog.'

'Did he bite people?'

'Sometimes.'

Thursday, July 19.—Lyndhurst, fine. Walk with
T., Fox Leas, Whitley Wood, Queen's Bower, brook
dry; a heron rises. Another brook, brisk and clear,
which pleases T. 'I should like to lie in that pool
for an hour. Nothing so delightful to the mind as
a brook.' I say good-bye, cross Ober Green and hurry
to train, thunder-shower in the evening.

Sunday, July 22.—T. and I walk to Swan Green,
turn off to Emery Down and into Compton Manor by
path which leads us into a Park and then flower-gardens.
We are posed, till a gardener shows us the way, with
the remark that, 'It is not liked that people should

come through the Manor.' We explain that we lost our way. See a jay. Cross a brook. Take a wrong turn to the left, and inquire at a cottage where the folk are at dinner and civilly offer us beer. The wood-paths puzzle us again.

T. says, 'I want some forest,' and leans over a gate while I go scouting to the top of the hill and scratch my new umbrella amid the brambles (important at the time!) Reach Stony Cross Inn and make inquiries, then back to T., who is lying under a hedge, reading. He reads aloud from his book, *Materialism of the Present Time*, by Paul Janet.

'Vis inertiæ—matter can do nothing by itself— there must be a Primary Motor.'

A huge hornet; T. kills it.

'A weekly paper called *The Hornet*—sweet name to choose!'

To the Stony Cross Inn; bread and cheese and shandygaff (*i.e.* beer and ginger-beer), good; civil girl. We look at rooms upstairs, and T. opens a door disclosing folk eating, and shuts it. View of woods below the ridge. We descend; felled trees, bare spaces.

W. M. Thackeray—his letter about the 'Idylls'— 'While I am reading your splendid verses, here I lie in bed'—his sufferings.

On large families—Mill, Malthus, etc.

We look about for the big yews, and can't find them. Ask Rural Postman, who says, 'The Sloden Yews are *all cut down.* They were offered me, the whole of 'em, for £50. It was the head place for Yews.' I think he said they were bought for £30 by an upholsterer at Southampton. We much vexed; T. said he would have paid £30 himself to have preserved this famous Yew Wood, old beyond memory, and fit to live beyond reckoning. The cutting probably done by order of some London official down for the day. But surely the Deputy Ranger here might have interposed? The

wood is valuable, but very hard to cut and work.
We now had wide prospects Eastwards, over forest
and field, dale and down, towards Southampton and
Winchester.

After dinner we talk of dreams. T. said, 'In my
boyhood I had *intuitions* of Immortality—inexpressible !
I have never been able to express them. I shall try
some day.'

I say that I too have felt something of that kind ;
whereat T. (being in one of his less amiable moods)
growls, 'I don't believe you have. You say it out
of rivalry.'

Tuesday, July 24.—Have got ten days' leave.

Wednesday, July 25.—To London by 10.20 train.

Thursday, July 26.—Note from Browning, just off
to Bretagne : on mourning paper ; his father dead.

July 27.—Dine at Tom Taylor's, Lavender Sweep.
In with them to Opera.

Monday, July 30.—Kensington Square. Studio.
Psyche drawings. Book planned, Morris, and 'lots
of stories and pictures.'

To D. G. R., Cheyne Walk. My old regard for
D. G. R. stirs within me, and would be as warm as
ever *if he would let it.* Fanny, Howell, D. G. R.,
H., and I walk to Sloane St. ; talk of dining at the
Wellington (corner of St. James's St.), but do dine
or feed at a little *a-la-mode* beef-house off Sloane
Square. His pleasant easy manners. He is now acting
as Secretary to Ruskin. He tells about the subscription
for old George Cruikshank, of which he is Treasurer.
I promise £1.

'C. is very badly off——'

'How can that be ? He has no children.'

'A number !'

When we separated I turned the corner into Cheyne
Row, and seeing light in No. 5 went in. Upstairs
room, Carlyle, Miss Welsh ('Maggie'), Miss Jewsbury, and an old bald man, to whom I was introduced

by C. 'This is David Laing, well known to all inquirers into Scottish affairs.' (Librarian to the Signet Library, Edinburgh.)

They were looking over some engraved portraits, and C. singled out one, asking pointedly, 'Whose face do you call this?' Laing suggested that it might be So-and so, or So-and-so, C. saying 'No, no, no!' and at last, 'I perceive that you can throw no light on the matter.' It is his own conviction that this (a shrewd humorous face with bald forehead and scanty beard) is the only authentic portrait of John Knox.

Miss Welsh is ever cheerful and chirpy. Miss Jewsbury asks me to visit her. Mr. Laing gone, C. and I sit on chairs in the little back garden, under the summer stars, he smoking.

The New Forest—adder, properly 'a nadder.' He repeats, 'the poison of asps is under their tongues.' He speaks approvingly of my paper on Petrie in *Fraser*. 'Perhaps *over*-appreciative—but that is as it should be in such a case.' C.'s last visit to Dublin and intercourse with Petrie there.

'Very amiable and good man; but can get no good of his writings.'

We walk out in the solitary streets.

'Success of Prussia—nothing has pleased me so well for forty years. I knew it must be. Bismarck a hero —his disregard of the babble of people and newspapers, and of his own parliament.

'*History of Ireland*—I recommend you to try it. You may do a very nice book in ten years; not long, about the length of my *French Revolution*. It's a book that would have a large sale. Whatever poetic faculty you may have would be shown in this form, etc.

'The death of Hugh de Lacy, where was that?'

'At Durrow in Meath. Hugh de Lacy was looking at a new castle he was building, when an Irishman standing by suddenly pulled an axe from under his loose coat, and at a blow struck off Hugh's head, stretched forward, doubtless. Head and body fell into the castle ditch.'

'I would have gone and looked at the spot if I could have found it.'

As we parted he said, 'Come again some evening, at eight.'

Then by solitary streets and devious ways I arrived at Kensington Square, and found Ned, sleepy, returned from a Reform Meeting in the Agricultural Hall, Islington, whither he went with Faulkner. N. J. is now a People's Man.

Tuesday, July 31.—Kensington Square. Rainy. 'Reform Meeting. Couldn't hear the speeches.' Studio, N. painting; imitates old Connoisseur talking of 'Greek Art,' etc. I in cab to D. G. R.'s. W. M. R., friendly—back from Naples, Vesuvius, Pompeii. Sandys, painter, large heavy man with short yellowish hair parted in the middle. Tells me he 'wants a dreary moor to paint—is there such a thing in the New Forest?' Enter Swinburne (his hair cut). Talk about ages: W. M. R. tells his experience of Vesuvius. Swinburne's new volume is on the table. Am asked to dine here on Friday. Swinburne asks leave to stay the night. Kensington Square about 3. Leave a note on table—'Your respectfully drowsy Friend—3 A.M.'

Sleep not comfortably on my sofa.

Wednesday, August 1.—Newspaper says cholera is increasing. I ask Ned to come down to Lymington, with wife and babes. Thinks of it. At dinner William Morris, pleasant, learned about wines and distilling. The Big Story Book, woodcut of Olympus by N. Jones. M. and friends intend to engrave the wood-blocks themselves—and M. will publish the book at his warehouse. I like Morris much. He is plain-spoken and emphatic, often boisterously, without an atom of irritating matter. He goes about 12.

Thursday, August 2.—Waterloo, 5.10 train. Lord

Cardigan (for Portsmouth), bustle in station, hats touched ; a thin old upright man with an air of command ; face cold, but not exactly repulsive. Bishop of Winchester (Wilberforce), shrewd, ruddy old round face, young man with him (his son?), and a clever looking little parson.

August 6.—Look at Miss Knight's rooms for the Joneses, think they will do. Write.

Wednesday, August 15.—Lodgings far from ready, bring books. Meet Aubrey De Vere in Ashly Lane, coming to call on me. Chat, ' going to Ireland, then back to Bournemouth—*Laurence Bloomfield*, etc.' ; with me to station. I to Brockenhurst. Here's Ned and Madam and Pip and Baby! They much like Stanwell House.

Friday, August 17.—Ned and I crossed to the Island and visited Tennyson, who received us very friendlily and took us up to his den.

Saturday, August 18.—Very fine, South wind. Ned, Georgie and I to Brockenhurst. Field-path, stiles, Ober Green, heather : Queen's Bower. Sit by the little bridge. Oakenshaw, big oak, brook, insects, big beech. Ned sketches. I read aloud *Robin Hood and the Monk.* Skirt New Park to other wood, they tired. Ned does not paint down here (it's his holiday), and only makes a few pencil sketches. He occupies himself, when in the mood, with designs for the Big Book of Stories in Verse by Morris, and has done several from Cupid and Psyche ; also pilgrims going to Róme, and others. He founds his style in these on old Woodcuts, especially those in *Hypnerotomachia,* of which he has a fine copy. His work in general, and that of Morris too, might perhaps be called a kind of *New Renaissance.*

Sunday, August 26.—Fine. Rail 4.5 to Brockenhurst. The old Church. Service over, we peep in and encounter the Vicar, Rev. ' Paddy ' Falls. I apologise, introduce my friends. ' Come in. Why not ? ' he says, with a strong brogue and funny twinkle of eye. ' I

was just saying a few words to a poor woman—pouring
the "leperous distilment" into her ear.' I remarked
that we *ought* to have come in service-time. 'Not at all,
sir, not at all!' says Paddy politely, and showed us
round the church. N. and G. were delighted with this
Vicar ('hot from the service,' as Georgie remarked),
and thought the quotation 'leperous distilment' very
happy.

Through Brockenhurst Park, where N. likes the
woods. Roydon. They tired—Boldre—Lymington
about 7, very tired. Ned comes to dine with me, not
Georgie. . . . He lauds Luini; speaks of the injustice of
the critics, 'wonder when people will begin to speak of
me decently.' With him to Stanwell : return and read
Carlyle's *Cromwell*.

Tuesday, August 28.—Rain, clears up, Yacht. Webb
comes by train, a room for him at Perry's. We dine
at Stanwell House.

Thursday, August 30.—Rail to Winchester, with N., G.,
and Webb—meet Morris there. All walk by the Close
and meadows to St. Cross. Old man, dining-hall ;
men's rooms, old cloisters, wooden arches—mixed up
with leaves and flowers. The Dole. Back by meadows
and streamlets. Dinner at 'The George,' tough mutton,
parsonic waiter, red-faced grinning Landlady, bill 19s.

Cathedral—west window, *bits* of old glass, choir,
side aisles, Lady chapel, wall paintings, etc. Morris
talked copiously and interestingly on all things, Webb
now and again on technicalities (also interesting). Ned
enjoyed the general charm and picturesqueness ; I also,
in my own way—but with the drawback of uncomfort-
ableness which I always feel from the incongruity of
past and present, of old intention and modern significance,
in these great and beautiful Edifices.

A Verger, tall, sallow, and melancholy, did not offer
his services, but made a remark or two which seemed
to imply, in a self-respecting manner, that he was ready
to go round with us officially if we cared for him.

But, taking slight notice of him, Morris discoursed away, and the Verger listened with the rest of us, at one point civilly correcting Morris on a detail, and pointing out the broken hand of a Knightly figure. I made some sort of apology aside to this man for not availing ourselves of his guidance. With a mournful pride he confessed his sympathy with our views, saying, ' I should do just the same myself. I never meet any one in a place like this that I would care to have go round with me.'

We went to the College. In the Chapel, bad glass in imitation of old. To Dining Hall by outside stairs, bread and butter on square slab of wood, beer, *and tea* (a modern innovation). The Boys. I have my usual feeling of no unkindly envy at the discipline and training (the evils, very real, at present invisible). Schoolroom—dormitory. Under gateway and out. Old walls, then clear brisk river, little houses with gardens, bridge, St. Giles's with little red-tiled steeple-spire,—wide space. High Street, the downs rising beyond. Old Hall, Assize Courts, Arthur's Round Table! View of City and Cathedral flushed with sunset. Field-path to Station. Ned, G., and Morris and I back to Lymington—Webb to London. M. being hot wants to sit in a draught. When we got to Stanwell House, Ned said, ' I'm very sorry, but I've been so lazy I've not done a single thing for the book,' to which Morris gave a slight grunt. Then Ned produced his eight or nine designs for the wood-blocks, whereupon Morris laughed right joyously and shook himself. Supper, then took M. to the ' Nag's Head ' for his bed. House-maid uncivil : a very stupid ill-mannered set of humans in these parts.

Friday, August 31.—Carriage from ' Nag's Head ' takes N., G., M., Phil and me to the sea at Milford. Milford Church, in, good, ' time of Henry I., about,' Morris says ; choir waggon-roofed. Hurst shingle, M. and N. sprawl, won't walk. We bury Morris up to the neck

in shingle. Surge, boats, sward. M. would like to 1866
find lodgings in Milford. Return—they dine with me
at 7. Look at folio Virgil with plates, and Raleigh's
History of the World, etc.

Tuesday, September 4.—N. and G. sup with me.
Heywood's *Woman Killed with Kindness,* and Heine's
honest Lottery Office Keeper (which delights N.).

After they go I read in Swinburne's volume, lent me
by Ned, but can't like it : great display of literary
power of a sort, to what result? so elaborated, so
violently emphatic, so really cold-blooded.

Wednesday 5.—Cloudy, showers. To Stanwell
House. The Joneses packing up. Baby Margaret,
asleep on large bed, her father has made like a grotesque
giantess, by means of gloves and shoes peeping out at
immense distances. Good-byes, including old Mrs.
G., who is eighty-eight, living at top of the house,
Nosegay, omnibus. Train for London, and so ends the
pleasant friendly visit. They would like, they say, to
come again, and to the same lodging. I walk back to
Lymington by the old church and Boldre.

Wednesday, September 19.—Southampton Exhibition.
Pictures—'Sir Joshua,' Hunt's ' Awakening Conscience,'
Lear's ' Florence,' Lee's ' Caprera,' etc. Antiquities—
Indian and Chinese things, etc. etc. An Exhibition
always troubles my mind—why?—it is heterogeneous
and confused, as a whole the very opposite of an artistic
thing. A Collection of whatever kind ought itself to be
a Work of Art—hard to manage this in a *temporary*
Exhibition, yet even here something might be done.

Monday, October 1.—Clough as poet is reflective and
didactic. His landscape painting is noteworthy for
its truth and solidity. It is often too truthful to be
good as art, resembling rather a coloured photograph
than a picture. Something of the land-surveyor, one
might say, mingles with the poet. In everything,
indeed, he aims at exactness, sometimes with too
obvious an effort.

143

Man, shape the moment! God will shape the life.

[Allingham received a sudden intimation of his Father's death—on October 7. He went at once to Ballyshannon.

This was his last visit to Ireland.]

November 9.—Walk—the old pathway to Brockenhurst Church, through Mr. Morant's park, obstructed by an oak lying across it, so that the rain has formed a small morass. The Squire evidently allows it to lie there for the annoyance of people using the path, which he would fain shut up. What an ugly trick. Hear guns, and see M. in shooting-dress, dark-haired, florid, rather dandified man between thirty and forty, something like an opera Baritone. Daresay he would like to shoot me for being on this path, which has certainly been public since before the Norman Conquest, while his family have only been here two or three generations. The old Doomsday Book Church, with its yew and hollow oak, always a delight to me. There is talk of building, mainly by the Squire's wish, a new one in another place—cutting one more of the threads that join Past with Present. Of what use is John M. in the world ? Towards the village he has closed up lately a beautiful bit of shady byroad.

On my return find a parcel by rail from Gabriel containing the portfolio of photographs from drawings by his poor Wife ; they are naturally full of his influence.[1] Also of two very beautiful pencil portraits of her by his hand, one a head, the other full-length.

Short, sad and strange her life ; it must have seemed to her like a troubled dream. She was sweet, gentle, and kindly, and sympathetic to art and poetry. As to art-power, it is not easy to make as much as a guess ; and this portfolio hardly helps. But it is very interesting, at least to those who knew her. Her pale face, abundant red hair, and long thin limbs were strange and affecting—never beautiful in my eyes.

Sunday, November 11.—Milder weather, mind dull and muddy. *History of Ireland*—lawlessness and turbulency, robbery and oppression, hatred and revenge, blind selfishness everywhere—no principle, no heroism. What can be done with it?

Monday, November 12.—Meet G. St. Barbe. He applied *viva voce*, to oblige me, to the Parson of Ellingham, whom he knows, for leave for me to look over the Parish Register. I want to see if I can discover any traces of my ancestors (Allingham and Ellingham are, I believe, identical), who came to the north-west of Ireland in, Petrie thought, Elizabeth's reign. The old Vicar answered gruffly, ' Shilling a year, shilling a year!' that is, I must pay a fee of a shilling for each year I look at. This might come to a good deal of money, so I give the thing up.

November 13.—Out after midnight to look for meteors, see many streaming like fiery arrows, mostly from east to west.

Wednesday, November 21.—Farringford. Breakfast. Letter for Tennyson from Poets sending specimens of their work, and autograph seekers. T. says, ' I should like to sneak about and get a cup of tea by myself.' At which Mrs. T. smiles sweetly on us. T. added, in a matter-of-fact way, ' I breakfasted alone for a quarter of a century.' Mrs. T. asks me to stay, but go to Lymington I must, so hurry off to Yarmouth, running part of the way, to catch steamer. Cross again in the afternoon, and walk to Farringford. Dinner. Parson F. defends Church and State. Parson's wife angry, and shows it.

Drawing-room.—T. on the death of children, without any reference to orthodox phrases or notions. Mrs. F., driven out of her wits almost, declares what he says to be ' mere chop-logic.' After this he goes upstairs leaving us silent and the parson's wife enraged.

T. and I upstairs—' Swinburne—he has a metrical swing. W. M. Rossetti's pamphlet.'

' You shocked Mrs. F.'

'Can't help it.'

Thursday, November 22.—Farringford. After breakfast T. reads a number of Songs of his under the general title of *The Window*, or, *The Loves of the Wrens*, prefacing it by the remark, 'They're quite silly!'

These songs were privately printed some little time ago at the press of Sir Ivor Guest. Arthur Sullivan saw a copy and managed to get a promise from T. to allow him to set them to music and publish them, all together, on some half-profit arrangement. T. repented of this and tried hard to back out. Some lines in them one remembers like a nursery rhyme—

> When the winds are up in the morning,
> Vine, vine and eglantine,
> Rose, rose and clĕmătis
> Kiss, kiss!

There are naïvetés and niaiseries—

> You are small, am I so tall?
> Cannot we come together?
> Why?
> For it's easy to find a rhyme—
> It's ay, ay, ay, ay, ay!

In reading this, T. jumped round most comically, like a cock-pigeon. He is the only person I ever saw who can do the most ludicrous things without any loss of dignity.

Reading the lines—

> After-loves of maids and men
> Are but meats cook'd up again,

he remarked, 'That's very like Shakespeare.'

December 2.—Letter from John. Irish Annals. Walk, Shirley Holmes,—heavy shower ; shelter under ivied porch of gatehouse, man looks out, I ask leave ——he replies 'I doesn't know as it's any 'arm to stand theer,'—a British welcome, or Anglo-Saxon rather. Yellow sky under rain-cloud.

Saturday, December 22.—To Tom Taylor's, Lavender

Sweep, for Christmas. Clapham Junction, all trains late.
Reach the hospitable house about 7, in good time for
dinner. Then T. T. hurries me off to the Junction
again, and from Waterloo we take a cab to the Adelphi,
and see *The Sister's Penance*, with Kate Terry. The
Indian Mutiny scene, Ahmedvolah. In a stage-box the
Terry family (including Nellie) and their Yorkshire
friends. We just catch train at Waterloo and get home
about half-past twelve.

December 24.—Lavender Sweep. After City, a
steak at the Cock, in honour of Will Waterproof—but
where is now the 'plump head-waiter'? Rail from
Blackfriars; in the train a widow telling a man of her
son's death, sour-looking man opposite interposes 'I
doubt if your son died a right and happy death,' and
then goes out. I speak to the widow and try to take
away the dismal effect of this fellow's harsh words.
She tells me of her son, how good he was. After the
widow got out, one woman in the carriage said to
another 'we want something to cheer us up after that'
—perhaps gin.

No people talk so freely as the lower class of
Londoners when thrown together.

Lavender Sweep. Children's party—The Terrys,
Burnands, etc. Game of Post Office, I blind the people.
Game of the Ring. Mistletoe. All gone. Chat by
the fire.

December 26.—Lavender Sweep. Goodbye. Bright
spring-like day. To Kensington Square. Ned. Studio.
He with me to Kensington Station and sees me off.

CHAPTER IX

1867

Friday, January 24.—Lymington. Fine and vernal.
Ferry to steamer—delightful colours of earth, sky and
sea, a bloom upon the landscape. From the Solent
see the woody background of Lymington recede, the
Island approach with a welcome ; a boat with red
sails passes in the sunshine. I feel tranquilly happy.
Yarmouth, send two bottles of whisky to A. T. by
Lambert's driver. Walk to Farringford, field-path,
warm. Drawing-room. Mrs. T. (looking ill), Miss
T., T. He and I walk on the downs ; very friendly
talk. I said I felt happy to-day, but he—' I'm not at
all happy—very unhappy.' He spoke of immortality
and virtue,—Man's pettiness.—' Sometimes I have a
kind of hope.' His anxiety has always been great to
get some real insight into the nature and prospects of
the Human Race. He asks every person that seems
in the least likely to help him in this, reads every book.
When *Vestiges of Creation* appeared he gathered from
the talk about it that it came nearer to an explanation
than anything before it. T. got the volume, and (he
said to me), ' I trembled as I cut the leaves.' But alas,
neither was satisfaction there.

Plato : T. says he has not really got anything from
him. Æschylus is great ; he quoted from a Chorus in
the *Agamemnon.*

148   Women in towns, dangers to health, horrible

diseases, quack-doctors, etc. T. would have a strict
Contagious Diseases Act in force everywhere.

We go through kitchen garden, lane and gate to
the road as usual, where we take leave after some talk
upon Christ and the People. T. loves the spirit of
Christianity, hates many of the dogmas.

Friday, February 1.—T. is unhappy from his uncer-
tainty regarding the condition and destiny of man. Is
it dispiriting to find a great Poet with no better grounds
of comfort than a common person? At first it is.
But how should the case be otherwise? The poet has
only the same materials of sensation and thought as
ordinary mortals ; he uses them better ; but to step
outside the human limitations is not granted even to
him. The secret is kept from one and all of us. We
must turn eyes and thoughts to the finer and nobler
aspects of things, and never let the scalpel of Science
overbear pen, pencil and plectrum. A Poet's doubts
and anxieties are more comforting than a scientist's
certainties and equanimities.

Saturday, February 2.—T. and Lionel just starting
for a walk ; we took the green road at foot of downs.
T. had in his pocket a volume, or pamphlet, of Edwin
Waugh's *Lancashire Songs*, and when we paused he
read, ' Coam whoam to thy childre and me,' with praise.
We went to the end of the downs overlooking the
Needles. T. spoke of Campbell—his vanity—' has
written fine things.'

Edge of cliff, wind blowing in from the sea ; a ship
ashore at Brook.

Sunday, February 3.—Walk with T. to Brook Bay,
ship ashore, the *Fannie Larabee* of Bath, large, three
masts, good model. There are people on the shore,
but T. doesn't seem to mind. We walked to next
point and saw a steamer ashore at Atherfield ; then
turned up to downs and came back by a path slanting
along the cliff side, like a frightful dream rather, my
head being lightish. T. tells of people who have fallen

over, and at one place is a monumental stone to commemorate such an accident. I said (walking close behind him) 'suppose I were to slip and catch hold of you, and we both rolled down together,' on which T. stopped and said, ' you'd better go on first.'

We talked of Dryden, Campbell, etc. T. told me he was prevented from doing his Arthur Epic, in twelve books, by John Sterling's Review of ' Morte d'Arthur ' in the *Quarterly*. ' I had it all in my mind, could have done it without any trouble. The King is the complete man, the Knights are the passions.' Home a little late for dinner. Afterwards T. rose to leave the room. Matilda (I think) asked, ' Where are you going ? '

' To read the Scriptures.'

Later in the drawing-room he read aloud some of Goethe's lyrics.

Monday, February 18.—Mist. Steamer to Yarmouth. Flags flying. The Queen expected from Osborne, coming to take a look at this part of the island. I to Farringford. I say to T., ' Perhaps the Queen will visit you to-day.' He thinks it possible.

' Then I had better go ? '

' No, stay by all means.'

Talking of the Queen, when T. was at Osborne Her Majesty said to him, ' Cockneys don't annoy *us*,' to which T. rejoined, ' If I could put a sentry at each of my gates I should be safe.'

' She was praising my poetry ; I said " Every one writes verses now. I daresay Your Majesty does." She smiled and said, " No ! I never could bring two lines together ! " '

The Queen, I find, has steamed past Yarmouth, landed at Alum Bay, and lunched there at the hotel.

March 30.—Ride to Hurst. Returning, I rode by the edge of the sea, till in one place the horse suddenly sank to his belly in the muddy sand. I had a real fright for half a minute, and then we scrambled out, I don't know how. At Keyhaven I got the horse well wisped.

Wednesday, April 3.—Farringford. Tennyson and
I busied ourselves in the shrubberies, transplanting
primroses with spade, knife, and wheelbarrow. After
dinner T. concocts an experimental punch with whisky
and claret—not successful. Talks of Publishers, anon
of higher things. He said, 'I feel myself to be a
centre—can't believe I shall die. Sometimes I have
doubts, of a morning. Time and Space appear thus
by reason of our boundedness.'

We spoke of Swedenborg, animals, etc., all with the
friendliest sympathy and mutual understanding. T. is
the most delightful man in the world to converse with,
even when he disagrees.

To my inn, where I woke in the dark, bitten, and
improvised two lines—

>Who in a country inn lies ill at ease
>On fozy feathers fill'd with furious fleas.

April 18 *to* 25.— In London, staying at Tom
Taylor's — old Mr. Barker is there. See Carlyle,
Browning, Ned Jones, etc.

Sunday, April 21.—Lunch with Browning at Warwick Crescent. Miss Browning. Swinburne's writing
'a fuzz of words.' Browning improvises,

>Don't play with sharp tools, these are edge 'uns,
>My Ned Jones!

B.'s pet owl sits on its perch in a corner, B. calls
him 'a good man,' petting and stroking him. We
speak of William Morris, and B. wishes he could see
him : I say, 'Come with me to him,' and B. hesitates,
but ends by not finding it possible to-day. Enter Pen.
As You Like It—Mrs. Scott Siddons was 'so bad!'
Shakespeare's language ; he *invented* a great number of
words and phrases which have become common property—

>The big round tears
>Cours'd one another down his innocent nose.

>Sweep on, you fat and greasy citizens!

151

Now Byron says 'swept,' and that's all very fine—but give me the man who first said 'sweep.'

To Cheyne Row. C. asks about my *Irish History*, but is not satisfied to find me taking much trouble about the ancient part, for which he cares very little, the old Saints excepted. I fear, indeed know, that my views and his are irreconcilable. He describes Mentone —clear air, good peasant people near it.

Saturday, *May* 4.—Lymington. By train to Brockenhurst and walk to Queen's Bower. The brook bestarred with white flowers (water crowfoot), little fishes gliding. Sit under the Big Oak reading *As You Like It,*—and this might be Jacques's very brook in Arden. Then through forest glades appears a carriage with Aïdé, George du Maurier and his wife, and Miss Middlecoat.

May 24.—To Winchester, St. Giles's Hill, Cathedral, St. Cross, etc.

May 25.—Farnham (see *Rambles* by Patricius Walker), Cobbett's Birthplace 'The Jolly Farmer.' Bishop's Park, fine old walls, great elms, deer, Moor Park and Waverley, river, ruins, Crooksbury Hill (dark firs).

May 26.—Guildford—Hog's Back, Liphook—Grayshot, and find the Tennyson house (they occupy the best part of a large farmhouse). Lionel shows me the piece of land which his Father thinks of buying to build on.

May 27.—Morris's *Jason*, 'from his friend the Author.' Medea off with the Fleece—admirable.

Sunday, *June* 9.—Find with joy a book on my table, by post, *May-Day*—gift from Emerson.

Monday, *June* 10.—Fine, warm. To Brockenhurst by invitation to the Bowden Smiths, croquet, roses, hot sun. Field-path to station, red campions and kingcups. Down train comes in with Mrs. Cameron, queenly in a carriage by herself surrounded by photographs. We go to Lymington together, she talking all the time.

'I want to do a large photograph of Tennyson, and he objects! Says I make bags under his eyes—and Carlyle refuses to give me a sitting, he says it's a kind of *Inferno*! The *greatest* men of the age (with strong emphasis), Sir John Herschel, Henry Taylor, Watts, say I have *immortalised* them—and these other men object!! What is one to do——Hm?'

This is a kind of interrogative interjection she often uses, but seldom waits for a reply. I saw her off in the Steamer, talking to the last. Dine 7.30—Sit on doorstep and hear corncrake in the moonlight. Haymaking now.

June 18.—Very fine. Picnic in Forest, Schoolgirls and grown folk, youths and maidens. A Club Day also—children in waggons—noise and laughter— wood walks. We dine on the grass at 2.15.

Friday 28.—Hot. Leave of absence : Burnett, my *locum tenens*, appears, and I start for London, to stay in Kensington Square. Find Georgie well, Ned at Morris's—supper.

Saturday 29.—Kensington Square. Hot—call at Lavender Sweep ; Mrs. Tom Taylor, Lucy, Wycliffe. Up Regent St. ; dusty, dry, ugly London. Dine at 7. Ned and I in garden of square ; to us enter Mr. John Simon (from next door) and his niece. Mr. S. a kind, bright pleasant man and good talker, as well as eminent surgeon, boyishly merry at times. He and his niece run a race to the house, then he jumps on the low wall and lies flat on it as if exhausted. Read Ruskin's Lecture at Royal Institution on Art and Life.

Sunday 30.—Ned's Studio, 'St. George and Dragon,' 'The First Mirror' (nude models). To Queen's Square ; Mrs. Morris, Jeannie and May. Enter Morris, frank and friendly as usual—Supper.

Tuesday, July 2.—Ned, Howell and I. Howell 'going to be married in August'—I congratulate him ; he says 'you are more encouraging than——, who, when I told him, said in an anxious tone—

' My dear fellow, can't you get out of it ? '

Morris and I to the Royalty Theatre, *Black-eyed Susan*. M. seldom goes to the Theatre, and is bored a good deal. Poor enough fun, indeed. With M. to Queen Square.

July 4.—Queen Square.—Morris and I to Westminster Abbey. Deanery, Cloisters—pleasant.

Wednesday, *July* 17.—Lymington. Fine ; hurry to steamer. Excursion to visit the French Fleet at Spithead. At Yarmouth a large Tennyson party comes on board—A. T., his brother Charles and Mrs. Charles, Hallam and Lionel, two daughters of Fredk. Tennyson, from Jersey, and Matilda T. A. T. and I collogue. At Cowes a bustle : the Queen embarking in her steam-yacht.

We see the Fleet at Spithead, ' like Milan Cathedral.' Rain comes on. The Queen having reached the French Fleet—Ironclads, huge, black and ugly,—royal salutes thunder, the yards are manned, but we can see very little for the thick weather. Ryde Pier, Tennyson and I land, among others ; the ladies ill and draggled. Pier Hotel. A. T., Charles T., and I go up High Street and out into a field beyond, where we sit on a balk of wood, looking at some cows grazing, and A. T. smoking. He quotes a sonnet of his brother's about elms and calls it *daimonisch*. We return by lower road and all go aboard again, where A. T., Sir Andrew Hammond and I dine. The weather still thick with frequent showers ; some want to turn homewards without running through the Fleet, etc., as arranged. Captain Cribb will do whatever the passengers wish,—whereupon a debate below. In an interval of silence a deep voice is heard grumbling out—' I know it's not the least use my saying anything, but I'm for going back.' This was A. T., but the majority were plainly for going on, and soon we steamed in the rain close to the dark sullen row of huge Ironclads. Then fireworks, and we turned homewards. We nestled down near the boiler,

A. T., Lionel, W. A., and the rest—chatted, asked
riddles, and so we reached Yarmouth, where they
landed and I was left lonely again. Got back half an
hour after midnight.

July 19.—Writing *Rambles*. Walk, riverside,
honeysuckle, scabious, bluebell, ferns, more contented.

August 5.—Farringford, Bradley, etc. I continue to
like B. more and more.

Monday, August 19.—After dinner a thunderstorm
with rain. Night grows pitch dark. Tremendous
thunder and lightning for a long time. I put out my
candle and sit at window watching. The lightning
over the Island. A *thunder-bolt* apparently falls on the
mainland eastwards. 'Tremble, thou wretch.'

Tuesday, August 20.—Hearing that the lightning did
mischief out eastwards, I cross Ferry, walk to Baddesley,
and find a two-story cottage burned, only the blackened
walls left; the ivy and flowers scorched, and the apples
on some trees close by *roasted on one side*. Among a
heap of half-burnt things, mixed with charred wood and
ashes, lay some fused photographs of the old daguerreo-
type sort in metal frames, such as hang on cottage walls.
The Father stood grave and reserved, a girl, his
daughter, near him, both seeming stunned. The man
told me he went to the upper room during the thunder-
storm and sat down on a chair near the fireplace.
His wife was in bed, and two sons in another bed.
Suddenly the lightning darted through the thatched
roof and down through the floor of the room, and the
whole place was in a blaze in a moment. Up started
wife and sons, the feather beds were thrown out of
window, all rushed out into the rain, and nothing else
was saved from the fire. I offered to lend a little
money, but it was declined.

This was the work perhaps of the thunderbolt which
I saw fall last night; the time fits. I could not find
that the lightning did anything as lightning save set the
house on fire; this it did very effectually.

Friday, August 23.—Very fine. Steamer 11.40 to Yarmouth. Tennyson on the quay, also his brother Frederick and two daughters. A. T. is going to Lyme Regis alone.

'I have wanted to see the Cobb there ever since I first read *Persuasion.* Will you come?'

Can I possibly? Yes, I will!

We cross to Lymington. I rush up and make hasty arrangements at Custom-House and lodgings; then off go A. T. and I, second class, to Dorchester. A. T. smokes. (T. is a great novel reader, very fond of Scott, but perhaps Miss Austen is his prime favourite.)

In our carriage a cockney Clock-winder, who gets out at every Station to regulate the Railway Company's clock.

Once safely *incognito* T. delights in talking to people, but touch his personality and he shuts up like an oyster. Ringwood, Wimborne, Poole harbour, Wareham (mounds), Dorchester. Walk in the warm afternoon, through stubble fields and reapers at work, to the grand old Keltic fortress now called 'Maiden Castle,' view the great green mounds, and lie on a slope looking over autumnal landscape. Then descend and return, finding corn-flowers and 'Succory to match the sky.' Shall we stay to-night at Dorchester? T. vacillates, at last agrees. We go to the 'Antelope,' rooms not good—out, and into the Museum, up a backyard,—British antiquities, Roman pottery, etc. High Street, at its foot a clear little river, *the Frome.* A tipsy cobbler accosts us. Riverside walk through meadows. County Jail looks like a pleasant residence. Return by back street to the 'Antelope,' which produces a pint of good port at dinner. The twilight being fine I propose that we should visit William Barnes, whom T. personally knows, and whose Poems in the Dorset dialect T. knows and likes. I show the way to Came Vicarage, where I had enjoyed hospitality from a Saturday to a Monday a year or two

before. The cottage-parsonage lies in a hollow among
trees about a mile from Dorchester, separated from the
public road by a little grass-plot and shrubbery. We
find the gate by starlight and reach the house door
between 9 and 10 o'clock. The worthy old Poet-
Vicar is truly delighted to see us, especially such a
guest as T. (whose poetry, he used to say, has a ' heart-
tone ' in it).

Barnes himself lets us in or comes out at once into
the passage—' Here's an honour ! ' Little Miss Barnes
and Mrs. Shaw, a married daughter, appear. B. says,
' put out something ! put out something ! ' with hospitable fervour, tho' we lack no bodily refreshment.
Barnes himself, by the way, though not a teetotaller, is
an abstemious man, very plain and inexpensive in his
diet. We are pressed to stay but can't. Talk of Maiden
Castle, Irish dūns and raths. T. tells his story of his
car-driver, ' The King of Connaught.' Then we go,
Barnes with us to near Dorchester, talking of British
Antiquities, Wareham, Sun-worship, etc.

Saturday, August 25. — Dorchester — To Maiden
Newton—Bridport. We start off to walk to Lyme
Regis, leaving bag to come by carrier. Uphill, view of
sea, down to Chidiock, pretty village, old church, flowery
houses. We push on (as like two tramps as need be)
along the dusty road to Martin's Lake, sea on one hand,
shore hills on the other. Down a long hill to Charmouth, where we have beer and cheese in a little inn,
then T. smokes in the porch and chats to the waitress.
She says she is from the Isle of Wight. ' So am I,'
says T.,—' what part ? ' ' From Cowes,' says the girl.
' I come from Freshwater,' says T., which surprises me,
—but he revels in the feeling of anonymosity. We
see Lyme below us and take a field-path.

· Down into Lyme Regis, narrow old streets, modest
little Marine Parade. ' The Cups ' receives us in the
fair plump good-humoured person of a House-Keeper
Barmaid. T. gets a good bedroom and I a tolerable

one; we go into garden sloping down-hill and out by some back steps to a Mrs. Porter's, where the F. Palgraves are lodging—not in.

Back to 'The Cups' and order dinner; then by myself up steep street to top of the town, pleasant, view of shore and headlands, little white town far off. Dinner. Then T. and I out and sit on bench facing the sea, talking with friendly openness. Marriage,—'how can I hope to marry? Some sweet good woman would take me, *if I could find her.*' T. says, 'O yes,' adding, 'I used to rage against the social conditions that made marriage so difficult.'

Sunday, August 25.—Lyme Regis. Very fine. T. up first and at my door. He has been on the Cobb, and eats a hearty breakfast. We go down to the Cobb, enjoying the sea, the breeze, the coast-view of Portland, etc., and while we sit on the wall I read to him, out of *Persuasion*, the passage where Louisa Musgrave hurts her ankle. Palgrave comes, and we three (after Manor House and some talk of Chatham) take a field-path that brings us to Devonshire Hedge and past that boundary into Devon. Lovely fields, an undercliff with tumbled heaps of verdure, honeysuckle, hawthorns and higher trees. Rocks peeping through the sward, in which I peculiarly delight, reminding me of the West of Ireland. I quote—

Bowery hollows crowned with summer sea.

T. (as usual), 'You don't say it properly '—and repeats it in his own sonorous manner, lingering with solemn sweetness on every vowel sound,—a peculiar *incomplete* cadence at the end. He modulates his cadences with notable subtlety. A delightful place. We climb to the top, find flat fields, and down again. Stile and path—agrimony—we sit on a bank, talk of Morris, Ned Jones, Swinburne, etc. Whitechapel Rock. Then return by winding paths to the town. Miss Austen, Scott, novel writing. P. counsels me to write a novel.

Inn, dinner, fat waitress, port. In the coffee-room a
gentleman, who joins in conversation—High Church,
etc., State of England,—and speaks well but guardedly.
T. talks freely—human instincts, Comte, etc.

We go to Palgrave's, who says, 'thought you were
not coming.' They smoke. When T. and I are walking back to the Inn he takes my arm, and by and by asks
me *not* to go back to Lymington. I (alas!) have to
reply that I must. 'Well then,' says T., 'arrange your
business there and come back.' I doubted if I could.
'Is it money?' says he,—'I'll pay your expenses.'
Most delicious! that the man whose company I love
best should care about mine. Most mortifying! for I
am tied by the leg.

Wednesday, August 28.—Lymington. Letter from
M. D. Conway, 'on a little tour of the South Coast—
coming to Lymington with *New York Tribune* man to
visit you and *try to persuade you to go to America.*' Letter
from Howell, at Hastings, giving an account of his
Wedding. Letter from Palgrave (dry): 'Tennyson
asks me to say he hopes you will join us at Moreton
Hampstead—Dartmoor—*au revoir.*'

August 30.—Yacht *Mirella.* Faraday is gone.

Monday, September 2.—Very fine. Pay pensioners
—Train 2.30 brings Conway, but not his *Tribune*
friend. Secure him a bed at the 'Nag's Head,' then we
walk out by Pennington. Talk much of Emerson—
Magazine-writing, etc. Letter from D. G. Rossetti!
'Shall I come to you?' I reply, 'Yes, by all means.'

Sunday, September 8.—Very fine. D. G. Rossetti
coming to-morrow, Read his *Early Italian Poets.*

Mem.—Use him nobly while your guest.

Wednesday, September 11.—Rainy. By 8.40 evening train behold D. G. R.! he wears a ventilating hat,
something like a policeman's helmet, in which he looks
short and broad, having grown stout. We have supper
and sit up talking till three. He has been troubled with
his eyes, but has brought down an unfinished picture,

half-length female figure, intending to paint in background of roses.

Thursday, September 12.—Very fine. My landlady grumpy—'didn't tell me of the gentleman,' etc. I explain. We walk by the river-side to Roydon Farm, path to Brockenhurst Church. Crown Inn. Rail to Lymington. Dine 7 ; Bed about 1. He had thought Lymington to be on the very edge of the Forest.

Friday, September 13.—D. G. R. and I walk out to Rope Hill, and Captain Barton shows us beautiful roses and offers us some for the picture—a very kind man. R. and I to Shirley Holmes and lie in the grassy circle surrounded with oaks, hollies, etc., pierced with little green alleys and tunnels, a fit place to act the *Midsummer Night's Dream* in. We talk of the Forest Gypsies ; this is one of their camping places. D. G. R. has some notion of taking lodgings at Lymington.

Saturday, September 14.—Call D. G. R. He has not yet opened his Picture case, so I undo the fastenings. He finds that none of Captain B.'s roses are exactly of the kind for him ; he wants the fresh-coloured loose-leaved China rose.

I to Custom-House and then call at the Skinners. Walk with Skinner, Q.C., and two daughters to Arnewood. The knowing and experienced talk of the eminent lawyer makes me feel small.

I find D. G. R. on the sofa, has not been out, nor looked at his picture, but been reading *The Mill on the Floss* all day.

Sunday, September 15.—Call D. G. R. Registered letter with bank notes, etc., £157 : 10s.—for 'copy' of *Lilith*. We write letters. Howell has proposed to come here, R. writes to him, ' Come if you will.' Out about 1.30 ; R. and I call at Pennington Cottage, and young Skinner joins us. Milford Church—congregation in it, but D. G. R. and S. go in all the same, take a look and come out again—path, millpond, cliff, sea ; delightful view. We talk of Home and other 'Spiritualists,'

about whom D. G. R. has at the least a curiosity.
Back by Keyhaven and the Marsh. We are late, but
D. G. R. *won't* hurry. He says in a conclusive tone :
' I never do anything I don't like.' Dine 6.30. We go
down and look at the river by moonlight. Bed about 2.
I argue that Maggie Tulliver's lover Stephen is made
too mean and commonplace : R. doesn't agree.

Monday, September 16.—Have had several pressing
notes from Mrs. Cameron to come and bring D. G. R.
to her—' photograph you both.' I ask him will he
come to-day. Decidedly, ' No ! ' We walk through
Sowley Copse and lie under an oak by the pond-side,
reed-beds. R. says, ' You ought to have been a landscape painter. You notice everything.' (Sometimes to
the length of boredom, perhaps he meant.)

Then to Norley and the cottage burnt by lightning-
stroke. The scorched walls and trees remain much as
when I saw them. An old woman, who had been in the
house when it took fire, told us she was ' all skivered
with sparks.' R.'s comment on the whole was this—
' What a damned world where such things can happen ! '

In the garden was a little clump of box clipt into
the form of an arm-chair ; R. wanted to buy this, have
it dug up and transplanted to his garden at Chelsea, but
the bargain did not take effect. The *live* chair tickled
his imagination. (He afterwards got a similar box-bush
chair transplanted to his garden, but it soon died there.)

September 17.—I try to get R. over to the Island and
coax him as far as the pier, but it is rather windy, and
he entirely objects to be sea-sick, and doesn't want to
see either Mrs. Cameron or Tennyson. He takes no
interest whatever in the sea, ships, boats, etc. We go
by 1.45 train to Brockenhurst and walk by Whitley
Wood to Lyndhurst—see Leighton's fresco in the church.
Returning, we go over a roomy cottage-villa on the
roadside, ' To Let,' with a garden behind, and Rossetti
says in his emphatic tone, ' I think I had better take it
at once ! '

Wednesday, September 18.—Fine—D. G. R. and I walk to Boldre Church, Gilpin's tomb and its inscription ; we talk of 'immortality,' but nothing new, and of 'suicide,' which R. thinks 'silly.' There are traces of superstition noticeable in him, none of religion. Back by Pilley and Walhampton House. I visit the Skinners : they are going to Arundel. Young Skinner walks back with me. We find D. G. R. on the sofa.

Thursday, September 19.—R. and I look round the furniture brokers, he buys an old mirror and several other things ' for a song,' but they will have to be done up, 'otherwise you fill your house with dinginess.' Then a walk. R. walks very characteristically, with a peculiar lounging gait, often trailing the point of his umbrella on the ground, but still obstinately pushing on and making way, he humming the while with closed teeth, in the intervals of talk, not a tune or anything like one but what sounds like a *sotto voce* note of defiance to the Universe. Then suddenly he will fling himself down somewhere and refuse to stir an inch further. His favourite attitude—on his back, one knee raised, hands behind head. On a sofa he often, too, curls himself up like a cat. He very seldom takes particular notice of anything as he goes, and cares nothing about natural history, or science in any form or degree. It is plain that the simple, the natural, the naïve are merely insipid in his mouth ; he must have strong savours, in art, in literature and in life. Colours, forms, sensations are required to be pungent, mordant. In poetry he desires spasmodic passion, and emphatic, partly archaic, diction. He cannot endure Wordsworth, any more than I can S. He sees nothing in Lovelace's ' Tell me not, Sweet, I am unkind.' In foreign poetry, he is drawn to Dante by inheritance (Milton, by the way, he dislikes) ; in France he is interested by Villon and some others of the old lyric writers, in Germany by nobody. To Greek Literature he seems to owe nothing, nor to Greek Art, directly. In Latin poetry he has

turned to one or two things of Catullus for sake of the
subjects. English imaginative literature—Poems and
Tales, here lies his pabulum : Shakespeare, the old
Ballads, Blake, Keats, Shelley, Browning, Mrs. Browning,
Tennyson, Poe being first favourites, and now Swinburne. *Wuthering Heights* is a Koh-i-noor among
novels, *Sidonia the Sorceress* 'a stunner.' *Any* writing
that with the least competency assumes an imaginative
form, or any criticism on the like, attracts his attention
more or less ; and he has discovered in obscurity, and
in some cases helped to rescue from it, at least in his
own circle, various unlucky books ; those, for example,
of Ebenezer Jones [*Studies of Sensation and Event*] and
Wells, author of *Joseph and His Brethren* and *Stories
after Nature*. About these and other matters Rossetti
is chivalrously bold in announcing and defending his
opinions, and he has the valuable quality of knowing
what he likes and sticking to it. In Painting the Early
Italians with their quaintness and strong rich colouring
have magnetised him. In Sculpture he only cares for
picturesque and grotesque qualities, and of Architecture
as such takes, I think, no notice at all.

Friday, September 20.—D. G. R. and I take a short
walk to Pennington, then early dinner, and he departs
by the 5.45 train, I going with him to Brockenhurst. He did up his picture again without having
put a single touch upon it; and while down here indeed
never once handled brush or pencil, partly to save his eyes.

September 30.—Custom-House accounts. French
lesson from M. Meurzet.

Tuesday, October 8.—Steamer to Yarmouth. To
Mrs. Cameron's, Henry Taylor, and his daughter Emily.
Luncheon. To Farringford, and walk with A. T. to
near Alum Bay. He thinks 'England is going down '
—'Christianity becoming extinct? There's something
miraculous in man.' 'There's more in Christianity
than people now think.'

Publisher P. and rumours of insolvency, etc.

Friday, October 11.—To London—Waterloo at 3. Cab to Chelsea, being invited to stay with D. G. R. Well received ; Dinner in lower room, Fanny, Howell, Madox Brown—Howell's stories, himself an actor in all ('actor' in the stage sense)? He was at York once at the time of a Convocation of Clergy, he had an uncle an Archdeacon, and was allowed to dine with the Clergy one evening, including several Bishops : 'They all got drunk,' said Howell with historic simplicity. Queer stories, such as Sir Robert Walpole used to encourage. In the evening Dunn, R.'s assistant and copyist. All sit late and supper being suggested, Howell and Dunn go down to the kitchen and bring up meat ; H. says he 'saw a mouse eating a haddock' downstairs. 3 o'clock, R. goes to bed, Howell and Dunn go out in the rain to look for a cab, Madox Brown and I wait, sleepy, in hall—cab at last.

Saturday, October 12.—Studio—Sibyl (with roses), Iseult, etc. ; D. G. R., F. Call at Ned's and walk with him in the Park : soppy and foggy.

Monday 14.—Note from Froude about Swift paper for *Fraser*.[1] Evening, with D. G. R. to Ned's. R. lolls and runs down Raffael, Ned and Webb remonstrate. No music. R. and I walking back take wrong turn—'This is bl—y!' He is very fond of this expletive —as well as other phrases (F. sometimes says, 'Rizetti, I shall leave the room !—I'll put you out in the scullery !' etc.). Lounging chat till 1 or 2, with rusks and sherry.

Tuesday, October 15.—Garden ; fierce Virginian owls which dash against the bars of their cage to get at you as you turn away: other creatures. Taylor's estimate of Household Expenses ('for Greengrocer, £58,' and so on), ending with, 'This does not include Wild Beasts.' I sit over proofs all day in the big room—post them ;

---

[1] Allingham's paper, afterwards published in his volume of *Varieties in Prose.*

Call at Morris's, 'out of town.' At Mrs. Rossetti's, Euston Square. The dear old lady looking strong still, with her handsome full-coloured face and rich-toned voice of sincere and touching intonations. She says nothing clever but it's always a pleasure to be near her. Miss R., Christina, and Miss Heaton. Mrs. R. expresses her pleasure at Gabriel's having visited me, thinks it has done him good, talks as if I were a sort of Mentor to him, which makes me feel rather ashamed. Away, rain, cab to Fitzroy Square ; upstairs, Madox Brown, Mrs. B., Lucy, in green dress, Katty, young half-sister with fair hair ; Marshall, Dunn. Piano, Grog.

Wednesday, October 16.—Call on Ned ; Italian Model, a peasant woman—at Mr. Simon's. Call on Froude. Back to Chelsea, then D. G. R. and I to the Café de l'Europe, Haymarket, where we meet Ned and dine. Ned goes, R. and I walk to Queen's Square, Morris out. On the way I buy (for 10s.) an old painting on panel, 'Virgin and Child,' which R. says is ' Flemish, before Rubens, Porbus time.' Cab to Euston Road, to Taylor's lodging. T. Morris, Webb, D. G. R. lounges. I say the rhyme about ' There's a louse on my back Twenty years old ! ' (which I heard Tennyson give). Morris repeats it with furious emphasis and gestures, making us all shout with laughter. Poor Taylor—tall, with eager hatchet face —is ghastly thin but full of mental energy—vociferates, then must stop to cough. ' Won't go away this winter.'

Cheyne Walk—call at Carlyle's. When the door opens, see him in the passage ; he says in an angry voice —' Go away, sir ! I can do nothing with you.' I go away, with reflections many and black. What can it mean ?

Call on Froude at Record Office, make up, and renew *Fraser* agreement in a way. He says ' Byron was the greatest man of the century—greater than Alfred ' (*i.e.* A. T.). I tell of Carlyle's rebuff, which surprises him ; says he has strange moods. Cheyne walk, D. G. R. and I (not like old times).

Thursday, October 17.—Cheyne Walk, pack up, R. lolling on the bed ; cab to Waterloo—train to Lymington.

N.B.—Very kind letter from Carlyle—did not know me that day I called ; 'must blame my poor old eyes. Allingham's company would have been very welcome to me.' How I have tormented myself !

November 11. — Lymington. Evening, reading Rousseau with M. Meurzet. Newsroom, Waterside.

Thursday, November 14.—Gloomy day. Carlyle's 'Shooting Niagara'—object to parts. *Carlylus Tyrannus.*

Friday, November 15.—Fine. Poetry again—in spite of T. C.

Walk, Walhampton Hill, Portmore firs, hedges, ferns, yellow oakleaves, harebells, children sweeping up fallen leaves. Ferry.

Monday, November 25.—Fine gray day ; Mrs Clough has written to say she is coming, I meet her at 11.17 train and cross with her to Island : with her, her little Blanche Athena, dark-eyed, pleasant, sweet little mouth. At Yarmouth the Tennyson carriage. Farringford, luncheon. A. T. on 'the Fenians.' Prince Consort's Book, the Queen's autograph inscription—

'Alfred Tennyson, Esq.,

Who so truly admired and appreciated the character of her beloved Husband. Victoria R.'

Tuesday, November 26.—My last visit to London was an unhappy one. In art, and still more in life, R. and I have discords not to be resolved. Should we ever have been or supposed ourselves such friends in early days if we had lived constantly near each other ? Has he changed ? If I have I am not aware of it. 'I loathe and despise family life ! ' he said.

I long and pray for it—and O, how the years slip away ! The only comfort is, 'You might have made a

mistake, an irremediable one—and it's not too late even
yet!' The 'Curtis' Ballad.

Tuesday, December 24.—Steamer; Parry[1] meets me,
we walk by muddy path and copse to Hook Hill: his
wife and baby (3 days old), both well; luncheon. Take
up my quarters with Mrs. Curry at Myrtle Cottage, then
to Farringford with Parry. I introduce him to Mrs.
Tennyson. He soon retires. A. T. comes in with Sir
John Simeon. I go up the Downs alone, to Beacon;
wide sea, misty landscape, western light, melancholy.
Myrtle Cottage — dine at Farringford, no guests. T.
rages against the Fenians—'Kelts are all mad furious
fools!'

Irish landscape—'I saw wonderful things there—
twenty different showers at once on a great expanse—a
vast yellow cloud with a little bit of rainbow stuck on
one corner' (T. swept his arm round for the cloud and
then gave a nick in the air with his thumb for the bit
of rainbow)—'I wish I could bring these things in! I
was travelling in Kerry through a great black landscape
—bogs. A lady beside me asked how I liked the
country; I said, it might be greener; to which she
replied indignantly, "And where then would the poor
man cut his bit of turf?"'

Away at 11 to Myrtle Cottage.

Wednesday, December 25.—Parry's; walk with him
to sea-side, black rocks, breakers ghostly white, light at
sea. Back with him, tea. His childhood, etc. We walk
along the dark road to Albion Hotel, Mr. and Mrs.
Murrow personal acquaintances of C. P. P. tells of
his tribulations when his wife was confined. No bed,
lay down by a fire and went to sleep, wakened by
woman putting on pots and kettles; went into another
room and fell asleep by the fire, wakened by some one
putting on pots and kettles there; went out, nearly
asleep, and lay down in a passage, wakened by the
Doctor wiping his boots upon him, at which the

[1] Clinton Parry, son of Gambier Parry, the architect.

Murrows laugh.   Walking back P. explains to me
that Murrow (a Welshman) is 'a high Freemason'—
'He doesn't call me "Sir" when we're alone.   If you're
a Mason your Servant may be a higher Mason than
you.   Garibaldi head of the Italian Masons, which
added greatly to his power.   L. Napoleon a High
Mason, etc.'

Has Freemasonry any real importance in the world's
affairs ? or is most of this mythical ?

Friday, December 27.—Myrtle Cottage, fine, misty.
Farringford.   T. in his big cloak on lawn.

'Poe on metres—he knows nothing about them.'

Tauchnitz—T.'s poems smuggled in ; T. complained ;
Treasury letter, 'the public complain of much searching.'   Boys at football.   Cold wind, fog, gray ; slender
moon in the west, and Venus.   Myrtle Cottage.   To
Farringford.   Dine in the study—jokes and puns—
after dinner, pleasant talk.

T. — 'We remember Summer Walks in Winter,
Winter in Summer.'

T. reads the newspaper into metre.

T. says : 'Boys become beasts for a time—no conscience : I don't know what it means.

'I hate publishing !   The Americans forced me into
it again.   I had my things nice and right, but when I
found they were going to publish the old forms I said,
By Jove, that won't do !—My whole living is from the
sale of my books.'

He went upstairs by himself.   When he came down
again spoke of Greek Poetry,—'The *Odyssey* the most
delightful book in the world.   Blank verse is the only
English metre to translate Homer in, and even that will
not do.   Lofty Scriptural prose would be best.'

Of Latin Poetry he said, 'Virgil's is the most
finished of any ; Catullus is exquisite ; Lucretius wonderful, but much of him hard and tiresome to read, and
very obscure.'   Away—stars—Bed about 1.

Saturday, December 28.—Myrtle Cottage, cold, hoar-

frost, misty. Farringford, Lionel and his fiddle.
Henry Cameron comes, for rabbit-hunting. I walk to
Yarmouth, pretty byroad to shore, hartstongue ferns,
a primrose in bloom. Quay, Hallam with carriage and
ponies. Cold, foggy wind, gray sea. Steamer comes
in with Woolner and Mr. W. G. Clark of Cambridge.
We three walk off by shore and byroad. Show them
primrose—'The rath primrose that forsaken dies.'
T.'s lines :—

> the gloomy brewer's soul
> Went by me, like a stork :

Why 'Stork?' Clark says because the Stork was
an antimonarchical emblem.

To Farringford. At dinner Mr. Clark talks of
Rome, Greece, foreign travel (pleasant life). T.
denounces publisher P. Says he is trying Hebrew.

'Do you (to Clark) know any Hebrew?'

C.—'Only the letters.'

T.—'Exactly! the priests can't read their own
sacred books.'

C. (rather disconcerted).—'The New Testament I
can, more or less.' (One forgets that C. is a Rev.)

Monday, December 30.—Dine at Farringford. T.
discourses on 'Maud': I make him laugh by misquoting
lines about the shell, thus—

> 'Did he stand at his own front-door
> With a diamond stud in his frill?'

Tuesday, 31.—Myrtle Cottage—fine. Take leave
at Farringford and at Mrs. Cameron's. Steamer to
Lymington, Custom-House, resume charge ; lodgings
—no dinner—all in confusion—'not expected'—
Christmas Tree in Kitchen ; make the best of it and
give a picture to the lottery. Look over *Midsummer
Night's Dream.* No feeling about the Old Year, save
of depression.

CHAPTER X

1868

January 1.—Lymington. Pay pensioners. Engaged to go to Lyndhurst to-day. 5.45 train to Brockenhurst, Aïdé's carriage, Forest Bank, A. and Mrs. A., dinner at 7. Then to Sir Charles Burrard's. We read the *Midsummer Night's Dream*, which goes well.

Monday, January 20.—Fine; walk to Pitt's Deep—vernal and pleasant; Coastguard station. Beautiful Sowley Copse—men destroying it by order of Lord Henry Scott, since he finds he cannot close up the foot-path—what a noble action !

Tuesday, January 21.—Fine; Steamer brings Mr. Cameron, white-haired Mrs. Prinsep, etc., for London. I go with them as far as Brockenhurst, pleasant. Walk to Lyndhurst, vernal, call at Miss Dickson's, poorly ; friendly chat. She says, 'I thought you surly at first, —like you now,—thrown away at Lymington.' Hurry to Brockenhurst, hot, catch train. Dine 7—rain—sleep better.

Wednesday, January 22.—Rainy. Sir Percy Shelley runs after me, and takes me aboard his yacht *Enchantress*, pleasant chat with Lady Shelley: 'Come to us to-morrow evening, if we're not gone.' Street—stars.

Thursday, January 23.—Fine, frostyish ; *Enchantress* gone. Walk, Pennington, etc.

Monday, February 3.—To London—very fine day.

Mr. Burnett at Custom-House; away 1.45. Clapham
Junction; lovely evening, moon, Jupiter and Venus.
Lavender Sweep—friendly welcome as ever. Talk
with Tom Taylor.

A Comedy in hand, *For Love or Money*; Mrs. T.
writing it from Tom's dictation; they do some this
evening.

Tuesday, February 4.—Lavender Sweep, called at
7.30; Wycliffe, Lucy—Breakfast. In with T. T. to
Victoria. National Gallery, Egyptian Hall, Dudley
Gallery. Bond St., Mrs. Cameron's Exhibition of
Photographs, in charge of a pretty Brunette (Miss Kate
Shepherd) with sweet smile. Lavender Sweep—dinner.
Evening, T. T. dictating comedy, Mrs. T. writing, I
suggesting sometimes. Sleepy, yet awake in the night.

Wednesday, February 5.—Fine but windy. Walk
through old Wandsworth, like a country town, to
Putney, where are some large Georgian houses. Call
on Arthur Hughes, whose house faces the river, most
friendly. Arty, a pretty boy, little boy, girl.

Studio, pleasant chat; yard, children feeding two
tame deer. A. H. walks with me to near Clapham.

T. T.'s, dress to dine at Conway's—find them at
dinner on the basement floor, Mr. and Mrs. C. and
Mr. Smalley, European Correspondent of New York
Tribune—lively chat. Then to Peter Taylor's, an
evening gathering. Conway and I walk, fine starry
night. Bed at his house; lie long awake.

Friday, February 7.—Lavender Sweep—rail to
Chelsea, cab to Onslow Gardens and breakfast with
Froude, Mrs. F., two daughters, governess; chat.
Study, where he has his cigar—State papers on Ireland,
praises my prose style. I feel awkward with him.
Call at Miss Thackeray's, close by; find her writing—
very friendly. Mrs. Cameron's Exhibition—' I blew
the trumpet for it in the Pall Mall.'

Enter Mr. Leslie Stephen, tall and pale. Away
(pleasant). Call on Carlyle at 3. Find him in upstairs

room, cap on, smoking. He talks of the *Ballad of Tranent Muir*, by Skirving, then takes me out with him to walk, Hyde Park, Bayswater, and back.

'Leigh Hunt a fine kind of man. I used to read the *Examiner* with much interest when I was living down in Scotland. Some used to talk of him as a frivolous fellow, but when I saw him I found he had a face as serious as death.' I asked C. if he dreamed much.

'Dreams! my dreams are always disagreeable— mere confusions— losing my clothes and the like, nothing beautiful. The same dreams go on night after night for a long time. I am a *worse* man in my dreams than when awake—do cowardly acts, dream of being tried for a crime. I long ago came to the conclusion that my dreams are of no importance to me whatever.

'Ireland—education at National Schools, not good, what I saw of it, except at Glasnevin. To teach reading and writing is not education : little good will follow from that. I *used* to think almost every good would follow from that. You must teach *work*, you must drill.

'Criminal classes : I went with a Colonel of the Guards to Whitechapel to see some of the dens, a few policemen with us ; it was very melancholy, the places were not *dirty* in general. The police know all the regular rogues. In one place we heard some girls laughing behind a screen ; I said in a rather loud voice, "God pity you !" upon which they suddenly fell silent. We seemed to give no offence where we came ; but one woman, tipsy, said to one of our policemen, "You're showing us to the Gentlemen, but if they want to see the greatest rascal in London they'll take a look at yourself, you—unmentionable !" which I thought to be not far from the truth.'

C. spent three days on the Grand Jury at Clerkenwell, over trivial cases, 'a great loss of time.'

'Your "Ramble in the New Forest" very pretty and

pleasant, the only thing in the Magazine I could read. But you are rather losing your time. Go on with your book on Ireland, I advise you.'

Back at 5 Cheyne Row, we find a carriage at the door and a demonstrative man in the hall, who exclaims, 'So I *have* found you!'

C. asks me to come again. I propose Sunday, my only free day, but he says 'engaged on that day,' and adds, 'it is unfortunate'—evidently regretting that we cannot meet again this time, as I also assuredly do. (To-morrow I am engaged to lunch at Browning's.) Over Battersea Bridge and up Pig Hill. Lavender Sweep. Dinner—very sleepy, yet cannot sleep much.

Saturday, February 8.—To Warwick Crescent. Browning in his study, with proof sheets of his new edition in six vols.

Tennyson and the Magazines; *The Spiteful Letter*, B. said, 'I like the kind tone of it, but I think it gives a wrong view about Fame. What absurdity to say, "Wait a little and all will be past!" You cannot say that of anything in life.

> Our echoes roll from soul to soul
> And live for ever and for ever.

I like that better!'

Then we sat down to a luncheon-dinner. R. B., Miss B. and self. B. said the Secretary of the A. Club had posted his name as a defaulter, tho' the subscription had been duly paid by his banker. 'I'll come down on him like thunder! It's not good to have the reputation of being an easy-going man. I'll ask him how this blunder came? "Blunder, sir?" he says—upon which I open fire!'

B. shows me, in bird's-eye view only, the MS. of a new Poem to be printed in July.

I go, meaning to walk to Chelsea and call on Rossetti. R. B. says he will walk with me and seems inclined to come on and see R. 'How long will it take?'

We cross Kensington Gardens, but opposite S. Kensington Museum R. B. finds he can't come further.—'Give my love to Rossetti.' I give up Chelsea and walk towards Fulham; find the Grange with some trouble, Ned J., Mrs. J., Mr. W.—dinner, pleasant chat. Mr. W., learned in such, sings old Italian music by Stradella and others. Baby Margaret. Pleasant House and large garden. Very friendly. Catch train, Lavender Sweep —the T. T.s not in yet.

Monday, February 10.—Very fine. Lavender Sweep, walk, Clapham Common, pretty. Train to Lymington. Custom-House, relieve Burnett and take up old routine.

Wednesday, February 12.—Very fine. Walk, Efford Copse, first primroses; the Island blue, sweet air, thrushes. Dine — out. Stars—from some bird a sudden single gush of song : a night-warbler? Spiritual Wives—Stuff !

Tuesday, February 18.—Browning's 'Sludge,' etc.

Mem.—Too often a want of solid basis for R. B.'s brilliant and astounding cleverness. *A Blot in the 'Scutcheon* is solid. How try to account for B.'s twists and turns? I cannot. He has been and still is very dear to me. But I can no longer commit myself to his hands in faith and trust. Neither can I allow the faintest shadow of a suspicion to dwell in my mind that his genius may have a leaven of quackery. Yet, alas! he is not solid—which is a very different thing from prosaic. *A Midsummer Night's Dream* is as solid as anything in literature ; has imaginative coherency and consistency in perfection. Looking at forms of poetic expression, there is not a single utterance in Shakespeare, or of Dante as far as I know, enigmatic in the same sense as so many of Browning's are. If you suspect, and sometimes find out, that riddles presented to you with Sphinxian solemnity have *no* answers that really fit them, your curiosity is apt to fall towards freezing point, if not below it. Yet I always end by

striking my breast in penitential mood and crying
out, ' O rich mind ! wonderful Poet ! strange great
man ! '

Thursday, February 20.—Lymington. Walk, Efford,
poor little moles executed, hanging on twigs. Talk
with the Gamekeeper, who is considerably like Carlyle
in person : Grouse — pheasants. I try to explain
something of Darwin's researches. Keeper's dog has
to be trained to fly at a man, so as to be ready for
poachers : ' I likes a good savage dog.'

Tuesday, March 17.—Windy. Steamer to Yarmouth,
walk to Farringford, A. T. friendly. His visit to
Cambridge ' delightful.'

' What a dream of bliss to an Undergraduate, to
have lodgings and board for half a week at the Lodge ! '

Upstairs, new window in corner of study : ' have
desired it for years, sixteen years—done while I was
away.'

Thursday, March 19.—Birthday. Begin sad ; grow
cheerfuller. C. Parry and wife from Island ; a great
rainbow. Tea at F. St. Barbe's.

Saturday, March 21.—More cheerful again, but
Emma vexatious. O for a house of one's own !
' Mary '—' Squire Curtis.' [1] Sleep better.

Thursday, April 9.—Cross to Freshwater ; Mrs.
Norman (Mrs. Cameron's daughter), with her husband
and children. He is of Baring Brothers. ' His God-
father,' Mrs. C. said, ' gave him £100,000 one
morning,' as a little surprise. Farringford—A. T. on
lawn, friendly as usual : ' Come to-night.'

Miss Thackeray asks me to dinner ; Fitzjames
Stephen coming to-morrow.'

Friday, April 10.— Good Friday — Mrs. Curry's.
Miss Thackeray's : Fitzjames Stephen, tall, burly,
pleasant, the ' makings ' of a judge, as we say in Ireland ;
plain in dress.

To Farringford by field-path, Miss T., Fitzjames S.

[1] Allingham's poems.

and I—beautiful sunlit prospects, Yarmouth in the distance, gleaming river. They go in—I flee. Luncheon at Miss T.'s. We find A. T. and walk to the Beacon ; meet one stranger, at sight of whom A. T. nearly turns back.

Lincolnshire stories. Preachers : 'Coom in your rags, coom in your filth, Jesus'll take ye, Jesus won't refuse ye.' 'Time has two ends, and the Law cooms down wi' a *bang* ! ' 'Glory ' a very favourite word.

Lincolnshire manners. 'One of my brothers met a man in the lane near our house and said in a friendly voice, "Good-night!" to which the man replied, "Good night—and *dom* you ! " I asked a man one day, " Do you know what o'clock it is ? " he answered, " Noa ! and I don't want to." '

Grace said by Dissenting Minister according to the nature of the feast. If a poor one, he snivelled and sneered in a thin voice, ' O Lord, bless these *miserable* creatures to our use,' etc. ; if a good spread, he rolled out in unctuous tones : ' We desire to thank Thee, O Lord, for all these mercies Thou hast provided for us.'

April 23.—Lymington. Launch of a yacht. Walk to Sowley Pond. Lord Henry Scott, after trying illegally to close the Path (charming shady short-cut from the dusty road) and failing, has now cut down the trees and grubbed up all the hazels and hollies, and left it a path through a bare field. Oaks lying on the ground, piles of oak bark. The Magistrates decided against his claim to shut the Path, the Judges at Winchester decided against it, and now, instead of humbly apologising, his Lordship does this !

Monday, May 4.—Fine. Cross to Yarmouth. Servant girl says, ' I took your advice, sir, not to go to London '; had forgotten it, but it was good advice— wonder whether my habit of talking with everybody ever does real good ? Perhaps.

Yarmouth, The King's Head, Mary Blandford, drawing beer, gives me a lily of the valley ! Beer not-

withstanding, a ladylike girl.   Over Bridge, Golden
Hill with gorse in bloom (whence the name ?), nightingale singing.   Myrtle Cottage : yes, Mrs. Curry can
give me a room.   Farringford—Mrs. T. just going to
drive, invites me into carriage, Mrs. T., Mr. Lecky
and I, Hallam on the box.   We go by Afton and
near Brook.

L. does not see any use in knowing Authors
personally.   In fact personality does not interest him
in any case, I suspect.   We don't agree, evidently.
Still, we agree to get on our legs and walk back
together over the Downs.   Ireland is low now (he
thinks), intellectually : Tyndall her best representative.
He greatly admires Macaulay, also Buckle.   Knows
Carlyle, but seldom if ever agrees with him.   Dean
Milman stands high in L.'s estimation, 'a learned man
and very liberal, etc.'

Joke (Milman's ?)—'Churchmen may be divided
into Platitudinarians, Latitudinarians, and Altitudi-
narians.'   I proposed to add 'Denarians,' *i.e.* loaves
and fishes men, but the vowel is changed.

Friday, May 15.—Having got leave of absence, I go
to London.

May 18.—To 16 Onslow Gardens to accept Miss
Thackeray's invitation.   Find her with John Leech's
daughter Ada, thirteen, in black, very tall and slender,
with large eyes, long hair, full lips, looking sad : (Miss
T. as usual the Samaritan).   Miss T. with proofs of a
story.   'Give it a name,' she says : 'Balm of Gilead'
suggested.   Invited to Mrs. Barnard's for this evening.
'I don't want to go,' says Miss T., and we all sit on in
a dim light, talking peacefully.

Tuesday, May 19.—18 Neville St.   To 16 Onslow
Gardens.   Breakfast 9.30, Miss T., Mrs. Stephen ; warm
day.   With Leslie S. to Mrs. Brookfield's ; children's
party.   Magdalen B., large fair girl of seventeen ; second
Miss Hallé in blue, merry ; younger, like a Vandyck ;
May Sartoris ; Margery and Annie T., shy, I carry

Annie ; Enter Miss Thackeray, Mrs. Marshall. Mrs. Brookfield asks me to stay, and a merry joyous feast it is, seven lively girls, the children at a long table—a picnic indoors. Upstairs and dance Sir Roger, May S. and I ; then a reel. She is going to a Ball to-night, this is merely a whet. Back to Neville Street, and with Miss Thackeray and Mrs. Stephen to Mrs. Procter's. Mrs. P., daughter Edith. Old Barry Cornwall, an indistinct and almost mute figure, sitting on the landing ; Robert Browning (who asks me for Friday) and his sister ; Samuel Laurence, Leighton, etc. Box of cab —16 Onslow Gardens. 'Do have something! but O, everything is locked up by Justine, and she's gone to bed ! So Good-night.'

Thursday, May 21.—18 Neville St. Cab to Albemarle St. and breakfast with Lecky. Books on Witchcraft, etc., and on Ireland. Rooms very quiet, no lookout, has them from year to year : Christianity—morals, pagan and mediæval.

Meet Palgrave, 'choosing a picture'; civil, walk with him to York Gate : 'stay and dine ?' yes.

To Prince's Gate, Mr. Huth, Mrs. and Miss H., various guests, including Miss Thackeray and her sister. Library, gorgeous and rare books ; all the early editions of Shakespeare. Mr. H. unlocks and lets me handle some.

To Mrs. Barnard's, South Eaton Place. Madame Sainton-Dolby, Miss Ingelow. Little Miss Parr, who writes novels as 'Holme Lee,' looked nice in a high dress of lavender silk, like a quiet little old-maidish governess. Miss Thackeray accosted her, and so did I ; we spoke of the Isle of Wight, New Forest, etc. 'London fatigues me,' she said : 'going to Dulwich to-morrow.' As we drove home Miss Thackeray exclaimed of one of the guests ; 'Horrid woman ! she said to me, "I have been much pleased with some of your efforts," and, "You must have felt leaving that nice house in Palace Gardens !" but little Holme Lee's a duck.'

May 22.—Breakfast with Froude, 5 Onslow Gardens —wife, two girls, little boy : Ireland, English cruelties, massacre of women and children on Raghlin Island, Sorley Buie looking on from mainland—'he tore and tormented himself.' Library : F. speaks of my *Fraser* articles, says 'Carlyle has a greater regard for you than for anybody almost.' Cab to Browning's, invited to luncheon. R. B. (grayer).

Tennyson, the Magazines, Morris's *Earthly Paradise*, etc.

'We ought to take up the ball at the furthest point to which it has been thrown. I should be sorry to think that any one was in advance in any way of me in my new Poem.' Perhaps not quite knowing what to say I remarked bashfully :—

'I have always been a believer in you,' or to that effect.

R. B.—'I am glad to believe that, for your own sake among other things.'

When he went out, I stayed for a chat with Miss Sarianna. 'Robert, after writing *Pauline*, went to St. Petersburg, overland, in connection with a diplomatic mission, expenses only paid, and returned the same way after six weeks' residence at St. Petersburg. He saw the breaking up of the ice on the Neva, and the ceremony of declaring the river open.'

Away—passing through Leicester Square, meet Alan Skinner, and walk with him in the flower avenue of Covent Garden, talking of the Home trial, the Eyre case, etc. Then we dine at Bertolini's pleasantly. I show him the local curiosity, old Mr. Seymour, now eighty-two, who has dined here every day for the last forty-three years : he comes at 5, stays till 8, sits always in the box on the left-hand of the fire-place as you go up the room, which is kept for him at this time of day ; has the joint, college pudding, a gill of Marsala ; puts his feet up and sleeps or snoozes for about twenty minutes, then reads the *Daily News*, fidgeting a good deal with the paper, for his hands tremble. Finally he puts on hat, buttons coat up to the throat, straightens his spine and walks down the middle of the room very stiff and wooden, driving off, the waiter says, to his house somewhere near the Regent's Park. I should mention that when he comes in every evening the waiter who receives him invariably says, 'Good evening, Mr. Seymour : you are looking very well this evening, Mr. Seymour.' Looks like a solitary old bachelor, lawyer or attorney, dried up, penurious ; the daily tavern dinner a sort of loophole glimpse of the outside world. Save a word or two to the waiters he never speaks to any one at Bert's. Skinner departed and I went into the Alhambra and see some good dancing, but the opera-glass is a terrible disenchanter. Next me a bald civil quiet gentleman with his wife and daughters. Leotard on the 'trapeze' wonderful.

May 25.—Lavender Sweep. To evening party at Hallé's. Mrs. Brookfield and her daughter, Mrs. and Miss Sartoris—Leighton, Aïdé, etc. —Santley, Titiens, Trebelli (charming), Bettini, her husband, like a German. Strauss plays violin.

I heard to-night some of the best music in London. Did it enchant or even delight me ? No. A grand musical party is neither concert nor home-music ; and besides, few public singers know how to sing in a private room.

May 26.—Lunch at Browning's. Talk runs chiefly on his forthcoming new Poem in many thousand lines. He takes me into his study, and shows me the original Book, a small brown quarto, printed account of the trial of Count Guido, with some original MS. letters, stitched in at the end pleading for his respite. B. bought it off a stall in Florence for a few pence. He has told the story over and over again to various friends ; offered it to A. Trollope to turn into a novel, but T. couldn't manage it ; then R. B. thought, 'why not take it myself?'

'I began it in rhymed couplets, like *Laurence*
Bloomfield, but thought by and by I might as well have
my fling, and so turned to blank verse.'

At luncheon he went over the headings of the
chapters or books into which this very long Poem is
divided. 'And now! can you advise me? I'm puzzled
about how to publish it. I want people not to turn
to the end, but to read through in proper order.
Magazine, you'll say: but no, I don't like the notion
of being sandwiched between Politics and Deer-
Stalking, say. I think of bringing it out in four
monthly volumes, giving people time to read and
digest it, part by part, but not to forget what has
gone before.'

Wednesday, May 27.—Lavender Sweep; very fine
—11.30 to Clapham Junction and take train to Epsom
to see the Derby Race. Only one other person in my
carriage, young man from Southport near Liverpool.
Epsom, people on road, carriages crawling through
clouds of dust. Gypsies, etc. Sit on grass at Totten-
ham Corner and see first race without trouble. Then
down course and stand at rails opposite Grand Stand.
A pocket picked, dirty man accused, who says in candid
matter-of-fact way, 'I ain't got it.'

To Queen Square, to dine with Morris, and find,
just alighting, Mrs. Ned in a gorgeous yellow gown :
'tis a full dress party! and I in velveteen jacket. Morris,
Ned J. (thin), D. G. R. (looking well), Boyce ('has been
ill'), F. M. Brown (oldened), Webb, Howell, Mr.
Wilfred Heeley, Publisher Ellis, and W. A. (ten men).
Mrs. Morris, Miss Burden, Mrs. Ned (gay), Mrs.
Howell, Mrs. Madox Brown (looks young with back
to the window), Lucy Brown, Miss Faulkner (I
between these), Mrs. Ellis, Miss Heeley (ten ladies).
Banquet,—'Earthly Paradise,' I suggest, and Ned writes
this atop of the menu. A storm of talking. I away
with D. G. R. about 1 ; walk first, then cab to Cheyne
Walk, in and stay chatting and lounging till 3 in old

fashion. 'Come to-morrow, and we'll go up together to my mother's.'

I walk to Lavender Sweep in daylight, passing some revellers from Cremorne, and to bed about 4.

June 8.—To Carlyle's about 3. He is writing, but soon comes out for a walk. On the door-step we find Sir Charles Dilke and Hepworth Dixon come to solicit C.'s vote for the former. C. does not ask them in, and on hearing their errand declares briefly, ' I never gave a vote in my life,' whereupon they depart. He talked to me of Parliament and its absurdity, and how foolish for any man to desire to sit night after night for many hours in an ill-ventilated room, listening to the most tedious stuff, etc. etc. I took leave of him at Albert Gate, 'going back to Lymington to-day.'

He said in shaking hands, ' You won't walk many more times with *me*,' which made me sad.

June 20.—Lymington. Coach to Freshwater, Mrs. Cameron's ; long wait for lunch. Mrs. C. and her household take no note of time. Meet girls going up-stairs in fancy dresses, Mrs. C. has been photographing a group, and appears carrying glass negative in her collodionised hands. ' Magnificent ! to focus them all in one picture, such an effort ! '

Enter Sir John Simeon with Mr. Austin Bruce (M.P. for Merthyr-Tydvil). Sir J. presses me to go back to Swainston with him. I hesitate, then agree, and we walk off over the Downs. Dine at 8—they talk of Parliament behind the scenes : Dizzy often *vinosus*—one evening he spoke in such a state (keeping his legs with much difficulty) that Sir J. S. feared a public scandal, and was in pain for the credit of the House. (*N.B.*—Simeon is no scandal-monger.)

Monday, July 20.—Hot. Tennyson and Mrs. T. on the steamer, I with them to Brockenhurst. ' To London, the dentist ; then Scotland.' T. said of Longfellow, ' A very gentlemanly man : seemed very tired. We had ten at luncheon. They slept at the

hotel, stayed two days. Little King Theodore of
Abyssinia now at Farringford with Captain Speedy.

'Longfellow—I didn't compliment him—told him
I didn't like his hexameters: he rather defended
them.'

We spoke of Swedenborg: T. says his Hell is
more striking than his Heaven; praises Hinton's book
on Man and Nature. The up-train; T. shakes my
hand warmly. It is always a real happiness to see him.
I walk to Queen's Bower, its brook and oak tree, back
by pretty path through New Park, and in by train.

Wednesday, July 22.—Mrs. Cameron has a standing
and, I fear, incurable pique against me for not recognising
Henry Taylor as a great poet. Most gladly do I, anywhere, at any time, recognise a great poet, but I cannot
do so at second hand. *Philip Van Artevelde* is a
solid piece of work, with both form and substance;
but, tho' written in verse, is the impression it leaves
more *poetical* than that left by *Ivanhoe,* say? The
'Interlude,' called *The Lay of Elena,* is a cultivated
effort, entirely out of place; nothing can be more
modern in style, a mixture of Wordsworth, Coleridge,
Campbell and Henry Taylor,—the latter contributing a
certain pompous stiffness which he takes for dignity.
There is no magic in H. T.'s pen, whether it write
blank verse or rhyme. Rossetti much admires the two
snatches of song in the second part of *Philip*;—they
have, for one thing, the flavour of quaintness which his
palate requires. 'Quoth tongue' is pithy and pathetic,
but as to

> Down lay in a nook my lady's brach,

how on earth came a lady's brach hunting in a
pack of boarhounds? and this first line is in itself
almost enough to justify a verdict against the writer
of—'No lyrical ear!' What born Balladist but would
have said—

> Down in a nook lay my lady's brach?

August 10.— Steamer to Yarmouth and coach to Freshwater. Lunch at Mrs. Cameron's ; Dr. Hooker of Kew, Mr. Erasmus Darwin, his niece, Miss D. Dr. Hooker is writing his Address as President of the British Association, to meet this year at Norwich. He comes with me to Farringford, where we find A. T. on the lawn, sitting at a small table with books and tobacco. Walk round garden, the three of us, Dr. H. giving the names of various plants as we go along, ' Kuyphofia,' etc. Tobacco plant about seven feet high—' never saw so fine a one in the tropics.'

August 11.—To Freshwater ; engage bedroom over little shop, and to the Darwins. Dr. Hooker in lower room writing away at his Address ; going to put ' Peter Bell's ' primrose into it and wants the exact words. Upstairs Mrs. Darwin, Miss D. and Mr. Charles Darwin himself,—tall, yellow, sickly, very quiet. He has his meals at his own times, sees people or not as he chooses, has invalid's privileges in full, a great help to a studious man. Dr. Hooker and I to Plumley's Hotel (where he is put up) ; T. and Hallam come in, and T. calls me ' an ass ' for not taking a bed at Farringford. I to little shop,—and then to Farringford. After dinner come in Mr. Erasmus Darwin, brother of Charles, an old bachelor and invalid, living in London ; Mrs. Darwin, and second Miss Darwin ; also Captain Speedy, six feet and a half high, who has pleasant manners. He talks of Abyssinia—the churches there, religion, slaughter of animals, the Trinity. The Hindoos and Beloochs ' wept for Theodore.'

Little Alamayu (means ' I have seen the world '), Theodore's son, is here at Freshwater in Speedy's charge, by the Queen's wish. The little prince has a native attendant, a young man who is devoted to him. Speedy the other day overheard them amusing themselves by mimicking English people. Attendant comes up in the character of an English lady, shakes hand— ' How you do ? '

Alamayu replies—'How you do?'
Attendant.—'How you like this country?'
Little Prince.—'Ver' mush.'
Attendant.—'Ah! you like ver' mush'—and so on.
T. complains of hotel charges, especially in England.
I say—'They ought to let you go free, as a Poet.'
T.—'They charge me double! and I can't be
anonymous (turning to Mrs. Cameron) by reason of
your confounded photographs.' The party breaks up
about twelve, 'an orgie,' T. calls it. He comes out
with me and we wander some distance. Jupiter and a
half-moon in the sky; talk of immortality. I go back
with him and find the door locked! He rings and says
'My wife will come,' but a servant woman comes.
Nobody guessed he was out.

August 12.—Freshwater. Pack bag, to Farringford.
Breakfast in the study, the boys pleasant; Lionel back
from bathing; A. T., letter from America for autograph.

Mrs. T., 'Lionel going to Eton.' She dislikes
Darwin's theory. I sit in study: A. T. teaching
Hallam Latin—Catiline.

Charles Darwin expected, but comes not. Has
been himself called 'The Missing Link.' Luncheon.
Then T. and I walk into croquet-ground, talking of
Christianity.

'What I want,' he said, 'is an assurance of immortality.'

For my part I believe in God: can say no more.

Friday, *August* 21.—Mrs. Cameron's: Captain
Speedy opens the door. Little Alamayu, pretty boy,
we make friends and have romps, he rides on my knee,
shows his toys. His Abyssinian attendant. They dress
to be photographed by Mrs. C., the Prince in a little
purple shirt and a necklace, Captain Speedy in a lion-skin
tippet, with a huge Abyssinian sword of reaping-hook
shape ('point goes into your skull'). Photographing room—Speedy grumbles a little, Mrs. C. poses

them. Photograph of Mrs. Tennyson's maid as
'Desdemona.'

Sunday, August 23.—Kind note from Miss Thackeray,
to which I reply. (Suggest possible match between
Alamayu and little Margery—future Queen of Abyssinia.)

Saturday, August 29.—To Esher (by invitation from
Mrs. Howitt). Arrive at 'The Orchard,' a pretty homely
cottage, where William Howitt, sturdy and white-haired,
welcomes me from the open window. Then Mary
Howitt, looking gray and worn. I am shown to my
trim little bedroom, adorned with various Christian
emblems. Outside, three tall poplars shoot up into
the blue sky.

Monday, August 31.—Good-bye. William Howitt to
the station with me and sees me off. Good people the
H.'s, but we should not long agree in the same house.

Stop at Basingstoke and walk into the town ; dullish,
snug houses with trim gardens. At Brockenhurst find
Aubrey de Vere, going to Freshwater, much talk till
he goes off in steamer.

Thursday, September 3.—Freshwater. Very fine.
Lionel and I on ponies, a gallop on the downs.

Hinton's *Life in Nature* (praised by A. T.).

I walk to Yarmouth, cross to Lymington, Custom
House, and back in the afternoon to dine at Farringford.
Dinner : A. T., Mrs. T., Lionel, Mr. Digby (tutor),
De Vere, and W. A.

De Vere—his talk of Catholicism, eloquently vague,
sliding into Newmanism and Jesuistry. The T.'s mildly
dissentient, I getting angry. T., De V. and I went
out under the stars ; I flared up at last and asked De V.,
'Do you yourself entirely believe the account given by
the Roman Catholic Church of God and man?'

De V.—'I believe it all as surely as that I tread this
ground and see those stars.'

W. A.—'And I don't believe one atom of it.'

186   Tennyson.—'You have no point of contact, then.'

De V. and I walked off in the moonlight and said
good-night at Plumley's ; he going on, he said, to walk
upon the down.

Friday, September 4.—Freshwater. Mrs. Carter's
lodging. Very fine and sunny. To Farringford, meet
William with the ponies. Breakfast, then out to
croquet-lawn, sit in shade, reading odd numbers of a
Conservative magazine. A. T. comes, friendly ; says,
' I saw a beast watching me ! I saw his legs behind
the ilex.'

September 20.—To Farringford.—Tennyson.—Is
writing his ' San Grail.'

' I'm spoiling it. Will you take a turn? '—then we
talk on Hinton's book, and on his brother Charles's
Sonnets. ' All is not chemistry and matter.'

We look at ducks and pigs. Little Alamayu sits
on my knee and looks at a book of animals. Zebra
especially interesting to him : that is the Abyssinian
name of the beast. The Elephant he calls ' zoon.'

T. said he had a rich cousin who drank hard and
talked loud. ' He used to quote Byron to me—

Over the waters of the dark blue sea—

and so forth, adding, " Poets have some sense." ' He
offered to lend me Castle B—— for our wedding
month—' will you come down to B——? then you
may go to Hell ! '

A. T. then went upstairs and dulness set in.

September 26.—*Vestiges of Creation.* Depressing
scientific views of life. Call on foreign gentleman—Mr.
Quintinella, a Brazilian : Brazil, Paraguay, Spain, etc.

Thursday, October 8.—Fine ; walk to Brockenhurst,
lonely. Dine 7—rain—out. Magee is made Bishop
of Peterborough, reflections thereupon ; when we met
at Ballyshannon he was a curate, and we stood on a
social level. But would you like to be a Bishop?
Would *anything* induce you to be a Bishop?

Saturday, October 10.—To Southampton. Lunch

at Dr. Bond's ; then with a party to the New Forest—
Miss Webster, Mr. and Mrs. Hankin, etc. Swan-Green,
Queen's Bower, rich red sunset through the trees ; old
oak and brook like old friends now, yet how little they
care for us ! This longing for Nature to return us some
friendship, some affection, created Naiads, Dryads, and
Oreads. Yet how should a Poet turn back to these ?
and what then is he to do nowadays with his faculty of
imaginative song ? Cross Ober or Over-Green and
pick some Butcher's-Broom.

October 11.—Very fine. Irish topography. Natural
History. Walk, Norley Wood : lakes of mist on
Beaulieu Heath.

October 12.—Dissatisfied : life slips by—to what
purpose ? Lindley on plants. Walk to Keyhaven by
marsh.

October 15.—To Freshwater. Miss Thackeray at
St. John's Cottage, with Marjorie and Annie, and
maid Justine. Guests—Frederick Walker, the artist,
small, compact, jockey-like figure, large bluish eyes,
short but thick brown hair combed down over his forehead ; his small hand gives you a sinewy grip.

Miss Emma Irving, Captain Irving from India. We
have games with the children—fishing for mermaids
with gingerbread, etc.

Call at Terrace and find there Mrs. Ritchie and
three daughters. To Mrs. Cameron's where we all
dine (though the poor woman has a bad cold and her
husband and Ewan are in bed) at two round tables
put together. Ladies go. Men talk of billiards,
Sayers and Heenan, etc. Professor Owen's true ghost
story of the nigger's head falling out of a medical
student's bag, hopping down a steep street (in Lancaster ?), and bumping against the door of a man who
had been a slave-dealer, and who, seeing it, was near
frightened to death. Story of parish clerk who in
parson's absence essayed to console a dying parishioner.
'He was a bad chap, your Reverence.' 'And what

did you say to comfort him?'—'I told him he was
sure to go to Hell, and that he ought to be thankful to
have a Hell to go to.'

October 16.—Saw little Alamayu in the road ; two
of the De Havilland children came up, whom he kissed,
and then came the snuffy old Postman with his bag,
and the little Prince kissed him too—partly, perhaps, as
an important functionary who often bears tidings of
interest. Breakfast at Miss Thackeray's, enlivened by
the children. Walker is going on with a little picture
of a Girl watering flowers.

Walk to Yarmouth and cross to Lymington ; back
in the afternoon ; roughish sea and coldish on the
coach. Myrtle Cottage. Dine at Miss Thackeray's ;
the Miss Ritchies, F. Walker. Talk of George Eliot,
etc. F. W. and I have cigarettes, and then to
drawing-room, where I read aloud Shelley's Sonnet
'Being your Slave,' and Leigh Hunt's 'Abou Ben
Adhem.' We fall to drawing pigs with our eyes shut
and dawdle away time till 12 o'clock.

October 17.—Freshwater. To breakfast at Miss
Thackeray's. To Farringford. A. T. and I down the
lane ; call at Miss T.'s, where they are at luncheon ;
then at Mrs. Cameron's. He says, as we approach
her house : 'Mrs. C. (using the initial, as he often
does) is so gushing !' She presently justified this by
saying fervently to T., while we spoke of F. Walker,
'His soul is at your feet !' Says T., 'I hope his soles
are at his own feet.' We go to the shore with the
Ritchies ; T. throws a stick into the sea for dog to
fetch.

Mem.—I doubt if —— holds poetry in any honour,
or poets as such. I sought A. T. and worshipped him
as the well-head of an enchanting river of song : charm
of personality and surroundings came in addition, a fine
setting to the priceless jewel of his genius. ——, I
imagine, admires the poetry mainly because she admires
and loves the man.

Monday, October 19.—Cross to Yarmouth. We find the Tennyson carriage at Miss Thackeray's ; Mrs. T. asks the ladies, ' Will you take compassion on him ? ' that is, allow A. T. to walk with them ; and they *do* consent. A. T. comes accordingly, and we walk off (Mrs. R., Miss Augusta, Miss Emily, Nellie, Miss Annie Prinsep, A. T., and W. A.) down old road, by Afton Park fence, field-path through turnips to Afton Down, see the barrows (ancient burial mounds), cross the rough new military road, and by path to shore ; geology—Wealden ; so on to Brook Point and the fossil trees. T. (enjoying the girls' company) says : ' If I could take a walk like this every day I shouldn't be tired of Freshwater.'

I mentioning Yarmouth, he turns quickly on me : ' A rhyme to Yarmouth ? quick, quick ! mustn't think ! ' ' Charmouth ' the only perfect rhyme that occurred. On the rocks an unknown demoiselle, to whom A. T. offers his hand to help her over some slight difficulty. She did not seem to know who he was.

Thursday, October 22.—Lymington. Walk to Setley, and find gypsies encamped. Coming back I overtake a little girl carrying with difficulty two bags of sand, and just as I am asking how far she is going, up drives Rev. P. F. in his gig, who offers me a lift. I say, ' Help this little girl with her two heavy bags,' upon which his Reverence reddens and drives off. I carry one of the bags.

Monday, October 26.—To Forest Bank, and (on suggestion of Aïdé) call on La Marchesa Taglia-Carne, who has taken the place for a time. She has been a widow more than twelve months.

October 28.—A. and E. Ritchie by steamer, with them to Brockenhurst, and show the old Church.

Walk alone into Forest, among coloured trees : Whitley Wood, Gretnam, Tollgate, back by brook-side, among beautiful beeches ; spindle tree seeds ; maple yellow like a ripe quince.

Daily News, 'Leigh Hunt Memorial—Browning in the chair.'

Evening, moonlight. Molière.

November 2.—Invited to Miss Dickson's. Pay pensioners. Kind Miss D. in her pretty rooms, but 'not well,'—I wish the good soul could be well. Out and walk in the dusk on Boldrewood Road, sunset fading, dark trees, owls do cry. Already a drift of withered leaves. Return and see, like a pale smoke, the moon-dawn mounting. At dinner with Miss D. and self, only Mr. Darwin, son of Charles Darwin.

Tuesday, November 3.—Lyndhurst. To Meet of the Foxhounds at Bolton's Bench, carriages, horses, hounds.

November 5.—Assembly Rooms, Election Meeting.

Sunday, November 29.—Gray. Cheerfuller. Received from Robert Browning by post Vol. I. of his new Poem, *The Ring and the Book.*

Friday, December 4. — Call on old Kirkwood, pensioner ; hands crippled, cheerful face and voice, cheerful heart to all appearance : tended by his old wife. What is the secret of the cheerfulness of old poor sick folk ? Complete resignation the basis of it ?

Wednesday, December 9.—Christchurch ; Boscombe. Lady Shelley, luncheon, Sir Percy. Upstairs, cast of Shelley monument at Christchurch. Bust of Mary Wollstonecraft, bust and oil picture of Mrs. Shelley —'the noblest of creatures (says Lady S. to me), entirely unselfish. I knew her before I married Percy ; I was with her when she died. She lay ten days motionless and speechless, only sometimes opening her eyes wide. When she died, *I felt sure Shelley was in the room.* Her look of joy was indescribable. Shelley's daughter Ianthe was brought up by low church clergymen, according to the wish of her Aunt Eliza ; she was married to Mr. Esdaile, a squire, once a sporting man, and her children have been brought up in Low Church Calvinism. She visited us here at Boscombe :

before she came she wanted to bargain that her father's name should never be mentioned in her presence or her children's, but this I refused to agree to. She came to us, but when we gave a children's party she would not let her children be present. She had prayers or a religious service with them every evening, lasting two hours. One day I left her alone in the Shelley room, with the portrait, hair, books, letters and other memorials of her father. She stayed a long time, and when she came out I saw that she had been weeping. She promised to send me some early poems in MS. in return for a copy of the portrait ; but after she got home she drew back from this, and I have not sent her the copy which I had made for the purpose : there it is.'

Take leave and walk to Christchurch, Sir Percy along with me half the way. Dismal road, empty barrack, wretched suburb, Station ; the ugliest old little English town I have seen, spite of a river and a Minster.

Commercial man in train describes Bournemouth as ' a rotten place ' commercially. Brockenhurst, train gone, got back to Lymington in a butcher's cart.

Saturday, December 12.—Sir Percy Shelley's steam-yacht *Nökken* at Inman's Quay, steward calls to invite me. I find on board Sir P., and in the cabin Lady S. and Miss ' Flossy ' Gibson. Engraving of Shelley for me. We start, rather cold—Cowes, we put off in a boat, Sir P. and a sailor row us in, and drive to Woodvale, a semi-marine house with gables and a hall. Dinner— music, drama, Norway, etc. Drawing-room, Norwegian book with picture of ' Leerfossen,' my cousin Thoning's waterfall.

Sunday, December 13.—I walk into Cowes by road near the sea, then upper road, muddy lanes, Floating Bridge, then wide road with streets and villas, and the rails and gates of Osborne House. I venture to ask the dignified porter if one might walk a little way into the park, to which he replied mildly and calmly, ' On no consideration, sir.'

Monday, December 21.—1.45 train to London.
Lodging at 44 Hans Place.

Tuesday, December 22.—Tom Taylor at Richmond
Terrace, friendly as usual : ' all well—come to us on
Christmas Day ' ; gives me card for Picture Galleries,
see Wallis's Exhibition in Pall Mall.

Thursday, December 24.—Call on Carlyle, ' out.'
On Froude, who is friendly, praises the *Rambles*.
On Miss Thackeray ; Mrs. Stephen, Marjorie,
Annie, Nellie Ritchie and brother : Christmas Tree.
Hans Place, — and to dinner at No. 19 : Mr.
Planché, with old, comic wrinkled face ; Mr. Walter
Cassell, good looking, kind, somewhat choice in
manner and voice. Ouida (Louise de la Ramée), in
green silk, sinister clever face, hair down, small hands
and feet, voice like a carving knife ; also her mother.
At dinner puns and jokes : Ouida silentish. The ladies
go to the drawing-room, upstairs, and when after an
interval we follow them we hear, before the door opens,
a voice going on inside like a saw, and on entering find
Ouida saying, in loud harsh tones—' women are un-
generous, cruel, pitiless ! ' Planché, taking refuge on
an ottoman with a face expressing humorous alarm,
' God bless my soul ! I think they're angels—I adore
them—they're the best half of the world.'

Ouida, with severity,—' I entirely disagree. The
woman nearly always leads the man astray,' etc. etc.
' Woman can't be impersonal.'

Mr. Cassell philosophises on the subject, rather
materialistically. Ouida departs, after inviting Planché
and me to visit her at the Langham Hotel, where she is
biding at present with her Mother and an immense Dog.
She carries a portrait of the latter round her neck in a
locket, which she detached after dinner and handed
round for inspection, with the remark, ' This is my
hero' (perhaps the hero of one of her books). She
asked somebody present ' Have you read my last
book ? '—' Not yet.'

'But you *must* read it, you know!'

She said she had found America 'a mine of wealth' to her, in the payments for her novels.

Friday, December 25.—Miss Thackeray's at 1.30, to luncheon: Leslie Stephen and his wife: 'Come next Sunday.' L. S.'s 'earliest recollections connected with Kensington Gardens, The Yew Wood, seemed very solemn'—America—Emerson—Authoress of *Charles Auchester*. L. S. likes Lowell.

Saturday, December 26.—To Froude's to luncheon. Then to Carlyle's at three, shown upstairs, where I see *The Ring and the Book*, part read, a Frederick snuff-box, blue and gold, photographs of Mrs. Carlyle, *Biographie Universelle*, Revisal of *Miscellanies* going on for Library Edition, 'volume in hand.'

Enter Carlyle, friendly; we walk to Kensington Gardens. *The Ring and the Book* 'a curiously minute picture of Italian Society: not poetry at all.'

Dine at Tom Taylor's: — we go in to Ella's, to a small music-party. Ella gives an abstract of a story with musical illustrations, and is most vivacious and amusing, as well as an attentive host. Then he gives us part of *William Tell*. He overflows with anecdotes of musical celebrities whom he has known. Miss ——, who is dull and evangelical, one day expressed herself shocked at E.'s vanity and frivolity, 'and at his age!' I defended him, liked to see age cheerful, and thought Ella had given much pleasure to others—and so he has. So-called *vain* people, not fools, are usually amiable, they wish to please.

Sunday, December 27.—Cab to Warwick Crescent, to lunch by invitation with the great Robert. After luncheon—Shelley, the drowning of S.—' not in his right senses—in the moon. Another man who lives in the moon is Sir George Bowyer. I called on him to ask some questions about *Romana Homicidiorum Lex* for my book, but as to intelligible answers—you might as well ask a butterfly to fly straight across this room!

He referred me to an Italian friend of his, who was ten times worse than himself.'

We go into the Study—small back-room looking on balcony and back-green below, still talking of *The Ring and the Book*, and R. B. asks me plump 'How do you like it?' to which I return praise, and for the present (with uneasy conscience) nothing but praise; don't know how to set about criticism, especially with but half of the Poem as yet seen. B. again shows me the original *Book*, and translates to me the letter of the lawyer, de Archangelis, written on the day of the execution, saying, among other things, 'Guido is lamented for by all respectable people.'

B. praises his own poem—'It's admirable! I've ever so much more to tell.'

Shows me proofs of 'Pompilia'; also two rings of *pure* gold, very soft; Castellani of Rome makes them. He gives me Volume II. of *The Ring and the Book*, remarking, 'Your first volume was one of *six* only. I gave one to Gabriel Rossetti. I should like to give to Morris and Ned Jones and William Rossetti. The *Athenæum* notice is good.' We walk out,—still talk of *The Ring and the Book*: 'a builder will tell you sometimes of a house, "there's twice as much work underground as above," and so it is with my poem. Guido's not escaping better, man won't give him post-horses; the Pope, as Providence; Guido has time for confession, etc.' We part. I sit in an arbour and read the first pages of 'Tertium Quid.'

To Hans Place, then walk to 12 Earl's Terrace, Kensington, to dine with Du Maurier, 6 P.M. D. M. in brown velvet coat, Mrs. D. M. in light robes; Poynter, T. Armstrong, and another. Children, little girl on my knee, sturdy boy: talk, animals—swallows, etc.

'Ned Jones doing most wonderful things—three Saints.'

Old Ballads—my *Ballad Book*.

D. M. on his fear of blindness.

Monday, December 28.—To Cheyne Row (heavy rain). Parlour : 'Scotch lassie,' niece of Carlyle, lives at Dumfries, has never been to London before, been here about three months (?) [1]—National Gallery, the Titians, etc. Speaks gravely and sensibly. Enter T. C., very friendly and familiar : ' Go up, sir, to that place there (drawing-room), and we'll see what can be done.' A yellow gleam shows through the rain as we go upstairs. Portrait of Landor on the stairs.

We started on our walk, passing through Hans Place in a shower of rain. He spoke of his own writings—' they gave me much trouble. I brought them into the world with labour and sorrow, and I must reckon most of them but small trash after all. Ay, there's far too much dogmatism going : English funeral service, for example. The Scotch way is better in that. People write to me to try to bring me to Christ—ah me ! If the Universe grinds me to nothing, I will hold that to be best and say " Not my will but thine be done." I don't pretend to understand the Universe— it's a great deal bigger than I am. The Darwinian Theory tried to meddle with things that are out of man's reach : and besides—I don't care a straw about all that ! People ought to be modester.'

In answer to a remark of mine one day Carlyle blazed up—' Write my autobiography ? I would as soon think of cutting my throat with my pen-knife when I get back home ! The Biographers too ! If those gentlemen would let me alone I should be much obliged to them. I would say, as Shakespeare would say to Peter Cunningham, " Sweet Friend, for Jesus' sake forbear." '

Tuesday, December 29.—Return to Lymington.

December 31.—Fine. Walk to Efford, sunset. Evening, Methodist chapel, Watch Night.

---

[1] Mary Carlyle Aitken, afterwards Mrs. Alexander Carlyle

CHAPTER XI

1869–1870

January 1.—Lymington.   Write to various friends.

March 31, *London.*—Carlyle.—Insomnia. *The Ring and the Book.*

C.—' A set of people who cannot see over Browning are determined to see in him all sorts of things.'

April.—Saw, one of these days, the Siamese Twins, old and withered men.   They were, by rumour, one of the marvels of my childhood.

May 6, *London.*— To Albemarle St., and breakfast with Lecky—his *Morals*, Morley's attack in *Fortnightly*.   I attack Lecky for civility to Dogmatism and talk rather sharply.   He *sees much on both sides* ; abhors the Utilitarians.   He says, ' I began to write in the usual way, with Poetry, and was much disappointed to find my poems unnoticed, I believed in them very strongly.'   He gives me a book of his called *Religious Aspects of the Present Time.*   When I point out some of the evils of Dogmatism, L. says, ' These things are a great comfort to ignorant people ' ; at another time he argues, when I press him as to orthodox dogmas, ' practically these views are now inoperative.'

Contradictory ? or is it that he thinks it better for the less ignorant to make believe as to all these ' views,' for the sake of comforting the ignorant ?

L. tells me he was ' intended for the Church,' to which I reply ' You would have been a Bishop.'

He is a man of probity and intelligence, reads diligently and remembers accurately; but our minds are not in touch — differently constituted as well as differently trained.

May 7.— Dine at Bertolini's, and see old Mr. Seymour in his accustomed corner.

May 9.—Mrs. Clough's. 20 Eaton Place,—Lady Simeon, Venables, etc.

May 16.—Lymington. Mrs. S.'s—Table turning. Mrs. S. attacks my want of faith. 'We *know*,' etc., 'cerebration,' etc. (what can one say in such case? and silence offends). We try a table, and it does tilt and knock and spells out a message to myself, 'You will be much loved' (!) after which it runs about, we dodging it up and down. What tiresome nonsense!

Tuesday, May 25.—Lymington. Invitation from Mrs. Tennyson for to-day to meet ' Mr. and Mrs. Fields and Miss (*Biglow Papers*) Lowell.' 3 o'clock steamer, I find them on board and introduce myself. Low water, land in boat, show the Americans the old George Inn, and the quaint little lock-up ; their delight in old houses, ivy, etc. pleasant to see. Dinner 6.30, brisk chat. Mr. F.'s stories of Thackeray in Boston—' all the Lecture tickets sold. Then I can't do less than put my feet out of the cab window,' and he did so. Big oyster—' feel as if I had swallowed a baby.'

Wednesday, May 26.—Farringford. Lovely view from bedroom window, over the trees Hurst Castle, Solent, and England. Birds singing.

I had the great pleasure of accompanying Miss Mabel Lowell in her first walk in English fields. There were only us two. A Daisy was one of the first marvels, and while she gathered it a Skylark sprang up singing into the bright clouds. But an old cottage almost covered with ivy surpassed everything. She stood gazing upon it, lost in wonder and delight. They have ivy in Mass[etts] as a potted plant only, taken indoors in winter.

Mrs. Cameron photographs M. L. I cross to

Lymington and return in the afternoon. After dinner,
a discussion on Ireland. A. T. as usual, while grant-
ing and liking the lyrical and humorous qualities of
the Kelts and their pleasant manners, calls it 'that
horrible island,' and will not allow that it has any
history of its own worth the least notice, knowing in
fact not a whit more of its history than does the
average Englishman—who knows, as nearly as possible,
nothing. To him, as to A. T., the very name of 'Brian
Boru' is a joke.

I try to make Brian be seen as a real and important
historic personage, and win audience from the Americans,
and perhaps some attention, but A. T. plays his part
of the deaf adder, and we have to wind all up with a
laugh.

Thursday, *May* 27.—Cross to Lymington with Miss
Lowell and the Fieldses. M. L. said Tennyson offered
her her choice among his books for a gift, and she
chose *Maud*—'I found it was all right, he thought it
a good choice.'

Wednesday, *June* 9. — Lymington. Letter from
'Annie Fields,' dated from 'Gads Hill Place,' thanking
me for 'Touchstone,'[1] which she asked me to send her
in autograph. It seems it was much talked of in
America because Emerson recited it in his funeral
oration for John Brown : most of the papers gave it
as his.

Bed 2.30. 'Hear the lark begin his flight.'

Friday, *July* 30. — Longman (by Tom Taylor's
advice) asks me to write verses to a set of fairy drawings by Doyle.

A job of this kind likes me not, yet I accepted the
offer, and have found some pleasure in trying, chiefly
during rambles in the Forest, to bring the unconnected
designs within the compass of a little story in dialogue,
with some lyrics interspersed. Both artist and publisher
have left me entirely to myself in the matter, and it

[1] Poem, in Allingham's *Flower Pieces*.

remains to be seen how they will like ' Prince Brightkin,' whom I have posted to-day to Paternoster Row.

Garden Party at the Tomlinsons, small ; Miss P., Admiral Castle, Mrs. Telfer—who tells me something of her history. We were talking of wild flowers ; she said, ' the English wild flowers are beautiful, but I never saw any in the world so lovely and profuse as those of Siberia.' ' Siberia ! ' said I. Then she told me that her Father was a young Russian Officer who, for his liberal opinions, was banished to Siberia by the Emperor Nicholas. He was not imprisoned but restricted to certain limits of habitation, and his correspondence had to pass through official hands. Before leaving St. Petersburg he was permitted to marry a young lady to whom he was engaged, and she accompanied him into exile. Their daughter (now Mrs. Telfer, *qui parle*), was born near Irkutsk ; they afterwards lived at Tobolsk, and thus in her childhood she was among the enchanting wild flowers of the Siberian Springs. ' *My Mother used to say they were the happiest years of her life.*' They were years of youth, love, enthusiasm, and the bright hope of one day returning to their country. They did return ; but those years of exile seemed in the light of memory sweeter than all others.

' I can understand,' said I, ' why you love the Siberian wild flowers.'

' But they really are the most beautiful in the world,' said she.

Tuesday, August 3.—Internal gloom. To Lyndhurst (invited) ; Whitehorn meets me with Miss Dickson's carriage : Bird's Nest, Miss D. and Mrs. Aïdé. I walk off over moor, Matley Wood—nothing good !

Begin to feel better. *Mem.*—' Songs of despair, O Poet, only songs of despair.' [1]

Return by road. Dinner at 8. Miss Dickson and I talk ' gloom, Lymington etc.' She speaks wisely and kindly as usual, but agrees that Lymington is no abiding-place.

[1] Poem, in Allingham's *Blackberries.*

August 6.—Walk to Whilley Ridge ; cowboy says the bull 'blared' (*i.e.* bellowed).

Sunday, August 22.—Out to Sway and Mead End, dine under old tree, near sunset time. Shall I go to Exeter, to British Association ?

August 23.—Start for Exeter (having arranged for Customs duty). Reception Room. Dr. Hooker, etc.

August 28. — Totnes, Dartmouth, Dean Prior (Herrick), Brent, and back to Exeter.

(See *Rambles* by Patricius Walker.)

August 30. — Bideford ; Westward Ho (absurd name). Clovelly.

August 31.—Back to Lymington. I love Devon.

October, Lymington. — The Tennant family go to Freshwater : they invite me to join in a little tour through the Island. Cross to Portsmouth, run up to Haslemere to visit Tennyson in his new house on Blackdown. Kind reception, magnificent prospect.

October 13.—Move to Wellington Place ; write on chimney-piece of bedroom :—

> I hope that in this House I may
> No evil do, no evil say.

Monday, November 1. — *In Fairyland* comes — a *muddle*, no consultation having been made or proposed between artist and poet. The former (in a huff probably) has put his own prose description to the pictures.

Old Irish airs on violin. I love Ireland : were she only not Catholic ! but would she be Ireland otherwise ?

News Room. *In Fairyland* [Prince Brightkin]. *Daily News* says ' charming poem.'

1870

[Through this year, the entries in Allingham's diaries are too bare to be linked together in any continuous narrative. He had been offered by Messrs. Longmans the post of sub-editor of *Fraser's Magazine* with Mr. Froude ; and in April he finally gave up the Customs and came to live in London. He stayed for a week with Mr. and Mrs. Tom Taylor, at Lavender Sweep, and then found rooms near Onslow Square, within easy distance of Cheyne Row. He was immediately busy with the work of the Magazine ; and for several weeks, in his diary many of the days have entered against them only one word—proofs.

He was often with the Burne-Joneses, now living at The Grange, in North End, Fulham, and there he met Morris and Webb : he writes of walking from his rooms to 'Ned's, by fields, with pear trees in blossom, green hedges.' From time to time he dined with Rossetti— and with Browning. There is a story of—'Old Mr. T——, meeting Browning for the first time at a dinner-table, said to him in his important manner—"Mr. Browning, I have read some of your poetry, but I can't make anything of it." B. replied, "I am delighted to hear you say so. I have never met a reader of my poetry who made that observation in such plain terms as you have to me, yet I am sure a great many of them don't really understand it one bit better than you do."'

Carlyle was very 'friendly and encouraging' about Allingham's new prospects. He was frequently at Cheyne Row ; but unfortunately there are no details of the talks during this year.

One note we give as it stands : 'Mary tells me she said to her Uncle—"People say Mr. Allingham is to be your Boswell," and he replied, "Well, let him try it. He's very accurate."']

CHAPTER XII

1871–1872

January 26.—Overtake Carlyle in King's Road. 'I am glad to see you, I was going along in solitary reflections in this black element of frost.

Speaking of some one lately dead, C. said, 'Ah yes, he's out of this confused puddle that we must still go floundering in a while longer.

'Death and the Future. We know nothing—must leave all that alone. I often think of Kant's notion— no real Time or Space, these are only appearances— and think it is true. I have often had a feeling (contrary as it is to all logic) that there is a Special Providence,—a leading by the Hand of a great friendly Power above us.'

Europe seems determined to try the experiment of doing without a God—'the world must be crucified and brought through extreme sorrow to a better mind.'

C. spoke of the Scotch : John Knox : 'they are degenerate now—in *many* ways (laughing) : the old-fashioned lairds used to get drunk for ten days at a time ! Even Burns had a true sincerity—not like Tommy Moore.'

'Maclise was a quiet shy man with much brogue. His drawing of me in *Fraser* had a very considerable likeness. Done from life in Fraser's back-parlour in about twenty minutes.'

February 2.—At Carlyle's meet Tourgueneff, and the

talk turns upon Russia. T. says that every one speaks good Russian in his country, not French, except the lower people. He speaks well, softly, naturally, tellingly, politely ; his gentle speech flowed round Carlyle's rocks—a big strong man, over fifty, about $6\frac{1}{2}$ feet, good linguist, and curious about English Literature of the time.

June 28.—In Battersea Park. We go by rose-garden ; ask the gardener a question, and he answers in a rude surly fashion ; we agree that these are 'Saxon' manners, and that the Irish have much sweeter. We passed some tall foxgloves, which I admired : ' Ah,' said he, without looking at them, ' old Mother Nature is profuse in her gifts ! ' His insensibility to the beauty of flowers is one of the odd things in C., he allows it as a fact but does not feel it.

Mem.—He has little or no sense of smell.

He told me of an old man, a pauper (' bandster '), who sang Border Ballads in the Annandale dialect ; C. imitated him. Of ignorant old Scots wife who, speaking of some family, said, ' There's twa sons, baith doin' weel in Glasgie ; tane's an Imposter, and t'ither's a Malefactor ' ; it was found that she meant ' Upholsterer ' and ' Manufacturer.'

Once more the longest day is past, we recollected. ' A day,' he mused, ' how strange ! A year—where is it gone ? Time—is it real, or not ? Kant says it is but our way of seeing things. I can conceive this, but am not able entirely to accept the thought. " Forty years make great odds in a lass "—ah, that's true enough.'

He then spoke affectionately of his Mother and her piety.

As we crossed Battersea Bridge coming back, C. said, ' Leigh Hunt used to walk with me in the first years after I came to Chelsea. He was sweet and dignified, and his talk like the song of a nightingale. He was delighted with everything in our house,—

my Wife's playing of Scotch melodies, Scotch brose for
supper,—praised everything : gradually, however, he
found I was not a Shelley—had a foundation of
Presbyterianism which was not agreeable to him. He
met with much contradiction, and ceased to come to
walk with me ; but we continued very friendly.'

[Another day the talk ran on various men and
books.]

Pope : Rev. W. Elwin's edition of Pope an
absurdity, running down his author all the way. Pope
a systematic liar—nonsense ! ' His mendacities about
his writings mattered nothing or next to nothing at
all ; were merely like those of a young lady who says
no when she means yes.'

C. spoke of *Life* of Peacock (whom he called a poor
creature)—of Lord Houghton, and ran down Keats
and Shelley : 'Keats wanted a world of treacle !'
Milnes's *Life*, etc.—a book that interested *me*, I said, to
which C. retorted, ' That shows you to be a soft-horn !'

Of Browning's *Balaustion*, C. said ' I read it all twice
through, and found out the meaning of it. Browning
most ingeniously twists up the English language into
riddles—" There ! there is some meaning in this—can
you make it out ? " I wish he had taken to prose.
Browning has far more ideas than Tennyson, but is
not so truthful. Tennyson means what he says, poor
fellow ! Browning has a meaning in his twisted sentences, but he does not really go into anything,
or believe much about it. He accepts conventional
values.'

C. found considerable beauties in *Ossian*. In early
days (he told me) he read everything he could put
hands on — *Roderick Random*, with immense delight,
a bundle of old numbers of *The Lady's Magazine*,
another of *The Belfast and County Almanack*, sewn
together. This had a department of Mathematical
Questions, all of which he worked out for himself.

We spoke of White's *Life of Swedenborg*, C. rather

with praise, in which I could not agree. C. thought there was a prurient element in Swedenborg which accounted for much : but he never cared at all for the great Swede, and had, I believe, no grasp of his character. He has been reading Dr. T. Brown's *Lectures on Moral Philosophy* :—'might as well have listened to a rookery.'

November 8.—With Carlyle. Old Saints. Shakespeare : C. said with emphasis, 'The longer I live, the higher I rate that much-belauded man.' He thought that Shakespeare was much impressed with Christianity ; to which I demurred. He repeated 'The cloud-capt Towers,' etc., dwelling solemnly once more on—

> We are such stuff
> As dreams are made of, and our little life
> Is rounded with a sleep—

He quoted Richter—'These words created whole volumes within me,' and mused, saying the words again to himself, 'such *stuff* as dreams are made of.'

To my mind, I confess this fine dramatic passage seems of no very particular value when separated from its context.

We agree about Scott as a poet, and, on the whole, about Byron—Moore, too.

Spoke of Gray—the *Elegy*, Letters from the Lakes, and passed to Goldsmith. At no time did C. show himself so happy and harmonious as when talking on some great literary subject with nothing in it to raise his pugnacity. The books and writers who charmed his youth—to return to these was to sail into sheltered waters.

C. said, 'Writing is an art. After I had been at it some time I began to perceive more and more clearly that it is an art.'

November 11.—C., and Sir ——, who talked again of the Poor Law. C. complained to me of having too much of this from the worthy Baronet. I told him of

the apprentice who, getting cow's liver for dinner day
after day, remarked at last that liver was very nice for
six months or so, but after that one wanted a change.
C. laughed, and thenceforward used to say, on occasion,
' I've had another dish of liver ! '

Story of the mulatto Scotch gentleman who told a
wandering Irishman asking help that he ought to go to
his own parish. Paddy looked him full in the face :
' I'm thinking your Honour's a long way from your
parish too ! '

1872

January 1.—Bright Day, to Cheyne Row at 3.
On my greeting him Carlyle said, ' Yes, this is a New
Year. I don't expect it to be a better one than last,
rather worse.'

I said (remotely hinting at the need of resignation
or stoicism—if nothing better may be had), ' Every
creature can but have its own life—no more than that ? '
C. assented, ' Yes, that is the case.'

January 2.—Bright, vernal. To C. at 3. We
walked to Hyde Park. He spoke about a curious
old Scotchwoman Susy, a blacksmith's daughter. She
could do quadratic equations in her head, without any
mathematics ; when she had to solve a question she
thwarted it, that was her explanation of her method.
She wrote poetry, and used to say, ' Burns and me are
pure nature.'

Sir Charles Johnston, ' a rich, wild man,' gave Susy
a cottage and kail-garden.

C. praised parts of *The Ring and the Book* very highly
—' showing a most intimate acquaintance with Italian
life—better, I think, than anything else of Browning,'
he said. ' But the whole is on a most absurd basis.
The real story is plain enough on looking into it ; the
girl and the handsome young priest were lovers.'

I said that B. had neither given us the real story as

he found it, nor, on the other hand, constructed a poem out of it, and in reading *The Ring and the Book* I felt (as I told B. himself) like a creature with one leg and one wing, half hopping, half flying ; at which C. laughed. C. said Thackeray's *Irish Ballads* were the best things he ever wrote, and quoted (as he often did) with great gusto and a strong brogue—

> 'Twould binifit your sowls
> To see the butther'd rowls,

laughing heartily afterwards.

For Thackeray's novels, except *Esmond*, he had little praise. The fact is he has not read most of them.

He praises *Laurence Bloomfield*.

Wednesday, January 24.—C. dictating to his niece introduction to the *Saga*—Heimskringla, Norse chiefs.

Wednesday, March 6. — Warm. Sit in Carlyle's room while he is punctuating the *Saga* translation. We walk to Hyde Park, dodging the carriages sometimes, at risk. (He may catch his death thus, for he usually insists on crossing when he has made up his mind to it, carrying his stick so as to poke it into a horse's nose at need.) Call at Lady Ashburton's, and back to Chelsea.

Monday, March 11.—Death of Mazzini.

Wednesday, March 13.—Carlyle's at 3—friendly.

'Poor Mazzini! lying dead there—all done, all over. What a bright young man when he came in here in 1836 and sat on that sofa! He got into "solidarity" and all manner of absurdities. He used to trouble himself about every wretched Italian who was in any way political. There was one Italian who fell in love with a *danseuse* and stabbed himself ; Mazzini took care of him, recovered him, and persuaded the girl to marry him. Mazzini was indolent, rose late, and smoked a good many cigars. His mother watched over him and sent him £200 a year, which he never took care of.'

Easter Monday, April 1. — Corner of Oakley Street, see Carlyle in omnibus, help him out and walk home with him. He speaks of a Scottish First of April custom—'Hunt the gowk! A-pril!'

Friday, April 12. — to Carlyle at 3 — with him to London Library : Ruskin's books, W. H. Brookfield, Thackeray, etc. etc. ; the idle classes ; few productive people. I had recommended Petrie's *Round Towers* as an authentic memorandum on ancient Ireland, but C. found it 'intolerably stupid.'

He cares to hear nothing about Ireland save what feeds his prejudices. His is the least judicial of minds.

Monday, April 22. — Fine. To C. at 3. We spoke of the Agricultural Labourers' Strike, and I was somewhat surprised to find C. sympathising with the men. Speaking of Slavery he said 'work by compulsion is little good. You must carry man's volition along with you if you are to command to any purpose.'

May 11.—Carlyle, Froude, and I. C. talked against painting, said it was all worthless except portrait-painting : F. chimed in with him, and remarked in his sub-sarcastic manner, 'The connoisseurs tell us a Portrait is no work of Art.'—I said, 'O no !'

F.—'Well, when I said to Ruskin that I cared for no pictures but portraits, he replied, " That proves you care nothing at all about art." '

W. A.—'But that was not saying that a good portrait is not a work of art.' I did not go on ; it was merely tedious and vexatious.

June 24. — To Cheyne Row — 3. C. in lower room writing behind screen, calls out 'Are you there ?' He has been reading *Fifine at the Fair*, and saying every now and again to Browning (though not present), 'What the *Devil* do you mean ?'

July.—To C.'s and see Dr. Carlyle lately from Vichy, looking hearty. C. speaks of his brother John. Translated Dante's *Inferno* ; was private physician to the Duke of Buccleuch. Went to Rome and had good practice there.

C. speaks of Falstaff in an odd way. ' It is no picture of a man at all—merely a stage caricature to make people laugh ; Doll Tearsheet, etc., inconceivable ! '

I could not in the least agree or, of course, in the least shake him. He was speaking of the Sir John of *Henry IV.*

' *Henry VI.* is not Shakespeare's ; the writer of that is a stupid man.'

He praises *Henry V.*, and especially Agincourt. He has often urged me to visit and describe the battle-field ; but I have no enthusiasm for *Henry V.*— a horror of him, rather.

One sometimes feels provoked—' You have said your say, and I'll say *my* say, not yours over again, great as you are ! ' but I believe he is really in his heart ready to allow any true honest feeling.

Sunday, September 22.—Returned from holiday at Lynmouth ; go to Cheyne Row at 3, and find C.— friendly. We walk to Kensington Gardens—sunshiny but cold. Saint Elizabeth, Marbach, etc. C. quotes Shakespeare's—

> Fear no more the heat o' the sun,
> Nor the furious winter's rages ;
> Thou thy worldly task hast done,
> Home art gone, and ta'en thy wages ;

' One of the prettiest things ever written—that. It is like the distant tinkle of evening bells. Much comes of the rhymes—rhymes are valuable sometimes, answering somehow to the melody within a man's thought and soul.'

(I was amused by this concession.)

But a man may have skill in metre, and little along with it, we agreed ; and I quoted Moore's ' Harp that
once through Tara's halls.' C. said, ' Could not be

better done—by a man who could not do it at all!—do
anything worth having.'

C.'s ignorance of the *technique* of Poetry—*i.e.* the
form and body of it, is astonishing, and by me inexplic-
able. He has read a vast quantity of Poetry, and
admired much that he found there ; countless phrases
from Shakespeare and Milton are embedded in his
writings ; he always speaks of Æschylus, Dante, Shakespeare, Goethe as men of the highest rank. Moreover,
he tried hard, tried over and over again, and in many
various metres, to write Poetry. In his verse you can
hear the sound of an original man, vigour, quaintness,
imagery are there, and for a few lines, less or more, the
movement may go right, but only by chance ; presently
it goes all awry. It is not a question of choosing or
happening to be rough, or of taking liberties : the
Writer, after reading many thousand lines of the best
Poets, remains entirely insensible to the *structure* of
verse, to the indispensable rules derived from the nature
of the human mind and ear.

He spoke of having once fainted—'torrents of sleep
descended on the brain ; death, I have thought, will
be like that.'

September.—C. : ' I hear that Burns's nieces, the Miss
Beggs, are paupers. If every Burns' Club throughout
the world would give them *one night's punch* !'

'Strauss's *Life of Jesus*, a revolutionary and ill-
advised enterprise, setting forth in words what all
wise men had had in their minds for fifty years past,
and thought it fittest to hold their peace about.' (I
could not agree.)

Schiller—an account of his father and family has
lately appeared, and C. is going to translate this, and
add it to the people's edition of his *Life of Schiller*.

' Perhaps you will let it first appear in *Fraser* ?'
' That cannot be, sir.' [1]
Duke of Wellington. I tell of his reprisals on the

---

[1] Carlyle afterwards allowed it to appear in *Fraser*.

farmer at Walmer who prevented the Duke from riding along a bridle-road on his farm. Duke rode straight to the barracks, spoke to the commanding officer, and in a few minutes a number of soldiers went into a turnip-field at the back of the barracks and pulled up all the turnips growing within a certain number of yards of the wall, and flung them into the other part of the field. The ground thus summarily cleared belonged to Government, and the farmer aforesaid had cultivated it on sufferance.

Cervantes : his poverty, his nobility and sweetness.

'*Don Quixote* is a very pretty book : Jarvis's translation I reckon best ; Smollett's is not good.'

He praised Smollett's own pathos, instancing the bit from *Humphrey Clinker* of the blacksmith's wife.

' Cervantes began the *Don*, I think, in a mere spirit of raillery, but gradually saw his way to making a fine character of him.'

C. read *Don Quixote* in Spanish at Craigenputtock.

October 3.—Carlyle's. Forster has lent C. *Democratic Vistas* by Walt Whitman. C. was accustomed to say of W. W., 'It is as though the town-bull had learnt to hold a pen.' To-day he had a modicum of praise for Walt.

' Professor Clifford thinks that three angles of a triangle may perhaps *not* be always equal to two right angles.'

C.—' Let him prove that, and I'll give him my head for an ounce of tobacco. God bless us all, what deluges of delirium are pouring out over the world ! '

October 5.—' Suicide of Justice ——.' C., as usual, speaks of suicide in a matter-of-fact and rather sympathetic tone : ' the Roman death—Venio, Proserpina ! etc.'

C. looks through all the principal English Periodicals and is uneasy to miss one, but seldom finds anything to praise. I was surprised to-day to find him speaking with some approval of a paper in the *Fortnightly Review* on ' The Morality of Marriage,' advising people to

restrict the number of children, on economic grounds. I
argued against the public discussion of such a subject in
such a tone.   The question, if it arises, is one for private
decision in each case (wife's health for instance may be
weighty consideration), and is not to be settled by
general rules of frugality or economy.   When children
are a burden, the constitution of society is accused.
Carlyle would not listen, and I was much hurt and
disturbed by his having, apparently, come round to a
grossly utilitarian view which he once abhorred, and
which he had strongly censured in Stuart Mill.   But I
believe that all C. wishes to inculcate is self-denial, and
that he thought of nothing else.

He objects to Taine's book on England, — The
account of the Derby Day—boxing, etc.—'I find it is
not true—it is incredible—inconceivable, etc. etc.!'
Now C. has never been at the Derby ; I have,—and
can believe it all.

October.—C. said, ' Plato has not been of much use to
me ; a high, refined man : " Odi profanum vulgus."
'Socrates—I didn't get much benefit from *him*.'

A.—'His Discourse before his Death ?'

C.—'Well, in such a case I should have made no
discourse ; should have wished to be left alone, to
profound reflections.'

We spoke of *Candide* and its author.

A.—'Voltaire is always crapulous, often nasty, when
speaking of the relation of the sexes.   Very different
from Fielding who, though he takes liberties, warmly
recognises true love.'

C.—'And I believe Fielding was much attached to
his own wife.'

A.—'I don't remember anything like love in
Voltaire's writings.'

C.—'Voltaire is a very questionable sort of article.'

A.—'But he hated injustice.'

C.—'Oh, he abhorred that with his whole soul ! . . .'

A.—'I saw *Macbeth* the other night ; with Phelps.

The *crowd* of witches put on the stage is a great mistake. The Incantation,—a poet nowadays would hardly describe the brewage in detail, " Eye of newt and toe of frog," etc. ; it would be thought vulgar and ludicrous. Goethe avoided the like in *Faust*.'

C.—' Yes ; but all that in the Cauldron Scene is very clever too. It struck me often in reading Shakespeare —this man knew a hundred times more about animals, plants, and all the visible world than I do : how did he learn it all ? What he needs for his purpose is ready to hand.'

We walked into Hyde Park by the powder magazine ; heavy rain came on, and we stood under a plane tree, C. talking all the time vehemently on Emigration and urging me to write upon it. I intimated that I felt little capacity that way, but would take down anything he dictated. C. laughed, and said Sir Baldwyn Leighton had offered to send him a short-hand writer who could write as fast as one spoke.

November 1.—Dined at Mr. John Forster's, Palace Gate House, Kensington. Mr. and Mrs. Forster, Carlyle and Mary Aitken, Edward Emerson (son of R. W. E.), and myself.

C.'s description of a charge at Waterloo got from some eye-witness : *two red lines*, one advancing, one fixed—of dead and wounded. I told the account of the battle given me by Tom Patten, an old soldier at Ballyshannon, which amounted to this—he was ' a'most smothered with smoke, and *mortial hungry* (nothing to ait all day) ' ; when the French ran away he prowled about for something to put between his teeth, and by good luck found a live goose squatting in a corner ; three or four other men came up and would have taken it off him, but he defended the goose at the point of the bayonet, and they agreed that it should be cooked and shared ; so they plucked it, made a little fire, and ' ait ' it half raw.

C. laughed, and agreed that we were apt to forget that

hunger and thirst are often among the trials of a battle-field.

November 3, *Sunday.*—Tennyson calls, with Knowles —sits, looks at books. T. looks well and *big*. K. asks me to dinner. Walk, Chelsea Bridge, up to Clapham Common, dusk, walk about. Dinner—T. repeats Lincolnshire Nursery Rhymes, etc.

Art in writing : 'A little thing well done will out-last a thousand great things not well done.'

Talk—Immortality. F. Harrison in *Fortnightly*.

T.—'If I ceased to believe in any chance of another life, and of a great Personality somewhere in the Universe, I should not care a pin for anything. People must have some religion.'

K.—'I said to Manning—we're all coming back to you by and by.'

T.—'I have often thought the day of Rome would come again.'

A.—'We ought at least to try and hinder the worst absurdities from coming back.'

I walk back, over Chelsea Bridge.

November 5.—To Carlyle's. We spoke of the 'Immortality Dinner,' otherwise Metaphysical Society. *Fraser*—paper on the stars.

C.—'It seems the stars are racing along at an inex-pressible rate of speed. But I care next to nothing about it, let them race as they will. There are much grander and more important subjects for contemplation.'

The Fenian meeting in Hyde Park on Saturday— 'Fitzjames Stephen and I passed through the tail of it; they were mainly London idlers. What are we coming to ? People intend to try Atheism awhile. They will not find it answer.'

A.—'When the main road of dogma has become a quagmire, people will get back to Religion by byways, as it were. Domestic love will not fail. The love of Nature, too, I own I think a powerful help to religious feeling.'

C. (as I knew he would).—'Ho! there's not much in that. A great deal of sham and affectation is in the raptures people express about Nature; ecstasies over mountains and waterfalls, et cetera. I perceive that most people really get much the same amount of good out of all that that I do myself: I have a kind of content in it; but any kind of Nature does well enough. I used to find the moorlands answer my purpose as well as anything,—great, brown shaggy expanses, here and there a huge boulder-stone—"There you lie, God knows how long!"'

I intimated dissent, but knew that discussion would be useless.

Coming back, we spoke of hand-writing; bad writing is hard on the printers, who lose wages by it.

C.—'I could not be taught to write at school; the master gave it up in despair. I taught myself afterwards. A hand should be legible, neat, and saving in space. I was very economical in paper, perhaps too much so—I used to bind myself to do so many pages of writing every day, before I went out to other affairs. I don't quite approve of your hand; it looks hurried. I like my own as well as any I have seen.'

November 6.—To C. at 3. Found him dictating to Mary about Schiller; description of S.,—long nose, long neck, awkward.

C. said, 'The veritable living Emerson was with me to-day; hair all gone from the back of his head, but cheerful. He asked about Matthew Arnold, but I could give him little satisfaction as to Matthew. He mentioned you.'

Saturday, *November* 9.—Note from Edward Emerson, 'Father at 11 Down St., hoping to see you in the evening.' Walk to Down St. Emerson and his daughter Ellen. He said, 'Carlyle called to-day—his humour runs into everything, hearty laugh, excellent company—has always something memorable to say in choice language.'

E.—'London—much improved to the eye.

'Matthew Arnold—his book on Homer good.

'Dr. Wendell Holmes,—a man with us who writes (perhaps you have not heard of him?), said he could find nothing to read ; everything appeared to him *slow.* I said, "I have a book at home which is not slow," and lent him Matthew Arnold on Homer. He said he could read any quantity of books like that.

'Matthew Arnold called on me when I was in London before, but our interview was interrupted before I got any good of him.

'Canada—Americans will not take any definite step, they feel that Canada must come into the Confederation, and will of herself. American party in Canada always at work.'

A.—'Tennyson and Carlyle are for keeping together the Empire—Canada, Australia, India, etc.'

E.—'Is not the case of India different ? I think the world would applaud England if, after due preparation, she withdrew from India.'

Going now to Italy, Athens, perhaps Egypt, to return to London in the Spring. 'My curiosity has increased with years.'

December 23.—Carlyle's. Drove to Athenæum Club. Natural scenery : 'any part of Nature is wonderful.'

His first view of the river Annan, 'running solemnly down with a slight rippling.'

I said I dreamed much of wonderful landscapes. Did he ?

C.—'I do work upon Scenery sometimes; I dreamed every night, for about six months, of Ecclefechan as a wild wide moorland.'

One day Carlyle said, 'I have for many years strictly avoided going to church, or having anything to do with Mumbo-Jumbo. I stood sponsor the other day to Sir Baldwyn Leighton's child ; I didn't like it, but was told it was only a form. I don't think it was right. I have an unfortunate difficulty in saying *No.*'

Speaking of *Memorials of a Quiet Life*, he said, ' I cried over it. It brought back my old world—I used to *ride* to Hurstmonceaux in summer—couldn't stay on the road. I was strong enough for anything then.

'I was forced into resistance to the intellectual position of the men (Julius and Augustus Hare), but as to the women all was clear and right. They had no doubts. Julius used to attack me for my heresies ; always giving me due and grave notice. But when the attack came, it was really so mild that it made no impression on me one way or another.'

One day I found him with the *Life of Beethoven*, edited by Moscheles.

He said, ' I have been wading through it. I can perceive that there may be a great deal of expression in Beethoven's music, if I could understand it—as I never could. We are to think that the greatest thing a man can do is to write a sonata, which I cannot at all believe ! '

[Another day]—' Goethe and Diderot are the only critics of pictures who seem to me to talk sense. Diderot explained what was told by the picture, and afterwards how it ought to have been done.'

Carlyle was entirely against the use of any sort of sedative and anæsthetic drug. The smallest dose of an opiate made him feel poisoned. He held chloroform in surgical operations to be a mistake : ' the pain a *natural* accompaniment and has its use.' The only medicine he believed in was blue-pill.

CHAPTER XIII

1873-1874

London, *January* 1, 1873.—To Carlyle's at 3. He gives me a book. We walk out.

This morning he said, 'after midnight, as Mary and I were sitting together, we heard a chorus of male voices outside the window singing *Auld Lang Syne*. We peeped out, and saw five or six figures on the other side of the street. I was really touched. I put up the window and said "Good-night!" one of them eagerly replied "Good-night!" and then they all vanished silently away.' Then with a laugh he added, 'Truly the songs of Judah in a Babylonish land'! and afterwards quoted Burns's burlesque lines :—

> We hung our fiddles up to dreep, etc.

He spoke of 'Hogmanay' in the streets of Edinburgh, hot punch and kissing.

There used to be gangs of *footpads* in Edinburgh. C. was once struck on the head by them and had his hat broken. He saw three young men of this kind hanged.

'Before that I had seen a man from Liddesdale, Armstrong by name, hanged for horse-stealing. He was a strong man, grimly silent. His body spun and twitched horribly. I saw it before my eyes in the dark and in daylight for weeks. At last I drew the horrible figure on paper as exactly as I could, and thenceforth it ceased to haunt me. I saw another execution—of an old woman who killed an infant, bastard of her son, and who had the reputation of a witch. She declared they *could not* hang her. She was a mere old wrinkled wretched bundle of some sort.'

January 21.—C. picked up a bit of bread in the street and put it on a ledge, blaming such 'waste of food.'

He often praised Cobbett's *Cottage Economy*, and spoke of a poor woman who took up straw-plaiting from it.

February 7.—Arranged with Messrs. Longman, Green and Co. for the publication of an edition of the *Rambles* of Patricius Walker.

March 16.—To C., Sir Baldwyn Leighton there, who asks, ' What has Emerson written ? '

C.—' Oh, many little books, which are very well worth reading. *English Traits* can be highly recommended to any Englishman's attention. Emerson often spins things out to an extreme tenuity ; but he has a fine lofty tone—the highest kind of thing America has to show us ; and Emerson himself is very sweet and equable in disposition.'

Carlyle and Emerson—they recognised each other as no common men, liked each other, praised each other ; each was idealised to the other by distance of space and difference of circumstance, and in a way represented to his friend a whole strange nation of peculiar interest.

In the published correspondence are plentiful hints that C. thought E. too much in the air, and E. thought C. too much on the ground.

You hear E. calling ' Come up ! ' and C. calling ' Come down ! '

Carlyle's genius wants the poetic flavour of the feminine.

Emerson to Carlyle—as an angel to a genie, as light to fire. E. holds up a mild steady lamp, like the full moon ; C. brandishes a huge torch.

Saturday, *April* 19.—To South Kensington Museum, Emerson and Browning in the porch, Miss E. inside. Walk round musical instruments. Browning looks fondly at Handel's favourite harpsicord, Michael Angelo's 'Slave,' Donatello's 'St. George,' etc. Japanese temples: devils as spouts.

B. says, 'Same on Christian temples, devils are made to serve.'

W. A.—'To remind people of what they must fear.'

Wednesday, *April* 23.—Call at Royal Institution, 2.40; upstairs Miss E., Tyndall, Huxley, Emerson; Huxley (looks ill), 'Indigestion—so depressing.'

W. A.—'Carlyle boasts of having had it continuously for fifty years—says it includes all the evils of life.'

H.—'I believe it does.'

Tyndall opens book of Icebergs.

'Your toes are tingling to climb them.'

'Old love of mine. When at Tennyson's I climbed down a precipice at Freshwater—nearly sacrificed another guest. That was P., the publisher, a pity he escaped.'

E., Miss E. and I in cab—past Garrick Club; E. an honorary member; Blue Coat Schoolboys at play; Guildhall, Gog and Magog, New Free Library, splendid room, write names.

Letter of Nelson from the Nile—'Britannia still rules the waves, and that she may ever do so is the sincere prayer of . . .'

Emerson much amused at this. Out by back way and by desire to St. Giles's, Cripplegate; Milton's tomb, slab in aisle—bust moved from pillar, and put under a foolish canopy against wall.

E.—'Do many persons come to look at Milton's grave?'

Sexton.—'Americans, sir.'

Crosby Hall, London Bridge, St. Saviour's; Gower, Massinger. Monument to (Wm.) 'Emerson, who lived and died an honest man, 1695.'

E. says he does not care for Massinger's writing ; there are some good lines of Gower.

The Tabard looks very shabby and mean.

(Missed the Bull and the Green Dragon) return in cab to Down St.

I show E. my little green edition of his *Eight Essays*, which I have long carried in my pocket ; he looks carefully at my pencil marks.

His daughter says, ' that's just what Father likes to see, hints of real opinions, etc. ; in a letter, that which is omitted in sending is what he mostly wishes to see.'

E. asks what my marks mean—' what is + 500 ? ' (Sin is but defeat).

A.—' That the statement is 500 times questionable.'

After a short discussion E. said smiling, ' I agree with the author.'

Talk till it is time for him to dress for dinner.

(At Lady Airlie's)—Poetry—'The Touchstone' ; E. offers to make a selection of my poems for publication in America—Good-bye.

Cold—hail, walk, Hyde Park.

Sunday, April 27.—Call at the Priory on Mr. and Mrs. Lewes—friendly reception. Mrs. Lewes had sent me her ' reproachful regards.'

Carlyle, Emerson, Max Müller on Language. Lewes agrees that language makes an impassable gulf between man and the lower animals, but this does not touch the Darwinian theory.

Mrs. Lewes says ' Emerson would have liked to hear some of Browning's opinions. Have *you* ever heard any of Browning's opinions ? '

April 28.—At Carlyle's house about 3. He spent about fifteen minutes in trying to clear the stem of a long clay pipe with a brass wire, and in the end did not succeed. The pipe was new, but somehow obstructed. At last he sent for another one and smoked, and we got out at last. (I never saw him smoke in public.) He said Emerson had called on him on Sunday, and he

meant to visit E. to-day at his lodging in Down Street.
We walked to Hyde Park by Queen's Gate, and west-
ward along the broad walk next to the ride, with the
Serpentine a field distant on the left hand. This was a
favourite route of his. I was well content to have the
expectation of seeing Emerson again, and, moreover,
Emerson and Carlyle together. We spoke of Masson's
Life of Milton, a volume of which was on C.'s table.
He said Masson's praise of Milton was exaggerated.
'Milton had a gift in poetry—of a particular kind.

'*Paradise Lost* is absurd ; I never could take to it at
all,—though now and again clouds of splendour rolled
in upon the scene——'

'But *L'Allegro* and *Il Penseroso*—you can find
nothing better.' I quoted—

> Over some wide-water'd shore
> Swinging slow with sullen roar.

C.—'That is very good. He did not find that at
Horton.'

W. A.—'At Cambridge, he might.'

C.—'No, no!'

W. A.—'The bell over the levels——'

C.—'It's the sound of the *sea*.'

W. A.—'The sound of a bell—the curfew.'

C.—'No, no! The sound of the *sea*,—*that* is what
he is speaking of—

> Swinging slow with sullen roar.'

We then discussed Emerson, whom C. described as
'a mild, pure, gentle spirit.'

Some one had said of Emerson that he spent his life
in 'making sentences'; 'an unfriendly remark,' said
C., 'yet with some truth in it.' But of whom may
not unfriendly things be said with some truth in them?
And Emerson has made golden sentences, diamond
sentences, sentences to be always grateful for.

At Hyde Park Corner C. stopped and looked at
the clock.

'You are going to Down St., sir ? '
'No, it's too late.'
'The place is close at hand.'
'No, no, it's half-past five.'

So he headed for Knightsbridge, and soon after I helped him into a Chelsea omnibus, banning internally the clay pipe (value a half-penny farthing) through which this chance (perhaps the last, for Emerson is going away soon) was lost.

The chance never did come again.

Friday, May 2.—Bright and mild. To Carlyle 3.15. We walk, Kensington Gardens. C. said, ' Here is May—poor May ! not forward with her work this time—Tyndall has not come near me lately ; I must touch him up. O yes, he's very fond of me—but perhaps he was vexed by an outburst of mine against Darwinism. I find no one who has the deep abhorrence of it that I have in my heart of hearts ! Science, falsely so called. Tyndall is Irish, but not an inaccurate Irishman. He is jocular, and not without a touch of blarney. Has Huxley indigestion? — lucky not to have had experience of it sooner. Huxley attacks Herbert Spencer, with many polite bows and recognitions.'

Kensington Gardens—we sit on felled trees, amid a strong odour of bark, which C. does not, I think, perceive. He praises Charles Norton : 'a serious man—he is attached to America, but sees well enough too the dreadful plague of money-worship there, and the manifold evils that are, and are to be, from that.'

Monday, May 12.—Fine and warm. To C. 3.15. 'Not seen you for a long time.'

He is smoking, throws a printed circular into the fire, and denounces the Promoters of Companies—promoters of Gambling—'damnable fellows deserving to be horse-whipt ' (emphasis on the second word).

Walk along the Fulham Road — Browning's *Red Cotton Night-Cap Country*. C. tells the story very

clearly (he always likes doing this kind of feat), and
says there are 'ingenious remarks here and there ; but
nobody out of Bedlam ever before thought of choosing
such a theme.'

Agrees that B. may possibly take up the Tichborne
Case next.

Tuesday, May 13.—To C. 3.10. Walk, Gloucester
Road, Kensington Gardens, sit.

'Browning *will* very likely do the Claimant by and by.'

'And call it, what ? *Gammon and Spinach*, perhaps.'

C. in Germany. *N.B.*—He has kept a longish diary
of his German tour.

In May and June I walked with Carlyle various
times, but made few notes of our conversations.

Monday, June 9.—Met Carlyle. We had been
talking, on some previous day or days, about Stratford
on Avon, to which I had paid a visit this May. When
I quoted the tombstone lines 'Good Friend, for Jesus
sake forbear,' etc., C. wished to correct me to 'Sweet
Friend,' and would not be gainsaid : indeed he has
used the 'Sweet Friend,' etc., several times in his
writings and very frequently in conversation, and would
not give it up save on compulsion. To-day I brought
proof in my pocket in the shape of a photograph of the
stone with its inscription clearly legible, and as we sat
on a tree-trunk I showed this to him in the quietest
possible way—(not the least air of triumph, overt or
covert). He looked at the photograph, said nothing or
very little (' Ah, well,' perhaps, or the like), and handed
it back without any formal retractation, though further
argument was plainly impossible ; and not long afterwards (I mean a few weeks later) he was using his
beloved old formula, 'Sweet Friend,' as if nothing had
happened, and so continued.

June 30.—To C. at 3. In a new book he found
'—*Whatever* are you doing ? '—' an abominable word.'

We walked to Hyde Park, talking of Russian Tales,
Gaelic Tales, J. F. Campbell, and Macpherson. The

Highlanders C. once more declared to be of Scandinavian origin.

Thornton Hunt is dead—' Leigh Hunt was saying one day, what a fine thing it would be if a subscription could be made *to abolish Hell*; but I remarked, " Decidedly a bad investment, that would be ! "—which grieved Hunt considerably.'

Saturday, July 19.—To C.'s, carrying some books of poetry to him. He is having a course of reading in English Poetry, and I have lent him Hazlitt's *Selections*, Campbell's, etc. Walk, Carlyle, Mr. Robert Tait and I ; C. speaks of Dryden's *Alexander's Feast*.

' Handel's music decupled the effect of the poetry : this is what music ought to do.'

Talking of scenery C. told of two rustic Scotchmen who found themselves by some chance at Ailsa Craig ; they stared in astonishment at the great sea-precipices. At last one said to the other, ' Eh, Jock, Nature's dcevilish !'

The Smith near C.'s father. C. describes minutely the situation of the smithy. ' Smith a great arguer ; used to say, " Tak' ayther side ye like, an' I'll *doon* ye !" He was popularly said to make a pudding for himself at Christmas time of horsenails, and this was supposed to keep his bones green. Poor John ! poor fellow !'

Monday, July 28.—C. urges me to visit Crecy and Agincourt on my holiday ; but the truth is that (while I know what the lust of battle is, and read eagerly the story of a well-fought fight, from Waterloo to Tom Sayers) these old invasions of France by the English seem to me acts of violent injustice,—disgusting and useless butchery.

July 29.—Carlyle tells me he is ' sitting ' to Whistler. If C. makes signs of changing his position W. screams out in an agonised tone, ' For God's sake, don't move !' C. afterwards said that all W.'s anxiety seemed to be to get the *coat* painted to ideal perfection ; the face

went for little.   He had begun by asking two or three
sittings, but managed to get a great many.

At last C. flatly rebelled.   He used to define W. as
the most absurd creature on the face of the earth.

C.—'I met Cary, translator of Dante, a wise looking
old man, but neglected to speak to him, through shyness.   The Kilmarnock weaver prayed, " The Lord gie
us a guid conceit o' oursells ! "—and I would have been
better of some additional share in every situation in my
life.   Still, real self-conceit is the most poisonous thing
can get into a man's mind.'

August 28.—Left London by boat for Honfleur and
arrived there on the 30th. . . . .

September 14.—Carlyle remarked, ' I believe I have
been a *Ritter* of some sort these twenty years or more.
The diploma is in the drawer yonder.'

W. A.—' Have you ever put on the decoration ? '

C.—' There's no decoration.'

Mary.—' O yes : the decoration's in the drawer with
the diploma.'

October 8. — I returned from a little tour in
Normandy, Brittany, Jersey and Guernsey.

October 9.—Carlyle.   ' Tom Paine has been entirely
misrepresented.   When I read *The Rights of Man* I
found I agreed with him.'

I amused him by quoting from a speech of Lord
Derby (on Education), reported in the newspaper, ' We
have no reason to despair of greatly limiting the area
and scope of imbecility in future.'   He laughed loud
and said, ' that would be a very excellent thing if it
could be managed.'

Carlyle had thought much of writing a life of
Napoleon, or book of some kind upon him ; ' but the
more I looked into him;' he said, ' the more I perceived
him to be of the Brigand species.'

October 10.—I found C. had been reading Lanfrey's
book.   He said, ' I am amazed at the character of
Napoleon,—it is most devilish ! '

Napoleon must have been dreadfully disconcerting to C.'s theory of Power and Goodness going together. He used to deny that Napoleon was a great general ; ' Circumstances (he would say) gave him unbounded means, and he lavished them recklessly, he cared not how many soldiers he lost : this is not Generalship.'

October 28.—Carlyle's.   W. W. Story the sculptor. S. and I speak of Browning.   J. S. Mill's autobiography.   I walk with Mr. Story to Alexandra Hotel. He is returning to Rome through Paris.

November 7.—Lady Ashburton about Latin tutor for her daughter.   C. praises Mary B.

' Tom Stanley going to stand for Maidstone against Lubbock.   Amberley, etc.'

C. preaches morals ; and then talks without censure of Goethe at Weimar and Frau von Stein.

Leslie Stephen writing on Jonathan Edwards.   C. : ' What is the use of it ?—sticking like a wood-louse to an old bed-post and boring one more hole in it.—There is deep truth in Calvinism.'

November 17.—C. speaks of the second part of *Faust*, which he has been reading again : ' All this is very inferior to Shakespeare.'

We talked of death—I recalled Goethe's conversation with Falk on the day of Wieland's funeral, and how he spoke of the continuance of existence after death as a thing of course, and said some very remarkable things.

C. said, ' I have thought little of this, pro or con.   I long ago despaired of any response to such an inquiry.'

On another day about the same time he said to me, ' Dying of old age is a painful process.   Still, this may be called an euthanasia,—and there are flaming glimpses and glories sometimes among the deepening clouds.'

One day Carlyle said to me, ' Life's a Dream.'

Tennyson (who was in town) said to me the very same words on, I think, the very same day, without any reference having been made to the conversation with C.,

and while talking on a different subject.

C. has no belief at all in the efficiency of the
British Army : 'nobody connected with it has the least
knowledge of the art of war. Our officers ought to be
sent to Germany to learn something of this, and one
or two of our Royal Princes ought to go.'

December 2. — Germany and Frederick — Carlyle
visited various battlefields and 'found something to go
on ; *Frederick* occupied me thirteen years ; about
eight in writing ; I knew I should have mountains of
dust and rubbish to swallow. I thought I could manage
somehow *brevi manu*. But it was infinitely worse than
I had ever prefigured. I thought of nothing else for
eight years : used to go about and say to myself, " What
kind of man is this Frederick ? What does all this
talk about him mean ? incredible most of it, clearly
incredible." '

W. A.—'Did you read about nothing else ? '

C.—'Hardly anything, — except something very
notable now and then. My mind was full of *Frederick*.
I used to ride a great deal then, and when I came in I
had usually an hour's bright talk or so (ah me !), and
then after dinner sat down to *Frederick*,—she silent in
another corner of the room. Often, I think, she would
have been glad to speak to me—ah dear ! . . . Well,
it nearly killed me. It was the desire and longing of
my life to finish it.

'When it was done I felt ill in body and much
discomposed.'

W. A.—'But it *is* done.'

C. (quietly and perhaps sadly)—'Yes, it is done.'

C. despised oratory, yet much of his writing is akin
to Oratory. Whatever he takes up he impresses upon
you with all the emphasis of his forcible nature, and all
his skill of language. When the Reader has recovered
breath he may sometimes suspect that a claim has been
made upon his attention and nervous system, disproportionate to the real importance of the matter.

The Frederick Book might be called the *reductio ad*

absurdum of Carlyleism.   Yet, on the other hand, take —that very Book.   Suppose you care little or nothing at all for the King of Prussia and his concerns,—if you care for Literature and for Genius, here is a supreme work of Literary Genius, here is the best that a truly Great Man of the literary sort found himself able to give you by the conscientious devotion of thirteen laborious years ; here is spread out legibly before you a world of wit, humour, picture, narrative, character, history, thought, wisdom, shrewdness, learning, insight. Open it where you will, the page is alive.

1874

January 23.—C. has a bad cold, very unusual with him.   We call at Froude's, who is gone out.   C. manages to get as far as Sloane St.—his laughing always ends in a cough.

Speaks of *Sartor Resartus*.   'I did not then, and never did, and do not now, think highly of *Sartor*. And when I get letters such as often come from young men—Oh, so impressed with *Sartor* ! it almost makes me sick.   But I thought I might perhaps get £150 for it.'

Sartor sold better than any of C.'s other books in the cheap edition.   He used to mention this, with a protest against ' the foolish people' who showed this preference for a book ' of very little value.'

He often said, ' The only book of mine I care at all about is the *Cromwell*.'

C. told me he at first got *Sartor* printed with capital letters to all the nouns, but on full consideration gave up the plan.   One complete copy was so printed, and in after years he sent this away in a box of books, gift to a needy individual whose name I forget (if he told me).   C. never heard more about said box, and thinks it was perhaps lost in transit.   So the Bookstall-hunter may set down this unique copy of *Sartor* among his possible discoveries.

Mem.—*Sartor Resartus :* was the title suggested by an old song called 'The Tailor Done-over'?

'The *Niebelungen Lied* is the prettiest thing we have out of the Middle Ages. There is no English translation of it. That would be a fine thing for you to do, it would be a lasting work. I felt, once, I had got into it, and could have done it if I had been able to write poetry.'

February 13.—Carlyle has received the German order *Pour le Mérite*—black ribbon with silver line near each edge ; he dictates to Mary letters to the Ambassador and to Berlin, but cannot phrase them to his mind.

We walked to Palace Gate : returning saw the red glare in the sky of a great fire. C. quoted—

> A little spark makes muckle wark.

It was the Storehouse called Pantechnicon, near Belgrave Square, which had boasted itself fire-proof.

'Lord Salisbury's article in the *Quarterly* ("Difficulties of the Liberal Party ") is good, and so quietly worded ! I thought with shame how impossible it would have been for me to avoid bursting out into the most violent language.'

C.—'Gordon Bennett, an Aberdeen man, pushed himself into notice by scurrility. Somebody once said to Daniel O'Connell in a London room, bringing forward a stranger, "May I introduce to you Mr. Gordon Bennett ? " O'Connell replied " No, you may not. Neither you nor any man alive may introduce to me Mr. Gordon Bennett." Best thing I ever heard of Dan.'

W. A.—'The blossoms are coming out.'

C.—'Ah, yes, poor things ! '

March 23.—To C.'s 3.30. C. lends me a pair of 'model braces.' He highly admires some practical little inventions, and thinks it must have been one of the most ingenious of modern men who thought of putting metal *eyes* into the lace-holes of boots and shoes. Walk to Hyde Park—'Forster's *Dickens*—next to

Boswell.' We crossed the crowded drive and Carlyle was nearly run over ; on reaching the opposite foot-path he laughed and quoted—

> There's a sweet little Cherub that sits up aloft,
> To keep watch o'er the life of poor Jack.

March 30.—Carlyle spoke of the first Nigger Minstrels in this country ; some one took him to a theatre to hear them. He was extremely tickled by their ' tempest of enthusiasm about nothing at all ' ; and imitated ' Who's dat knocking at the door ' with energy.

Saturday, April 5.—Easter Day. Carlyle, Mary and I to Millais' Studio, ' North Pole ' (Trelawney).[1]

J. E. M. big and stout, with cap on.

Tuesday, April 20. — C. and I walk past Rajah's fountain ; Carlyle (as his habit is) takes his hat off at the spot where he supposes his Wife to have died, and keeps it off for a quarter of a minute or so.

May 24.—Carlyle spoke of his College days. ' The Mathematical Professor had no single word of encouragement or advice to give me. I studied the *Evidences of Christianity* for several years, with the greatest desire to be convinced, but in vain. I read Gibbon, and then first clearly saw that Christianity was not true. Then came the most trying time of my life. I should either have gone mad or made an end of myself had I not fallen in with some very superior minds.'

He then imitated very comically the Professor of Theology at Edinburgh, who was extremely emphatic in addressing his class. ' The Devil, after succeeding in his vile machinations retires to his infernal den and grins with horrid satisfaction ! ' . . . This led to talk on elocution, and C. repeated the lines—

> There was a man of Thessaly,
> And he was wondrous wise, etc.,

in the manner of Macready, and did it with great point and effect.

---

[1] Edward John Trelawney, the friend of Byron and Shelley, sat to Millais for the old mariner in his picture, ' The North Pole.'

May 27.—The post of Historiographer Royal for Scotland was 'about to be offered' to Carlyle, but the attack on Dizzy in *Shooting Niagara* put a stop to this. So C. told me to-day.

There was a throng at Hyde Park Corner, but C. ran into the middle of the street, at a risk, to catch a Chelsea omnibus.

June 2.—Walk with C. and Professor Bain to Hyde Park. Talk of size of heads. C. said (I think) that his own head was 23½ inches round, one inch more than Burns's. Goethe's head was large, Byron's small. Browning's is small. Whewell's brain was found to be shrunk. The brain of ordinary persons begins to shrink at sixty, of superior men not till seventy. Grote's head was large, but his brain was found to be *light*. Greatest weight of a brain about 62 oz.

C.'s present height, five feet eleven—'I used to reckon myself six feet.'

Thursday, June 25.—C. and I walked on the Chelsea Embankment. He praised Wren, always a favourite of his : 'I was some years in Chelsea before I took particular notice of the Hospital, and then I perceived it to be an honest, dignified structure, admirably adapted to its uses. St. Paul's is a very fine thing.'

I hinted that the visible Dome is but a wooden shell covering something like a glass-house chimney ; C. did not take any notice of this fact, but went on with his eulogy.

'I remember (this was on his first visit to London) catching a glimpse from Cheapside of the huge Dome, its gold finger pointing to Heaven ; human creatures creeping about (I one of them) on our petty errands. It was and is the grandest building I ever saw.'

For Westminster Abbey, or for any Gothic building, C., I think, cared nothing.

[In June of this year Allingham became editor of *Fraser's Magazine*, and on August 22 he was married to Helen Paterson. The diary begins again in October, when they are back in London, at their new home, 12 Trafalgar Square, Chelsea.]

Thursday, October 8.—Helen and I about 9.30 to 5 Cheyne Row. Upstairs : Carlyle in gray dressing-gown, reading. Mary Aitken ; C. returned lately from Scotland.

'Saw many things that were interesting and pathetic to me—at Kirkcaldy, the Provost extremely attentive. To Edinburgh ; wished to speak to no one, but could not manage that. St. Andrews, curious place—ruins, getting larger now.'

Tuesday, October 13.—C. : 'Dizzy the most ambitious of living men—was dreadfully unhappy in his time of obscurity ; believes in nothing whatever but success. Has undoubted toughness, the Jew quality—as Goethe noted. His novels worth little or nothing. His address to the young men of Glasgow almost as empty as if " the people's William " had made it. Dizzy no humour, no *love* in his jesting. Even Swift had real humour, could really banter and *enjoy* a joke, the grimmest real humourist I know of. *Gulliver* merry reading.'

October or *November*.—Emerson Tennent—he went to Greece in 1824, to help the cause. He had an album in which Campbell promised to write something ; it came back to Tennant with the following line inscribed in it—

My dear Sir, you are going away to Greece, and you have the best wishes of, my dear Sir, Yours faithfully, Thomas Campbell.

C.—'Spedding's *Bacon* : a most admirable work, has brought together every fact with the utmost diligence, honesty, and good judgment, and produced a book of great value, which is almost unreadable from its flatness and prolixity. He shows Bacon as a thoroughly respectable character and an opulent mind. Bacon had a power of swift deliberation—if that be not a contradiction in terms. But he was an unfruitful man in matters of science.'

CHAPTER XIV

1875

January 7.—Walk with Carlyle to Piccadilly. He said, ' Froude's *History of England* is too long, ought to be melted down to a third part. Fr. is hardly just to Elizabeth, has brought up all her foibles. His treatment of Mary is harsh. The sneer at her faded charms in the execution scene gave me a shudder.'

January 11.—Helen and I call at Cheyne Row about half past ten in the evening—show him proof of *Early Kings of Norway*, second article. (He is particular to the minutest point, and rages against printers. Mary copied out all the MS., with no small labour.)

January 15.—Carlyle calls at my house about 4. I go with him in omnibus to Oxford Circus, and we walk to Wells Street for Samuel Laurence's Studio. The painter is gone for the day, but a civil pleasant woman shows us in, and we see L.'s copy of the picture which C. maintains to be of John Knox—also portrait of Thackeray. We walk down Regent Street to Piccadilly. C. in a very kind mood ; he into omnibus.

February 1.—To C.'s at 10 in the evening. He sitting with Mary, at work (correcting new edition of *Frederick*).

' This is a good number of *Fraser*. Froude is coming home.' Vegetarianism.

Has received from Disraeli an offer of the Grand Cross of the Bath ; also intimation that the Queen would provide money by pension or otherwise. . . . 'This is magnanimous of Dizzy !'

I doubted that ; thought it would be a great triumph to D. to be able to confer public favours on those who had publicly despised him, and put famed and haughty men under obligation to him.

April 2.—C. spoke of Sydney Smith, to whom he was able to give no praise at all. 'The nature of true *Wit* is very much misunderstood. Sydney said nothing worth remembering. He said "it took a surgical operation to get a joke into a Scotchman's head"; the thing is, that what Sydney presented was not a joke worth admitting into any one's head, and the Scotchman refused to have anything to do with it. The Scotch are a people with a large appreciation of fun very generally among them. . . . I remember seeing Sydney Smith setting himself to make a company laugh, and I left him there at it, reflecting what a wretched ambition it was in any man.'

June 12.—With Carlyle and Dr. John Carlyle to Hyde Park Corner. Ruskin's pamphlet on the Royal Academy—'more coherent and reasonable than some he has written.

'I never was at a Royal Academy Exhibition. I was taken in once to the Hall to see a bust of myself— a wretched, absurd thing,—and should have been glad at any time to hear of its having been dragged out by a rope round its neck and pounded into lime-dust.'

He spoke of a debate long ago at the London Library about the appointment of a Librarian. C. was for one man, Gladstone for a certain Italian. C. said : 'I discovered then that Gladstone had the art of speaking. He and I were like Valentine and Orson. I laid about me with a rough club, he got up in shining armour and drew his sword. But all in vain, too ; by no sleight of fence could he carry his point.

'The London Library is choked with foolish books.'

July 6.—Thomas Campbell. C., a youth at

Edinburgh University, was greatly struck by Campbell's
lyrics — especially 'The Battle of the Baltic' and
'Lochiel'; and when coming to London procured an
introduction to the Poet. 'I found him one day in his
house somewhere near the Edgeware Road, and was
much disappointed ;—a little man in a black scratch
wig, luminous eyes, but unkind looking, with a belli-
gerent expression. He was unhappy and snappish,—
thought I wanted something of him in the way of
magazine work or literary introductions,—which I did
not at all ; and I soon took my leave.'

Friday, July 23.—To Cheyne Row about 10.15 in
the evening. Carlyle, Dr. C., Mary. My sketch of
Campbell to Bell's new edition. C. praised it on the
whole, but thought me 'rather stingy' in my estimate
of Campbell's poetry. Talked of Dr. Beattie : 'It was
a curious thing, that shriek of joy which Beattie reports
as the last thing. No one but Beattie could give any
opinion as to what it meant. Probably it meant nothing
at all,—was a mere physical convulsion.'

'Your poor friend Plimsoll'—C. sympathised with
him. (He often calls the selfish shipowners 'Cannibals.')

Carlyle spoke with respect of sailors ; their occupation brought them into close contact with the eternal
verities of the universe. But, as matter of experience,
is the average sailor a superior man ?

He learned smoking as a schoolboy. It is the only
'creature comfort' that has given him any satisfaction.
After working for some hours he always has 'an interlude of tobacco.' He smokes long clay pipes, made at
Paisley, whence he gets them by the box. 'No pipes
good for anything can be got in England.' He likes
best a new pipe, and used, when first I knew him, to
smoke a new pipe every day, its predecessor being put
out at night on the door-step for who would to carry
away.

I have more than once heard Carlyle talk about
Tennyson's smoking, and also T. of Carlyle's. Each

thought the other smoked too much—or at all events too strong tobacco. T. carefully dries his tobacco before putting it into the pipe, which, he says, lessens the strength, while C. asserts that this process makes it stronger. T. has a wooden frame for his pipes, holding, I think, fourteen, which hangs over the chimney-piece of his study, and he smokes No. 1 to-day, No. 2 to-morrow, and so on, coming round in a fortnight to No. 1 again.

Saturday, July 24. — Mr. William Black the novelist wrote to me some days ago to ask if I could take him to Carlyle—' one of the few ambitions of my life.' I asked leave ; and to-day Mr. B. lunched with Helen and me, and I took him down to Cheyne Row. C. received him civilly, and we three walked by the Embankment, Chelsea Hospital, King's Road, Ebury Square and back to Oakley Street. The talk was mostly about Scotland. C. asked Mr. Black : ' Well, sir, and when are you going to seriously set about writing a book ? '

Mr. B. afterwards sent *A Princess of Thule* to Cheyne Row.

August 4.—C., the Dr. and I walk. C. : ' Michelet —very wise and truthful—a curious kind of historian —puts in a good deal of strulduddery.' Bradlaugh and Kenealy — Newman's ' Primitive Christianity ' (article in *Fraser*). ' I could not read it. I know Primitive Christianity was some sort of high and holy enthusiasm. I do not in the least believe that *God* came down upon earth and was a joiner and made chairs and hog-troughs ; or came down at any time more than He comes down now into the soul of every devout man. There is no use in saying anything more in the matter. Let it rest here.'

A.—' People are still busy with the old dogmas, and they still interfere with life, individual and social.'

C.—' I don't want to see Christianity falling all away to ruin—a bit faster than it is doing.'

J. S. Mill on Religion—C. : 'It is like the last mew of a drowning kitten! people speak as if "Comfort" were the one thing ; as if Divine Providence had not intended a man to go through many things and learn much thereby, by labour and self-denial and mis-fortune and even misery—John Mill wasted away his soul.'

Tuesday, October 5.—Back from Eastbourne—at C.'s 3.20. Carlyle and Mary back from Keston Lodge. C. and I go out, rain, shelter in public-house, allowed with scant civility, and then go *back* for his coat.

Carlyle never carried an umbrella ; in wet weather a waterproof coat. He very seldom caught cold.

C.—' We had a successful stay at Keston. Saw Sir John Lubbock ; Charles Darwin several times.

' I had not seen him for twenty years. He is a pleasant *jolly*-minded man (I thought this a very curious phrase), with much observation and a clear way of expressing it. Has long been an invalid. I asked him if he thought there was a possibility of men turning into apes again. He laughed much at this, and came back to it over and over again.'

C. praises Owen's paper on ' Petroleum ' in *Fraser.*

October 12.—C.'s. Walk with him to Piccadilly.

Goethe's *Sprüche* very hard to translate. ' I found, when I was translating from the German writers that each man has *a tune* : Goethe has his ; Richter has his, and, when I got into it, all went on well. That was the pleasantest kind of work I ever did. I could do it in any mood—like basket-making. Goethe's style is by far the most refined and most difficult to render.'

Carlyle's intellectual position and attitude are, from his own point of view, rightly chosen and unassailable. He is not a learned man in the scholastic sense, being anything but a purist in classical matters. He neither had, nor cared to have, more than a rough working knowledge of Greek and Latin, but he never let any quotation or reference pass, if he cared to look at it at all, without getting at the real substance of it.

C.—'I have often been invited to places with the temptation of meeting Manning; but he is perhaps of all human creatures the one I would most decidedly refuse to meet. If we did, it might possibly end in actual blows, old as I am.'

November 5.—Helen went to Carlyle's to-day at 2, to go on with his portrait. Browning came in. Lately returned from Normandy. Had read in the newspapers of C.'s being ill—not true : 'happy for your sake, and still more for my own ; I have often lamented not to have availed myself more of your company of late.'

He reminded C. how, long ago, C. used to come to their house (at Camberwell) and 'talk Scotch' to B.'s mother (who was a Scotchwoman).

'You told me the Scotch name for buns—*cookies*.'

C. said, 'I hear you have been bringing out several new Books rather lately. I always read your Books and find them well worth it, but I have not seen these.'

B.—'I'm afraid of you in that way! I'd sooner trust my body to you than my book.'

C.—'What is the last about ?'

B.—'It's called *Aristophanes' Apology*. I felt in a manner bound to write it, so many blunders about Aristophanes afloat, even among the so-called learned.'

C. praised B.'s translation from Euripides (*Alcestis*). 'The very best translation I ever read,' and recommended him to do more.

B. looked at the portrait and said, 'Very like.'

C. passed my house about 4 to-day. I overtook him in the Fulham Road and walked with him to Lady Ashburton's door at Knightsbridge. He said, 'Browning in his young days wore a turn-down shirt collar with a ribbon for neck-tie, and a green coat. I first met him one evening at Leigh Hunt's, a modest youth, with a good strong face and a head of dark hair. He said little, but what he said was good.'

Carlyle and Lecky in King's Road walking along, C.
looking small beside L., who overtopped and bent over
C. in speaking and listening.

C. asked for ' Madame and the Homunculus.'[1] ' A
Baby is the most wonderful of all phenomena in this
variegated world. Some of the women told Mary it
was a most lovely creature (smiling). Babies have no
features at first—they're small red things, but gradually
you come to discern some features.'

After this we spoke of Historians. ' Ranke a diligent
man, gave much about diplomacies useful in its way, no
picture of men or things. He hangs up a kind of—
well—a gray shadow, you might say, like an Ossian
ghost, " the stars dim twinkling through." Macaulay
like a Russian Steppe—green enough, but not a rock or
tree to break the monotony.'

I.—' Macaulay tried much to make an effect by style.'

C. (smiling).—' Then we can only say he did not
succeed.'

The Slav people—C.: 'An ugly, dirty, ill-conditioned
set of creatures, with all the worst qualities attributed
to the Irish, and none of the good. Their language
a mere jargon, with nothing in it worth knowing.'

L.—' You have been among them?'

C.—' O yes, for some three weeks.'

L. (very mildly).—' Is that long enough to judge of
a nation?'

C.—' Oh, I did not judge them by that alone. They
are most miserable, their houses filthy and unventilated
beyond imagination—smells centuries old!'

December 1.—Carlyle and I walk in the snow and
dusk in Cromwell Road. We meet Leslie Stephen,
whose wife died on Sunday ; he turns and shakes hands,
but does not speak. Carlyle says 'I am very sorry
for you, sir. My own loss did not come in so
grievous a way.' S. departs without a word.

[1] Gerald Carlyle Allingham, born November 8, 1875.

Carlyle, to me : 'We feel some pity in such cases, —but small, small, small it is. I look back often to those times of poverty in my life, and richer they seem than all California! And *She* going through it all so nobly and so queenly,—without any recognition almost! Ah me! . . . That winter I went to Mentone was the saddest of my life. I used to go into an olive grove and meditate most sadly on many things.'

'Browning came on my birthday and talked loud. He agreed with me about Shelley and his poetry.'

December 27—C. returned to Shelley again to-day, a subject I would fain avoid with him. 'Shelley had not the least poetic faculty. I never could read anything he wrote. It was all a shriek merely.'

I hope it is not wrong in me to avoid battles in such a case. C. knows perfectly well that my opinion is not his—that Shelley is a star in my sky. As to Browning, I have with pain heard him of later years speak slightingly of Shelley. The longer I know B. (great and lovable as I must always hold him) the less do I know how much weight to give to his utterances.

Shelley's conduct to his poor Harriet is entirely inexcusable. It was the act of a wildly impulsive, impatient, unregulated mind, always hurried headlong by its moods. C. was only three years and four months younger than Shelley, and his mind was already formed before the latter became at all known to him.

It may be noted here that Emerson once told me he could see nothing in Shelley's poetry, beyond some pretty verses in 'The Skylark' and 'The Cloud.' I tried him with 'Ozymandias' (he was just back from Egypt). 'That is fine,' he said, and asked leave to look at it, but I fear was hardly likely to alter his verdict. Emerson said on this occasion, 'If I don't know what Poetry is, I don't know anything.'

Perhaps I had secretly a similar prejudice in favour of somebody else's judgment!

CHAPTER XV

1876

Wednesday, January 26.—Spring-like. Walk with Carlyle and Froude, Hyde Park.

'School proposed for Haddington in memory of John Knox.'

Lord Amberley's death. (To W. A.)—'Emerson has quoted from you about sleep.' Game Laws—'do animals enjoy being hunted? I asked a man how he would feel if he had to run for his life with twelve devils at his heels?'

C. declared game laws bad, caused a 'waste of food-producing power.'

Saturday, January 29.—To C. 12.30, and stayed three hours, examining with him Goethe's *Sprüche*, the original, and an English translation by a lady.

C. said, 'She has rubbed down all the points with a bathbrick.'

Froude comes in.

F.—'Jowett's Plato, a bald, tame, prosaic translation.'

C.—'Plato's style is admirable, but he has nothing particular to tell you.'

A.—'One wonders how much is Socrates.'

C.—'Socrates one suspects to be a myth mainly. I could get nothing out of Plato! What do you mean then?—the devil a word!'

F.—'You would have liked to meet him?'

243

C.—'O yes, I daresay I should have found him highly interesting in himself.'

Wednesday, February 16.—We walk to Hyde Park. C. helps a blind beggar-man over a wide crossing. We meet Leighton, old King Cole,[1] and the Hon. and Rev. Byng. Sit on bench in Park, where a man speaks to us, but none of us know anything of him.

C. has had a letter from Mr. Norton (Mass.), 'turning much on Emerson, describing him as cheerful and hopeful ; but E. says he has lately been affected with a disease called Old Age (smiles). His memory for names is defective. He is not inclined to write more ; Emerson's last book, like the rest, full of fine airy sayings.

'Browning's *Inn Album* is the worst of all he has given us ; and he has been growing worse and worse— with the exception of his Greek translations. *The Ring and the Book*—what a thing it is ! Browning has a great quantity of miscellaneous reading about him, but no solid basis of knowledge in anything. Tennyson's later things are better than B.'s. But Browning is a man of great abilities.'

Thursday, February 17.—Helen, Miss Edith Martineau and I walking along Chelsea Embankment, meet Carlyle with Mary. I ask C.'s leave aside to introduce Miss E. M. to him. 'The sister of theologic Martineau ? ' he inquires. 'Daughter '—on which he speaks to Edith : 'How is your Father ? I used to go to your house in Liverpool.' Asks after Harriet Martineau, now about seventy-three.

E. asks if her father may come and see Carlyle.

'O yes, I shall be delighted to see him and hear what he has to say of things.'

To Helen : 'Take care of your little son.'

Saturday, February 19.—Rev. James Martineau called on me. Tyndall, Haeckel, and modern materialism in general.

[1] Sir Henry Cole.

We went together to 5 Cheyne Row and were shown into the parlour, where, after a few minutes, enter Carlyle. He had already two waiting to walk with him, and we walked slowly along the Embankment eastward, and nearly as far as Vauxhall Bridge, a body of five—Carlyle, Martineau, Froude, Lecky and W. A.—too many for hearing well what C. said. Froude and he turned back; M., L. and I went on to Westminster. Spoke of Newton's *Principia*. M. thought he saw faults in the logic, *e.g.* 'Gravitation in proportion to Mass'—now, mass is weight, and weight is gravitation.

Wednesday, February 23.—Walk with Carlyle and Froude. I ask C. has he read Mr. Martineau on Tyndall in the *Contemporary Review*? 'No, I care nothing about it. It is an utterly contemptible theory, that out of dead blind dust could spring the sense of right and wrong! Fit only for a dog, if a dog could speculate. Don't come to me to certify that you have an intellect, with such notions as these in your head.'

Monday, March 6.—Walk with Carlyle and Froude, meet Longman and Spedding. We speak of Ruskin's *Fors* ('my pets,' money accounts, etc.).

St. George's Society, which C. thinks an absurdity, and gives nothing to.

Froude says Ruskin lamented to him the way he was brought up—not like other boys, no out-door games, etc. 'I might have had a son of my own and been happy.'

I alone into St. James' Park, at liberty to greet the new spring. Cool west wind, leaves budding, almond bushes in bloom; pleasant (though C. would never admit it!)

I to Water Colour Gallery and find Helen. 'Ruskin just gone—introduced himself, thanked me for Carlyle portrait, asked me to do another showing the stronger aspect.'

March 10.—At Hyde Park Corner meet Browning.

'How odd ! made sure I had just seen you in another part of town and differently dressed. I don't quite believe in *doppelgangers*.'

Browning asks me about Byron article in *Fraser*, and praises it most warmly. 'Shouldn't mind if my name were at the bottom of it. Only you did not say half a hundredth part as much as might be said of Byron's baseness and brutality.

'I might have rated Byron higher intellectually than you have done, in some respects, but what you have said of him morally is mild to what he deserves.'

He then spoke of Disraeli. 'What a humbug he is ! Won't I give it him one of these days !' Royal Academy dinner, Dizzy's speech. 'What struck him most was "the *imagination* of the British School of Art, amid ugly streets and dull skies, etc. etc."'

Afterwards Disraeli came up to Browning and said, 'What do you think of this Exhibition?'

Browning wished to hear Disraeli's opinion. Disraeli said—'What strikes me is the utter and hopeless want of imagination' (as much as to say, you didn't think me such a fool as I seemed in my speech !)

Browning told this to Gladstone, who said pungently, 'It's hellish ! He is like that in the House too—it's hellish !'

'And so it is,' added Browning.

Friday, March 24.—To Carlyle's. Lecky there (L. up in all the newspaper and club gossip). He said *The World* gave what professed to be the substance of Bismarck's letter to Carlyle, and all wrong from beginning to end. C. said 'it was a most flattering thing to receive such a letter, saying that I had "raised a living statue of their great King"—could not be a finer compliment. Nothing to make him write such a letter but his own free will ; not a word of humbug in it that one could see.'

Macaulay's *Life* by Trevelyan on the table : C. has just begun it. Lecky asked him, 'You read the first

two volumes of Macaulay's *History*, I believe?' C.
assented, and L. no doubt chuckled internally.

I said, 'How variable a thing National Character
seems to be; take the England of Shakespeare, of
Cromwell, of Charles II.'

C. said, 'Shakespeare and Cromwell were brothers,
profoundly wise and sympathetic souls.'

W. A.—'I meant Shakespeare's *time*. He was above
his time.'

C. (emphatically).—'He was above everybody of
every time. No such man has been seen in the world.

We are such stuff as dreams are made of—

nothing so profound anywhere out of the Bible, or in it,
that I recollect. "Such *stuff*"—the same kind of thing.
I put *The Tempest* first of all (profound philosophy of
life in robes of romance).'

Lecky.—'His last play, was it not?'

C.—'I recollect when I first heard of Shakespeare,
when I went to school at Annan, where there was
rather more acquaintance with things in general than
in our house. I had never heard of Shakespeare there :
my Father never, I believe, read a word of him in his
life. But one day in the street of Annan I found a
wandering Italian resting a board with very bad imagery
—"images" (C. imitated the cry), and among them a
figure leaning on a pedestal with "The Cloudcapt
towers," etc. Various passers-by looked on, and a
woman read aloud the verses, very badly, and then the
name below, "Shankespeare," that was the way she gave
it, "Shankespeare" (laughing).'

I tell the joke of the sailor reading, 'The Cloud—
Captain Towers—don't know the ship.'

Carlyle laughed and said, 'I've heard that.'

When Carlyle first came to London in 1824 he
went very seldom to the theatre—saw Kean once in
Shylock, thought he exaggerated everything, and was
like a wild beast. Had seen him in Edinburgh in the

same part of the Jew—Macready gave him a season ticket for three seasons, and then he went often (he always praises Macready).

Spoke again to-day with bitter contempt of 'Darwinism.' Lecture at Zion College to the Clergy against Spontaneous Generation.

C.—'No argument at all for it. But (he said, half in soliloquy and with a tone of conviction) we shall get rid at last of all forms, and that will be a blessed thing.'

Scotland greatly changed since his youth, a hundred times as much wealth, and not a hundredth part as much solid worth.

(L. queries and suggests dissent, but does not argue, and rarely opposes.)

I say, the whole world of mankind is mixing—it cannot be helped. Old local peculiarities are disappearing. C. agrees.

April 1.—Carlyle said, ' Just after I had got out of my bath this morning and was drying myself—getting into a kind of fury or exaltation of mind, I exclaimed, " What the devil then am I, at all, at all? after all these eighty years I know nothing about it." '

April 6.—Browning paid us a visit 3.15 to 4.30 about. He breakfasts every morning at 8, not later, has luncheon at 1. He tells me he has no dreams worth remembering—no beautiful or clever dreams, ' Except that a few times I have dreamed that I was among the mountains near Asolo (of *Pippa Passes*), and I said to myself, " I have often wished to see Asolo a second time, but now here I am and I'll go and do it." Once I dreamed I was seeing the elder Kean in *Richard the Third*, and he uttered a line which struck me as immensely finer than anything else in the play, or than I had ever heard perhaps, and I perceived it was not Shakespeare's, but my own invention. It was in the scene where the ghosts' rise. When I woke I still had hold of the stupendous line, and it was this—

And when I wake my dreams are madness—Damn me.

'I never dream but when out of sorts in health.'

Browning looked at a photograph of himself on my chimney-piece and said, 'There I am—and I don't recollect when or where it was done, or anything about it. I find gaps in my memory. The other day I came by chance on an old letter of my own, telling how I had seen Ristori in Camma—if that was the word, and I could not and cannot recollect in the very least what Camma is, or what I refer to : yet there it was in my own handwriting—a judgment on me for my opinion of my Grandfather, when I asked him if he had seen Garrick in *Richard the Third* and he replied "I *suppose* I have," and I thought "Bless my soul! shall *I* ever come to this." People compliment me on my prodigious memory, because I have a knack of remembering rhymes—"hog" and "dog," and so forth ; but it's breaking down.'

B. took down Quarles's *Emblems* from the shelf, and turned it over. 'Whose pencil marks are these?'

'Mine,' I told him.

B. said, 'Quarles did a great deal for me—he was a man of great genius.' He read aloud passages here and there—*e.g.*

> She's empty : hark, she sounds, there's nothing there
> But noise to fill thy ear, etc.

Trust not this hollow world ; she's empty ; hark, she sounds.

And with especial relish the close of the dialogue of Eve and the Serpent—

> *Eve.*—   fruit's made for food :
> I'll pull, and taste, and tempt my Adam too
> To know the secrets of this dainty.
>
> *Serpent.*—Do.

'That's exquisite!' Browning said.

We talked of music. B. goes to all the best

concerts and musical parties he can. Spoke of people who know nothing at all of music. ' Last night at a private house—Joachim playing "Beethoven" ; Mrs. P., sitting next me, knew and cared absolutely nothing about it.'

I tried to say that there are people with *no* ear and also people with some, though not much, and these latter may, having sensitive and imaginative souls, be much moved by what *does* reach them ; and I instanced Carlyle—but had no sooner uttered the name than B., *more suo*, snatched the ball out of my hands, and ran off with it in another direction.

' Carlyle talks the most utter rubbish about Beethoven, knows absolutely nothing about it, etc. etc.' And went on to declare, in his rapid way, that no untrained person could know or feel anything of this high music. ' It cannot be reached *per saltum*—instead of a melody in a song or ballad, you have, in the harmonies and transitions, countless melodies melted and flowing and mingling,' and so on.

Browning asked for Gerald, took him in his arms and kissed him ; looked at Carlyle's mug.[1]

Hardly looked at Helen's drawing—talked contemptuously of Dizzy. 'Snobbishly changed his name from D'Israeli to Disraeli. D. a great tyrant to everybody. Told me he had never seen Carlyle, and I brought him up to Boehm's Statue.'

April 18.—Carlyle called at my house to-day. Looking into little Gerald's face he placed his hand lightly on the baby's head, saying solemnly, ' May God bless thee ! ' He then placed his arm across his own heart in a peculiar way, bowed his head and muttered or sighed something.

September 6.—We came back from Margate on Saturday. I called at Carlyle's on Sunday, and again

---

[1] A silver mug given to Gerald, on which is inscribed, in facsimile of Carlyle's hand-writing : 'Gerald Carlyle Allingham, his little Cuppie. (T. C. 1875.)'

on Tuesday about three, but he was gone out both times. To-day, about half past two, he and Mary called here ; they went into the parlour. C. looking well and very neatly dressed—a long dark frock-coat and a straw hat dyed black. Says he is rather better than he was. Goes out every day about two, takes an omnibus to the top of Regent Street, walks along Portland Place and back again southward, and takes a Brompton omnibus back again. To-day he wished to walk with me. We went through S. K. station and up through Brompton Churchyard to Hyde Park, and by his favourite road, that between the Ride and the Serpentine, sitting down a while on a free bench. He has not been at the sea this year. 'Mary found a lodging at Littlehampton which she thought would do, but I dreaded noise. Have suffered dreadfully from sleeplessness lately.'

We talked of the mischievousness and cruelty of many human beings.

'Many children are taught no kind of feeling for others, and they come to care nothing about seeing or doing hurt ; it amuses them. When I was in the habit of riding about the suburbs of London, I found the populace looked upon me as a kind of strange unfortunate being, and the object they proposed to themselves for the moment was to make me as much more uncomfortable as possible. One evening a crowd of idlers did their best to make my horse jump over the parapet of a small bridge. They didn't want me to be killed or smashed, I suppose—didn't think about it, only wanted some "fun." I rode through them, keeping my whip ready—I may very likely have administered a lash or two, I don't remember. Can you lend me some books ? I am much at a loss for a good book. I took to Marlowe the other day, having heard much praise of him. He's utterly absurd and intolerable. Yes, his language is fine sometimes, but generally inflated beyond all measure.'

> And hollow pamper'd jades of Asia,
> Which cannot go but thirty miles a day !

a quiz on Marlowe, and C. laughed.   Faustus—scene
with the devils. 'He's in terrible fear of the devils,
and yet he doesn't believe in any devils.'

W. A.—'The Old Dramatists in general are very
disappointing.'

C.—'Very, and Marlowe's the worst I have come
across—entirely illogical and unreasonable.   In fact not
one but Shakespeare is worth anything.   Well, Ben is
sensible and able—rather prosaic.'

[C. said one day]—'Ben Jonson had quite recog-
nisably an Annandale face.   His Father was an
Annandale man, who spelt his name " Johnson."   He
moved to Carlisle, where Ben was born.'

W. A.—'Was his mother an Annandale woman ? '

C.—'I know not, but very likely she was.   When
Johnson died, she married a bricklayer, who brought
up young Ben to his trade.'

October 6.—Carlyle has been reading *As You Like
It*.   He said that 'After Swift (whom he had been
looking into lately) it was like a sea-bath ; Shakespeare
was a man of many *thŏ'ts*, most delicate and sweet.'
Carlyle always pronounced *thoughts* thus.   It is touching to find him, in his old age, turning so warmly
to Shakespeare the Poet, and in his most poetical
utterances.

CHAPTER XVI

1877

January 12.—With Carlyle—Christianity—age fifteen, spoke to his mother—her horror. 'Did God Almighty come down and make wheelbarrows in a shop?' She lay awake at night for hours praying and weeping bitterly.

'This went on about ten years. Goethe drove me out of it, taught me that the true things in Christianity survived and were eternally true ; pointed out to me the real nature of life and things—not that he did this directly ; but incidentally, and let me see it rather than told me. This gave me peace and great satisfaction.'

In omnibus—'I have a notion of a carriage for myself.' I approved—'but, oh dear! I care little. I see nothing but the shadows of coming events and images of the past. They come back—very strange— most vividly, early things in my life.

'I am much disappointed in my reading in the Greek dramatists—now reading Aristophanes, a blackguard fellow. Disappointed with the Tragic Dramatists, too. Æschylus's *Prometheus* very striking. One thing struck me, the awful sense those Athenians, too, had of this Human Life of ours.'

W. A.—'Alfieri—like Byron?'

C.—'Yes, something, more sense. Racine much the highest of the French Dramatists.'

He then spoke of 'that woman too — what call

you her ? Prunty ? Brontë ? they are writing in such a solemn tone about. God bless me ! I remember reading her first novel and saying " this is a woman, and very nearly mad." 'Tis in that she gives us a wooden figure in the shape of a man, that gesticulates and curses by machinery.'

' Rochester ? '

' Ay, that's it ; not an atom of flesh and blood in it.'

I told him Swinburne's verdict, ' the one supreme masculine figure,' or something like that ; which amused him a little. I added that there was a good deal of real experience infused into *Jane Eyre*—and then let it drop. We parted at the hall door, he saying, ' I'm glad you are near me again. Come again soon.'

Some consider Carlyle's Scottish dogmatic breeding to have been fortunate for him, but I cannot think so, even though he believed this himself. It was burned and branded into his youthful conscience and imagination. It could not be made to fit in with ' facts '— hence, what sufferings ! what rages ! He was contemptuous to those who held to Christian dogmas ; he was angry with those who gave them up ; he was furious with those who attacked him. If equanimity be the mark of a Philosopher, he was, of all great-minded men, the least of a Philosopher.

January 27.—To Carlyle about 10 in the evening— very friendly and sympathetic about *Fraser*—says he cannot at all understand Fr.'s conduct. ' It may prove to be a good thing for you, after all. I often thought with dissatisfaction that you were giving up your time to this Magazine. You must write something valuable, as you are capable of doing.' He then praised *Seven Hundred Years Ago*. ' I have read nothing so good since in any Magazine.' [1]

[1] After Mr. Froude's return from his official Colonial tour, the renewal of his editorship of *Fraser's Magazine* was suggested, but the plan fell through, and Allingham was asked to continue the management : this he did until the publication of the Magazine ceased altogether, a few months later.

He came down to the street door and shook hands with me again on the door-step.

Saturday, March 3.—To C. about 2.30. Mary and Madame Venturi in parlour. Portrait of De Quincy—'untruthful man; story of girl in *Opium Eater* all untrue.'

At the top of Oakley Street we pause a moment at the crossing to let a hansom-cab go by, but the Driver on his part politely pulls up to give us time, saying, 'All right, Mr. Carlyle!' C. and I get inside an omnibus. Passing the Chinese Embassy we saw a servant in yellow silk, and C. was reminded of the Learned Man in *The Two Fair Cousins*, a Chinese novel which he always had pleasure in recalling. He began telling the story, and spoke as usual of the Author 'as a Man of Genius of the dragon pattern.' He asked, 'Do you know the root of the word *ten*? I made a guess at it when I was washing my feet the other morning. *Zehen* is "toes" in German, and *Zehn* "ten" = "toe-en," as it were. I took up the Arabic numerals one day, and made out the meaning of the signs.'

I told him of my guess of the forms of many letters of the alphabet coming from the shapes of the mouth in saying them; which was new to him and not without interest.

April 11.—C. very sympathetic about H.'s serious illness.[1] Millais is to paint him.

April 13.—Carlyle and Mary call : sorry about H.

Wednesday, May 16.—C. and I in Brompton and Islington omnibus ; rain begins, and turns to a heavy pour : so not alighting at Oxford Circus we go on and on, to the Angel at last, and the omnibus stables, whence, after a wait in the yard, we return S.W. with fresh horses. C. shows me the street, next St. James's, Pentonville, where he had his first London lodging. Edward Irving lived in Myddelton Square.

---

[1] After the birth of her daughter, Eva Margaret, on February 21st of this year, Mrs. Allingham was ill for several months.

Turkey—'Dizzy wants a war, to show himself like a second Chatham. He's a very bad man.'

Thursday, *May* 24.—Modern Atheism—Clifford, etc. C. said, 'I know nothing whatever of God except what I find within myself—a feeling of the eternal difference between right and wrong.'

June 24.—Carlyle is going through Gibbon's *Decline and Fall* (not read since his youth). 'I find it entirely below my expectations, the style is laboriously antithetical—and he doesn't lay out his history well ; there are many chapters where a mere tabular statement ought to have sufficed. I should have liked him also to hang out more frequent general elucidations in the way of dates. On the whole, it is very disappointing.'

I reminded C. that Gibbon was one of the writers whom he strongly recommended to me, many years ago, saying, 'Gibbon is always worth meeting.' He replied, 'Oh, one must read Gibbon to get any insight into this wild history of mankind.'

The New Republic rather amused him, but he 'could not believe the writer meant a single word he said.'

October.—To C.'s about 3.30. Mrs. Lecky there. To Queen Anne St. and call on Erasmus Darwin. Talk of Mr. Martin's Biography. Carlyle wrote to *Athenæum* : 'Mr. Frederick Martin has no authority to concern himself with my life—of which he knows nothing.' He remarked that many old things came back clearly which he had not thought of for a great many years.

I asked how far back his memory went. He told of something that happened when he was less than two years old. 'An uncle of mine sent me the gift of a small wooden can—they called it a noggie—to eat my porridge from. The can had two bottoms and some small pebbles between that rattled,—but this was a profound secret to me at the time, the source of the rattling. One day finding myself alone in the kitchen with my noggie, I conceived the scheme of making some porridge for myself, and for the first stage I poured water into my noggie and set this on the kitchen fire to boil. After a little, however, it all suddenly blazed up, and out I rushed shrieking with terror—I was under two, I don't know how much. It must have been some months later, probably in 1798, that we moved from one house to another. A pathway and short-cut led between the two, across a field known to the satirical villagers as Pepper Field, because the owner was said to have made his fortune in the West Indies. I was allowed to suppose myself helping in the flitting, and I recollect very well carrying the stoup or nozzle of a watering pot across Pepper Field and blowing through it like a horn, feeling at the same time a great exultation—some kind of false joy, I suppose, for I don't think I was very happy at the time.'

Going out we found it was a quarter to six. 'Bless me !' said C., 'what an old fool I have been to sit there talking useless stuff when I ought to be at home,' and we hurried to the omnibus as fast as age allowed. He usually takes half an hour's sleep before dinner, and is very methodical in all his ways.

C. to-day praised highly 'Modern Prophets' in *Fraser*, said it would be a satisfaction to many minds. 'You have left these Prophets "sitting on their seats of honour," but you have been more good-natured to them than I could have been—though there is plenty of satirical pungency too.'

He asks leave to send the article to his brother, and I tell him he is welcome to the copy.

Saturday, *October* 27.—To C. about 4. C. and I to King's Road. Chelsea omnibus to Charing Cross. We walk down the Embankment as far as Somerset House, 'one of the most dignified buildings in London.'

Browning's *Agamemnon*. 'Oh yes, he called down some months ago to ask if he might dedicate it to me. I told him I should feel highly honoured. But—O bless me ! *Can you understand it, at all?* I went carefully into some parts of it and for my soul's salvation (laughs) couldn't make out the meaning. If any one tells me this is because the thing is so remote from us—I say things far remoter from our minds and experiences have been well translated into English. The book of Job, for instance. It's bad Hebrew, I understand, the original of it, and a very strange thing to us. But the translator said to himself, " the first thing I have to do is to make this as intelligible as possible to the English reader ; if I do not this I shall be—h'm—I shall be—in fact *damned*." But he succeeded most admirably, and there are very few books so well worth reading as our Book of Job.

'Yes, Browning says I ordered him to do this translation—he winds up his preface (highly to his own satisfaction, in a neat epigrammatic manner) by saying so,—summing it all up in a last word ; and I did often enough tell him he might do a most excellent book, by far the best he had ever done, by translating the Greek Dramatists—but O dear ! he's a very foolish fellow. He picks you out the English for the Greek word by word, and now and again sticks two or three words together with hyphens ; then again he snips up the sense and jingles it into rhyme ! I could have told him he could do no good whatever under such conditions.'

C. spoke of Swinburne—'there is not the least intellectual value in anything he writes.'

We spoke of the convicts Baxter and Swindlehurst, and agreed that many business people of high repute (even including some publishers) deserved no better a fate.

November.—Carlyle, Lecky and I take omnibus to Oxford Street, then walk up Portland Place.

The Brougham—'Oh, I shall give that up—I find instead of it being *mine*, I should be *its*. I cannot go whither I would—the man cannot find out the places. Mary, I believe, has some other plot : I must keep my eye on her !'

Sunday, November 25.—Ask Tollman at new bridge,
'Seen Mr. Carlyle?'

'Yes, gone round other bridge, with two gentlemen.'
I over and meet them in Battersea Park. Carlyle, Sir
James Stephen, and a quick-eyed, good-looking, semi-
American old young man who talks very fluently and
well on China and Japan. 'The Japanese are trying
the languages and systems of England, France,
Germany, Holland.' Describes the suicide, by order
of the Tycoon, of a noble who fired on some foreigners :
temple, by night—dirk or knife wrapt in silver paper
on small table of white wood. Speech—bows—throws
off upper garment—cuts his belly across—head cut off
by friend.

It is Mr. Mitford (*Tales of Old Japan*), now in the
Woods and Forests Department.

November 29.—Carlyle is very weary and depressed
—'unwilling to live longer—but must be patient.
Mary is planning a horse and carriage. Omnibus has
advantages and is decidedly economical—but a carriage
might help me. But nothing can give me any
satisfaction at this date I have arrived at,' he adds.
'But I am better off than many a one. I am free of
an irritability of nerves that tortured me a year ago.
Things hurt me and rankled in me, I know not at all
why. The recollection, for instance, of some man I
knew forty years ago perhaps—often some one I had
but the slightest acquaintance with, or only knew by
eye—would suddenly, without any reason at all, come
into my mind, and prick into me in the most painful
manner. That is all over now.'

December.—H. and I dined at Surgeon Clover's ;
Mr. and Mrs. Stebbing, Mr. and Mrs. Townsend
(*Spectator*). Clover was at Chislehurst during last
illness of the 'Emperor.' 'Empress very easy and
pleasant, and seemed so well pleased with anything I
said that I never felt more at ease in my life.

'Emperor said, " Now, you'll do what you think fit

(about the chloroform), I know nothing about it."
Once, after waking up from sleep, he sighed and said,
" I thought I was at Sedan."

'He forgot much of his English, not an unusual
thing in illness. His brain was *very large* : it was
weighed after his death and found to approach Cuvier's
in weight.' I told Clover what I heard Owen say of
him : Prince Louis Napoleon visited the Museum of
the College of Surgeons while Owen was Curator.
Owen observed him narrowly—'And I came to the
conclusion, from·his whole appearance, and especially
his *bony conformation*, that he was certainly not of the
Napoleon family.'

December 5. — C.'s about 3.20 — dressing. Enter
Mary : ' Flowers for Birthday yesterday, and letters.

' Mme. Venturi came at ¼ past 11 at night—couldn't
let her up ; we actually quarrelled, for the first time.'

Carlyle and I in the Chelsea omnibus to Charing
Cross : 'This is the second day of my eighty-third
year—no doubt of that ! Browning came down yesterday, he has a great deal to say about many things. I
must go and see him. I told him frankly about the
Agamemnon, after praising his fidelity, that I could make
nothing of his translation—could not understand it—
had to turn to the Jesuit's book. R. B. admitted that
all said it was of no use.'

(I spoke of *Athenæum* and *Academy*, which praised
it.)

C.—'I still exhorted him to give us, as the best
possible thing, a Greek Theatre, done like that from
Euripides in *Balaustion*. He said the *Agamemnon* text
is exceedingly corrupt (only one MS. known in the
world), much mauled by commentators.'

We walk to Bedford Street—Civil Service Stores.
Can't at first find the clothing department. Carlyle has
a coat tried on (after careful inquiries as to whether
this is the coat ordered at such a time—and 'is this the
man that took my measure? etc. etc.'). Walk back

to Charing Cross. He speaks of Johnson's house in
Gough Square, praises once more the *English Dictionary*.
Asks me what number of *Fraser* ' Modern Prophets '
is in? a blind old gentleman in Scotland wishes to
have it read to him.

C. asks me about MacMahon, and says, ' In a
century or less all Europe will be republican—democratic; nothing can stop that. And they are finding
out their old religions, too, to be mere putrid heaps of
lies.'

Friday, December 21. — To Carlyle's. Louis
Napoleon—' Met him at dinner—he made up to me
rather, understanding me to be a writer, who might
perhaps be of help to him somehow. His talk was a
puddle of revolutionary nonsense. He was internally
a mass of darkness. I used to meet him often in the
street, mostly about Sloane Square, driving a cab, with
a little tiger behind ; his face had a melancholy look
that was rather affecting at first, but I soon recognised
that it was the sadness of an Opera Singer who cannot
get an engagement. When I heard of him afterwards
as Emperor, I said to myself, " Gad, sir, you've got an
opera engagement such as no one could possibly have
expected ! " '

[One day the following talk took place.]
Carlyle, Lecky and I.

C. praised Sir Robert Peel, ' the only tolerably good
minister I have known.' Catholic Emancipation :
' Peel resisted that a long time,' L. said.

C.—' He could not venture sooner. You have no
notion what a feeling there was against it. In our
country, at least in the southern part, I knew of only
one other person besides myself who was in favour of it.'

L.—' Lord Melbourne said, " All the wise men in
the kingdom were of one opinion on this, and all the
d——d fools of the other ; and it turned out that all
the d——d fools were right ! " '

C.—' Quite true.'

CHAPTER XVII

1878–1879

Thursday, January 10.—Fine but cold. To C. about 2.30, and drive with him in brougham, Lecky with us, by Clapham, etc. He insists that Wandsworth is 'Wodensworth'; I bring up the River Wandle, and he makes out Wandle to be 'Woden's Dale.' He then speaks of Ireland and Cromwell, we (especially L.) silently dissenting. We drive in Richmond Park, see deer ; get out and walk a little. Pass near Owen's cottage and see a man like O., but who turns out not to be any such man.

C. speaks with his usual contempt of Parliament, but allows that it gives a safety-valve.

January 23.—Carlyle and I drive in brougham to Richmond Park : 'People set about writing History in an entirely wrong manner. They ought to try and *see* the people and events, and set them forth in due order and all possible clearness.'

On health C. said, ' I have had stomachic disturbance ever since I was twenty ; otherwise quite healthy. It is very curious, the head is still the same, only the interest in things is nearly gone. I long ago felt that the greatest comfort was to be able to say, "This will not last for ever." Death is welcome whenever it comes. One thing is firmly held to—God, who arranges and decides all : this I am thankful to say I keep. And whoever uses honestly the light placed in his own mind,

acts as the voice of God tells him, will find satisfaction
therein, and not otherwise.'

Saturday, February 20.—To C. We drive to Queen
Anne St. and visit Erasmus Darwin in his warm
house (which he does not leave at this season). Talk
of Lecky's book ; of Turkey, etc. C. says, ' Dizzy was
on the point, months ago, of sending a fleet to Constantinople. I wrote a letter in the newspaper—it was
no merit in me ; the information was given me from
unquestionable authority, and his scheme was blown up as
by a torpedo ! He thought of bringing me before the
House of Commons to be questioned as to my authority ;
but I was very easy about this, as I understood from a
competent adviser that I had nothing to do but say, " I
will not tell you." '

Saturday, March 2.—Carlyle, Dr. Carlyle and I to
King's Road and have our hair cut. I keep a lock of
C.'s, which has still some brown in it. He says, 'Curious !
—that head (the Doctor's) is five or six years younger
than mine, the hair much whiter—softer too.'

We go in omnibus to Charing Cross.

C.—' Dizzy will not be allowed by the country to go
to war. People show the most complete ignorance of
Russia—talk like so many raging jackasses.'

We spoke of Lionel Tennyson's wedding ; going to
Spain for the honeymoon.

Monday, March 11.—To Cheyne Row 2.30. Drive
to Dover St. C. speaks with admiration of Ruskin.
' A celestial brightness in him. His description of the
wings of birds the most beautiful thing of the kind that
can possibly be. His morality, too, is the highest and
purest. And with all this a wonderful folly at times !
The St. George's Company is utterly absurd. I thought
it a joke at first.'

March 29.—To C. at 2.30 ; with him and Mrs.
Lecky in brougham to Browning's, 19 Warwick
Crescent. B. (in rough gray dress) received C. with
great emphasis.

'How good and dear of you to come! dear Mr. Carlyle! How dear!' and took him upstairs on his arm.

Pen's large picture in drawing-room, 'The Worker in Brass, Antwerp,' intended for Royal Academy. Old man with hammer and punch finishing a metal dish with rim of dolphins—medallion of Rubens on the floor —pipe on stool—watch hanging on wall.

C., placed in an arm-chair, looked at the picture without speaking; B. went on describing it, from time to time. At last C. said, looking at B., '*Antwerpen*— on the wharf—that is the meaning of the name. It used to be said there was *hand* in it, but that is not so. *On the wharf* is the meaning.'

C. asked questions about Pen; asked me, is the medallion like Rubens? but said nothing of the Picture.

C. asked B. the name of his new poem, but B. evaded. 'I'll let it speak for itself.' We departed; B. giving his arm to C. downstairs and out to the carriage.

C. spoke of Darwinism. 'I don't care three ha'pence for the Darwinian Theory.' By and by he said, 'It is impossible to believe otherwise than that this world is the work of an Intelligent Mind. The Power which has formed us—He (or It—if that appears to any one more suitable) has known how to put into the human soul an ineradicable love of justice and truth. The best bit for me in Kant is that saying of his, "Two things strike me dumb with astonishment—the Starry Heavens and the Sense of Right and Wrong in the Human Soul."

'These physical gentlemen ought to be struck dumb if they properly consider the nature of the Universe.'

Mrs. Lecky suggested that investigation as well as reverence was natural to man, and would not Mr. Carlyle permit inquiry? 'Oh yes,' he said (half jestingly), 'man is full of curiosity—but I would order these

people to say as little as possible. Friedrich Wilhelm's
plan would be the right one with them, " Hold your
tongue or else— " '

Carlyle has taken again to reading Goethe.

Saturday, March 30.—Helen and I to an evening
party at Tennyson's at 14 Eaton Square. Arrive 9.30.
Mrs. Tennyson on sofa. Mrs. Thackeray Ritchie and
husband, Browning, Gladstone and Mrs. Gladstone,
Paget, Duke of Argyll and daughter, Messrs. Matthew
Arnold, Lewis Morris, E. Gurney, F. Pollock.
Joachim plays ; T. and myself at end of piano.

He asks, ' Have you any politics ? ' Says, ' I can't
agree with you about Russia—you're a damned Irishman ! I've hated Russia ever since I was born, and
I'll hate her till I die ! '

W. A.—' What do you think of Dizzy ? '

T.—' I hate Dizzy, and I love Gladstone ; still, I
want Russia snubbed.'

Spedding joined the conversation, and was also
against Russia as Russia. (Carlyle always supports
Russia as Russia.)

F. Locker, Aïdé, Mrs. Huxley (asks us for Sunday
week), Huxley girls.

May 2.—We all go to Shere, H. and I, Sonny and
Sissy. Cottage delightful—woods—bluebells.

[The Allinghams stayed all the summer in Mr.
Bray's pretty old cottage—Allingham, as usual, busy
with his own work, besides *Fraser* ; his wife painting
' every day most assiduously.' There were pleasant
meetings with friends, too—Mr. Vernon Lushington,
Mrs. and Miss Procter (Mrs. P. ' loved the country—
for a few days ' !), Mr. and Mrs. Richmond Ritchie,
Mrs. Coleman Angell and her husband. But there are
no notes of talks at this time.

Allingham ' visited old John Linnell at his house
near Red Hill—eighty-six in June—deaf—hand steady':
also went to see George Eliot, at the Heights, Witley.]

October 24.—Chelsea. Returned after six months

in the country (Shere and Dover). Mary Aitken came in the evening. Her uncle is well.

October 26.—To Carlyle's to-day about three, and find him looking well. Mr. Paul Friedmann.

C., F., and I drive to Regent's Park, where I get out. We talk of Shere Ali ; of Dizzy ; 'England is disgraced ; never before has she had such a man at her head.'

Heligoland agitating to join Germany. Carlyle asks, 'was there an old religious establishment there ?'

Friedmann explains, 'Not *Heil*igo but *Heli*goland, which in old German means a rocky and sandy island. The people,' he added, 'were pirates and wreckers and would fain be so still. They will probably repent of joining Germany. England may some day give the island to Germany as *quid pro quo.*'

Monday, October 28.—Go down to C.'s at 5 P.M. on business (M.'s American Railway Shares). C. (returned from his drive) comes into the drawing-room in his dressing-gown and sits down on the floor by the fireside, his back to the wall, his face guarded from the heat by a small screen hanging from the chimney-piece. Rose, a sturdy young serving-wench of rather rough manners, puts on his cap (which is shown in some of H.'s drawings), hands him his pipe, ready filled, and a spill—then a second spill, to provide against failure of the first. He lights his pipe and smokes.

'Mrs. Oliphant's book gives no picture of Irving, except in the letters to his wife—Irving was, on the whole, the finest fellow I have ever come across' (and yet, one must again reflect, what a futility was his life !)

Wednesday, October 30.—10 P.M. Carlyle and Mary call at our house and come upstairs—talk about Albury, 'Henry Drummond ; he invited me to Albury for a certain Saturday. I went, but D. was not there. The servant evidently took me to have felonious intentions ; but discovered by degrees I was not for stealing anything.'

C. tastes Helen's cup of milk. I show him engraved

portrait of old Mr. William Bray,[1] in his ninety-seventh
year, and tell him of my visit to old John Linnell
(himself approaching ninety now), the painter and
engraver of it, and how I saw a portrait of Carlyle in
the studio, done some fifty years ago. C. remembers
sitting for it.

'Entire failure as a likeness : was done for a Mr.
Cunningham, who would not have anything to do with
it when finished.'

Carlyle, coming away one day from a friend's house
where they had had a good luncheon, patted his niece
on the shoulder saying, 'Well Mary, we've had a
pleasant visit—but we're both rather drunk !' Mary
declared *she* had only taken water.

Wednesday, November 6.—H. went again to-day
about 12.30 to C.'s, and brought back two life-like
sketches in colour. He was mild and genial to-day,
and bade her come again.

C. said to me, 'Your wife is the *only* person who
has made a successful portrait of me, though many
have tried.'

November 14.—To Carlyle's at 2.30, and found
him stepping—slowly climbing—into the usual hired
carriage. He said, 'I feel I may die any time.'

I asked, 'Did you ever in early life think yourself
near death ? '

'Never,' he answered ; and then went on to tell
me of his Uncle Tom, the youngest of the brothers
—of a fine Roman character ; 'I looked up to him
with the greatest admiration and respect. He was ill,
and my mother used to sit up with him at night. (He
seems to have lived either in the same house or an
adjoining one.) One night I took the watch upon me,
to relieve her—I was about nineteen years of age—
and in the middle of the night it became clear that my
uncle was dying. He fixed his eyes upon me with a

[1] Given to Allingham by Mr. Bray of Shere.

wild stare—bright blue eyes—and tried to lift his head from the pillow, but could not do it, and the eyes kept wide open till life went out of them—ah dear!—it was about three in the morning. It was then I first began to make reflections upon death. He had no disease—a general break-up, mostly from hard work.'

'Had you any kind of orthodox belief in your mind at that time?'

'No, I had given all that up some time before, but I said nothing about it one way or another. I had asked my mother one day how it was known that Solomon's Song was symbolical, representing Christ and the Church, and she showed such boundless horror at my question that I resolved on silence thenceforth.'

C. spoke of the folly of Tyndall and others who went on about the origin of things; 'I long ago perceived that no man could know anything about that; but that the Universe could come together by chance was, and is, altogether incredible. The evidence to me of God—and the only evidence—is the feeling I have deep down in the very bottom of my heart of right and truth and justice. I believe that all things are governed by Eternal Goodness and Wisdom, and not otherwise; but we cannot see and never shall see *how* it is all managed.'

December 3.—To Carlyle's. Found Browning in the drawing-room, talking earnestly to him—'and here's Allingham'—talk, Lord Beaconsfield. Browning—'I met him at dinner last spring, and he was got up to look as much like a young man as he could.'

I.—'Had you any talk with him?'

B.—'Oh yes; he came up and said, "I daresay you don't recollect me"; I assured him I did.

'Then he said, "Oh yes, I remember you did me the honour to introduce yourself to me at the Academy dinner."

'I said, "I beg your pardon, it was *you* who did *me* that honour."'

December 4.—Carlyle's birthday. Helen and I went down about 2.30., and met the carriage, which pulled up and allowed us to shake hands. Mary, Mrs. Lecky and Mr. Graham were with him. He does not like more than just a greeting on his birthday.

December 5.—Carlyle, Mary and I in carriage—drove along the Embankment and stopped to see Cleopatra's Needle. C. put his head out of window and took one look, then leaned back, 'Ah yes—old Egyptian hands made that a long time ago.'

We drove to Tower Hill.

I asked him a question to-day I had often wished to ask : 'Do your thoughts ever turn to another life?' He answered : 'Oh, every day and every hour.' Then he went on to say, in slow semi-soliloquy, 'We know nothing. All is, and must be, utterly incomprehensible. Annihilation would be preferable to me to this state I am in. But I hold with Goethe' (and he repeated the verses in his own translation)—

> The Future hides in it
> Gladness and sorrow ;
> We press still thorow,
> Nought that abides in it
> Daunting us,—onward.
>
> And solemn before us,
> Veiled, the dark Portal,
> Goal of all mortal :—
> Stars silent rest o'er us,
> Graves under us silent !

'That is very fine,' he said, giving these two lines again—

> Stars silent rest o'er us,
> Graves under us silent !

Then went on—

> While earnest thou gazest,
> Comes boding of terror,
> Come phantasm and error,
> Perplexes the bravest
> With doubt and misgiving.

But heard are the Voices,—
Heard are the Sages,
The Worlds and the Ages :
'Choose well ; your choice is
Brief and yet endless.

Here eyes do regard you,
In Eternity's stillness ;
Here is all fulness,
Ye brave, to reward you ;
Work, and despair not.'

The last seven lines he gave with special distinctness.
Meanwhile we were driving slowly, with frequent stops,
through the dingy crowded Minories and Leadenhall
Street.

By and by he said, 'A thought that bewilders me
sometimes is the prodigious number of human beings
who have come and gone.'

W. A.—'Against this we can set the immeasurable
Space around us and its innumerable Worlds.'

C.—'I care very little about the stars. I look
round upon my fellow-creatures.'

W. A.—'But the multitude of mighty Globes is a
physical fact, as much as any other.'

C.—'Yes' (letting the subject drop).

Again he resumed. 'One thing Browning told me
the other day was a saying of Huxley's, "In the
beginning was hydrogen." Any man who spoke thus in
my presence I would request to be silent—"No more of
that stuff, sir, to me! (angrily). If you persevere I
will take means, such as are in my power, to get quit of
you without delay."'

To Carlyle's. Mr. Paul Friedmann. We three
drove out. Talk on Prussian affairs, and especially
Bismarck, whom F. thinks a despot. I was surprised
at C.'s not coming forward to defend the Chancellor,
but he seems to have got fresh lights on B.'s character
lately. He remarked, 'I hear he is a terrible fellow at
eating and drinking.' F. confirmed this, adding 'he

says himself he never gets drunk, but his friends do not

say so.' The book of conversations with B.'s secretary,
just published, was mentioned. I asked, 'was it
authentic?' 'Oh yes, it could not have been published
without B.'s full consent. His object is to keep himself
before the public.'

We then spoke of Morganatic marriages, on which F.
gave copious and apparently accurate information. He
said the ceremony is in no way peculiar, (he never heard
of the left hand being used) nor the status of the wife : the
only difference being in the succession of the children.

C. and F. entirely agreed with me as to the absurdity
of writing histories of centuries, or of treating those
artificial sections as real. The practice is very modern.
Histories of reigns, of great wars, or of famous person-
ages, were the usual forms of writing.

C. often declared that the driver was going wrong—
at last thrust his head suddenly out of the window, and
roared 'Where in the Devil's Grandmother's name are
you going?'

Carlyle has allowed Helen to sketch him as he reads
in his drawing-room from 12 to 2.30, and she has had
six sittings up to December 9. Helen writes—

'The first morning I went at Mary's invitation ;
after shaking hands with me C. left the room ; when he
returned I had arranged my things on the sofa, and M.
then called his attention to " our special artist." He
said " What ? " and added, when he understood, " I'll
have nothing to do with any sketching."

'At last M. persuaded him to let me stay, and he
sat down before the fire to read a translation of a
Russian poem (lent by Madame de Novikoff) ; he called
the poet a " blathering blellum."

'He often expressed a weariness of life, and wished
to be out of it ; and one day taking leave said, " Well,
ma'am, I wish you all prosperity, and that you may not
live to be seventy-two " (meaning eighty-two).

'One day he said, " As far as I can make out, the
best portrait-painter who ever lived was one Cooper, in

Cromwell's time. When painting Cromwell, Cromwell told him to put in the wart, and he did. I have spent much time in studying Cromwell's physiognomy."'

'Every day he asked after "Allingham and the bairns."'

Sunday, December 29.—Carlyle and I in omnibus. Rain, so we did not alight at Charing Cross, and I suggested our going into St. Paul's—to which, to my surprise, he agreed. He had not been there for many years. We ascended the west steps and went in by right-hand door. C. immediately pulled off his broad hat and we soon, arm-in-arm, turned into centre aisle. The Cathedral was lighted up and a sermon going on under the Dome.

C. said, ' Ah, this is a fine place ! '

I found seats on the edge of the seated congregation, where we had a good view up into the dim dome and along the vista of the choir. We could hear the preacher's voice but not the words. I tried to keep him till the end and the organ music.

'There is no doubt a very fine organ,' he said, ' and the Amen comes like nothing else in the world.' But by and by he became impatient : ' We can hear nothing— let us go.' So we glided out of our places, and went to look at the Wellington Monument, but he declared he could make out nothing of it.

He was full of praises of Wren and his work—' the grandest Cathedral he had ever seen,'—and spoke of his first day in London.

He arrived by water from Leith, and went up to Islington to Edward Irving whose guest he was. In the evening he found himself in view of St. Paul's, and has never forgotten the sight of it rising above the crowd of little houses.

We walked up and down St. Paul's Churchyard, and looked up at the dome—' Ay, it's a bonny thing.'

' Wren—a grand man—I lived for many years beside this Hospital of his before I took much notice of it, and then I began to perceive that it was a building of most thorough adaptation for its purpose—well contrived, well built in every particular.'

I remarked and C. agreed it was odd there should be no street in all London called after the great Architect.

When we parted he said, ' You have brought me along in a most beautiful manner to-day—many thanks.'

1879

In the cold weather of the early part of the year I saw Carlyle seldom. But in the end of January and in February I had three or four drives with him.

Our visit to St. Paul's pleased him so well that he went there on the five or six Sunday afternoons following with Mary, and was much impressed by the organ.

One Saturday we drove in Richmond Park, C., Mr. Friedmann and I.

F. spoke of Kant, and that the Germans were returning to him, which I was very glad to hear. C. said [as often before], ' Kant's notions of time and space struck me very much : I have felt greatly oppressed in thinking of the long duration of Time Past, and Kant offered a relief in the suggestion that Time may be something altogether different from what we imagine. I have no kind of definite belief or expectation whatever as to the Future—only that all will be managed with wisdom, the very flower of wisdom.'

Another day, he and I drove through Clerkenwell by a half-finished new street, and turned up to King's Cross : I reminded him of Swedenborg as we passed the corner of the jail, on which by the by is inscribed ' Mount Pleasant.'

He said, ' Ah yes, Swedenborg was fond of London. I never got much good of him. Emerson says he came nearer the secret of the world than almost anybody, but I never could see that he came near any secret at all. Still, I have a respect for him : I read his books with considerable interest.'

A long time ago, speaking to me of Swedenborg, C. said, ' he upset his platter ' : this is probably a proverbial expression.

February 22.—Drove with Carlyle.—Darwin and Haeckel. C. : ' For Darwin personally I have great respect ; but all that of " Origin of Species," etc., is of little interest to me. What we desire to know is, who is the Maker ? and what is to come to us when we have shuffled off this mortal coil. Whoever looks into himself must be aware that at the centre of things is a mysterious Demiurgus—who is *God*, and who cannot in the least be adequately spoken of in any human words.'

March.—I asked C. if he was going to St. Paul's to-morrow.—' I think not, after what I got at Westminster Abbey last Sunday ! '

W. A.—' How did you like the preacher ? '

C.—' Like him (glaring). I felt a very strong appetite to lay my stick about his head ! I did not say this aloud, but I thought it emphatically.'

' What was the sermon about ? '

' Oh, something about adversity and affliction, and what fine things they are. I should say *he* would be highly unwilling to undergo the slightest affliction he could escape.' Then, raising his voice, ' Oh, it's perfectly horrible—what was once a religious worship ! He would have been greatly surprised if he could have looked into me and have seen the strokes that were prepared for him, and the kicks on his seat of honour.'

We then spoke of Dean Stanley, and C. repeated his old saying about him that ' he skated on the thinnest ice of any theologian he had ever heard of.' He added, ' but you can see when you look at his face that he has no misgivings about the part he is playing : he holds there are fine things underlying all this.'

Drove with Carlyle. C. and I spoke of Hamlet.

C. said he was much struck on reading Hamlet again.
He made light of the difficulty about 'no traveller
returns.'—'Oh, Shakespeare found it would not do to
bring in the ghost when he was discussing these grave
matters : Hamlet did not really believe in the ghost.'
I told him of the curious point as to the description
of the plot of the strolling actors' play beforehand by
one of the players : that it had been discovered that
this was customary in Denmark in old times, though
no instance of it is known in England.

About this time Carlyle's health suddenly worsened :
beginning it was thought from a chill, and the action of
his heart. He became alarmingly weak. He ceased
for a time to drive out : was very languid and slept
much : he sometimes looked very sunken and low.

One day I went down and creeping into the
drawing-room found him asleep on the sofa :—creeping
back again I met Ruskin coming up the stairs, by
appointment. Mary said it was time to awaken him
and did so. They greeted each other affectionately,
and Ruskin knelt on the floor, leaning over Carlyle as
they talked. Carlyle began to speak of Irish saints,
and referred to me for some account of Saint Bridget
and her shrine at Kildare, to which I added that Bride-
well, that is St. Bride's well, had come to mean a prison.

This seemed to interest Ruskin particularly, and he
remarked, 'We make prisons of the holiest and most
beautiful things!'

He then took leave, very affectionately kissing
Carlyle's hands ; and he and I walked together to my
house where he greeted Helen with much *empresse-
ment*, and sat for about half an hour looking at her
drawings. He examined them through a pocket-micro-
scope : 'I am glad to see you paint sunshine : I am
always wanting Walter [Severn] to do so : he can paint
rainbows, but he prefers to paint gray days.' A lady
present remarked, 'There are so many gray days.'

Ruskin.—'The Devil sends them.'

The lady thought they had a charm; but Ruskin insisted that they always came from diabolical influence. *Sunday, May* 4.—To Cheyne Row about 2.15. C. complained, in her presence, of Mary's having ordered the carriage to come to-day : he wanted to go in the omnibus. I proposed to take him; and, the carriage not appearing in time, we walked slowly to Oakley Street and got into his favourite vehicle—his first trip of the kind these many weeks. The conductor showed special attention, and C. got his favourite seat, namely, next the door on the left-hand side—that on which the conductor's perch is. At Temple Bar we got out, and he consented to come into the Middle Temple, where he said he had never been before in his life. We entered, after a slight demur of the janitor (it being Sunday), by the gate and lane leading to the porch of the Temple Church. 'Close by,' I said, 'is Goldsmith's grave.' 'Where is it?' said C., and crept slowly on my arm till we stood beside the simple but sufficient monument, a stone about coffin length, and eighteen inches high. I read aloud the inscriptions; C. took off his broad-flapped black hat saying, 'A salute.' I followed his example, and thus we stood for a few seconds. When our hats were on and we were turning away, C. laughed and said, 'Strange times, Mr. Rigmarole!' Then, 'Poor Oliver!—he said on his deathbed, "I am not at ease in my mind."'

We now heard the organ rolling in the Church, and C. said, 'Can't we go in and sit down there?' We went to the porch, the great door yielded and showed us, better than I hoped, plenty of seats just inside. We sat down in the middle of the round part. I showed C. the recumbent figures of Templars, and he said, with rather alarming audibility, 'Aye, they were so poor that two of them rode on one horse, and they were the richest and powerfullest of orders in their day.' Then the organ and chanting began and filled

us both with responsive waves of feeling.

Carlyle said one day, 'Black's *Oliver Goldsmith* is worth nothing at all, he gives no credible Goldsmith.'

Friedmann. — '*The Vicar of Wakefield* is given to young Germans for their first book in English.'

C.—'I read the *Vicar* again lately, and was disappointed.'

W. A. thought the latter part of it much below the beginning.

Monday, June 10.—Helen, I and Sonny call at Carlyle's about 2. Sonny (aged 3½) says, 'How do you do, Mr. Carlyle?' C. shakes hands with him, and puts a hand on the curly head, saying 'O, this is a very good kind of article.'

[One day Mr. Lecky and Allingham drove out with Carlyle.]

Carlyle discoursed on Cromwell and Ireland : L. and I disagreeing with almost everything he said, but chiefly in silence. What use in speaking? on Irish affairs he finds nobody but Froude to agree with him. The Duke of Wellington—'Lord Stanhope (L. told us) asked the Duke one day in company, Why in a certain Peninsular battle the French did not move in such and such a way?' —obviously, he implied, the proper thing to have done. (Any one who has seen Lord Stanhope can easily picture the self-satisfied manner in which the noble historian would put this question.) The old Duke replied gruffly, 'Because they were not damned fools!'

September 2.—Left home about 9—Lancaster—Carnforth—to the westward wide hills and vales and misty mountain-land, ante-room and portals to the Lake region.

Kendal, scatter of houses along the hill-side ; and Lake-land, lying under clouds and mists.

Ullswater in the twilight, water gray and wintry, woods and mountains beautiful, old trees hanging into lake.

September 3.—To Patterdale—Aira Force—Penrith. —Dumfries, Hotel. Read in Burns's *Life*.

September 4. — Dumfries. Seek Burns Street, not easy to find — formerly 'Mill Hole.' New School House with bust of R. B.; and next door Burns's little house, unaltered. Into the house. Portrait of R. B. in lower room. Upstairs, — little room where he died (certain?), little closet where 'tis said he used to write. Walk over Old Bridge, lane, thatched cottages — cornfields, hills, Criffel, wide cheerful prospect.

Cassilands — ' Mr. Carlyle gone — to the Hill,' I walk down to town — speak to decent elderly man. ' Mr. Carlyle? — yes — he's been stopping here at Cassilands. I never heard much about him till last year — I understan' he's vera clever. No Sir, I never read any o' his warks. What may he hae written?' (I told him.)

To the Hill, pretty red-stone house, in shrubbery, with peep of the hills to eastward.

Portraits of Carlyle, Mary — Enter Mrs. Aitken. The Doctor very ill, poor fellow : they don't know what it is. A doctor has been here, ' but you know he (*i.e.* Dr. Carlyle) has no belief in medical skill.' T. C. with Mary and Alick, at Moffat.[1]

Out. River, sweeping round, houses, low wall — beautiful. Up Nith pathway, trees, fields, swift river (reminds me of Erne).

' Globe Tavern ' — small snug rooms, Burns's corner and chair (boarded in), narrow forked entrance — rough stable-yard — upstairs, writing on panes.

> Gin a body meet a body
> Comin' through the grain,
> Gin a body kiss a body
> The thing's a body's ain.

(There was, and perhaps is, a way through the stable-yard and back lanes from the ' Globe ' to Burns's house in Mill Hole.)

I also saw where he lived in Bank Street (*i.e.* river-

[1] Mr. and Mrs. Alexander Carlyle, newly married, had just been joined by Mr. Carlyle at Moffat.

bank?) a few doors from the corner of the wide space
by the River (which reminded me of Ballyshannon).

September 5.—To Beattock—Moffat. Buccleuch
Arms—enter Mary, friendly greetings—then Alexander. We go up into Carlyle's room—he shakes
hands in friendly wise.

After luncheon we four drive to the De'il's Beef-Tub.

Mary recalled Carlyle's first journey to Edinburgh,
on foot, at the age of fourteen.

C.—'Ah yes—about seventy years ago, I came
through here, in the charge of a very decent man who
was driving two carts of potatoes up to Edinburgh.
When I got tired, he let me lie on the potatoes and
happed me in some sort of covering he had.'

On this youthful journey Carlyle peeped at the
source of the Annan in the De'il's Beef-Tub—a hollow
under Hartfell with steep sloping green sides, here and
there a streak of loose stones, and some little threads of
water slipping down.

Over the hill, not far, is the source of Tweed, which
I would fain have seen (there is a strong attraction in
river sources), but rain threatened. We saw a long
way down Annandale : Annan is doubtless the same as
Avon, Evan, etc. etc.—various forms of one of the
Gaelic words for water.

To-night we took up Burns, and Carlyle urged me
to read something—'Let me see how you'll read it.'
I began 'The muckle deevil wi' a woodie Harle.'

He stopt me at every line, catechising. He then
read and repeated several pieces, showing great tenacity
and readiness of memory. He uttered a verse of 'Auld
Lang Syne' in a kind of chant, evidently intended to
suggest that he was singing it, or could sing it if he
liked. One word of his version was different from
the words in the usual copies, and perhaps better :
instead of

> An' here's a hand, my trusty fiere,
> An' gie's a hand o' thine—

C. said,

— gie's a haud (a hold) o' thine.

September 6.—Moffat. Fine. In open carriage, C., M., A., and I for Ecclefechan ; they going on to Newlands to meet James Carlyle and others.

At Lockerbie we stopt half an hour to bait the horses. I walked through the village and returning to the carriage found him seated there (horses gone) with his thick gray hair uncovered. Barefooted children ran about, people stood at shop-doors, no one appeared to recognise him. As we approached Ecclefechan he talked a little of the localities, pointed out the wooded hill called Woodcockair, and Repentance Tower—also the conspicuous flat-topt hill known as ' Burnswark ' [Birrenswark], from which one can ' look down into Yorkshire,' and on which stood a Roman city. We skirted Ecclefechan, and they drove on after dropping me. A few steps brought me into the village street and before the humble house, or half-house, in which Thomas Carlyle was born. The small stone building has a gateway through the middle of it. On each side of this gateway is a tenement—of three rooms. In the right-hand tenement, in the [larger] room upstairs, the son of James and Margaret Carlyle was born on the 4th December 1795. The ascent to the upper rooms is by a steep flight of stone steps direct from the front door to a very small landing, from which the little room (birth-room) opens. Behind the tenement are two or three other rooms.

A brook emerges from an arch a little above the Carlyle house, and runs down past half a dozen houses —a source of perpetual pleasure to the bairns, some of whom are always ' paidling ' and trying to catch little fishes, which they call ' beardies.' In the other half of the house I found a girl of nineteen. After some chat I inquired had she ever seen Mr. Carlyle ? ' O aye, often enough.' ' Would you like to see him again ? ' ' No.'

At half-past four, as agreed, the carriage came, and stopt to take me up. Two or three small groups of villagers looked our way, but there was no kind of greeting or palpable recognition whatever. Imagine an Irishman of equal fame seen in his native place !

The scene of the family meeting, at which were fourteen small nephews and nieces, was Newlands, a farm occupied by one of James's sons. James is also tenant of Thomas's Farm, Craigenputtock. ' James never knew such bad times for farmers,' C. told me on the way back.

At Lockerbie we again stopt half an hour. C. sat in the carriage as before, I leant over the side and talked to him. While we talked a biggish man came out of the inn,—like a comfortable farmer, and bearing a general resemblance to C. as many of the men do here —he advanced to the carriage, took off his hat, and said in a slow distinct voice without any expression in his face or tone, ' I request the honour of shaking hands with you, Sir ; I understand you're Mr. Carlyle.' C. looked at him, and after some seconds said, ' Who *are* you, Sir ? '—the other, a little taken aback, ' O, I'm only a farmer in the neighbourhood—I'm an admirer of your writings, Sir, and I wished to shake hands with you. I asked permission to shake hands with the grandson of our national poet, Robert Burns, at Lockerbie Station, and it was granted to me.' C. slowly took off his glove and gave him a thin, brown hand. ' Ye're lookin' fresh, Mr. Carlyle,' says the farmer. ' Fresh,' returns C.—' I'm very old and very weak '—whereon the farmer, taking his hat off again, withdrew, while C. muttered, ' I wish you well, Sir.' We got back to Moffat about half-past eight—the weather having threatened rain, but kept up all through.

Sunday, September 7.—I walked in the morning up hill and by field path to Spa, some two miles, and drank a glass of the water—pretty glen and rocky brook.

In Moffat Street meet C. and Alick coming slowly across—rain begins—C. sits on a doorstep—we notice name on signboard ' Jannetson,' which C. says he never saw elsewhere. Back to inn, where C. comes with me into the common parlour and I read to him from the guide book an account of the source of Annan, etc.

In the evening I came into his room. Burns again —' poor fellow—utterly misplaced—the best songster ever lived.'

I said Burns showed no signs of improvement in conduct as he grew older. Did his wife make any attempts to reform him? No, C. thought, she tried little or nothing that way, thought it no use.

' I was once brought to see Mrs. Burns in her old age—she said little, nor did I. I had unspeakable feelings in looking upon her, as though it were one of the Greek tragic heroines—Clytemnestra herself!— Bonnie Jean !—She was a quiet, grave person, no good looks left.' C. spoke of how Burns took his death, coming late out of the ' Globe,' drunk, and sitting down on a stone (a louping-on-stane probably), which is still in the close, on a cold, freezing winter's night.

Strange that no one looked after him. It was doubtless too frequent a case to excite attention.

C. said, ' I remember a man in Annandale telling me that he saw Burns lying dead-drunk in the back-yard of the " King's Head," and totally unheeded, save by a passing look.'

Old John Tait, the sexton or bedral, shewed me the Mausoleum in St. Michael's churchyard of Dumfries, a foolish kind of greenhouse or glass-case enclosing a relievo of a clumsy Burns.

Burns's body was moved hither from its original resting-place under a simple, and far more expressive, slab.

Carlyle told me, ' I went up one morning early, before the graveyard was open, and climbed over the wall ; there were many tombstones of Covenanters to

be seen ; searching about in the grass I suddenly came
upon a flat stone with " Robert Burns " on it and the
dates : it was the most impressive experience of the
kind I have had in my life.'

Old Sexton Tait told me something of a grandson
of the Poet, who died in Dumfries a few weeks ago at
the age of fifty-eight.   He drank daily as much whisky
as he could get by ' sponging,' chiefly at the ' Globe
Tavern,' on folk who ' treated ' him in memory of the
National Bard.

He had in his middle life a recognisable likeness to
the Poet, and his father was still more like, ' with the
same black eyes (Carlyle told me)—only the *soul*
entirely wanting in them ; they had no depth,—their
darkness was like that of polished cannel coal.'   This
third Robert, lately dead, ' used to say (the Sexton told
me) he would like to have his grave here '—namely,
under a small tree in a corner of the enclosed ground,
in front of the mausoleum or glass-case.   ' He kennt
weel he wadna be allowed inside.'

There are illegitimate Burnses, I believe, still breathing vital air at Dumfries.   Better for his countrymen, for
mankind, and indeed for his own memory, if much less
noise had been made about the unlucky one's grave, if
the stone had been left in the churchyard grass to be
found by one and another pilgrim, not without tears.

I quoted to Carlyle Goethe's remark that, to win
high popular success and fame a man must have, not
only genius, but opportunity,—Napoleon inherited the
French Revolution, Burns the old Scottish Songs.   C.
did not appear to know how much Burns owed to the
old songs, as Mary and I went over some of the
instances.

C. said that while the Poet in his last illness was
staying at the Brow, some miles from Dumfries, he
heard one day a farm-labourer speaking of various
things he was busy upon, and Burns said with a deep

283

sigh, ' Ah ! those were my happy days '—meaning, when he was thus occupied. To which Carlyle added, ' Gilbert Burns used often to say that his brother's conversation was never afterwards so delightful as when they two were working in the field, or digging peat together. Robert was full of poetry and enthusiasm.'

September 8.—To the Grey Mare's Tail.

September 9.—Home—all well. Ready to start to-morrow for Broadstairs.

October 18.—We returned to town from Broadstairs, Oct. 15. I walked with my little son to Cheyne Row, and met Mr. Carlyle coming out of the door to his carriage ; he shook hands with Sonny, saying, ' Ah, he's a bonny lad ! ' C. looks well, and even says ' Things might be worse.'

December 4.—Helen and I to Cheyne Row. Carlyle's eighty-fourth birthday. Mrs. Lecky there. Browning and Ruskin are gone. C. on his sofa by the window, warm and quiet, wearing a new purple and gold cap. Gifts of flowers on the table. Birthday—' O dear.' He speaks of Ruskin, who, he says, is in better spirits than he was. Asks me what I think of R.'s paper on the clergy, in *Contemporary Review*. I own myself puzzled as to his real meanings. C. : ' Oh yes, he believes all that—Can you lend me some book to read ? —a large book, that I can have satisfaction with.'

[Allingham notes during the winter :—]

H. and I called on George Eliot, North Bank, first time since Lewes's death. She seemed well and cheerful. Herbert Spencer there. He talked of Art— ' people don't know what to admire—the Old Masters —folly ! The R.A. Exhibition better than all the Old Masters. The art of painting greatly advanced, etc. etc. St. Mark's a barbarous and unpleasing edifice.' George Eliot denounced ' the rain, or perpetual drizzle of criticism under which we live.'

—— George Eliot called. Carlyle portraits : H. wished to do *hers* : G. E. said she would ' consider.'

CHAPTER XVIII

1880

Wednesday, March 10.—I meet Carlyle's carriage in the street and get in. Mary alights, Alick stays. We drive through the Parks, looking green, to Swiss Cottage. Carlyle, poor man, lies back crookedly in his corner, noticing nothing of the outer world. Yet he seems rather better than last time, a dim fire still in his eyes, a dusky red in his cheeks. He talks of Erasmus Darwin, the elder, with respect—has been reading a life of him. '*The Loves of the Triangles* is a poor thing. The writer (Canning) knew very little about triangles.' On politics he remarked, ' This time will be memorable as the time when England was governed by a perfect Charlatan.'

March 18.—Mary and Alick came to us in the evening—Professor Tyndall and Mrs. T. had called on Carlyle, who brightened up. They talked of the *Fahrbenlehre*. C. hoped that Tyndall would get something out of all the labour Goethe had given to this subject. The Professor said Goethe had many excellent observations, but his theory was wrong.

Tyndall said, aside, to Mary, ' Say what he will (of weakness), I never saw him looking grander.'

April 19.—To Carlyle's about 2.30, found him on sofa, just awaked : Lecky by him. We got into the carriage, and were driven through Hyde Park and Regent's Park to Belsize Avenue, his most usual route ;

then turned. L. had met Renan and found him very agreeable. Renan reads English, but does not speak it. C. said, 'I am reading Shakespeare again. I read *Othello* yesterday all through, and it quite distressed me. O what a fellow that is—honest Iago! I was once at this Play at Drury Lane (it would be in Macready's time—but *he* did not do me any good in it), and when Emilia said—

> O the more angel she
> And you the blacker devil!

a murmur swelled up from the whole audience into a passionate burst of approval, the voices of the men rising—in your imagination—like a red mountain, with the women's voices floating round it like blue vapour, you might say. I never heard the like of it.' (I thought this a curious remark—the interpretation of sound by colour in it.)

Lecky recalled Macaulay's remark that an Italian audience would look on Iago as a comic character ; adding, 'I have seen the play in Italy and found it was as Macaulay said. Tricking husbands is the habitual occupation of the Comic Man of the Italian stage.'

I out in St. John's Wood, and call on George Eliot. She was looking well in a high cap and black silk dress. I told her of C. and Othello—'the red mountain and blue vapour.' 'Like an imaginative child's description,' she said.

[In the spring of this year the Allinghams went to Haslemere, where they remained through the summer. Tennyson and his Son were in Italy, and the family came to Blackdown later than usual.]

August 5.—Haslemere—very fine ; Helen and I started about 3.30 to walk to Tennyson's, as invited. In the shady lane the carriage overtook us, T. had kindly called for us. He was in the carriage with his little grandson, Alfred, in his nurse's lap, and Mr. Fields, an American guest. Little Alfred, aged three, had on the great Alfred's black sombrero, and the child's straw hat with a blue ribbon was stuck on the top of the poet's huge head, and so they drove gravely along. I followed on foot along the heath-fringed road on Blackdown, overlooking the vast expanses of light and shadow, golden cornfields, blue distances, from Leith Hill to Chanctonbury Ring. Walked through the house,[1] long hall open at each end, and found tea on the further lawn, smooth, shut in with shrubs. The view of the lower windows of the house is now shut out by the growth of twigs and leaves. A. T. in sombrero and gray suit, broad shouldered. He has been at Venice, Cadore, etc., with Hallam.

T. took me to a top room and out on the balcony to see 'the enormous view.' 'I sometimes see a spire out yonder (due east), but I don't know what it is.' Horsham I suggest, adding, 'Field Place is near it, Shelley's birthplace.' Below, H. sketched Don, the handsome old setter, Hallam keeping him quiet.

T.—'I gave Irving my *Thomas à Becket*. He said it was magnificent, but it would cost £3000 to mount it,—*he* couldn't afford the risk. If well put on the stage, it would act for a time, and it would bring me credit—but it wouldn't pay. The success of a piece doesn't depend on its literary merit or even on its stage effect, but on its *hitting* somehow. Miss Terry said "we act mechanically after a long run—but on a first night nobody suspects how we have our hearts in our mouths!"'

T. did not much approve Irving's *Shylock*. 'He made you pity Shylock too much. I told Miss Terry she ought, as advocate, to stand on the steps to gain advantage, instead of standing on the level—a little female thing—and looking up at him. The worst of writing for the stage is you must keep some actor always in your mind.'

Sunday, August 8.—Helen and I walked up—

---

[1] Aldworth.

reached the house about 4. Tennyson on the front terrace with his two dogs, Don and Grig. He asked Helen had she brought her paints to finish Don's portrait. 'No—why not? Sunday? No one with wits in their brain would object. It's as allowable as lawn-tennis. Boys play cricket now on a Sunday. It's High Church to play cricket.'

Lord Lytton's return from India. T. spoke in his favour. I object—the Afghan War, etc.

T.—'How can we know the rights and wrongs?'

W. A.—'An intelligent man has both the means and the right to form an opinion on public affairs now-a-days. The main particulars are soon published.'

T.—'I was arguing with the Duke of Argyll about Roumania and Turkey, and said to him, Why don't you answer me? He said, "You haven't read the Blue Books."'

Matthew Arnold—'"Something outside of us that makes for righteousness"—ugh!' (This is a sort of grunt of disgust very usual with T.)

'I was asked by some one in London, "Shall I ask M. A.?" I said I didn't much like dining with Gods!'

T. praised in a general way *Thyrsis* and *The Scholar-Gipsy*.

'*Thyrsis* very artificial,' I thought.

'So is *Lycidas*,' he said.

'But *Lycidas* came first and was in the spirit of its age.'

I brought in my hand Ferguson's Poems, the volume published in May. T. looked into it but soon put it down. He read 'The Widow's Cloak'—'I don't much care for it; I can't read anything, much less poetry. On account of my eyes—yes—the doctor says I must only read for half an hour at a time. I shouldn't like both eyes to go. Everything now looks as in a very dusky twilight.'

He asked had I read Browning's new volume? '"Clive" is the best.'

A letter from Browning this morning, about 'Clive,'
is produced. He says some reviewers have charged
him with altering the story of the duel because his
version is not that in the memoir by ———— ; but *there* it
is clumsily done, and Clive's suicide is so slurred over, in
the same book, that you might take it to have been an
ordinary death. Browning had his version from Mrs.
Jameson (while travelling in her company on the
Continent)—she having just heard it told by Macaulay
at Lord Lansdowne's table.

At dinner—the account in a New York paper (*The
Tribune*) of Lionel's wedding—'the Poet Laureate,
bent figure and tottering gait.'

'Why, there were five steps to come down,—no one
had told me of them ; I was looking for them in the
obscurity, lest I should tumble on my nose.'

Then T. spoke of satire in general. 'It's quite
dreadful to think of how satire will endure, no matter
how unfair, if well written. Look at Pope—

> Now night descending, the proud scene was o'er,
> But liv'd in Settle's numbers one day more.

The perfection of that brings tears into one's eyes—and
it pillories Settle for ever ! Everything will be in the
British Museum—even the newspapers.'

We agreed on the absurdity of accumulating newspapers there, too many books even. But how select ?
—Who is to be empowered to do it ?

A.—'Carlyle declares his father was the strongest-
minded man he knew, yet he would admit no poetry
into his house.'

T.—'He was right.'

A.—'Nor fiction of any sort.'

T.—'There he was wrong. But I suppose he was
an old Puritan.'

T. denounced vivisection most fiercely : declared he
would not owe his own life to a cruel experiment on a
dog.

He made Helen taste his wine (Vouvray) from his own glass, and took her into the drawing-room.

'If the pronunciation of the English language were forgotten, Browning would be held the greatest of modern poets, having treated the greatest variety of subjects in a powerful manner.'

(Calverley called Browning 'a well of English defiled.')

Wednesday, August 11.—About 4 Tennyson calls with little Alfred and baby Charley (whom T. calls 'The Philosopher ').

'Don died on Sunday night. Hallam heard him howling, and thought there might be strangers about.'

Tea in the garden under apple tree ; T. praises the house, likes the steps in the garden, etc.

'Done by an artist—that accounts for it.' [1]

Friday, August 13.—Helen and I with the babes to Tennyson's. He sits on chair beside us. Two Miss ——s call (very old family). Tennyson tells us afterwards 'A former Lord H——, queer old fellow—was found on his knees near the kitchen one day riddling the cinders—he looked up and said, " Dick never riddles 'em right." He kept his two daughters in the nursery till they were thirty, and then they climbed over the garden wall and ran away. The young ladies to-day would have my autograph — ugh ! I said, " the glory of your presence has got it. I would never have sent it if you had asked by letter." '

Fair and dark people — dark people are thinner skinned.

T.—' I am. A countryman in the North said, " A wouldn't be as black as him for summat ! " At Dieppe the touter appealed to me as French, Spanish, Italian—and at last said in astonishment " *Vous êtes Anglais !* " But my brother Frederick, a white and rosy man, got much more admiration when we travelled together—he was adored by all the landladies and chambermaids.'

[1] Cecil Lawson's cottage at Haslemere.

'The New Forest is the finest thing in England, the most peculiar. There are mountains elsewhere, and cliffs, and lakes. When Palgrave and I came back from Spain we went to the New Forest, and as we lay under great trees with a green heaven above our heads I said, "We saw nothing so fine as this in Spain," and he said, "No."'

August 20.—Helen and I walk to T.'s. Blackdown now purple with ling and heather. Lawn: Mrs. Tennyson in invalid chair.

Mr. Edward Lear coming on Monday—one of twenty children—drew birds at fourteen to help his family. Improvises on pianoforte.

A. T. and Hallam—Browning's *Dramatic Idylls*.

T.—'I wish he hadn't taken my word Idyll. I said the other day and you took it as a jest, but I meant it seriously, "if the pronunciation of the English language were lost, Browning would be considered the greatest of modern poets."'

W. A.—'A basis of good sense is often wanting in him.'

T.—'I don't perceive that.'

W. A.—'What do you make of *Fifine*?'

T.—'I couldn't make anything of it. I tried it several times, and took it in my pocket on a walk— that's the best way to try.'

W. A.—'"Clive" is simpler. But why was Clive afraid once in his life, as he confessed?'

T.—'Because he had a pistol put to his head.'

W. A.—'Not at all. When his friend thought so, Clive swore at him furiously. Clive was afraid that his antagonist might make him a present of his life—in which case there would have been nothing for it but suicide.'

Hallam.—'No doubt that's it.'

Sunday, August 22.—Hallam and Lionel Tennyson, with Miss Ritchie, call on us after church. Helen and I walk up to T.'s. At dinner, talk of Ireland.

The Church of Rome—I speak of its singleness of aim but flexibility to circumstances, and variety of resources.

Miss Ritchie began—'They embrace so wonderfully'—when T. cut in : ' Did they ever embrace you? Were you ever kissed by a dozen priests?' The young lady laughed.

Miss Ritchie played Beethoven's 'Aurora' Sonata finely. T. came in and listened.

'I wish I could understand it—I could perceive a rushing as of a torrent—and flashes of light.'

Miss R.—' I think it's exactly like sunrise—and very like your poem too, "Out of the Deep."'

Sunday, *August* 29.—Hallam calls. Helen and I walk up to Aldworth. Find A. T. on seat at end of lower terrace, reading a large type New Testament. We sit beside him.

Tennyson shows me a paper by Mr. Crookes (Roy. Soc.) on 'Four Kinds of Matter,' Solid, Liquid, Gaseous, and another which is imperceptible to the senses (sometimes called 'Ether'). Molecules and atoms.

T. said (or something like this)—' I believe we never see Matter : what we count the material world is only an appearance.'

Huxley's question, 'Has a frog a Soul?'

W. A.—' I should first ask, "What do you mean by Soul?" But Huxley says questions about "Soul" and "the Future" don't interest him.'

T.—' Then, surely, that shows defect in him! Tyndall's metaphysics are very shaky, I think. They don't see that they are destroying their country.

'Old Sedgwick told me he visited Laplace in his last days and the old Astronomer said to him—"You are an Englishman, suffer me to say to you a word or two on politics. Never emancipate the Catholics, and never tamper with your glorious constitution."'

Tennyson dislikes our quitting Afghanistan—'the

want of continuity in our policy is the curse of our country; I believe Parliaments will be its ruin. We might have ruled the Afghans and made them good subjects, like the Sikhs.'

I said England had no business in Afghanistan. Lord Beaconsfield's policy was disapproved by Lord Lawrence, Lord Northbrook, and a majority of the Council of India. T. stuck to his own views. I told him, 'you always declare England to be right, whatever she does.'

T.—'I think she's often shockingly wrong. In this case it's unsafe to draw back.'

Speaking of the Irish agitator who said, 'I think their cattle will not much prosper,'—a speech followed by the maiming of many animals,—he exclaimed, 'How I hate that man—Ireland's a dreadful country! I heartily wish it was in the middle of the Atlantic.'

'Below the surface?' I asked.

'No, no, a thousand miles away from England. I like the Irish—I admit the charm of their manners—but they're a fearful nuisance.'

'Very troublesome,' I admitted, 'but there's some truth in the popular Irish notion that nothing can be got from England except by agitation.'

T. is a constant novel reader. 'What I dislike is beginning a new novel. I should like to have a novel to read in a million volumes, to last me my life.'

September 2.—Drove up to Tennyson's to dinner. H. and I., Aubrey de Vere, Dr. Bradley, Mrs. and Miss Bradley.

A. T., Aubrey de Vere and I talk of poetry.

T. and I agree on the odiousness of various readings inserted on a poet's page—and of critical notes.

De Vere blames Ruskin for his recent remarks on Wordsworth,—'a Westmorland peasant, etc.'

De V. wishes Wordsworth had written his *magnum opus*, of which the Prelude was the beginning.

T.—'His small things are the best. Even his

" Tintern Abbey," fine as it is, should have been much compressed.'

De V.—' But if it pleased the artistic sense more, might it not appeal less to the sympathies ? '

T.—' A great deal might be left out.'

W. A.—' One could turn the largest part of the *Excursion* into prose, very seldom altering a word, merely re-arranging. Here and there a line or a passage of poetry would be left, like a quotation. It is much easier to write bad blank verse than good prose.'

T.—' And it is much easier to write rhyme than good blank verse. I should not be sorry to lose anything from a poet which is not beautiful poetry. One plods over Wordsworth's long dreary plains of prose—one knows there's a mountain somewhere, and now and again you come to astonishing things. In old times, when copying was costly, Catullus, Horace, and the others gave only their best.'

De V.—' Wordsworth ought to have done great and perfect things, one fancies. He lived a poetic life, he devoted himself to poetry,—How was it ? '

W. A.—' For many years he never read any poetry but his own. His mind became monotonous.'

De V.—' I believe that is true. And he was continually touching and altering, and sometimes injuring what he had written.'

W. A.—' His experience of real life was neither wide nor various. His material ran short.'

De V.—' And yet, if he gives us a good deal of dulness, might not the same be said of Homer and of Milton ? '

T. (grunts)—' No, no ! '

De V.—' Well, I find a great deal of Homer very dull—and surely the last six books of *Paradise Lost* are much below the first six ? '

T —' Possibly—but there's the charm of Milton's style. He invented his verse—just as much as Virgil
invented his.'

De V.—'I read to Wordsworth your

Of old sat Freedom on the heights,

and—

You ask me, why, tho' ill at ease,

and he said, "Fine poetry and very stately diction." '

T. said 'H'm!' contentedly.

W. A.—'Coleridge was more essentially a Poet than Wordsworth.'

T.—'I don't know that.'

De V.—'I think so. But how melancholy to think that all his finest poems were produced in one single year of his life. Then he went to Germany and took to Metaphysics—such a pity!'

T.—'But the man I count greater than them all—Wordsworth, Coleridge, Byron, Shelley, every one of 'em—is Keats, who died at twenty-five—thousands of faults! (twiddling the fingers of one hand in the air)—but he's wonderful!'

De V.—'He doesn't pall upon you?'

T.—'No.'

De V.—'Shelley used to be a great idol of yours.'

T.—'O yes. We lived near the most prosaic village in the world, a little beast! where they had never heard of anything. One day we went there to meet my brother Frederick, who was coming back from somewhere, and as we were driving home he whispered, "I've got a poet who's much grander than Byron," and repeated one line—

Waterfalls leap among wild islands green,

which I thought delicious.

'*Alastor* was the first poem of his I read. I said, "This is what I want!"—and still I like it the best, though one can't tell how much these first loves are to be trusted. *The Revolt of Islam* is splendid but gives me a headache—it's fatiguing—all mountain tops and glories.'

De V. agreed, and named as his favourites *The Ode to*

the West Wind—Ode to Naples—(of which he recited some lines, and another piece).

Tennyson quoted a passage from Shelley and said 'what can you do with a man who has such command of language? But Keats was not wild and wilful, he had always an intention. At the same time he was *daimonisch*,—he had a touch (he was a livery-stable keeper's son—I don't know where he got it from, unless from Heaven).

> Perhaps the self-same song that found a path
> Through the sad heart of Ruth when, sick for home,
> She stood in tears amid the alien corn ;
> The same that oft-times hath
> Charm'd magic casements opening on the foam
> Of perilous seas, in faery lands forlorn.

'What can be lovelier? (He said the last two lines again.) I once saw it printed "In fairyland forlorn," which totally ruined it—one doesn't know why.'

W. A.—' "Fairyland" has been much used.'

When I shook hands with him he said, 'Good-night, Statuette!' I laughed and said, 'I know what you mean.' (A little poem in my *Songs, Ballads and Stories*, a volume Hallam borrowed of me yesterday and which T. had not seen before.)

T.—'It's modest—and it may be quite true. No one can in the least tell who will survive.'

We went out to the porch, T., Hallam, De Vere, Helen and I, with lantern—brilliant starry night.

T.—'Millions upon millions of suns.'

W. A.—'And Whewell argues that the earth is probably the only seat of conscious life. Suppose one looking from a distance at the Earth, a dot among other dots.'

T.—'That's just what I said at the time.'

We parted, and H. and I followed our lantern-gleam on the heath and down the shady lane to Haslemere.

September 19.—Rain—clears. H. and I walk to

Aldworth—glorious prospects, breadth of sunshine and
shadow—green woodlands, bounding hills, blue distances
—sweet cool air. Mrs. Tennyson very friendly.

T.—' A lady the other day here—a very nice woman
(I don't altogether like the word, but I want it), was
praising a friend of yours. " Nice " is objectionable, but
it is useful—a " nice " person is one that you're satisfied
with.'

W. A.—' It used to mean fastidious,—discriminative,
but there's not much harm in its being turned about
and applied to the object.'

T.—' No : it's something or somebody that satisfies
your niceness.'

Hallam takes H. and me down hill and shows us
old house which belonged to Denzil Holles.

Dinner, pleasant and lively talk.

T.—' A Russian noble, who spoke English well,
said one morning to an English guest, " I've shot two
peasants this morning."—" Pardon me, you mean
pheasants." " No, indeed, two men—they were insolent and I shot them." '

W. A.—' In Ireland it's the other way.'

T.—' Couldn't they blow up that horrible island with
dynamite and carry it off in pieces—a long way off ? '

W. A.—' Why did the English go there ? '

T.—' Why did the Normans come to England ?
The Normans came over here and seized the country,
and in a hundred years the English had forgotten all
about it, and they were all living together on good
terms.'

(I demurred : T. went on, raising his voice).—' The
same Normans went to Ireland, and the Irish with
their damned unreasonableness are raging and foaming
to this hour ! '

W. A.—' The Norman Duke had a claim on the
crown of England.'

T.—' No rightful claim.'

W. A.—' But suppose all these to be bygones. You

speak of a century, a short time in history—think what Ireland had to complain of only in the last century— the penal laws, and the deliberate destruction of their growing industry by the English Government : what do you say to that ? '

T.—' That was brutal ! Our ancestors *were* horrible brutes ! And the Kelts are very charming and sweet and poetic. I love their Ossians and their Finns and so forth—but they are most damnably unreasonable ! '

W. A.—' They are most unfortunate.'

Hallam.—' What would you do ? '

W. A.—' This last phase of discontent is perhaps the worst—flavoured with Americanism and general irreverence ; but what I would have done long ago I would try still—encourage peasant proprietorship to the utmost possible.'

Hallam.—' Get rid of all the landlords and give the land to the people ? '

W. A.—' Not at all. There are many good Irish landlords, and they usually get on well with their tenants. The peasant proprietors would have to be made gradually, and on business principles.'

T.—' What is the difference between an English landlord and an Irish landlord ? '

W. A.—' Is it a conundrum ? '

T.—' Not at all.'

(I tried to explain some great differences. T. came back to his old point.)

T.—' The Kelts are so utterly unreasonable ! The stupid clumsy Englishman—knock him down, kick him under the tail, kick him under the chin, do anything to him, he gets on his legs again and goes on ; the Kelt rages and shrieks and tears everything to pieces ! '

Tennyson spoke of the ' sea of silver mist ' seen at early morning from his windows at this season—also of the effect of mist spread over the wide green woodland and the sun shining on it—' incredible ! Turner would
have tried it.'

Mrs. T. thought it a great pity that the French Government was interfering with the Religious Orders— even those that nursed the sick. I said they were dealing with the Church of Rome as a great political power, known to be adverse to the Republic.

T. spoke of Venice. ' We stayed too short a time —the Giant's Stairs are very fine. Milan Cathedral struck me far more than St. Marks.'

I quoted—

> A mount of marble ! a hundred spires !

T.—' Well, that's what it seemed like. Plenty to object to, no doubt—but the great coloured windows are wonderful. Putting together the little I have seen of Italy, this time and the first time, I think the great charm is the number of old cities, so various, each with a character of its own.'

We talked of London. T. has a vague notion that he would like to live there. ' Chelsea Embankment is a charming place—I could live there all the year.' Hallam (*sotto voce*).—' He always gets tired of London in a fortnight.'

I referred to Emerson's essay (in *Society and Solitude*), that the feeling of Age is often less in ourselves than in our consciousness of being looked upon as old by others.

T. (partly agreeing).—' Yes ; I feel younger in some ways than when I was fifty.'

In talking of London, we spoke of old nooks and corners, old taverns, ' Bertolini's,' off Leicester Square, now shut up ; old Mr. Seymour—who dined there fifty years, etc. ; ' The Cock '—' Dick's.'

T.—' I had a room at " Dick's " once—I often dined at " The Rainbow." '

He has, amid his ruralism, longings now and again for the humours of London streets ; but alas he cannot easily go about without provoking notice. An Irish flower girl said to T. in Regent St., ' Ah, sure now, Misther Tinnison, ye'll buy this little nosegay ! '

September 23.—H. and I walked up to Aldworth to dinner.

Dr. Johnson.—T. : 'I don't think I should have liked his company, but I like Boswell's book.'

Byron.—T. : 'When a boy I used to worship him. But I do think Byron great. His *Vision of Judgment* is the most wonderful thing in the world.' Then T. quoted from *Don Juan*—

> Then rose from sea to sky the wild farewell, etc.

I said 'The Shipwreck' as a whole was not good.

T.—'The famous lines about the sea in *Childe Harold* are abominably bad.'

We examined them. I suggested—

> Thy waters washĕd them while they were free—

as possible, but T. truly thought 'washĕd' was not like Byron ; he was more likely to write 'wasted,' sense or no sense.

Ruskin's criticisms on Byron in the *Nineteenth Century*. 'After reading them I read "The Island" through the other night.'

'Well, did you find much in it ?'

'No.'

'And what Ruskin calls the finest line ever written by an Englishman about the sea—

> ——the swell
> Of Ocean's Alpine azure rose and fell.'

T.—'The open vowels are good. I don't know what is meant by "Alpine azure." And certainly that about the rivulet falling from the cliff being like a goat's eye is very bad.'

W. A.—'What did you think of Ruskin's article altogether ?'

T.—'I thought his remarks on the passage in Shakespeare very good—on the fitness of the placing of words.'

Tennyson drives into Haslemere ; he sits in our

garden[1] and looks at newspaper—admires the up-hill
garden and fir trees : 'it is like one at Florence. The
south of England is like Italy. When I came back
this summer and looked from the terrace at Blackdown, I thought it was exactly like Italy.'

[In the evening at Aldworth.] T. read us the
'Bugle Song.' I said 'That's Killarney.'

T.—'Yes, it was Killarney suggested it. The bugle
echoes were wonderful—nine times—at last like a chant
of angels in the sky. But when I was there afterwards
I could only hear two echoes,—from the state of the
air. I complained of this and said, "when I was here
before I heard nine." "Oh!" says the bugler, "then
you're the gintleman that's brought so much money
to the place!"' (The 'Bugle Song' increased the
number of tourists to Killarney.)

He said an Irish lady asked him how he liked the
scenery—'Too much bog,' he thought, 'black and
dismal.' 'O then, where,' she retorted in tones of
indignation—'where would you have the poor people
cut their turf?'

Afterwards Tennyson read to us from his new un-
published volume, 'The Cobbler with his gin bottle,'
'The Entail or the village wife'—'one of those gos-
siping beasts!' he said.

Wednesday, October 13.—Tennyson and I drive in
his carriage up Hindhead as far as the Huts, to look for
gypsies, but find none.

T.—'Old Hallam used to say the longer one lived
the higher one rated Dryden as a poet.'

W. A.—'I should say that to rate Dryden very high
is proof of a non-poetic mind.'

Helen, at his wish, made a sketch of the landscape as
seen through one of the arches of the porch. T.,
looking over her, said : 'I suppose I owe you £20 for
this?' H. said the payment would be to give her a
sitting or two, and he gave in rather grumblingly ;

[1] The Allinghams were now in a house under Court's Hill, Haslemere

hitherto he had refused, and said one day, 'I'll go out of the room if you look at me!'

H. had two or three short sittings in his study, with fading light, and made a couple of beginnings. He promised to sit again when we next met. I talked to him while he sat, and tried to keep him from looking unhappy. He gave Helen a copy of the collected edition of his brother Charles's Sonnets, about to be published, and one day read several of them to her with great feeling and warm praise. He read the Sonnet I said had impressed me a year ago. T. said: 'I know the place, the road, everything.'

He spoke of the objection that the Sonnets were not in perfect sonnet form, and said, 'I never care to read a perfect sonnet. I look down the rhymes and that's enough. I thought the other day of writing a sonnet beginning—

I hate the perfect Sonnet!

After going on for four lines I should say

And now there's "down" and "crown" and "frown" and "brown":
    I'll take the latter. Then there's "cheer" and "fear"—
    And several others,—

and so forth, would it be worth doing?'

T. often speaks of the absolute need of delicacy of elocution to give the true beauty of poetry.

T.—'Rogers used to quote with approval the praise of good verse by some Frenchman who declared it to be *beau comme prose*, that is, as easy and natural.'

T.—'I'm seventy-*nine* (this was a joke), but I don't feel the weight of age on my shoulders. I can run up-hill; I can waltz—but when I said this to Fanny Kemble she replied in a ghastly voice, "I hope I shall never see you do it!"'

He read us very powerfully the poem of the mother and the gibbet. I objected to the title of 'Rizpah' (in private life he called it 'Bones'), and also to an explanatory note (now omitted) prefixed to the piece.

The lady who gave him the story called it ' The Modern
Rizpah.' She gave it as true, the scene near Bright-
helmstown, but dates and other particulars vague.

Tennyson said : ' I used to write long letters—
beautiful letters. I used to write to Sir Vere de Vere,
who's now dead. I once wrote to him (I forget the
sentence, which was imaginative in its turn), and in his
reply he said, " My dear fellow, what rubbish you do
write to me ! " '

October 21.—Haslemere. Our last visit (this time)
to Aldworth. Snow on the ground. We all drive up.

The Wordsworth Society.—T. entirely objects to it.
' They'll give one a disgust for Wordsworth. Why
can't people be quiet ? Ugh !

' Reading magazines breaks one's mind all to bits.
One ought to leave off newspapers.

' A servant woman that left us told somebody in her
next place: " She is an *angel*, but he—why he's only a
public writer." ' (T. often says English people have
no respect for poets.)

Looking at the chimney-piece, T. said : ' When I
began to read Italian, I wrote down every word that
puzzled me on the sides and front of the chimney-
piece where I lodged—painted white—and made a kind
of dictionary for myself. I went away for two or three
days and when I came back it was all washed off.
" Thought it was dirt," the woman said.

' Worse than that—when I was twenty-two I wrote
a beautiful poem on Poland, hundreds of lines long,
and the housemaid lit the fire with it. I never could
recover it.'

Tennyson repeated some lines of his own from an old
idyll never published, they were something like this—

> The rich wed richer, and the poor the poor,
> The mount of gold accumulating still,
> The gulf of want enlarging, deepening, till
> The one into the other sink at last
> With all confusion.

'That's not quite the thing—"all confusion." Oh, I've written thousands of lines that went up the chimney.'

After dinner Tennyson called on Hallam to sing 'John Brown,' which he accordingly began in a strong bass voice, T. joining in (the first time I ever heard him try any musical performance), and sometimes thumping with his fists on the table—

> John Brown's body lies mouldering in the grave,
> But his soul is marching on !

He urged Hallam to go on, saying, ' I like it, I like it,' but Hallam thought the noise too great, and drew off. The soul marching on delighted Tennyson.

In the evening he read us in the drawing-room ' The Voyage of Maildun' (from Joyce's *Old Celtic Romances*).

T.—'At first I made half the men kill the other half in every fray, and Maildun himself return *alone.*'

I said the Irish were fond of extravagant stories, somewhat in the manner of Rabelais, and told him of another, where the hero travelled by land. We talked of subjects for poems, and T. said ' I want something quite mad.'

After eleven we went home in T.'s carriage, happy with the good company and friendly kindness.

[While at Haslemere the Allinghams had heard with great sorrow of the death of ' the kindest of friends,' Mr. Tom Taylor. They had always been made welcome at his delightful house, meeting there noted and interesting people, Sir Henry Irving, Miss Ellen Terry, and many others. It is not, however, so much as host and hostess—gifted and hospitable though they were—that Mr. and Mrs. Tom Taylor will be remembered—but as the truest and most sympathetic of friends, with the overflowing kindness that springs from warm hearts united in family affection.]

October 24.—Chelsea. Yesterday, returned to town. Carlyle's about five o'clock—feebler in look and voice. I told him of Haslemere—Tennyson.

Wednesday, October 27.—Took Mary home from our house about 11 P.M., and found Carlyle in his drawing-room reading a new edition of Burns. He often reads in it (Mary said), notes and all, without his spectacles. He again said he found Burns 'the greatest since Shakespeare.' We talked of Campbell.

C. praised Campbell's 'Lochiel,' 'The Mariners of England,' etc., and presently began to repeat 'The Battle of the Baltic,' giving four or five verses.

' I was greatly taken with these as a lad, and repeated some of them to my Father, who usually cared nothing at all for such things.'

' Was he impressed ? ' I asked.

C.—' O yes ' (repeating)—

> . . . when each gun
> From its adamantine lips

(he thought he had never heard so grand an expression as that)

> Spread a death-shade round the ships,
> Like a hurricane eclipse
> Of the sun !

Then we spoke of Nelson.

C.—'Never was any one so sagacious in divining his enemy's plans and whereabouts. I well remember hearing of Nelson's death.' (C. was in his tenth year.)

' A neighbour woman was in one evening talking with my mother about the War and the Fleet, and what great things were supposed to be at hand ; the next day she came in and said all their speculations had been vain, a tremendous battle had already been fought, the French and Spanish Fleets were smashed to pieces, and —Nelson was killed. I could not understand all, but I recollect I had much more grief for his death than joy for the victory.'

October 29.—H. and I to Hammersmith, Stephens's. Holly's birthday. W. Rossetti and wife, Jenny and May Morris. Talk with W. M. R.—Shelley, Browning, etc. Home : stars (I think of Ballyshannon and the sound of the Atlantic).

Saturday, December 4.—Helen and I call on Carlyle. His eighty-fifth birthday.

C. seems better and easier ; more himself. He asks what I am doing.

December 19.—H. and I to visit Sir Theodore and Lady Martin. (Burton just going out—' Fergusons well.') Talk—theatricals—Warner—the Batemans— 'no poetic actress now.' I suggest Modjeska, who throws sweetness into everything—friendly.

December 23.—Death of George Eliot. Alas! that little visit at Witley was the last. Her affectionate demeanour then we shall remember.[1]

Friday, December 24.—To Carlyle's at 2. He was lying on the sofa in the drawing-room. When I spoke to him he held out his hand and shook hands with me, but said nothing. I was not sure that he knew me. A stout Scotch servant girl and I lifted him to his feet to go to the carriage. In the hall his heavy seal-skin coat was put on with difficulty, and he was got into the carriage, Alick and I with him. We drove twice round Hyde Park. The old man dozed much.

[From this time forth Carlyle grew steadily weaker. Mrs. Alexander Carlyle, whose wise and tender care of him had been unceasing for the past thirteen years, was now joined by her Husband in her devoted attendance on her Uncle.

This may perhaps be a fitting place to say something about Allingham's own literary work during the period—now drawing to a close—of his life in London. Besides the routine of editing, he contributed, from

---

[1] The Allinghams had called on George Eliot, then Mrs. Cross, at the Heights, shortly before they returned from Haslemere.

time to time, an article to the magazine—'Seven
Hundred Years Ago' (chapters on early Irish history,
much and often commended by Carlyle), 'Modern
Prophets,' 'Painter and Critic,' etc.—and, frequently,
a column of critical and other notes and remarks, under
the general title of 'Ivy Leaves.'

In 1877 he brought out (with Messrs. George Bell
and Sons) a collection of his poems—*Songs, Ballads,
and Stories*.

He had other work in preparation—*An Evil May
Day*, a poem embodying his views on religion, in relation
to dogma and science—and *Ashby Manor*, an historical
play, to which Allingham gives a note at the end of his
volume, *Thought and Word*. He sent a copy of this
play to several London managers, one of whom entered
into a correspondence with him and 'highly praised the
play.' Some months after this manager produced a
'kind of clumsy parody of *Ashby Manor*—with sense-
less melodramatic additions and an entirely irrelevant
fifth act.' On this being pointed out to him he asserted
that he 'scarcely recollected anything about *Ashby Manor*.'
Later, an almost similar fate befell another little play of
Allingham's, *Hopgood and Co.*[1]

During these years pleasant intercourse was kept
up—though the meetings were not always mentioned
in detail in the diary—with Allingham's old friends of
the earlier time—with the Burne-Joneses and Morrises—
the Holman Hunts, Arthur Hugheses, F. G. Stephenses,
Moncure Conways, and especially with Madame Bodichon. Sir Percy and Lady Shelley had built a house
on the Chelsea Embankment, and friendly meetings
are noted with them and with the De Morgans, G. P.
Boyces, W. Bell Scotts, Mr. and Mrs. Christison, and
many other near neighbours.]

---

[1] Allingham had always taken a great interest in the drama : although
not a constant theatre-goer, he rarely missed seeing a notable actor or
performance.

CHAPTER XIX

1881-1883

January 17.—Helen visited Mary C. to-day. Carlyle keeps his bed yesterday and to-day. He lies now on a water-bed, which is placed in the drawing-room (first-floor front looking on Cheyne Row). The Scotch maid stays in the room all night. Mary said she looked at his clothes, and thought he might never put them on again.

After taking finally to his bed the venerable man spoke hardly at all ; there was no physical obstruction of the organs of speech, but almost total absence of will or wish to say anything. Sometimes when Mary was doing something for him he would say, in a low tone, ' Ah, poor little woman.' He was heard to say ' Poor little Tommy'—thinking of his grand-nephew of a few months old. Once, he supposed the female hands that tended him, lifting his head perhaps, to be those of his good old Mother—' Ah, Mother, is it you?' he murmured, or some such words. I think it was on the day before the last day that Mary heard him saying to himself, ' So this is Death : well—'

The ' well!' pronounced as if meaning, ' So be it! we shall see what it is like.'

After this nothing was heard from him, except his nephew's name, ' Alick,' once or twice.

During these melancholy days of the end of January and beginning of February 1881, Helen and I were in the habit of going down in the evenings to inquire at

Cheyne Row, usually seeing Mary, who was becoming terribly tired, yet could scarcely be persuaded to have help in her and her husband's long and sad night watchings. 'To-morrow night, we shall see,'—was the usual answer ; 'to-night, we can manage.'

One of the nights our nurse Elizabeth Haddon stayed at Cheyne Row, going in sometimes to the sick-room.

The newspaper reporters or penny-a-liners used to ring at the street-door nearly all through the night, but at last bulletins pinned up abated the nuisance.

On the evening of Friday, February 4, Helen and I went to Cheyne Row about half-past ten—Mary and Alick. Helen much wished to stay all night and help in the watching, but I could not agree to this, as she was not well herself.

Next morning (Saturday, February 5), a note from Mary—all was over.

He had lain motionless and, to all appearance, unconscious for hours, and quietly ceased to breathe about half-past eight this morning, Mary with him.

I went down about half-past eleven. Went into the room for a short time. Sad ! sad !—not wretched ; the sadness of Humanity.

I looked upon the honoured face, thin, with hoary hair and beard ; the face of a weary Pilgrim, at the end of a long journey, arrived and at rest. The large beautiful eyelids were closed for ever on a pair of eyes that, whether for carrying messages inwards or outwards, had scarce met their equals on earth or left such behind.

Helen made two pencil sketches. As we sat in the parlour the street-door bell rang, and a 'Messenger from the Queen' was said to be in the passage ; I went out at Mary's request, and found a Scotchman of middle age, who said he was 'sent by the Queen to inquire after Mr. Carlyle' ; I told him of the death, asked him no questions. He may have been John Brown.

A walk as in a dream. How strange all the moving crowds, all the busy trivialities going on ! No change felt on earth or in air. I thought, looking at this stranger and that, 'If I said to you "Carlyle is dead," would you care?'

February 6.—H. and I at Cheyne Row with Mary and Alick. The Funeral to be entirely private.

March 20.—H. and I to Mrs. Procter's. Lift— Mrs. and Miss P., Browning, Mr. Theodore Watts. B. said, 'I never minded what Carlyle said of things outside his own little circle (drawing a circle in the air with his forefinger)—what was it to me what he thought of Poetry or Music? One day I was talking of Keats, and Carlyle's opinion of him, to Mrs. Carlyle; she asked me to lend her something of Keats's, and I brought her *Isabella* and *The Eve of St. Agnes* (I was too knowing to try her with *Endymion*). She wrote me a letter— "Almost any young gentleman with a sweet tooth might be expected to write such things. *Isabella* might have been written by a seamstress who had eaten something too rich for supper and slept upon her back." Do you think (B. said) I cared about this more than for the barking of a little dog?

'I went with Odo Russell to see Carlyle. C. said, "You are British Minister at Rome? You ought to say to the Pope, 'you Infallible Chimera! We cannot for a moment listen to you, etc. etc.'" Odo heard with diplomatic calmness. When we went out he said to me, "What nonsense he did talk."' (But C. knew well enough what diplomatic formality requires.)

Watts.—'I never saw Mr. Carlyle.'

Browning.—'Then you could not know him. His personality was most attaching. I shall never get over it.

'He first made my acquaintance, not I his. I first saw him at Leigh Hunt's, and very properly sat silent for my part all the time. When he lectured, I subscribed and went, and coming out one day he spoke to me, "How do you do, Mr. Browning?" I said I had hardly thought he could recollect me. "O yes, I recollect you very well—will you come and see me? I live down in Chelsea."

'I did call, and he told me afterwards that he had on that occasion conceived an unfavourable opinion of me, because I wore (what was usual then) a green riding-coat of cut-away shape. If he had seen me no more I might have figured in his diary as a kind of sporting-man in aspect. He was always thoroughly kind to me.'

Browning came down in the lift with us, and we walked together as far as the corner of Buckingham Palace. He dined at Tennyson's last night. 'T. in great force. He said, "this pair of dress boots is forty years old." We all looked at them, and I said it was good evidence of the immortality of the sole.'

Browning also said Carlyle had written him the most beautiful letter possible—'among other things counselling me to give up verse-writing. I have my own character written by Carlyle,—my wife copied it, and it's in her handwriting.'

March 21.—To Cheyne Row—upstairs, into all the rooms. Everything in place, quiet, unchanged—with one exception!—grave, pathetic, venerable.

[In June of this year, 1881, the Allinghams moved to Sandhills, Witley, in Surrey.

Allingham writes of Sandhills—'the slope of heather and gorse, topped with fir-trees, looks far and wide over the Weald of Surrey and Sussex, Hind-Head, a mountain-like hill, closing the view on the right hand, Blackdown in front; then, as the eye travels eastward, come the rising grounds near Midhurst and Petworth, Chanctonbury Ring, with its tuft of trees, called locally "The Squire's Hunting-Cap," and on a clear day the downs near Brighton and Lewes.'

Here the life was quiet and tranquil, and Allingham had leisure for his own writing and reading.

During July the notes in the diary are of 'days hot and bright'—of 'lilies and roses'—'buying garden tools '—' of walks up the common, in shady lanes.' 'To Chiddingfold, Village Green, old cottages, hay-field, evening sun, little church spire—long shadows on the grass—peaceful, pathetic.']

July 14.—Meet Mary Carlyle and Tommy—Tommy happy.

July 23.—Dine at Birket Foster's—Keene's sketches, etc.

August 21.—Sandhills. H. and I to Blackdown —Foxholes. H. draws. Tennyson and I sit with her.

Beauty and picturesqueness—T. says, 'take a trim, snug, unbeautiful house, half ruin it, and you make it picturesque ; same as to ragged clothes, etc.' I argue that neglect alone will not make a thing picturesque, there must be beauty *in* it. For a thing to be absolutely 'beautiful' it must have regularity. The beauty in a picturesque neglected object comes from nature regaining her sway over it. T. would not be drawn out of the commonplaces of the subject.

T.—'I said to Tyndall, "You can but scratch the surface of things. You are like a swallow that dips on the water." He seemed to agree to this.'

T. sitting on the faggot complained of the 'bees' (flies) being 'as fell as ought.' I said I would break him a bit of oak, not *esh*, and I did so. He said, 'There was a real farmer in our parts—in Lincolnshire—that used to say he heard his horse's hooves saying "Propetty! Propetty! Propetty!" His name was Thimbleby. His wife, when she came into a room, would slap her pockets and say, "The day I married Thimbleby I brought him £5000 on each shoulder!"'

August 30.—To York [The British Association].

September 3.—Fryston. Breakfast 8.30. Lord Houghton reads out part of letter from Carlyle to his wife, written here at Fryston (for which he paid £10 : 10s.). It begins, 'My dear Bairn,' describes the

Milnes family and life at Fryston. R. M. M.'s sister

'about Richard's height, a fair height for a gown.'
Roebuck dined here, ' flew at me over and over again
like a cockatrice, and was duly flung off, more to the
satisfaction of the company than of me.'

Odd to think of this letter coming back here.

Ld. Houghton said, ' when I brought Carlyle here,
we came into this room (the hall). My father, who
was a most courteous man, expressed his great pleasure
at seeing him, and how much he was obliged to me for
bringing him : then, showing his cigar, said, " I hope, Mr.
Carlyle, you don't object to this occupation." C. replied
with emphasis, " I think sir it is a very natural occupation, and I should like to join in it as soon as possible ! " '

Sunday, October 16.—Sandhills. Very fine—cold
—Carlyle memoranda. I and the children walk to
fir-wood. Buss's Corner, children and nurse return up
path. I sit on log and call out good-byes. In passing
I call and ask Charles Lewes if he will walk ? He has
a cold. He lends me my own *Songs, Ballads,* etc., the
copy I gave to George Eliot in May 1877.

As I sit on the tree trunk at Buss's Corner I take
out the book and turn its leaves. Up this very path,
on the edge of which I am sitting, George Eliot, G. H.
Lewes and myself walked one fine autumnal afternoon,
September 25, 1878. I had come over from Shere,
where we had a cottage for the season ; called, stayed
for luncheon ; and they both, when I started to walk
home, came with me down their garden, into the little
lane, across the railway line, to this corner where I
sit, over Hambledon Hill, and up the hollow road ;
at the end of which we parted, talking at the last
moment of Carlyle. Sitting on the log and looking
up the path eastwards, I recollect distinctly that just
here we talked of death, and George Eliot said, ' I used
to try to imagine myself dying—how I should feel
when dying, but of course I could not.'

I said that when a child I firmly believed I should
in some way escape dying.

George Eliot.—' You cannot think of yourself as dead.'

G. H. Lewes was deeply silent at all this. I suspected him at the time of thinking the topic frivolous and uninteresting, but now I think he perhaps avoided it as painful. Charles Lewes has told Helen that his father could not bear to think of George Eliot's dying first. That September walk was my last sight of Lewes. Both are gone. And here I sit turning over my own book and looking at her pencil markings.

She wrote me a letter, which I have, on receiving this book. I put it in my pocket and walk on.

Neglected my diary till end of year. Weather mostly very mild—Periwinkle flowers in garden— found two primroses in fields. Tennyson and Hallam called. Sonny showed T. his garden.

At Blackdown. Talk—Browning.

I praised the Russian Scenery of ' Ivan Ivanovitch' in the new volume, remarking that the story was in substance an old one (a version of it appeared, I think, in a miscellany called *The Mirror*).

T. said, ' I think the woman was right. The wolves would have eaten them all. She might have saved part by what she did.'

T. told me that he had planned out his Arthuriad, and could have written it all off without any trouble. But in 1842 he published, with other poems, the ' Morte d'Arthur,' which was one book of his Epic (though not really the eleventh), and the review in the *Quarterly* disheartened him, so that he put the scheme aside. He afterwards took it up again, but not as with the first inspiration. This unlucky article in the *Quarterly* was written by John Sterling, who was then thirty-six years old, just three years older than Tennyson. It may be interesting now to read what it said of the ' Morte d'Arthur ' : ' The first poem in the second volume seems to us less costly jewel-work, with fewer

of the broad flashes of passionate imagery, than some

others, and not compensating for this inferiority by any stronger human interest. The miraculous legend of *Excalibur* does not come very near to us, and as reproduced by any modern writer must be a mere ingenious exercise of fancy. The poem, however, is full of distinct and striking description, perfectly expressed, and a tone of mild dignified sweetness attracts, though it hardly avails to enchant us.'

This, it will be observed, chimes in with the doubts expressed by the Poet himself in the lines written by way of prologue. Blame or doubt in regard to his own writings always weighed more with Tennyson than praise. He often said that he forgot praise and remembered all censure.

Sterling's review, meant to be friendly, was a thin pretentious piece and of no value whatever : a pity it should have chanced to prove so mis-effectual !

1882

January 1.—Sandhills. Last night at a few minutes before 12 o'clock we, that is Helen and I, with Elizabeth, Annie, and Sophie, went into the garden ; the sky clear and starry, with moonlight, weather mild, and heard the bells of Chiddingfold, some two miles off, ringing out the Old Year—five bells they sounded like, sweet and soft. The chime stopped and we shook hands and wished each other a 'Happy New Year'—then it began again, and also a distant band. The dear children are fast asleep—a toy waiting beside each bed.

January 13.—H. and I to Blackdown.

A. T. in study. H. tries to sketch him, but he *won't.* 'You're staring at me—I can't bear it ! He's keeping me in talk, it's a plot ! I hate it ! My back bone is weak ! You mustn't, Mrs. A.'

Autograph hunters—some one applied repeatedly— he sent 'Ask me no more.—A. Tennyson.'

Tuesday, February 28. — Lord Houghton struck with paralysis at Athens—gone, I fear.

March 4.—Visit Hook, R.A.—friendly and jocular.

[Miss De Morgan came down one day to look for lodgings—to Tobitt's Farm.]

' Mrs. Tobitt has let her rooms.'

' To an artist ? ' asks Mary.

' O no, M^m, *quite a gentleman.*'

[In the local directory Mr. Birket Foster was entered as ' Tradesman.']

Thursday, April 20.—Splendid day. Sat in Study with open window and wrote for P.M.G. ' Foot-paths.'

To-night hear nightingale for first time.

Newspapers—Death of Darwin.

May Day.—Overcast. A few cottage children came in carrying sticks with flowers tied to them— neither sung nor spoke, but stood shyly holding their flower sticks ; got 6d. and went away. A curiously silent folk, the English peasants. Sonny and Evey get flower sticks next day.

Abundance of wild flowers, nightingales and cuckoos heard all night.

May 8.—Murder of Lord F. Cavendish and Mr. Burke in the Phœnix Park. O wretched country !

Tuesday, May 9.[1]—Storm of wind, trees blown down. Hear of serious illness, then of the death of Emerson—eighty next month—a calm happy truly philosophic life. No grief, scarcely sadness, in such a departure ; but it leaves the world lonelier, and us the readier to go when our day comes.

June 13.—Walking with William Morris from the Society of Arts to Bloomsbury last Friday, we talked, among other things, of believing or not believing in a God, and he said ' It's so unimportant, it seems to me,' and he went on to say that all we can get to, do what we will, is a form of words.

I think we agree in part, not entirely ; but in the street and in a hurry explanation was impossible.

[1] On May 11th Allingham's youngest child, Henry William Allingham, was born.

'Le Sujet de Dieu' might be called unimportant in
a sense, because, as the French editor said, 'il manque
l'actualité.'

One knows that it is impossible to arrive at anything definite, and those who do not trouble their heads
about the matter can get on as well as other people,
so far as one sees.

It must be remembered, however, that our whole
society is based upon traditionary belief in a God, and,
believe what we will, we continue to get the benefit of
this in many ways. But there are, and always will be,
many people who cannot help asking often and anxiously,
'Is there a God?—Is there no God?' and the sort of
answer that comes home may be highly important to
them and others in its practical results, especially in
certain crises, common to human life, but new and
intensely interesting to each human being. In crises, too,
of national life the subject may have a terrible actuality.

But this does not justify dogmatism upon it. Here
also I think sincerity best, with oneself and others. I
will have nothing to do with the Church of Rome, or
indeed with any form of Christianity, in spite of all the
beauty and power, all the comforting and controlling
influences, because I know the structure is built on false
dogmas. No verbal Revelation of any date, in any
tongue, has the least authority with me. Nor do I
want a puppet God constructed or kept up because it
may scare some from robbery and revolution, murder
and suicide; and it seems to me that whoever goes
about to describe or define the Deity, sets up an idol or
puppet, a man's work, whether it be mean as African
fetish or majestic as the Jupiter of Pheidias. We
cannot in the least describe, or comprehend, or even
think Deity. And yet we can believe in Deity, and
that belief is not fantastic, but natural, sound, and
reasonable. There is to me no conception of the
Universe possible save as the dominion of Power and
Wisdom, unfathomably great, yet in sympathy with my

own intelligent nature ; a Greatness presenting itself to me (when I dare at all to shape it) as a true Personality, comprising all that man at his best in measured degree feels, thinks, and is ; and much more.

Almighty God,—to whom turns my soul, sharing, I know not how, the mystic divine nature ; whose reality is indubitable, whose quality is incomprehensible, whose plans are inscrutable. This conception is in harmony and consistency with my whole moral, reasonable, and imaginative being. It bears little talking about, and that only in the choicest moments. Logic has no hold here. Rhetoric is out of place. I do not know that I am bound to turn my mind towards the problem of the universe, or that any one is bound to send his thoughts outside of his daily life and business. But my mind does naturally and voluntarily so turn, and when it does so turn it finds before it the idea of *God*, and therefrom receives a sense of strength and serenity. Nor is this experience contradicted in the least by anything that I know, feel, or imagine.

August 23.—To Southampton [British Association].

Tuesday, August 31.—Broadlands ; Romsey. Lord and Lady Mount-Temple, Mr. Geo. Russell, M.P. The Gladstones starting for Stonehenge to join excursion. I in Lord Palmerston's library for several hours.

Talk about Dizzy—Lord M. said he was in the House the night Disraeli made his first speech. He spoke in a florid, hustings style, and the House laughed, more and more as he went on. He began a sentence— ' I think I see Britannia, with the Cap of Liberty in one hand, and in the other——' but shouts of laughter drowned his voice. At last, after a pause, he said, ' It is useless for me to continue—but the time will come when you *shall* hear me,' and he sat down. Every one heard the concluding words. Mr. Campbell (afterwards Lord C.), who was sitting near him, said in a stage whisper ' Mr. Disraeli, I'm very anxious to know what it was Britannia had in her other hand,' but received no reply.

D. was very dressy, with curled hair, and rings worn
over his gloves.   Mr. Russell said that after this Dizzy
began to cultivate the country-gentleman style of speaking, very practical and unadorned, taking for his subjects
the Corn Laws, Hop duties, and so forth.

D.'s family was originally Spanish, of the ancient
house of Lara ; an ancestor changed his name and
abode, and settled at Venice as D'Israeli.

1883

Towards the end of the year.

I have neglected my diary a long while.   At the
time it seldom seems worth doing   Let me try back.

Mr. George Philip of Liverpool, publisher, came
and lunched with us.   He agreed to publish *Blackberries*
and *Day and Night Songs*—bought Helen's ' Cottage
Garden, Spring.'

I went to Haslemere one day to get names to a
letter to Lord Derby, asking him not to enclose certain
roadsides hereabouts on the property he has lately
bought towards Hindhead.   Caught Dr. Tyndall at
station, who signed, saying that Lord Derby told him
himself he intended to do all he could to keep the
beauty of these places unspoilt.   Walked up to
Aldworth, saw Hallam, then Tennyson, who signed.

T.—' I don't know whether you can help me '—
taking a book off the table—' I'm not satisfied with
this '—then he read—

Low-flowing breezes are roaming the broad valley dimm'd in the
    gloaming.

W. A.—' That's a very old favourite of mine—hope
you won't alter it.'

T.—' Some of the things don't seem to agree with the
time spoken of.'

W. A.—' The total effect is harmonious.   It's like a
landscape in an old Italian picture.'

T.—' I know : but I fear the water-gnats are not
right : they would not be out so late.'

I suggested transposing the line—

> Over the pools in the burn water-gnats murmur and mourn—

so as to bring it in earlier in the piece, which need not be supposed to show one moment merely, but a deepening twilight. He tried this in several ways then put it by for further consideration, and came out upon Blackdown and saw the close of one of these strange rich volcanic sunsets, now in our skies—floating ghost, perhaps, of a mountain blown to atoms. He spoke of Edward Fitzgerald—had not seen him for years before his death ; Fitzgerald could not be got to visit.

'But no sort of quarrel ?'

'O no ! fancy my quarrelling with dear old Fitz !'

We talked a little about the steam voyage with Gladstone.

'Why did you read "The Grandmother" to the great folk ?'

T.—'The Princess of Wales asked for it ; she had heard Mrs. Greville read it. I read it in a cabin on deck : the Princess sat close to me on one side and a young lady whom I didn't know on the other. The wind came through an open window and the Princess whispered "Put on your hat"—but I said I ought if possible to make myself balder than ever before so many Royalties ! She said again, "Oh put it on !" so I did, and I heard afterwards that the King of Denmark's Court-Fool who was in the background (they really keep a Court-Fool) remarked, "He may be Laureate, but he has not learnt Court manners."

'When I was done the ladies praised me, and I patted the unknown one on the back by way of reply, and presently I found out she was the Empress of Russia.'

'Had you any talk with the Czar ?'

'Hardly any—he said he couldn't speak English. Perhaps he was disgusted at my patting his wife on the back. His head was up in the cabin ceiling as he walked about below.'

Tennyson said the finest thing he saw on the voyage
was one night as he stood at the bow of the great
steamer and saw, as it were, the whole sea rushing
past like an immeasurable river to some unknown gulf.

We came to Sussex Gate, as I call it, on the
boundary of the two counties. 'Come into Surrey,' I
said ; 'No, I can't,' says he, 'but I'll strike the gate-
post with my stick ; I generally do—like Johnson
with the posts in Fleet Street.' So we parted. I went
on to Mr. Hodgson's, who signed the letter.

August.—William De Morgan came. Argument
about Genius—he thought it meant inspiration, as by
a familiar spirit or demon.

September 12.—We dined at Pinewood, Sir Henry and
Lady Holland, etc.—Irish Members, South Africa.

[There was also an interesting evening at Mr. (now
Sir Robert) Hunter's, where the Allinghams met Mr.
and Mrs. Henry Fawcett.]

The Poynters at Bowler's Green : our intercourse
was pleasant and friendly.

Caldecott looks in from hunting, his mare having
cast a shoe.

Charles Keene calls—we walk. He speaks of
Edward Fitzgerald—odd—dressed roughly—disliked
London. 'You fellows in clubs and so on praise each
other's things, poor as they may be !' F. went with K.
to a studio, and after coming away asked, 'Why did you
say "very nice"? You know you didn't like them.'

K. once sent him a little sketch out of his pocket-
book of some cottages near Woodbridge. F. returned
it with the remark, 'I could do as well myself.' He
kept a Commonplace Book of extracts, *Half-hours with
the Worst Authors.* K. hopes it will be published. 'F.
had his favourite murders, and I had mine.'

I read to Sonny and Evey *The Tempest, Midsr. Night's
D., As You Like It* (the plot of the last much strained).

John, Mayor of Waterford (for 1884) : goes to
Parnell Banquet.

CHAPTER XX

1884

[EARLY in this year the Allinghams spent some weeks at Hampstead, near to Mrs. Paterson (Mrs. Allingham's Mother) and her son and daughter. There are notes of visits to many old friends in Town,—and of a night at the Corner House, Shortlands, with Mr. and Mrs. George Craik.]

March 23.—Sandhills. The 'Forward Oak' is beginning to show a green top about this time.

March 26.—H. and I to the Evans's—Miss Kate Greenaway.

Sunday, March 30.—Mild. With Sonny and Sissy down Haselmere Lane and into 'Primrose Land'—copse abounding in primroses, wood-anemones, some violets—wood-spurge sprouting. Home with basket of flowers.

Wednesday, April 2.—Fine. Visitors—Mrs. and Miss Mangles, Mrs. Hunter, Mr. Burdon.

The wallflowers now are rich, germander speedwells fine blue.

April 3.—Pruning currant-bushes. Walk with Sonny and Evey, Brook Road, little common. Skirt Banacle Copse, violets, stitchwort. Ants.

June.—I low in spirits : the going over and in part burning old letters and papers very doleful and trying.

Have I been half kind enough, or grateful enough, or humble enough ? How much kindness and friendship I have received !

Nine years of subediting and editing *Fraser*, and what a list of people I have offended for life, by declining their contributions or in other ways! My name was known in connection with the Magazine, and people applied to me personally and took personal offence, even when J. A. F. was the really responsible person. Enough of it!

June 25.—Helen and I by invitation to the wedding of Hallam and Miss Audrey Boyle. The T. party were in our train in another carriage. We met at Waterloo Station. We in hansom to Dean's Yard— take our places in Henry VII.'s Chapel. Enter old Mrs. Procter and daughter, who sat next us; Lord Houghton, Mr. Lewis Morris, Mr. Matthew Arnold, Lecky, etc. Browning up in a Stall; he caught my eye and gave a friendly wink. Tennyson came in, cool and self-possessed, with Mrs. F. Locker on his arm. Lady Tennyson, supported by Lionel.

Ceremony. Then we all moved out slowly to the Deanery. Caldecott joined us in the aisle. Lecky, Mrs. Lecky, etc., etc. We had little more than a glimpse of the Bride—Happiness to them! worthy young people, they deserve it.

A shakehands with Dean Bradley, who asks me to find him a cottage in our neighbourhood to run down to.

In the Chapel we had just in front of us, and spoke to, T.'s sisters, Matilda—always most simple, friendly, and a pleasure to talk to—and Mrs. Lushington, whom we know but from one evening together at Dover. Mr. Lushington, after all these years, recollected me well and some talk we had together (which I have forgotten)—he looks little older, and bears his age like a cheerful wise man.

Witley, July 26.—After much urging from H. (I have always a rooted belief that people don't really want to see me) I went to Haslemere to-day: cool with showers: and walked up to Aldworth, arriving about 3 P.M. Found an arch in Avenue, 'Welcome Home'—so the Bride and Bridegroom are back. 'Lady Tennyson'—'Yes sir,'—on her sofa, sweet, pale and friendly.

Enter Hallam, looking stouter and face broadened. He tries his Father's door. 'Come in,' and there was T., just wakened from his usual nap—glad to see me, and says, 'I've done an Irish poem and I want you to help me with the brogue. But you're from the North.'

I told him I knew various Irish brogues—had he chosen any one in particular?

'No.'

He took up Carleton's *Traits and Stories*, which he was reading for the first time (to get up the brogue), and was delighted with, all the more for its caricature. Then he produced the MS. of 'Molly Maghee' (I asked him to strike out the 'h'), and we spent about an hour over it. First Tennyson read the piece to me, I commenting on it; then I read it to him, he looking over my arm the while. Aubrey de Vere gave him the subject, as a fact—the body of a man drowned in a bog-hole found undecayed after forty years or so. His old sweetheart recognises him and drops down 'dead on the dead.' The same incident is told of a Cornish miner, and I published a prose story upon it in Leigh Hunt's Journal. Hamilton Aïdé has a poem on the same subject. I suggested many corrections in the brogue, and some in other points. I told T. the Irish would not like it, but he didn't see why not.

I am pressed to stay for dinner, and then to stay the night—consent, and send telegram to Helen. Then T. and I, in rain, make a little run in the copses to a new summer-house with a writing-table and pens, and a vista cut in front to see the vast view of the weald, etc. Dinner at 6.30. Stay a little with Lady T. and Hallam: then drawing-room, where T. at table close to window with Mrs. Hallam—wine and strawberries.

He thinks England is entering on gloomy times—

perhaps coming to the end of her grandeur and glory.
'Goschen feels the same—is much depressed about it,
the Lord Chancellor too. I voted for the Franchise to
avoid worse things.'

I said I wished he had voted against Pigeon Torture.
Hallam.—'So do I.'

T. said nothing, but I stuck to the subject.

'Hope you'll vote for the Bill next time.'

'Don't think I'll ever go into the House again.'

'Well, you can pair.'

'Lecky says the Irish want a despot,' and T. agrees.

'The English are not poetical or musical or clever
—they're very stupid and heavy—but they are for
reasonable and constitutional liberty, that a man should
have his own opinion without being knocked on the
head for it. In Ireland, if I don't agree with a man,
he shoots me or knocks my brains out! I never knew
a rational Irishman in my life! except you' (this
sounded very parenthetical), 'and you don't care a pin
for the grand Empire of England. You ought to be
proud surely to be part of it. There you are, with an
English name, English in every way, but you happened
to be born in Ireland, therefore you are for it.'

I pleaded that I was more impartial than most
people; 'if I were Nationalist I might be popular in
Ireland and perhaps get into Parliament if I liked.
My brother was offered a seat for Waterford free of
cost.'

T.—'I hate to think of Ireland. Here they are,
after 700 years raging and roaring.'

W. A.—'A most unlucky country!' (to which
Hallam agreed). 'Suppose England tried leaving them
to themselves.'

T.—'Civil War!'

W. A.—'Then let them settle it. England would
be able to take care of herself.'

T.—'Ireland might join with France against
England.'

W. A.—' Another plan : take away all franchise and representation from Ireland for seven years, letting her manage her local affairs as she pleases.'

T.—' They would roar incessantly. I hate speaking of it ! ' (da capo).

T. was shocked to hear of William Morris's Democratic Socialism, and asked to see a copy of *Justice*. (Morris's *Justice*, I partly agree with and partly detest. It is incendiary and atheistic, and would upset everything. How about America, which started a hundred years ago as a democracy with almost ideal advantages ? I want reforms and thorough-going ones, but not by the hands of atheists and anarchists.)

By the evening post came a packet from ' O. Weber,' Copenhagen, asking Lord Tennyson to present the enclosed MS. translation into Danish of his splendid dramas *The Cup* and *The Falcon* to H.R.H. the Princess of Wales.

Sunday, July 27.—Aldworth. About eleven T. and I came out to walk, first to the stables, where he unchained a Deerhound, a black Setter and two smaller dogs, then with these on Blackdown — along road, returning by Chase Farm uphill through plantations.

Poetry—Browning : ' one is constantly aware of the greatness of the man, yet somehow baulked of satisfaction.

' He offered me the subject of *The Ring and the Book*. " My Last Duchess " is very fine.'

As he stood looking at the pond by Chase Farm, I spoke of Ruskin's essay on versification, and his selection of Coleridge as the exemplar of a bad Versifier, and of these lines from 'Christabel ' as an example of bad verse—

> But vainly thou warrest,
>   For this is alone in
> Thy power to declare,
>   That in the dim forest
> Thou heard'st a low moaning,

> And found'st a bright lady, surpassingly fair ;
> And did'st bring her home with thee in love and in charity,
> To shield her and shelter her from the damp air.

'Nobody,' I said, 'but a true and heaven-born Metrist could have written that—'twas like a legato passage on the violin, flowing through from beginning to end with one bow.' T. did not entirely agree. He objected to—

> Did'st bring her home with thee in love and in charity.

I said the whole passage had an air of spontaneousness, of naïvety, and this to me was the last perfection of poetry.

T.—'The last perfection is the wild and wonderful—

> Charm'd magic casements, opening on the foam,
> Of perilous seas, in faery lands forlorn.'

W. A.—'Coleridge was a great poet.—Well, he was an endless talker, but not a bothering one ; 'twas like a fountain running, you went away from it when you pleased. He did not care about convincing or converting or convicting you.'

T.—'Ruskin's dictum is not to be relied on.'

W. A.—'Especially on poetry. He printed a volume of poems of his own ; but that (he wrote to me once) is "the disgrace of whatever faculty I possess."—Recently he has republished his Oxford Prize Poem on the "Caves of Elephanta "—entirely worthless.'

When on the upper road, looking over the gate where you see the Valewood ponds below, we still spoke of poetry.

'One believes in a poet,' I said, 'whose lines are perpetually coming into one's mind. Yours do with me.'

T.—'Repeat a line.'

W. A.—'Dozens, if you like.'

T.—'I was praising one of Rogers's poems to him once and he said, "Repeat a passage—ha, you can't," and I couldn't at the moment.'

W. A.—' Well, that's barley, not wheat, but here's a line it brings to my mind—

> And waves of shadow went over the wheat.

' After the thunder-storm the other day, as many a time before, I repeated to myself—

> Sweet after showers, ambrosial air,
> That rollest from the gorgeous gloom
> Of evening——'

T. interrupted me and, as he spoke, stood still and faced me (a custom of his)—

' You can't say it so sweetly as I can ! ' and repeated the whole stanza, and on, to ' the round of space.'

I always rejoice to hear him recite.

' It all goes together,' said he.

' Yes,' said I, ' especially when you sit down to the organ.   You won't listen to me and so I hurry.'

As we turned down Pack Horse Lane, T. spoke of Eternal Punishment as an obsolete belief.

I said, ' At Witley Station hangs on the wall a large book of Bible Texts, one page for each day of the month.   To-day I read—" All the dead shall arise, the righteous to eternal life, the wicked to everlasting damnation." '

T.—' It's not a right translation.'

W. A.—' But it's the authoritative teaching of the Church.'

T.—' Have you read Farrar's book ? '

W. A.—' I never read such books.'

T.—' Oh, but here he proves from original sources that no such doctrine existed in the early days of Christianity.'

I told T. that Bishop Wilberforce was very proud of having saved the Athanasian Creed when the Archbishop of Canterbury was for giving it up, which interested him.

' Did he ?   My father (I think it was his father)
would never read the Athanasian Creed.'

As we entered the back wicket and went along the shady little walk to the house T. said, 'You're not orthodox, and I can't call myself orthodox. Two things however I have always been firmly convinced of,—God,—and that death will not end my existence.'

W. A.—'So I believe.'

T. (stopping and turning round)—'Do you hold these?'

W. A.—'I do.'

He was going up for his usual sleep, and asked me not to go till he came down again about half-past three. So I sat and read in the middle parlour. Then went up and found him just after wakening. He came out, unloosed the dogs again, and walked with me along the road till we met Mrs. Hodgson coming to call. T. asked me to turn back, but I took leave and walked off to Witley, glad to have seen so much of the dear man, and sad not to see more.

August 2.—Warm—with breeze. H., I and Sonny and Evey to Godalming, by invitation, to the Wallaces,[1] Frith Hill, beside the Water Tower. Hot climb. Mr. and Mrs. Wallace in garden. Willy, Violet—children race about.

W. shows us round his garden—rare plants and flowers—little 'Californian tulip,' light yellow, three petals—green hairs inside—Canadian lily—Flowers of one day. Eucalyptus, three kinds, very tender.

Sit with Wallace under tree and talk a long while on Spiritualism, apparitions, mediums, etc.—'the Cock Lane Ghost was real (as Johnson believed), but they teased the girl into imposture at last.' He said about one person in ten, probably, is a medium.

He spoke with unqualified praise of every book and writer on the spiritualistic side — William Howitt, Professor De Morgan, Professor Barrett, F. W. H. Myers, etc.—showed us, in a magazine, drawings done by thought-readers. He gave an account, essentially

[1] Mr. Alfred Russell Wallace.

Swedenborgian, of the state of spirits in the next world
—but he does not take Swedenborg for a prophet.

I told him of my mentally seeing *The Times* with a
black border one morning before I went into the room
where it lay. It was for Prince Leopold's death. He
asked do I usually 'visualise' the things I think of?
'Yes, always.' 'I do not at all (he said)—my mind has
only thoughts.' Then spoke of Galton's division of all
minds into the visualising and the non-visualising class.

August 4.—To Lythe Hill, Mrs. Stewart Hodgson's
— Roomful — Corney Grain performing. Lord
Tennyson, Hallam, Mrs. Hallam, Mr. Buckton, Mr.
Macmillan, Wife and Daughter, Mrs. Pratt, etc. Mrs.
Hunter drives us to station, and asks us to dine on
Saturday.

Thursday, August 7.—A hot day. Helen and I all
the afternoon at Aldworth. Various visitors and
callers, so I had little talk with T.

Some numbers of *Justice*—Democrat Socialist paper
which I lent him—made him 'vomit mentally,' he said.
He would agree to the heavy taxing of large incomes
if it could be done. I told him about Alfred Wallace,
whom we visited last Saturday, and Spiritualism.
Wallace a thorough-going believer — but has had *no*
experiences himself. Also, he never visualises his
thoughts. I suggested that to such a man the mere
visualising power of some other minds might appear
supernatural, he having nothing like it in his experience.

T.—'I said long ago, " A poet never sees a Ghost." '
Still, he is most anxious to believe in ghosts.

'As to visualising,' he said, 'I often see the most
magnificent landscapes.'

'In dreams?'

'Yes, and on closing my eyes. To-day when I
lay down I saw a line of huge wonderful cliffs rising
out of a great sweep of forest—finer than anything in
nature.'

Other gifts he has, but T. is especially and preeminently a landscape-painter in words, a colourist, rich, full and subtle.

He has, latently, a very practical side to his character, and in using this his profound quietude of temperament and manner helps immensely.

We talked of Carlyle. T. said, 'He used to tell me, "You must do this—You mustn't do that"—but I never minded him in the least. I repeated some of Marvell's lines about Holland to Carlyle—

> They with mad labour fished the land to shore—

but he saw no humour in them, and said it was wrong to ridicule a serious diligent Nation.'

Mem.—Tennyson read Baudelaire's *Fleurs du Mal*, and thought him 'a kind of moralist,' though his subjects, he allowed, are shocking. I could not agree (and had, I think, studied Baudelaire more closely); he seems to me to take pleasure in seeing evil committed, and also in seeing evil-doers punished—a devil rather than a moralist.

September 8.—H. and I to Aldworth. In the drawing-room we find Lady Tennyson—then T. comes in. His two little grandsons run in. Tennyson went to his bedroom and returned with a soap-dish and piece of soap, which he rubbed into a lather, and proceeded to blow bubbles, himself much delighted with the little crystal worlds and their prismatic tints—'Never was anything seen so beautiful! You artists (to H.) can't get such colours as these.'

The children jumped and laughed, and we fanned the bubbles to the ceiling and watched them burst in various parts of the room. Then T., inverting his pipe, blew up a magic cluster of diamond domes on the saucer, which rolled over and wetted his knees, till we put a newspaper to save him. Next he took his trusty tobacco pipe, lighted it and blew opaque bubbles which burst with a tiny puff of smoke, like shells over a besieged fortress.

I said, 'Do you remember Vivier, the French horn-player, doing that in Tom Taylor's garden?'

T.—'I was just thinking of that.'

We were asked more than once to stay, but hurried off to the train.

September.—After the hot summer, rain—then fine autumnal weather.

The Oulesses at Grayswood : walks and calls.

Thursday, November 6.—Tennyson wished me to bring Mr. Alfred R. Wallace to visit him. It was arranged that W. and I should go over to-day. Mr. Wallace came by the 12.35 train from Godalming, and Helen and I (she specially invited by Hallam) joined at Witley. At Haslemere we found Hallam with a pony-carriage.

T. 'not well'—looking languid and rather sad.

At luncheon, talk about the tropic woods : Wallace said you would find one kind of tree in flower for about a week, and at another time another kind of tree in flower for a short time, but you might come again and again and find no flowers at all ; there were never in the Tropics such masses of floral colour as in an English Spring.

T. was disappointed at this, and asked about the trailing plants. W. called them 'glorious,' but more for the rich drapery than the colours. The palm-tops are mostly a grayish green.

We digressed to novels. Mr. W. (rather to my surprise) reads 'a good many in the course of the year,' but does not hurry over them. He and Hallam exchanged names of novels to be ordered from the Circulating Library, Lord Tennyson being an incessant novel-reader. While we were speaking of woods etc. T. said, 'Bayard Taylor, who has been everywhere, said the most beautiful sight he ever saw was a wood in Lapland covered with frozen rain and the sun shining on it.'

Also, 'Sir Robert Kane said the most awful thing

he ever experienced was the absolute silence of an Arctic winter.'

Mr. Wallace, Hallam and I went round the grounds, looking at various conifers.

To the Study.   W. gave details of table-rapping, table-prancing, and so forth, his own experiences and other people's.   He never doubts any statement whatever in favour of 'Spiritualism,' and has an answer to every objection.   'Maskelyne and Cooke do wonderful things.'—'Yes, partly by the help of mediumship.'

'The "Spirits" often give foolish and misleading answers.'—'Yes, as might be expected; that only proves them to be human beings.'

'Why noises and motions of tables?   Why these particular "Mediums"?'—'Such are the conditions; why, we do not know.'

W. said it was absurd to suppose that Matter could move itself.   I ventured to remark that Matter, so far as we can penetrate, does move itself, indeed is perpetually in motion.

He rejoined that in table-rapping etc. the phenomena were manifestly governed by an intelligence like our own.   The means of communication between the Unseen World and ours were few and difficult.

Here Tennyson said, 'A great ocean pressing round us on every side, and only leaking in by a few chinks'?— of which Wallace took no notice, but went on to describe instances of spirit-writing on slates, by Slade and others.

(I fear my tone all through was hardly respectful to the spirits.)

Somehow or other a sudden digression was made to politics, and W. came out with a strong opinion of the worthlessness of the House of Lords and the absurdity of the hereditary principle.

T. said, 'I think I respect it more than the other House.'

W.—'The other House wants reforming very badly, no doubt.'

The Duke of Marlborough was mentioned. Wallace denounced the purchase of his Raphael with the public money as ' scandalous '—would not buy any pictures or works of art with the taxpayers' money—' let wealthy men buy and present them to the nation if they think fit.'

Egypt somehow came in, and Wallace thought we ought to leave the Mahdi alone. He is perhaps a great man, and at all events we know no harm of him.

T.—' I know no good of him.'

W. A.—' Would you not like to see the Nile ? '

T.—' I'd much rather see tropical nature, but now I never shall.'

And then he questioned W. again about tropical scenery, producing a poem in MS., from which he read two or three lines about palms and purple seas. He wanted to know if the palm-trees could be seen rising distinct above the rest of the forest.

W.—' Yes, on a hill-side.'

' What colour are they ? '

' Rather light—gray-green.'

' Is an expanse of tropical forest *dark*, seen from above ? '

' Not particularly ; less so than an English wood-land.'

T.—' Then I must change the word " dark." '

He writes his poetry now in trim small quarto books, in limp covers, the writing as neat as ever, tho' sometimes a little shaky. He keeps these books handy and takes them up very often, both at set times and odd moments, considering and correcting, and frequently reading new poems aloud from them, first to his family and afterwards to visitors. After the compositions are put into type he usually keeps them by him in proof for a long time, months or even years, reconsidering and perfecting every part.

T. referred with praise to Wallace's book, *Tropical Nature*, and remarked, ' You have said something very bold about Matter ? I think Matter more mysterious than Spirit. I can conceive, in a way, what Spirit is, but not Matter.'

W.—'I conceive Matter not as a substance at all, but as *points of energy*, and that if these were withdrawn Matter would disappear.'

T. said this was something like his own notion.

W.—'So far from a material atom being indestructible, I believe that all the Matter in existence might be immediately destroyed by the withdrawal of the sustaining Force.'

Tuesday, November 25.—On a sudden impulse I walked up from Sandhills about 3 o'clock, to call at Aldworth, the roads greasy with a thaw, ice on pools. On Blackdown met Hallam, and then Tennyson. They hospitably determined that I was to stay the night, and would telegraph to Witley accordingly. They had come along the road to meet Miss Ritchie coming from London, who soon appeared, and we walked to the house together. In the ante-room, Miss Matilda and tea, and we all looked at a large coloured caricature, 'The Tower of Babel,' with portraits of peers, M.P.'s, etc. etc.

Miss R. said, 'What a pity Mr. Gladstone sees so many sides of a subject.'

T.—'No, that he doesn't do—he cannot see all round a thing. Bacon could. Bacon says, "It were good if men in their innovations would follow the example of Time itself, which indeed innovateth greatly, but quietly, and by degrees scarce to be perceived."'

I said, 'Yes, but we ought not to wait to be forced on.'

T. rejoined, 'Bacon says that too,' and went on to complain of the crude and dangerous haste of modern Reformers.

(Bacon's *Essays*, by the way, are mostly bundles of antitheses, and offer weapons to opposite combatants.)

In the evening Tennyson questioned me again about Irish brogue, ' How do they pronounce " door " ? '

I answer, like ' boor ' : ' floor ' sometimes thus, and sometimes with a sharper *u*—like ' flute.'

T. has rhymed ' door ' to ' asthore ' in his Irish poem, and is uneasy in his mind about it, notwithstanding Aubrey de Vere's thinking it all right.

In ' Mary Donnelly ' I have—

> When she stood up for dancing her steps were so complete
> The music nearly killed itself to listen to her feet—

but I avoid writing brogue, and leave it to the speaker or singer. An Irishman could read these lines without a jar in the rhymes and at the same time without saying ' complate ' in a broadly vulgar manner. But T. insists on the brogue all through his piece ; it's a brogue poem, and the rhymes ought to help emphatically.

Hallam showed me his father's lines in the *St. James's Gazette* about the cataract. T. coming to us, said it was a cataract like those on the Nile (not precipitous), the river is supposed to divide round an island. The first word, printed ' Statesman,' he has altered into ' Steersman.'

We spoke of Gladstone's oratory : I said I thought Brougham's (whom I heard two or three times) the most like it in practised verbosity and the long sentences out of which the speaker wound himself at last without a break—few memorable passages in either case.

Tennyson is very fond of Gladstone as a private friend.

Then spoke of Carlyle : Froude's quotation of the bitterness against Gladstone. I told Carlyle's saying about Dizzy : ' I wonder how long John Bull will allow this Jew to dance on his belly ! ' which amused Tennyson.

T. or Hallam said that Gladstone (his own account) gave Carlyle offence at Rogers's table by refusing to agree in Carlyle's estimate of Goethe, and C. never forgave him. Gladstone laughed at the description of himself as ' the contemptiblest man.'

T. thinks Byron's morals ought not to be considered in judging his poetry. 'Unless they come into his poetry' (I maintain), and they certainly do. But it is less as voluptuary than as sneerer that I can't bear Lord Byron. T. thinks he was perhaps the cleverest man of his time. The more shame for him to be what he was.

Byron was just before T.'s time, so there are no personal feelings one way or other such as are almost inevitably mixed with contemporary estimates.

W. A.—' Did you ever meet Coleridge?'

T.—' No, I was asked to visit him, but I wouldn't.'

W. A.—' Coleridge was a " noticeable man, with large gray eyes." '

T.—' Oh yes.'

We talked a good deal about metres—nothing new. T. brought on again the question of the rhymes in his Irish piece.

I said, ' Have Maria (an Irish housemaid here) and try her with them.'

T. on this told us a little story—' A Suffolk vicar going into a parishioner's cottage found a Catholic engraving on the wall, the Virgin with St. Joseph on one side and St. Somebody else on the other. The woman of the house had got it by some chance.'

' Did she know what it meant?'

' Well, yes, she'd made it out : " There's the young woman, and two men making up to her, and the one man he says to t'other at last, ' 'Ave Maria!' That's what's wrote up, you see, sir." '

Miss Ritchie played us some Beethoven finely. At Hallam's request she tried Edward Fitzgerald's music (MS.) to ' Locksley Hall,' but found it amateurish in structure.

Next day, wonderfully fine, T. started at his usual time (11.30) for a walk, Miss Ritchie, Hallam and I with him, and two dogs. We went by Chase Farm, fine yellow russets still on the woods. T. stopped us to see the white doves on the outhouse. Then on the western ridge of Blackdown, looking over Valewood, Lynchmere, etc., mistily rich, hills folded on hills. In the foreground some bushes of gorse in good bloom. T. went up to one taller than himself, covered with new golden blossoms, and stood looking at it : I have the picture in my mind.

Speaking of the new Franchise Bill, Miss R. said, 'I suppose there's no country where the people care so much for politics as in England?'

T.—'I hate politics! I'm for the *Empire*, but I hate politics. The Queen said to me, "*I* hate politics," and no wonder she does. As to this Bill, I don't believe the people care anything about it.'

In the evening Miss Tennyson reminded Alfred of the stories he used to tell his brothers and sisters. One called 'The Old Horse' lasted for months.

December 5.—A fine day. H. and I to Blackdown. We found her last year's point of view, and she sat courageously for two hours sketching in the cold, for 'twas an eager air tho' the sun shone. An immense level of thin cloud stretched moveless from north to south over the great Sussex landscape—green fields, houses, villages, stood forth in the sunlight ; clear, remote, all silent ; near at hand a bold sweeping slope of rusty fern, gorse clumps coming into Christmas blossom, mixed with a few hollies and stunted firs.

On the next ridge, a mile off or so as the crow flies, push up through sheathing woods the gray stone chimneys and blue roofs of the Poet's mansion, looking this way with an upper window or two. Then far and wide the map-like prospect from Haslemere and Leith Hill to the South Downs. I walked to the south end of Blackdown, glorious views ; came back with a chimney-sweeper who was taking a short-cut to Haslemere and complained that the farmers do not know the value of soot for land.

Found H. very cold, but working still; and away we walked to Aldworth to find her a cup of tea. On the road we met T. himself, most friendly, who turned back with us and left H. in charge of his Sister; then he came out again and finished his walk in my company.

T.—'I'm an old fellow and must exercise. One may do without it in youth, but not in age.'

W. A.—'Carlyle used to praise London for affording night walks in winter.'

T.—'I can't walk in London by night. The lights dazzle me.'

We spoke of William Morris (from whom I had just had a long letter).

T. said, 'He has gone crazy.' I said I agreed with many of Morris's notions. Labour does not get its fair share.

T.—'There's brain labour as well as hand labour.'

W. A.—'And there are many who get money without any labour. The question, how to hinder money from accumulating into lumps, is a puzzling one.'

T.—'You must let a man leave money to his children. I was once in a coffee-shop in the Westminster Road at 4 o'clock in the morning. A man was raging "Why has So-and-So a hundred pounds, and I haven't a shilling?" I said to him, "If your father had left you £100 you wouldn't give it away to somebody else." He hadn't a word to answer. I knew he hadn't.'

T. said, 'It's a very strange thing that, according to Wallace, none of the Spirits that communicate with men ever mention God, or Christ.'

I said I always felt that the Deity was *infinitely* above us. Another step will bring us no nearer.

T.—'Wallace says the system he believes in is a far finer one than Christianity : it is Eternal Progress— I have always felt that there must be somewhere *Some one who knows*—that is, *God*. But I am in hopes that I shall find something human in Him too.

'Gladstone and Tyndall were sitting at my table, Gladstone on my right hand, Tyndall on my left. Tyndall began talking in his loose way about "This Poem—or Poetic Idea—God." Gladstone looked at him and said with severity, "Professor Tyndall, leave God to the Poets and Philosophers, and attend to your own business." Tyndall fell quite silent for several minutes.'

Dinner—T. in good spirits and humour ; compares the cheese to Alpine scenery. I quote Marcus Aurelius about the inequalities of a loaf.

T.—'C. C. would say I plagiarised from Marcus Aurelius. Some one has said that "As the husband is the wife is" is evidently from Scott. "The wife takes her husband's rank."'

Lady Tennyson came down to dinner, very pale— spoke and was spoken to little, went upstairs again, almost carried by Hallam. A dear, almost angelic woman.

We were quoting odd and rough verses when the pony-carriage came—and William drove us rapidly to the station, feeling happy with our friendly visit.

[There is a note of an evening at Aldworth when] Tennyson was amusing in his vehement denunciation of the old Tory aristocracy of his boyhood—the 'county families'—their pride, prejudice, narrowness, and bitter partisanship. 'At a public ball at Lincoln the Whig families would sit by themselves on one side of the room, Tory on the other, noticing each other as little as possible. But the youth of each sometimes danced together in the middle. Two ladies of opposite politics found themselves on the same sofa and avoided each other mutually as much as they might without turning their backs. But the curiosity of one lady induced her to take up a piece of the gorgeous flowing dress of her neighbour to look at it more closely, when she thought the owner's head was turned away. Round comes the rival lady's face with a sneering smile upon it : "Madam, if you'll allow me, I'll send you my

mantua-maker's bill to look at. . . ." We are
certainly better-off in manners nowadays!'

Charles Keene at Birket Foster's for Christmas—
calls one day. We walk by Park Lane, Bowler's Green,
and Screw Corner. ' *Loud* smells not unwholesome.'
C. K. himself has, he tells me, very little sense of smell
—and no topographical faculty. His visit to a knacker's
yard. Edward Fitzgerald—Ed. F. used to call the
critics ' a case of monkeys '—had a boy to read aloud
to him every day (in a strong Suffolk brogue) while
he lay on a chair and smoked.

December.—Carlyle's *Life.* Melancholy book. F.
has manipulated his materials cunningly.

[A few words may be said here of the relations—
always cordial—between Allingham and his family and
old friends in Ireland. There was a regular, if not
very frequent correspondence, and little gifts were exchanged at the end of the year. His sister Catherine's
letters from Ballyshannon were always interesting to
Allingham—though sad, too, for they came to be
mainly records of the deaths of those he had known
there. Visitors from ' the old country ' always had a
warm welcome.

At this time—1884—were living John, Catherine,
Jane : and, of the second family, Edward, Hugh, and
Lizzie.

Now—1907—of these are left only John and Hugh.

John at Waterford, with Wife, Son, and Daughter.

Hugh and his Daughters, at Ballyshannon, where he
is in his Father's place as Manager of the Provincial
Bank of Ireland.

Hugh Allingham is the author of an unpretentious
little book, *Ballyshannon, its History and Antiquities* ; he
is now busy on a more extended local history, in the
researches for which he had valuable help from his
late Wife.

Sons and Daughters of Mrs. Johnston (Sister Jane)
are living and prospering in various places.]

CHAPTER XXI

1885–1886

[THE life at Sandhills went on much as usual during the spring and summer of 1885. The Tennysons had spent the winter at Aldworth, and Allingham went over several times : but there are no notes of the talks to copy.

Pleasant visits were exchanged with Mr. and Mrs. Harry Furniss, who stayed in Haslemere in June—and with many other friends.

In September the Allinghams went to Sandown for a month.]

October 13.—To Aldworth. Novels. *Vanity Fair* : I said I was now reading some of Trollope's, and felt my estimate of his powers to be higher than it used to be.

Tennyson.—' But they're so dull—so prosaic : never a touch of poetry.'

Lyme Regis—I reminded him that I was at Lyme in his company, and how we visited Mr. Barnes at his vicarage near Dorchester.—' How is old Barnes ? ' asked T. in a kindly tone—' Do you ever hear from him ? ' ' Yes, I had a letter lately.'

We spoke of Lord Houghton, his kindly nature. I repeated a verse of ' I wandered by the brookside,' and told what the author told me ; that he wrote it on an Irish jaunting-car driving to Edgeworthstown to visit Miss Edgeworth. A line or two came into his head, somehow ; he made the whole piece, almost without thinking of it, and it seemed to him (then) to have not the least value.

SANDHILLS,
WITLEY,
GODALMING.

Iuly 16
1885

My dear Mr Barnes

I think of you very often,
and long to hear some news
of you.   We have been
living here four years in a
beautiful region of woods
hills & commons. Tennyson's
hill, Blackdown, is opposite
our windows , 6 miles off, and
we often see him , tho it is
further than we could wish.
He is close on his 76th birthday
unchanged in mind and not

much changed in body by
these last ten years. He walks
2 or 3 hours every day, and
goes on writing — has lately
done an Irish piece, & honoured
me by much. consultation about
'brogue'. But the truth is, I
don't much like 'brogue' pieces,
& have myself tried to manage
Irish subjects with a minimum
of that flavouring. A 'brogue'
is not a dialect. I suppose the
word has been transferred, to ex:
press a rustic & clumsy gait
in speech, from its original
meaning — a rough shoe.

I hope, my dear & honoured
friend, that you are well
and able still to feel that
Poetry is one of the realest
and richest possessions of Man.
You have very certainly added
to the general store of that
wealth.

My wife, who belongs to the
Old Water Colour Society, is
happier here than ever before
in her life, painting out of
doors as much as possible.
What a good lot, to feel the
truest pleasure in one's work
& at the same time that one

is

is providing for the pleasure of others.
She is now engaged on a series of
"Surrey Cottages", for exhn by themselves
next year in London, & in this
making record of many beautiful
old things that are disappearing
from the earth.   For myself,
I continue to write, in verse &
prose, but with yearly increasing
distaste for the existing conditions
of literature (so called) & publication
I am writing twelve Sonnets
'Flowers & Months' – some of wh have
appeared in the Athenm. Accept a copy
of the last written, & just coming out –
Janry has the Daisy; Febry the Snowdrop;
March, Daffodil; April, Primrose; May,
Hawthorn; June, Wildrose; July, Honeysuckle;
August, Meadowsweet; Sept, Heather; October–?
With warmest regards and good wishes
I am ever sincerely yours
W Allingham

> Adieu, dear Yorkshire Milnes! we think not now
> Of coronet or laurel on thy brow;
> The kindest, faithfullest of friends wert thou.

T. asked, 'Whose is that?'

'Mine,' I told him.

'That's very good,' he said.

(A rare treat to have praise from him.)

Friday, November 6.—Fine, walked from Sandhills to Aldworth, through Haslemere, muddy roads, yellow russet woods. The Bucktons there. T. and Mr. B. on Natural History. T. asks 'How can Evolution account for the ant?' Mr. B. says the theory presents many difficulties. He is studying the English cicadæ. We go to hall door to see the B.'s off, then Tennyson and I take a short walk. He asks me to stay the night, and I accept.

After dinner, 'To-morrow' (late 'Molly Magee') is again produced, this time in print. The whole of the new volume is in print, but, as usual, stays thus for a time, sometimes a long time, for final corrections. Carleton's *Traits and Stories of the Irish Peasantry*—with which he is delighted. I said I knew Carleton a little. 'Then you knew a man of genius,' said T. He thinks C. is not appreciated. I told him that in Ireland he is, highly. Also that C., Catholic born, turned Protestant in youth, wrote the *Traits*, then returned to his old Church and wrote many stories, in which priests and other matters were handled in a different way.

'Those are not so good, I should think,' T. said.

I told him that Irish brogue has many *nuances*, especially in sound; it differs in different parts of the island; and there are vulgar and unvulgar brogues; and the possessor of a vulgar brogue is a subject of frequent imitation and ridicule among his own countrymen. But a mild brogue in the mouth of an educated person, and especially of a pretty woman, is sweet and soothing, pleasant and coaxing. Her way of spē-aking is very different from the way an ignorant Connaught or Munster peasant would *shpayke*. I could not bring myself to use the vulgar brogue in verse, unless it were for a broadly comic purpose.

T. said the Irish way of speaking was wonderfully like the Lincolnshire.

He once more spoke a good deal about the want of some fixed standard of English pronunciation, or even some fixed way of indicating a poet's intention as to the pronunciation of his verses. 'It doesn't matter so much (he said) in poetry written for the intellect— as much of Browning's is, perhaps ; but in mine it's necessary to know how to sound it properly.'

I suggested that he might put on record a code for pronouncing his own poetry, with symbolised examples, and he seemed to think this might be done.

After tea he turned over the leaves of the new volume, I looking over his arm. Put last now (it was first) is a Sonnet against raking together and publishing the fragments of a deceased Poet. This is to 'swamp the Poets with themselves' (a favourite turn of phrase with T.) Then he turned to a longish poem called 'The Flight' and said, 'This was written fifty years ago.' I asked him to read it : he said 'Oh, it isn't worth reading '—but he read it. It is not very notable among his varied riches, but simpler and more straightforward in style than some of his later pieces. I said I liked it, and he said he was glad of that. (I had read 'Vastness' in *Macmillan's Magazine* without any sense of gain.)

Saturday, November 7.—Aldworth, 8.15—misty. Walked with T. down the lane to Lythe Hill and back. I asked him what he had seen of Gordon. Saw him once only : he came to luncheon one day to T.'s, in London. He was shy and rather silent, but he had a pleasant look.

W. A.—'Have you read Gordon's *Journals*?'

T.—'No. The Queen told me I ought to read
them.'

W. A.—'You ought indeed.' Then I rapidly but
at some length gave him a sketch of the contents of
that curious book, and of Gordon's character—man of
great powers, immense wilfulness, whence followed a
great catastrophe. T. listened much more patiently
than I expected, and laughed at G.'s entry—'I am
insubordinate, incorrigible ; if I were my own superior
I would certainly never employ myself!'

He told a droll thing about Lord F. at a Farmers'
Dinner at Exeter the other day. Speaking to some
toast, his Lordship had occasion to name one of the
most important farmers present, and alluded with
sympathy to 'a recent family affliction' which had
befallen him—the man's wife having died a short time
before. The farmer, having to speak by and by,
thanked his Lordship very kindly for the way he had
spoken of him, but 'as for my old woman (he went
on) she were a teasy twoad, and the Lord's welcome to
her!'

We talked of Rabelais. T. made light of his
stercoraceous qualities, and said he used to read him
aloud at Cambridge to some of his friends and they
all nearly tumbled off their chairs with laughing. The
foulness was but a mask to hide his free-thinking. But,
I said, he evidently enjoyed it, revelled in it.

Friday, November 13.—Hallam met Helen yesterday
at Haslemere and invited us to come to luncheon to-day.
We found T. just untying the dogs for his morning
walk. He proposed to take Helen and me to an old
ruinous cottage, Dickhurst, he had often told us of,
and thought H. might like to paint. So we three went
down the new road, a few apples still in the orchard,
out by the lower gate, and a mile or so along the roads
of the Sussex Weald ; a fine day, though with some
mist, and the half-bare copses and hedges still rich with
their tarnished-gold russet.

T. said he never was in an oak country in Spring till last year and was astonished at the colours.   A highish field gate was locked, and T. climbed over—then trudging through a swampy field we came to the deserted half-ruinous cottage, with long slope of tiled roof, broken windows and empty barns.   H. made a pencil sketch, and T. and I went on further, but could not get through the copse.   Hallam appeared with a pony-carriage and drove off Helen and his cousin Mrs. Pope.   T. and I walked back.   He spoke of the Lincolnshire farmers of his early days, and what ' beasts ' they were.

I said : 'You ought to be more tolerant to poor Paddy—he has better manners at least.'

T.—'I count Paddy a child. But his mutilation of animals is shocking ;—worse than shooting men.'

W. A.—' I have heard it said that in Catholic countries there is less humanity towards animals than in Protestant: Catholicism teaches that animals are created solely for man's use.' We spoke of the cruelties of the Inquisition. T. said, ' A Catholic priest said to me, all those were political, not ecclesiastical.'

W. A.—'That takes away the sole possible excuse for them, namely that they were done in defence of the one true Faith and to save souls from perdition.' We then went back to Irish and Keltic peoples in general.   I said, ' Perhaps England owes most of its finer qualities, its poetry, music, and art, to the Ancient British elements.'

T. said, but not very confidently, ' I doubt that.'

[About this time, Allingham notes :—]

Savoy. *Mikado*—pretty dresses—music skilful, harmonious, and agreeable — not an atom of melodic invention. S.'s only way of getting at the semblance of a tune is to set words with a very marked rhythm, and by dint of time-beat and harmonisation to give a sort of impression of an air—but 'tis a mere bubble. In ' Yum-Yum ' (and elsewhere) the phrase is old and familiar.

Have entirely neglected diary from December 1885 till
to-day, February 16th! A variable cold winter—all kinds
of weather in a week. But is anything disagreeable as
we look back save one's own faults and mistakes?

We sometimes call in at the Evans's on a Sunday.
Sonny and I often walk to Godalming.

Helen diligent at her Cottages.

I finish the twelve Flower Sonnets in *Athenæum*.

Rhyme book.[1] Harry Furniss's two drawings.
Iu-Kiao-Li,[2] etc.

March 10.—Gladstone cooking his Irish Stew.

March 19.—To London. Japanese Exhibition, etc.

March 21.—The Grange. Georgie truly friendly :
Margaret in flowery flowing robe : Phil (with keen chin
and bright eyes) : Ned comes in.

April 25.—G. and E. to church with Elizabeth.
G. said ' I read all the " I believes " and I didn't believe
any of them.' They said ' church was nice.' ' Would
they like to go every Sunday?' ' O no.'

July 9.—Diary not touched for more than two
months. Mrs. Paterson at Sandhills. Visits of Carrie,
of Arthur, of Basil and Clara Martineau.

July 31.—To Busbridge. Hungarian Band. Mr.
Ramsden, Mr. Stone, Mr. Molyneux, etc. To Miss
Jekyll's—round her garden (I always like to be with
Miss Jekyll). Her studio, and forge.

Tuesday, *August* 3.—Miss —— having frequently
failed to come on the appointed days to teach the
children, we bring the arrangement to an end, and I
intend to take up the teaching for the present.

---

[1] *Rhymes for the Young Folk*: illustrations by Kate Greenaway, Harry
Furniss, C. Paterson, and H. Allingham.
[2] A Chinese novel, much praised by Carlyle. The only English translation,
'from the French version of M. Abel Remusat,' was published in 1827.
Allingham urged several publishers to bring out a new edition of the book (for
which he wrote a preface), but without success.

August 7.—Mrs. Tom Taylor and Wycliffe come—
Saturday to Monday. Gerald and I at station—fine day.
Gathering gooseberries, Wycliffe, Henny, and I ; Mrs.
T. and H. on seat at top of field. Luncheon, Mary Carlyle
suddenly appears, very welcome : ' busy over proofs of
new edition of *Reminiscences*—tired, and thought she'd
run down on chance.' We all drive off for Hindhead.
Evanses and K. G.—echo—Devil's Punch Bowl.

Mrs. Colvin going to help nurse Mrs. Moorey [of
Redland's Farm, Sandhills.] Death of Mrs. Moorey.
They kept the body a week—put on a shroud made by
herself before she was married.

H. and I met Mrs. M. a couple of evenings before
her fit, when she spoke of the beauty of Sandhills.

Tuesday, August 10.—*Times* obituary this morning—
' We have to record the death of Sir Samuel Ferguson,
Q.C., LL.D., Deputy Keeper of the Public Records in
Ireland '—at Bray, yesterday. They go on : ' had been
for some years a Vice-President of the Royal Irish
Academy ' (a Vice-President !) Not one word or hint of
his poetry or other writings. Truly, the union between
England and Ireland is not made of flesh and blood,
but of the harsh material of politics and economics ; and
only when this bond drags and irritates does the larger
island think of the lesser. No thrills of national sympathy run through the connecting tie. Even as a
subject of intellectual interest or curiosity Ireland has a
very small share of England's attention. The songs,
stories, and plays on Irish subjects, written to amuse
England, have had their success, but no more of the
kind are wanted, and no other kind is marketable.

Ireland herself is too poor and unsettled, and in too
backward a stage of civilisation to afford a public for
literature, unconnected with party controversies. On
the whole—whatever may be unthinkingly said to the
contrary, Ireland presents an ungrateful soil for the
cultivation of the higher *belles lettres.* No London paper
speaks of Ferguson as a Man of Letters.

August 22.—Our Wedding Day—twelve years ago.
Bless my dear wife and children.

August 25.—Lucy Toulmin Smith, meet her at train.
Garden—grammar, British Museum, Petrie's music,
etc.

August 27.—To Aldworth. Tennyson on lawn with
Dr. Grailey Hewitt, who has taken a house down here.

Ghosts—T. said, ' My grandfather, one night sit-
ing up late reading, at College, looked up and saw,
close to him, the ugliest old woman he ever saw in his
life ; and he also saw his cap and gown, which were
hanging on the wall, going round and round the room.
He shut up his book and said, " I'd better not read
any more for the present." '

Tennyson looked very fine to-day, grandly simple,
gently dignified : the marks round his mouth soft in
expression as dimples.

Friday, September 3.—Gathering plums and green-
gages—warm again. To Godalming with H. and
three children, to Wild Beast Show. Camels on grass.
Lions, African elephant fanning herself with her ears.

Monkeys, etc. : Irish giant, and ' Missing Link,' 2d.
extra.

Nothing entered till October 12. In September I
went to London for the day. Called at Quaritch's to see
the Blake facsimiles : some talk with Q. He said ' I
never look at pictures, except on vellum. I have as large
a collection of these as any bookseller, perhaps. I know
nothing about picture exhibitions : my business is with
books and I keep my mind fixed upon that.' By and
by I referred to a passage in some book and said ' you
remember that, of course ' ; to which he replied with
brevity and emphasis ' I never read books.'

The Old Book *Trade* is his subject, and he is said to
be master of it. I ordered 'Songs of Experience.' He
was interested in talking about Evans, a printseller in
Great Queen Street, who had a large collection of Blake
drawings, which Rossetti and I looked over. ' That

must have been twenty-nine years ago, at the least,' says Quaritch—and so it was.

October 29.—To Aldworth. Hallam. Show him letter from Miss Barnes about her father's death.

T. tells the story of a Dog, lost in St. Petersburg, finding its way to its master in the country. Also of a Bastile Prisoner and his lark. It had lived with him in prison ; when he was set free he took the cage out to the fields, and opened the door—the lark hopped out, flew up into the air singing—suddenly stopt, and fell dead at the man's feet.

[Another day] Tennyson said, ' No man can really feel the poetry of any language but his own.'

W. A.—Clough told me he could not dissociate Greek Poetry from grammar and ' grinding.'

T.—' I never appreciated Horace till I was forty.'

November 24. — To Aldworth. Tennyson spoke gloomily (as usual) about the future of England—war, etc. I said, ' We could escape from nearly all chance of War by a bold and honest step.'

' How ? ' asked T.

' Step out of India.'

T.—' That would be ruin.'

W. A.—' Not at all. Bind Australia and Canada to you—your own people : India you never can.'

T.—' We are doing everything possible for them in India, and they roar and rage against us.'

W. A.—' Just so, and will be your destruction at last.'

I tell him I have written a ballad on the ' Banshee.'

T.—' I intend to write one. I have always been much struck with the " Banshee." '

W. A.—' I must take care to get out before you ! '

Christmas Day, sunshine, 89° in the sun.

Monday, December 27.—Thick snow, dazzling. Trees broken, laurels bowed to the ground. Our children shovelling in the garden. Snow man.

Friday, 31st.—Snow—frost. Bells of Chiddingfold.

CHAPTER XXII

1887

January 1.—Frost and snow.   New Year's gifts.

January 4.—Pure white world, dun mist and soft snow.   People look like blackamoors.   Read *Faust* to H.   Letter from Henry Irving with Box for *Faust*. Pension received.[1]

January 5.—Thaw—slush.   Read Gulliver in the nursery.

January 17.—H., G., E. and I to pond.   I put skates on after at least seventeen years—clumsy.

February 1.—Snowdrops, polyanthuses.

Saturday, February 5.—Out after dinner—bright stars—half-moon—frost in the morning.   Aconite in flower, hazels hung with green catkins.

Monday, February 21.—Evey's birthday—H. and I with the three children into copse below Moorey's, and find a few small primroses.   Tea, cake, games, etc.

H. busy over the Bond Street Exhibition drawings.

Saturday, March 5.—Revising Poems all through.

April 3.—Very fine and vernal.   In garden, pruning.

Monday, April 11.—Easter Monday—Fine, G., E. and I walk ; Toll House, field-lane, some prim- roses.   Bank studded with wood-anemones, primroses, violets.

Dream : I went down the street holding in my left

---

[1] Allingham's Pension had been raised to £100 a year.

hand, by a red silken rope, five gold bells beautifully chased and carved, and, stroking them with my right hand, brought out delicious music ; and felt heavenly happiness. Then I woke—with a face-ache !—as I had gone to sleep with it.

Was it in a cessation of pain that the lovely dream appeared ? A pause of pain sometimes makes positive pleasure.

Friday, April 22.—After midnight went into garden —feeling rather depressed. Sprinkle of rain.

Hear first nightingale down in copse—feel cheered.

Monday, April 25.—Helen and I to London with cargo of drawings for her Exhibition. Drove to Bond Street, settling frames, etc.

In the evening to Old Swan House, and were kindly received by Mr. and Mrs. Wickham Flower. Beautiful house. Reading and looking at books till 12. About 6 A.M. I peeped out, saw the morning sun on the river just under our windows, and a little tug drawing two barges along ; on opposite shore the lawns and low trees of Battersea Park.

April 27.—Old Swan House. I visit Carlyle statue. Mrs. De Morgan (sweet-looking old lady) and Mary. 'Spiritualism—The Haslemere people whose fire is lighted by ghosts.' Wallace—the Carlyles—friendly talk.

April 29.—R. A. Private View. H. and K. Greenaway, Brett ('didn't know K. G. was a real person'), Fildes, Mrs. Stephens, etc. Albert Moore (dines with me at Liberal Club).

April 30.—Old Swan House. Pack up. Private View, Grosvenor—Hennessy, Holman Hunt, Browning: he tells story of Fontenelle—'miserly noble dropt alms into the bag ; being asked again, said "I gave." "I believe it," said the applicant, "though I didn't see it." "And I," whispered Fontenelle, "saw it, but don't believe it."'

May 1.—3 Eldon Road, Hampstead. The Russell

Scotts call.   To Gayton Road, Mrs. Paterson, Arthur,
Carrie.   With Clara and H. to Kate Greenaway's new
house, Frognal ; pleasant large studio.   Her original
drawings much prettier than the reproductions.

May 2.—H. and I call on Huxleys—tea, pleasant
talk—at Marks's.   Alma Tadema's new house, Grove
End Road—Mrs. Tadema friendly.   The studio like a
Byzantine church.   Mrs. T.'s studio built and furnished
like an old Netherlandish room.

May 5.—Dine at Mr. Walter Besant's.   Mr. B.
thinks the *Cloister and the Hearth* the best historical
novel in the world.   He thinks a novelist can't be a
dramatist.   (But in France 'tis otherwise : *e.g.* V. Hugo,
Dumas fils, and others.)

Friday, May 6.—Eldon Road, Dr. Martineau comes
to luncheon (82)—tall, thin, courteous, deliberate.
Curiously modelled, deep-lined face ; close-shaven ; hair
still bushy in effect, though thinned.   He speaks with
invariable readiness and gentle precision.   'Metaphysical
Society, so called—was there any result from it ? '

'Only in this way—it drew men together and made
them judge each other and each other's opinions more
fairly.   I believe it modified Huxley's views, and
perhaps Tyndall's.'

Comte : Dr. Martineau admires his classification of
the Sciences.   Fisk—Frederic Harrison.

All this time he was sitting to Clara, who is at work
on a third life-size portrait of him, head and shoulders.
After an hour he took out his watch, and soon departed,
in a shower of rain.   Said he should be 'most happy
to have the honour' of proposing me at the Athenæum
Club, if I thought of becoming a candidate, unless, I
'should select some fitter person.'

Dr. Martineau spoke much of Gladstone—met him
at dinner at Tennyson's, in London (about two years
ago?) The lady beside Dr. Martineau asking his opinion
on Irish affairs, Dr. M. said he thought Ireland of late
had rather been petted than oppressed.   Gladstone

overheard this, and asked the Doctor to explain. Martineau thought that wherever any legislative difference was made between England and Ireland, it was in favour of Ireland.

On this Gladstone took up the cudgels : 'but (said M.) I soon drew out of the discussion, and left my side of it in the hands of some politicians who were present. A day or two after I was with Tennyson ; he said, "Gladstone didn't like what you said about Ireland." "No—but it's true." "That's why he didn't like it," said Tennyson. The present Bishop of St. Andrews, Wordsworth, was tutor to Gladstone : he told me he was one day congratulating old Mr. Gladstone on his son's success at college : the old man replied, with a serious look, "I have no doubt of William's ability : I wish I were equally sure of his stability."'

May 11.—Sandhills. Henny's Birthday. Sweet happy little boy—five years old.

Sunday, June 5.—Fine, cool wind. H. and I drive, by invitation, to Manor House, Haslemere, which we reach about 4.15. Miss Wolseley receives us, then Lady Wolseley comes, lively, pretty, and pleasant. Soon after the General, in gray jacket, corduroy breeches (with flap), black riding-boots and spurs ; a light figure, about five feet seven in stature ; bright, almost boyish face of roundish shape, with small ashen-coloured moustache, the forehead full and smooth, the hair close-cut, of a steel gray. With easy friendly smile he shook hands and began to talk, without accent of any sort, but certain turns of phrase as well as his whole manner unmistakably Irish. After a little H. went off with Lady and Miss W., and I had the honour of half or three-quarters of an hour's conversation with the famous man, winding on without the least trouble from one turn to another. He was interested to hear of Banacle [1] as a semaphore station in bygone days.

[1] Banacle Hill, near Witley.

'The semaphore remained in the Admiralty till not long ago.'

I said some one had lately told me that there was still some use of it.

'O no,' said Lord W., 'you might as well think of using bows and arrows in war.'

Somebody, I remarked, did recommend going back to bows and arrows.

'O yes, there are people who think the world is going to the bad every day—a friend of mine thinks England has been ruined by railways; he can't even get anything fit to eat nowadays,—"do you call this stuff *mutton*!"—and so on.'

Painting—Lord Wolseley said he was very fond of it : 'If I had my time to myself it would be a toss-up whether I should turn to water-colours or to writing.'

The Life of Marlborough : 'Yes—I'm not at work upon it, but I have done something now and again these many years. I don't want to write about his campaigns —that has been done sufficiently, and by competent hands—but about the man himself.'

'You can perhaps brush away some of the dirt that has been thrown upon his name?'

'Certainly : judging him by the standard of the time, I find no foundation for the charges made against him by bitter enemies.'

'Thackeray's hard sayings in *Esmond* and elsewhere, "His Grace would rob a private soldier of his pay,"— any truth in this?'

'Not a bit. Marlborough did exactly what was usual ; the system was a bad one, but the outcry against Marlborough was made solely for party purposes, and when Ormonde succeeded him, Ormonde did just the same. Macaulay's style enchanted me in my youth, it was like music ; but his statements are not to be trusted in the least. Marlborough, at the age of fifty-four, was a poor man, and in the next ten years he grew very rich, there's no doubt about that. The truth is, it is very hard to get any idea of what Marlborough was personally : we know he was handsome, and that's about all. I have read great quantities of his letters and despatches.'

'Have they much individuality ?'

'Little or none.'

We came back to drawing. Lord Wolseley spoke of the sketches he made in various parts of the world, how they brought back all the minute circumstances in which each was done; most of them were burnt in the fire at the Pantechnicon—also his books. After the fire things were put in a chapel close by, and people allowed to pick out what belonged to them. Lord W. picked up a bronze of his, has it now, bruised and marked with fire. 'I'm sorry I didn't take some of my books—they were lying in a pulpy state, injured chiefly by water—but I left them there. I had to pay the Pantechnicon too for *taking care* of my things ! We protested against this, but the law so decided. Whenever I come near books I am attracted to them, and am ready to lose myself in them. I am very fond of my own books : I hate lending them—I tell people so plainly.'

Lady W. and her daughter returned with Helen, and we all had tea. Lord W. complained jocularly of the scanty supply of bread-and-butter, rang the bell, and said to the footman in prompt military manner ' More bread-and-butter.'

Lady W.—'We are not usually so ill-supplied. That tremendous young person (*i.e.* Miss W., a large, pleasant young lady of fifteen, as tall as her father) is not fed upon air.' Then they talked of the amusing parsimony in small things at a certain country house in Surrey (an Earl's)—only a shovelful of coals, for instance, in the bed-room coal-scuttles. Col. —— staying there, in cold weather, went into several empty bed-rooms near his and carried off all their coals in his own scuttle. Sometimes this comes from old habits.

Lord W. spoke of a man he knew, very rich and not at all miserly, but who had been very poor in early life and accustomed to practise strict economy : 'I know how absurd it is,' he often said, 'but I can't bear to throw away even an old tooth-brush!'

After tea we were shown some beautifully bound books (Lord W. let one drop—'O Garnet!')—several done by Mr. Cobden Sanderson.

While talking of Marlborough, I asked whether any of the present people (they were Spencers till lately, but descend from Marlborough's daughter) had the least physical likeness to the great Duke? Lord W. said no. I remarked that race did not necessarily carry likeness with it.

Lord W.—'But likeness crops up amazingly. Some years ago I was in Brussels, at the King's, and an Austrian grand-duke was there also, who was exactly like a portrait three hundred years old which hung in the palace, representing his ancestor.'

We all four went into the old-fashioned garden, Lord W. with large, soft but high-crowned gray hat, thrown loosely on to one side, handkerchief hanging half out of his breast-pocket, corduroy breeches, bright eyes and merry face, seeming as if he wanted only a shillelagh to enable him to present, if so inclined, a genteel version of the typical Paddy. Not that there is the least touch of burlesque or absurdity about him.

We spoke of Tennyson, and our thinking of visiting Aldworth this week.

Lord W.—'Queer old chap!'—admires his poetry, but thinks it 'effeminate.' (If I have the chance I must try to sift Lord W.'s notions on poetry.)

I must not forget that at tea Lord W. said in his usual easy cheerful way that it was a great modern absurdity to value human life too highly—people had made idols of first one thing and then another, and now their idol was human life.

I said, 'surely the notion of the mystic sacredness of human life is very old, there's Cain and Abel.'

Lord W. allowed this instance, but with a twinkle of the eye went on : 'but look at the Lord God, how he slew thousands upon thousands, smote them hip and thigh.' Helen put in, 'That was a long time ago,' and we all smiled.

I said a man I knew, Dr. Bodichon of Algiers, had a serious theory for improving the world in the shortest possible time, by the painless extinction of all useless human beings. He would have juries, including a large proportion of men of science, to decide on the fitness of this person or that to live.

Lord W.—'I entirely agree with your Algerian friend. I would have supplies of chloroform for gaols and hospitals, for cripples and so forth, and the world would be *débarrassé* of much trouble and expense.'

I argued that this would lead to many abuses, and that the general level of morality would be lowered. But Lord W. maintained that we have nowadays an absurd and superstitious respect for human life, and seemed to mean it. To lighten off the discussion I repeated to Lady W. what Madame Bodichon said to me in the midst of one of her husband's discourses on scientific homicide,—' he wouldn't himself drown a kitten!'

While H. went in with the ladies for her parasol before starting, Lord W. and I stood at the old porch looking at a nest of bees among the ivy ; then he pointed at Lady W.'s pug. 'There's an absurd creature! it has a tail and it's alive, that's all you can say. I'm fond of dogs, but such a thing as that is good for no purpose.'

'Pugs would come under the chloroform act?' I suggested.

'Every one of 'em!' said he ; and then out came the ladies, and H. and I took leave, and walked home four miles through the beautiful green country, glad of an interesting visit. Clear, prompt, direct, cheerful,— gifted with physical and mental vivacity, in manners

simplicity itself, in conversation easy and quick,—such
appeared to us the famous General to-day.

He can walk in the country, Lady W. told us, much
better than in London, where the hard pavements jar
his wounded leg.

Monday, June 13.—Invitation from Lady Wolseley
to see the Jubilee Procession from Lord W.'s window
at the War Office.

Tuesday, June 21.—At Mary Carlyle's, Chalcot
Gardens, Haverstock Hill.—Up at seven, breakfast at
quarter to eight. H. and I walk away quietly over
Primrose Hill and down Regent's Park, green, almost
empty, in the fine summer's morning. As we emerge
on the road a troop of the Life Guards passes. Portland Place, Chinese Embassy, two Yellow Dragon flags
and the Union Jack between them, lifted a *little higher.*
Cavendish Sqr., Hanover Sqr., Piccadilly,—crowd,
policemen make way for us across. Then St. James's
Sqr. and Pall Mall, cross and to St. James's Park, where
we find the back-way into the War Office, shaded with
elder and other greenery.

Lord Wolseley's room.—Mr. and Mrs. Frank Holl.
Miss Violet Paget introduces herself to me, and we
have much talk. She says I was the first person who
presented her to the public as authoress : ' I carried
about your postcard in my pocket for many days ; I
was younger then, I'm sorry to say, than I am now.'
She thinks Painters generally talk better than Authors
—I don't agree, nor does Mrs. Frank Holl.

Clubs drest up, Junior Carlton opposite, Army and
Navy (' *my* club,' says handsome man to his wife), copied
from Library at Venice, marble tint ' caused by silica
varnish.'

Claret cup and sweet cake. Band, also Ethiopian
Serenaders. Sparse red lines of soldiery—police—
officials cantering to and fro. Procession at last.
Princesses in white, bowing like automatons. Prince of
Wales, all gold and feathers ; German Crown Prince,

tall, in white uniform. The cream horses, and the Queen (white-haired ?) Princess of Wales opposite—glittering river of liveries and trappings. Continuous hurrahs—Queen's carriage stops opposite War Office.

Foreign Kings in *covered* carriages—long wait ; soldiers march off—all over ?—No, here come the Indian Princes—some in livery-stables turn-out ; two hansoms—mismanagement somewhere.

Lord Wolseley's room, part of an eighteenth-century dwelling-house, old mantelpiece. Pieces of armour on the walls, weapons, savage spears and shields, Egyptian flag, maps, books.

Downstairs, rough people. H. and I by St. James's Park, past Westminster Abbey, disfigured with stands, and so to Waterloo station. Home about 5.30—all well, glad to be back. Bonfires lighted about ten, on Hindhead, Blackdown, and at many points in the Weald. I go up hill with G. and E., and as far as Winkford gate—many fires, rockets, etc. Fire at Aldershot. Hindhead catches fire, and burns all night.

Wednesday, June 29.—Visitors. Miss Wolseley told us that Lady Wolseley and she, on 21st, breakfasted at six o'clock in the morning and sat in the Abbey till 4 P.M., without any food but some bits of chocolate. Lady W. could not see the Queen on the dais, only in passing up the aisle. Both (Lady and Miss W.) were knocked up. Lord W. also knocked up—against a wall by his horse, at Gloster House, when going to call for the Duke of C., hurt his bad leg, *believed it to be broken*, but rode to Buckingham Palace and in the Procession as per programme ; anxious about alighting at the Abbey—did alight, found his leg *not* broken and able to carry him to his seat.

July 20.—Dine at Busbridge. Mr. and Mrs. Ramsden—Lady Galway, tall, in black. Catches my hand in both hers, thanking me for lines on her Brother. (' Farewell, dear Yorkshire Milnes,' etc.)

July 22.—Miss M. Betham Edwards. G. and I

meet her at train. She republican and Home ruler. I
drive her round by Brook, Lea, and Witley Village.

Saturday, July 23.—Very fine and breezy. Miss
B. Edwards on garden seat with children. Gerald and
I to Portsmouth by 12.5 special—empty at first, then
fills. Station—crowded street, tramcars, flags. We
walk to Southsea Common—burnt up. Shingle, people,
sparkling tide, boats, etc. Line of Fleet not distinct, but
numbers of big ships at Spithead and along the Solent—
masts and flags. Long wait, watching the people, girls
and children, soldiers and sailors, bands, fruit-sellers,
etc. etc. Salute, like taps on a huge drum, followed by
rolling white smoke, which gradually drifts towards us.
As time went on we saw Fleet better, but nothing of
Royal Yachts.

Return by back streets, dull. Station—crowd ; sit
on board and eat ; no train for us till 8.8. Out again
—Witley about 10 o'clock.

Monday, July 25.—H. to train for her mother,
with Henny; Evey and I wait at gate, pick laurel leaves.

Friday, August 12.—Cooler, but not a drop of
moisture (no dew even). H. drove to Manor House
with Henny, picking up Mrs. Thompson and daughter;
Gerald and I walked over, and found H. painting
a corner of the lawn. To us came out Lord
Wolseley, in riding-boots and breeches, bright and
genial as usual, with his boyish smile and touch of
Dublin way of speaking, careless and easy. He hugged
Gerald, while asking him, ' How old are you, sir ? ' and
other questions. He looked at H.'s drawing, discussed
pigments, etc. Said he should much like to ride over
and call at Sandhills some day. Ran upstairs to fetch
me *The Reign of Queen Victoria*, edited by Humphry
Ward, but has only second volume, which I carry off.
Lord W. walked with us as far as Grayswood
Common. We talked of Carlyle and Mrs. Carlyle.
He said, ' I only saw Carlyle once, and I was much
interested.' H., G. and I walk home.

Saturday, August 13.—Fine, cooler.   H. and I, with Evey, drive to Mrs. Simmons's garden party, Shotter Mill.   George Craik and Dinah, Mr. and Mrs. Pratt, the Bucktons, two Miss Griffiths, etc. etc.   Lawn-tennis. Deodar, under which George Eliot used to write. H. and I cross the road to small house, formerly Mrs. Gilchrist's, and where George Eliot stayed a while. Mrs. Clarke and two daughters the present tenants.

Thursday, August 18.—H. to Manor House to paint. I with Gerald to fetch her home in pony-carriage. They all come to the gate and into the road bare-headed to see us off.   I say, 'Looks as if we might be bound for Australia.'   Lord W. says the low wheels are heavy to pull.—I lend him Garnett's *Life of Carlyle.*

Friday, August 19.—H. and I drive Toby to Thursley, with Mary Stewart, to call on Lowes Dickinson, find him with daughter at cross-roads going out to paint.   Wheeler's Farm—(Toby in coach-house), view to back, sloping fields, church, etc.   Talk, P. R. B. ; education doesn't alter character.   Sons at Charterhouse, have done well at Cambridge.

(L. D. a little like Hook, but with a sad and languid air in comparison, and dark eyes instead of gray-blue) —a friendly meeting ; drive home by Lea Park and Witley Village.

August 20.—Arthur, H.'s brother from London— drives her, with Mary Stewart, to Chiddingfold. ' Story written with Besant '—Arthur's own novel.

Sunday, August 21.—Arthur rides Toby to Hind-head Cross—goes with Mr. Colvin to Boro' Farm. Lowes Dickinson and two daughters come ; tea in garden ; friendly talk.

Tuesday, August 23.—Drive H. and Gerald to Boro' Farm, under Bodboro' Hill, past rifle-ground, moor, lane.   Alfresco-ists under big ash, the Glovers, the Colvins, children.   Miss Glover, in her brother's hat, sings *The Wearin' o' the Green*, also Spanish and Italian canzonettes, airily, easily, merrily—to Neapolitan Guitar

decorated with a great bunch of various coloured ribbons ;
asks me for a green one—we talk brogue. Swing on
big ash-tree. Tea for children and Miss G. on grass.
We in house (Humphry Ward's summer retreat).
Choice engravings on wall.

Proofs of *Irish Songs* dribbling in.

August 30.—[To Mrs. Turner's, Barlow Fold,
Poynton—British Association at Manchester.] Mr.
Rollo Russell, fellow-guest, has come from Haslemere
in same train.

September 1.—Reception Room at Owens College.
Free Trade Hall, Sir H. Roscoe's address. Exhibition,
Picture Galleries — Rossetti, Burne-Jones, Watts,
Tadema, Walker, Mason, etc. etc. : H.'s 'Carlyle'
badly placed.

September 6.—Poynton. H. and I in pony-cart to
Prestbury, then she to white cottage on Macclesfield
Road, where she puts up and paints. I into Prestbury,
church and old chapel. In the street, one hen visible.
Strange and beautiful little old house—knock. Young
woman shows me into house—poor inside ; bed-room
(her father's and her own) windows shut, bed-clothes
only turned down a little on rising, and so left. Other
half of house—'Can I get in ?—will you ask ? '

'Well, she's rather strange, you'd better ask her
yourself.'

I knock—'Who's that ?—well, you can come in.'

I found a woman, not very old, but worn and wild
looking : toothless, unkempt, no gown on, sitting by
wretched fireplace, of which she began to complain—
'smoke, soot, rain through roof. Agent won't do
anything —rent £4, taxes 10s. (other half the same).

Her husband left her years ago—not a good man ;
doesn't know is he living or dead—went to Westmore-
land. Son a sailor—sent her £1 a month last year.
Daughter married in London,—'that's like her'
(coloured engraving on wall).

'Don't people want to see the old house ? '

'Ay, they looks in—but you're the first this summer that's given me anything.'

There she lives alone, not friends even with her next neighbours—capable of sharp words, doubtless. Poor woman—many a one sketches the outside of this beautiful ancient House when she is crouching by the dull fire within, thinking of—what? I went up the broken and almost dangerous stairs to the roof—the rooms were empty; some dusty papers lay in a corner, one showing its title in bold print—*Glad Tidings*; on the wall hung an old coat and waistcoat—her husband's? Outside, the sun shone on the pretty village street and its trees. I found a path to where Helen was painting; settled plans, she to drive back. Then by path to station, and train to Manchester. Cab to Exchange, get in and see Madox Brown's Frescoes, which look well. Owens College about 5.30.

Wednesday, September 7.—Fine; garden — brook (wild angelica about 12 feet high), shady dark paths, bridge. H. painting apple-tree from field; Mrs. Turner drives us to Bramhall, to call on Mr. and Mrs. Nevill—fine old timber mansion, on rising ground. We are shown round—plans, restorations, old wall paintings, Japanese work.

Friday, September 9.—Drive to Stockport station with Mrs. Turner—good-bye.

Sunday, September 11.—Sandhills. Fine. Drive H. to Aldworth. Tennyson better—walk with him on lawn; asks, 'were you edified?' (at British Association). Lord Wolseley and daughter appear, having walked up from Manor House.

T.—'Is there a chair for the great Soldier?'

Lord W. speaks of the Nile—'pretty flowers'—has brought home specimens of them; doesn't know their names.

'Saw the mummy unrolled of *the* Pharaoh, the friend of Moses—face unchanged.'

T. asks, 'Which Pharaoh was that?'

W. doesn't know. 'There were so many Rameses. Overflow of the Nile, threatening even the Museum at Boulac. I rather wished for a scarabæus or two; the Khedive said to me, "Go down to the Museum and take as many as you like!"'

Hallam asks us to come to meet his Uncle Arthur.

T. (to H.)—'Didn't you begin a portrait of me once. Well you might perhaps try again sometime.'

Thursday, September 15.—Start with H. for Aldworth at noon in Toby-carriage, arrive about 1.15. Carriage passes us with Mr. Arthur Tennyson and wife. Luncheon. Arthur T. opposite me—hair bushy and still dark? curiously like Alfred, but younger and slighter.

Upstairs with Hallam and Arthur: they smoke. A.'s way of speaking thoroughly Tennysonian both in matter and manner—great love of natural beauty, naïve and original opinions. Out with him and Mrs. Arthur, flower garden, walk, back-gate—to spring. Arthur praises warmly the beauty of Surrey, and of this place, but thinks a beautiful lonely place not best suited for some people to live in—is apt to make them dreamy and indolent.

'Don't you find this effect from living in beautiful lonely scenery?'

'I have children to interest me.'

'Ah, yes, that makes a difference. I have not been granted any children.'

At the spring (where Lord Egmont has had several conspicuous trees cut down, leaving a woful blank) we saw the three grandchildren, Alfred, Charley, and Michael; Alfred leaping his pony over bars.

A. and I turn back. We agree in disliking flesh-food and in wishing we had been brought up vegetarians. 'We found the flesh-board provided (he said), and got used to it without thinking.'

We meet Alfred and Mrs. Arthur, and turn.

We go up the close-wooded valley till turned back by rain.

Arthur is a couple of inches shorter than Alfred, and much narrower in the shoulders.   He walks much, he tells me.

September 23.—To Dunrozel [Hindhead.]   Countess Russell and daughter.   Colonel and Mrs. Moncreiff. Talk with Colonel M. 'Indians—their way of moving —kind of leaping on their toes, five miles an hour ; good people and intelligent.'

[On the 24th of this month the Allinghams went to Sandown for a holiday with their children, staying there until October 25.]

Wednesday, October 26.—Fine—Henny and I up common.   Crowd of visitors—Lady Midleton and daughters and guests (seven in all), Mrs. Stewart Hodgson and Mrs. Freeman (*née* Merivale), Miss Longman and married sister, Mr. and Mrs. Colvin, Mrs Evans and Mrs. Cooper, Mrs. Hammond Jones. Drawings looked at.

November.—Winter has come on us by a forced march.   Trees red and yellow — now mostly bare. Wet, foggy, frosty weather, with a few fine days patched in.   London riotous and getting worse.   H. at work on her drawings, I at proofs of *Laurence Bloomfield*, and trying to get *Irish Songs*, etc. out. Binding not right, mistake in printing discovered, already tired of the book.

Our good nurse Elizabeth Haddon married on Tuesday, November 15, to Harry Cave (both of Naseby), brother to Alice Wisdom, the nurse.[1]   Day fine, children at Witley church, and Gerald signed the book by his own particular desire.   After the lunch H. and I went in, and I said a few words.   We saw them off.

---

[1] A little dispensary had been established at Sandhills by Lady Knutsford : and Mrs. Alice Wisdom, to whom she had given the necessary training, had been appointed by her as nurse : a great boon to the neighbourhood.

On frosty days the orange sunsets fine, Hindhead
looking mountainous against them; walks to Godalming, Park Lane, etc.—but often tedious.

H. and I called on Leonard Huxley, assistant-
master at Charterhouse.

'Must boys have been confirmed?'

L. H.—'I think so—they all must go "through the
mill."' [The Allinghams had some idea of sending
their son as a day-boy to Charterhouse.]

To Mr. Buckton's. Mr. B. shows whistle of several
degrees (nine) of shrillness: I can't hear the two
shrillest, but I hear the third, which B. cannot hear.
Helen hears No. 1.

November 23.—Indigestion continually, tedious
nights. If I only knew for certain what to eat and
drink!

Thursday, November 24.—H., G., and I to Haslemere by 4.7 train and walk to Valewood by Mason's
fields, farm, locked gate, old walnut. Three Counties'
Bridge, Valewood ponds and hills impressive in the
dusk. House—drawing-room, Mrs. Mangles, Daffarn,
Mrs. Daffarn, Daphne. Chat, tea.

Friday, November 25.—Fine—some sunshine. H.
and I by 12.45 to Haslemere and walk up Blackdown.
Shooting heard. Beaters in lane, eating bread and
cheese. H. lunches among the heather. Then stables,
no one; man cutting furze. Hallam hails us from
upper window. His room—he smokes—chat. He
and Audrey have just been at Cambridge to see
Œdipus acted, and took Mary Anderson with them;
she drilled the young fellows—was surprised at the
poorness of their legs; thought that but for the great
power of Sophocles the play would be intolerable;
was disgusted with the bloody eyes; all thought them
horrible.

Then about four to Tennyson's room; find him
sitting at window in a red woollen cape, of fisherman's
shape, reading. Contrary to reports — looking well

and cheerful. He gives Helen *The Brook*, illustrated;
asks if she will illustrate *Locksley Hall* for Macmillan,
but she excuses herself—is out of practice, and does not
know Lincolnshire.

Tennyson praises the picturesqueness of the great
fens, and the sun rising over the eastern sea. I say I can
tell them the right man for fen scenery—Macbeth.

T. says the drawings in the little book don't show
the Brook he thought of—it was partly an abstract, but
mainly from one in the country where he was born.

'Have you seen *Darwin's Life*?'

T.—'No, I hate biographies.'

Darwin—his dicta on religion—once cared for
poetry, etc.

T. was reading *Elaine*, a Play in five Acts, founded
on his Idyll. He said, 'I am told this has been played
for many nights in America. The language is partly
mine, partly not. It came this morning from New
York.'

'Have you got any money out of it?'

'Money—no!'

He went out on the lawn for his half-hour's afternoon walk, I with him. We talked of Darwin—of
human nature—of the difficulties of the period of
puberty and following years. He spoke with praise
of Paul Janet. I hardly recollected about him. T.
said, 'Why, I remember reading Paul Janet to you in
the New Forest.'

'The only tolerable view of this life,' he said, 'is as
the vestibule to a better.'

In parting Tennyson held my wife's hand and said,
'I am very glad to have seen you again. Perhaps
you'll never see me again till I'm dead.' Then to me—
'Do you know what old Mrs. Procter said to me the
other day? I said to her, "I'm seventy-eight and you're
eighty-seven, and perhaps we shall never meet again till
we're dead," and she answered, "You young fellows
mustn't be insolent to your seniors!"'

We walked away, agreeing that he appeared well and cheerful, and so down the lane in a misty moonlight and to Haslemere station.

[About this time the Allinghams spent a pleasant evening at Mr. Jonathan Hutchinson's on Hindhead, when Mr. Hutchinson spoke of his deep debt of gratitude to Carlyle for the influence of his teaching on his own early life. At the end of this year the following notes are written, undated, in the diary :—]

Have neglected my diary again for many weeks. See no particular good in keeping it up, yet feel uneasy when I don't.

A lady called to look at this house, hearing we were thinking of leaving it. The house and surroundings seem pleasanter than ever now that parting draws on—but how help it? We think of various places. It is horrid to feel one's roots tampered with.

H. away for about a week (I loth, as usual, to let her go) to Birmingham, where she saw old Mrs. Phipson and various others, all over eighty and all still enjoying life, which speaks well for the air ; then she visited Hampstead, staying at Clara Martineau's ; and St. Albans, finding her dear old Grannie, though feeble, glad to see her and able to talk a little. Could not see her Aunt Louie—who has since died, after a shadowed life. H. describes Birmingham as wonderfully improved—fine Public Library and Picture Gallery, cheerful look in general ; the inhabitants are ambitious to make it a provincial capital.

The winter, with some frosts, ran on quickly to Christmas and New Year—the children sending and receiving cards, putting up holly and ivy, etc. They had tea, separately, at *Nursey's* cottage, as they still call her. Went to a children's party at Mrs. Evans's.

In 1887 (October) departed Mrs. George Craik, whom I first knew many years ago as Dinah Muloch. Helen has a grateful recollection of her and her husband's kindness in H.'s early London days.

The R. Catholic Archbishop of Armagh (Daniel M'Gettigan) departed in December. From Curate he was made 'Bishop of Raphoe' and came to live at Ballyshannon, where I used to meet him often on friendly terms—a tall, handsome, portly man, with an engaging simplicity of manner and voice. He had a sweet brogue, and spoke the Irish language fluently. He lived a frugal, blameless life, diligent in his office, tranquil, simple, dignified, more like by far to one's notion of a 'primitive Bishop' than any other prelate I have seen. I was perhaps the only Protestant in the place who, in intercourse with him, used the terms due in courtesy to his rank; but he met nobody (as he knew very well) less likely to become a 'convert.'

Other departures.

Jenny Lind (November), good soul, with music in it as well as in her voice, whom I much longed to meet in private life, but never did. I saw her in *Norma*, *Sonnambula*, *Lucia*, *Figlia del Reggimento*. In a juvenile Universal Reformer mood I wrote and sent her a letter, urging her to leave the stage, as a profession unworthy her naïvely noble character. This was at Dublin.

Old Miss Gillies (July) the water-colour painter; in her earlier days a friend of various literary people, among others of the Howitts, when they lived at Highgate.

Dr. Quain (September), doctor and diner-out, ready to doctor literary people and artists for nothing, pleasant and talkative. Last time I saw him was at Emerson's lodging in Down Street, Piccadilly.

Richard Jefferies (August)—I never saw him, but had much correspondence with him (then quite unknown) when I edited *Fraser*. I put in various pieces of his, as good as anything he afterwards wrote, but no one took any notice; save indeed that Barbara L. S. B. was struck with the truth of his picture or photograph of women in the farming classes.

CHAPTER XXIII

1888-1889

January 1888.—Witley—More than half the first month of the New Year has already slipped away.

Alternate frosts and thaws. Great fogs in London, etc., and greatish even here. Ice on Sweetwater Pond. Helen sitting out to paint whenever she possibly can.

Hear good reports from Catherine, Jane, John also.

One Wednesday Lady Wolseley called on us, also Mrs. Mangles and others.

Mary Carlyle sends me *Academy* with notice of *Irish Songs*—well-meant, but 'cheeky' and blundering. The writer (a law student?) wrote to me, begging a copy of the D.G.R. woodcut.

Helen and I discuss Hampstead [with a view to going there to live]. Feel low and unsettled.

February 8.—Mild and vernal—abundant snowdrops and violets—aconites too, and crocuses in bud.

February 22.—H. and I to London, to Mr. Stewart Hodgson's, 1 South Audley Street ; dinner, drive to Lyceum — *Winter's Tale* ; Mary Anderson's grace and beauty, with a taking naïveté. (Must not Lady Hamilton have been something like her?) Her voice sweet, enunciation deliberate ; no thrills, but all well studied and well done.

Sunday, April 1.—A spring day. Walk with Helen and the children down lane—to Moorey's Gate, and into copse—bare trees, dark blue distances, fresh cool air, some sun, a few primrose tufts. Children out in garden after tea with great delight, at battle-dore, etc.

May 10.—Dry but clouded, and distances dim. Mr. and Mrs. Forbes,[1] with Edith and Waldo, by 12.50 train. Garden, luncheon. Walk, Haslemere Lane, copse crowded with primroses, wood anemones, violets, Mrs. Forbes delighted. Nightingale sings. Home, tea—we talked of Emerson, Cabot's Life, etc.

May 17.—On common. At home. Find Webb,[2] come over from Cranleigh. Together to Guildford. See Almshouses—which he likes.

June 4.—To London. National Liberal Club. Terrace, and saw Prince of Wales unveil statue of Sir B. Frere (looked most appropriate when standing before the public in its white sheet). Princess and daughters, Old Duke of Cambridge, Archbishop of Canterbury, Lord Knutsford, Sir Richard Temple, etc.

June 8.—Irish Exhibition. To Queen Anne's Lodge. James Knowles's house full of fine things. J. K., wife and daughter, Lucy Taylor, Lady Pollock, Helen. Tea. Portrait of Gladstone : Claude—Turner, etc. Urn (ashes and bits of bones).

June 9.—To Whitley Stokes's ; W. S. cordial.

To 40 Kensington Square. Sir John and Lady Simon. Dinner. Marcus Aurelius—Lady S. prefers 'that old-fashioned and despised book, the Bible.' Sir John agrees with me that it is desirable to inculcate morals without dogma. Ruskin : Simon attended him some years ago.

Sunday, June 10.—To 29 De Vere Gardens—Up-stairs, tapestry, bust of E. B. B., one of R. B. (young).

Enter R. B., friendly and vigorous. He asked me, Did I often come up to town?

'Very seldom.'

On which he remarked (I think premeditatedly), that in his early life he had much secluded himself, and had often since regretted it. He sees that he lost much by it.[3]

---

[1] Emerson's daughter.   [2] Mr. Philip Webb the architect.
[3] This remark of Browning's chimed in with what was often in Allingham's mind. Although fond of the country, he had keenly missed there

Then he took up a book from the table, *Oannes, an Ancient Myth, as told by Berosus*, by J. Garth Wilkinson.

'Here's a thing has been sent to me'—and read half a page or so (without spectacles, I noticed), to the purport that in remote times a creature, half man and half fish, came to a certain island, and taught the islanders various arts—his name was Oannes.'

W. A.—'It might be taken as a foreshadowing of Darwinism—the origin of man in an amphibious lepidosyren.'

B.—'Yes, altogether different from Wilkinson's notions.'

W. A.—'A gentleman whom the Vicar of Wakefield met was fond of quoting Berosus.'

B. (smiling).—'Ay, sir, the world is in its dotage.'

Then we talked a little about Darwin, B. saying that, whatever his merits as investigator, his philosophy was of little or no importance.

I told him of our neighbour Alfred Wallace, and how he had arrived, as it were, at the opposite goal from Darwin in what are called 'Supernatural questions'; D. at last believing almost nothing, W. almost anything!

Miss Rehan in *Shrew*—I praise her. B. going to meet her at lunch at Boughton's next Sunday. We talk of plays and actors.

B. says—'The acting of my four plays by professionals, *unpaid*, for the Browning Society, is surely one of the greatest and most wonderful honours ever paid to a dramatic writer. People burning to have their plays produced—paying to have them produced; if something even of Tennyson's is to be done you hear of the curtain's costing £2000! and here in my case the actors play for love, and give every word of the longest parts, and the audience listen to the very end!'

the intellectual life and interests of London. He had made the move to Witley chiefly on account of his wife and children—and never regretted it. But now that the education difficulty made another change desirable (for he wished to avoid boarding-schools if possible), his thoughts turned again towards London.

Miss Alma Murray, he maintains, is the most poetical actress now on the stage; her Beatrice, in *The Cenci*, thrilling; at the end she appears, and is, exhausted and barely able to speak. Vezin as the wicked count, most admirable.

B. reckons up the four Plays—*In a Balcony*, *The Blot in the 'Scutcheon*, *Colombe's Birthday*, and they're going to do *The Return of the Druses*.

'Charles Kean accepted *Colombe's Birthday*, but said he couldn't bring it out for two years, and I declined to hold it over so long. He wanted the name of the play altered to *The Advocate of Cleves*. "You've got the best part, Ellen," he said to his wife, "but the play must be called *The Advocate of Cleves*."'

In quitting the subject B. said, 'the Theatre is a great force; but its conditions need to be entirely altered.'

W. A.—'Would a subsidised Theatre be any good in England?'

B.—'Not the least!'

B. ate as usual a hearty dinner-luncheon, talking all the time—what a man!

B.—'C. said many things that I mentally dissented from, and he said something about a certain lady (E. B. B. I knew this was) which was reported to me and made me, for a time, hold aloof from him altogether. But I feel towards him as John Forster did to Landor: Landor used sometimes to write most unreasonable and exasperating letters to Forster, and one day that I was with Forster and he had been talking of Landor almost with indignation, he suddenly exclaimed "If he were standing here before me—I'd hug the old man!" —and so would I Carlyle.'

In saying this B. hugged me closely with his broad chest and strong arms, and laughed merrily. The notion of his being seventy-six!

B.—'He called one day at Warwick Crescent when I was out, and said from his carriage window to my

sister, "I should like to see him once more."' (I
believe I was with C. in the carriage that day.)

B.—'The last time I went to Cheyne Row his niece
said he was not speaking to any one, but I might go
up and see him. He was lying on the sofa, wrapt
in a shawl. I stooped over him and said a word
or two, and he put his arm round my neck. That was
all.'

In going away both B. and his sister asked me
repeatedly and warmly to come soon again—any day
I chose.

Up through Kensington Gardens to Hyde Park,
very fresh and green, and on to Zoological Gardens,
where I saw a monkey with artificial flowers snatched
from a hat, fourteen crocodiles, young kangaroo getting
into mother's pouch, etc.

As I sat in shady nook by the water-fowl, reading a
newspaper, Mr. Stewart Hodgson accosted me, and
we had some pleasant chat—he had heard we were going
to leave Sandhills.

Walk to Hampstead Road—train; people with
branches of hawthorn; 18 Gayton Road.

Mrs. Paterson, and Carrie and H.—We take a look
at Lested Lodge, garden tangled.—Walk to Adelaide
—Club.

Wrote to-day at Club a note to Miss Rehan, signed
An old Playgoer, entreating her *not to greet the audience*
after sweeping in round the stage in a passion on her
first appearance in *The Shrew*.

Monday, June 11.—To 'Gaiety' and get four
tickets. Show Helen the Club—with her to National
Gallery, then to Stores and lunch. Mrs. Woolner
accosts me. To Lady Dorothy Nevill's—her curiosities,
Walpole miniatures, Sussex fire-irons, etc., own portrait
by Watts. Lady Warwick and daughter—pleasant—
Dine at Gatti's, 'Gaiety'—Clara and Carrie waiting;
Upper boxes—*Taming of the Shrew*. Enjoyed and
admired Miss Rehan much.

N.B.—She swept in round the stage and *took no notice of the audience* : Brava!

Tuesday, June 12.—Train—Witley 5.20 ; all well, much the better for my trip to London.

June 17.—Sandhills.   Walk by Park Lane and steep wood to Hindhead, touch Cross at 4 o'clock precisely ; two boys and a girl selling ginger-beer.   Cold wind.

Hennessy and F. Pollock appear.   To Tyndall's, meet Mrs. Clifford at door—in.

Tyndall, Mrs. Tyndall, and her mother, mild and handsome.   Friend (who came on bicycle from Albury) with pleasant out-of-door face.

Apparent size of the moon—Tyndall said, 'Spedding said the full moon looked to him the size of a three-penny bit ; I told him it looked to me the size of a] dinner plate, but he couldn't believe it.   I was travelling from Vienna on a fine moonlight night with Hooker and Mrs. Hooker, and we said how large each of us thought the moon appeared to be, Mrs. Hooker said the size of sixpence, Hooker the size of half-a-crown, I the size of a dinner plate.'

Tyndall took us to top of house, snuggery and large outside balcony or platform.   I said as we stept out, ' This expands the soul.'

He.—' That's just what I feel—both here and in the Alps.'

He leaned back over the balcony rail while talking, in a rather dangerous looking way.   Downstairs and away.   When at gate, saw close by, walking along the heath, two brown bears, with them five men, seemingly foreigners.   Walk home, by Southern lane and copses —beautiful walk.

June 23.—Waggonette to Hindhead—Helen and I with Mrs. Flight.   I walk up steep wood—the Cross, schoolgirls running about.   Distance misty. Drive to Mrs. Clifford's—friendly and pleasant.

To Tyndall's—I introduce Mrs. Flight as widow

of Dr. Flight[1] and cousin of Du Bois Reymond. 'Walter Flight? Oh, I knew him intimately.' Speaks with interest to Mrs. F.—'dear Du Bois'—takes her and Helen to top of house. Away, T. comes to gate with us ; 'Dr. Martineau—we have exchanged some shrewd blows, but I don't think he hates me !'

I walk home from Hindhead by Witley Park copses, lovely—but oaks stript by caterpillars.

Weather turns cold and rainy. Ill and rather miserable for about a week.

Going on with proofs of *Flower Pieces*, etc.

July 5.—Hire pony from Luff, of King's Arms. Wet—wet—wet, with a gleam now and again : almost literally

> June,
> Without a sun or moon !
> July, August,
> Many a raw gust.

July 12.—Ride round by Sweetwater Pond—pick chantarelles. Have not had a ride for sixteen years !

Friday, July 13.—Ride Jenny to Aldworth. Party in flower garden, T., Hallam, Miss Ritchie and friend. Tea, talk of Clifford—his mathematical paradoxes. Tennyson goes in with Miss Ritchie 'to read a new poem.' I ride home ; not stiff or tired—did me good.

July —.—I saw the Duke of Argyll at railway station, and Hallam T., who asked us to come up to-day. We drove to Aldworth. I showed some chantarelles gathered in the lane, Duke knew them, handed them on to T., who sent them to cook with directions. 'Silos': farmers slow to take to them.

T. tells of old Lincolnshire farmer near his father's. T. said to him one day civilly : 'Mr. —— *why* don't you mend your fences ?' The old fellow stooped down and tied his shoe carefully, then straightened himself and said, 'I've never mended a fence, and I never will !'

[1] Walter Flight, D.Sc.(Lond.), F.R.S., analytical chemist in British Museum. He had studied under Tyndall at Queenwood College.

[Tennyson had a story of a Lincolnshire farmer who said, when he came out of church—'burned for ever and for ever! I can't believe that: no constitution could stand it!']

Wednesday, August 8.—Mrs Humphry Ward visits us, looks at drawings—asks us for Sunday week.

Sunday, August 19.—H. and I drive to Borough Farm, heather bloom. Tea-party at door, outside, Mrs. Humphry Ward, Mr. Ward, Miss Sellars (tall and beautiful), and Mr. Henry James. The Anglo-American Novelist had just arrived from London, and was going back by a late train.

He described himself as an 'unmitigated Cockney,' was surprised at the colour of the heather, and hearing ling spoken of, asked to look at it.

While we were at tea, a flock of sheep, herded by a long-limbed half-wild looking girl of fourteen, streamed down the green-sward track just in front of us, between an old weed-grown wall and some grassy knolls, with a great ash tree and two or three other trees : a picture. The pony, still in the shafts, grazed peaceably. 'Tis a beautiful wild place—much vext by the rifle-range close by.

Saturday, August 25.—Ride to Blackdown, in lane meet Tennyson carriage. He with Miss Boyle and Hallam, who says, ' we were going to *you*.' I ride after them. Find Miss B. seated in our garden, T. wandering in the field. ' I wonder you can leave this place.'

Take him in and show him some drawings, which he likes.

' That's Carlyle—looking very grumpy.'

Tea in garden. He admires the tall mullein. I bring up Emerson's comparison of Salisbury spire to the great mullein. T. grunted, and said ' This doesn't taper.'

I gave him a white rose, and said ' Perhaps the ladies would rather have jasmin.'

T.—' You called me Jasmin, once.'

I said ' I don't think you were quite satisfied with it.'

T. murmured something which I took to mean, ' No,
—*not* satisfied with it.'

I said jasmin grew on a cottage I lived in when a child, and it had most delightful associations in my mind.

While looking at a drawing with daffodils, T. said ' Millais put daffodils along with wild-roses in his *Ophelia* picture. I pointed this out to him. He said he had painted the rose-bush from nature ; and some time after when he was finishing he wanted a bit of yellow and sent to Covent Garden and got the daffodils. I told him it was quite wrong.'

I took T. part way up the path on our common to see the view and showed him his own hill ; ' this is a beautiful country,' he said.

In shaking hands with me he said ' I don't think I shall do the " Banshee." You have done one ? '

' Yes, and published it lately in a volume.'

' I've not seen it. I'm so much obliged to you for not sending it to me—get heaps every day.'

I said ' Oh, I promised long ago never to send you anything.'

Miss Boyle and I laughed.

September 1.—To Aldworth, find Tennyson in garden, reading *Times*—' going to station to meet Mary Anderson.'

He tells of old Monsieur C., one hundred and two yesterday, how he eats and sleeps.

In carriage with T., Hallam and Miss Boyle.

I show him chantarelles gathered in the lane, he wishes to taste them. ' I have a fine taste in matters of cooking,' he remarked. His cook would not cook the ones I gave him before—ignored them. T. asks me to go and reason with the cook, which I decline, not having a personal acquaintance with her. Station— T. walks off towards the village, I with him. He tells me Miss A. is going to give *The Cup* in Birmingham and Dublin. Carriage overtakes us with the lovely

Mary in dark-blue cotton dress, her healthy brown complexion un-actress like—presented, and have a handshake and a smile. (They will discuss and try over *The Cup*.) Home.

Monday, September 3.—H. and I drive to Grayswood—Mr. Pratten's house, Miss Swanwick comes out to hall door to welcome us ; room with fine prospect, east, over trees. Enter Mrs. Stewart Hodgson and Mrs. Forsyth, talk on literature, etc.

Browning told Miss Swanwick he knew nothing about the *Sonnets from the Portuguese* till two or three years after his marriage, when his wife showed them to him. He said to her, 'If I consulted my personal wishes I should keep these all to myself, but as the guardian of your literary fame I must counsel you to publish them.'

Monday, September 10.—I to Hampstead, to the Carlyles, 23 Rudall Crescent.

Tuesday, September 11.—Mrs. Paterson calls. Eldon House. Like it.

Thursday, September 13.—Hampstead—telegram from H., 'Coming up by first train.' To Eldon House, which she takes to by degrees. Home.

Friday, September 14.—Sandhills—fine ; ride pony, Lea Park, moor near Hammer Pond ; meet boys, one of whom lifts hand with switch in it to Jenny's nose. She starts violently, flings me off and kicks left arm—gallops off. Back and arm hurt.[1]

Tuesday, September 18.—Fine, common, H. painting. Splendid views of Hindhead and Weald ; harvesting. Country lovely. Miss Tynan sends me criticism from *Providence Journal*—'The Poet of Ballyshannon.' (non-national, how sad !)

Thursday, September 20.—Write to take my name off list of subscribers to Haslemere Commons Committee.

Friday, October 26.—Gap of over a month in diary.

---

[1] Allingham was inclined to connect this accident with the illness which attacked him later.

In London with H. (at B. Martineau's) for several
days. Hampstead looks pleasant.

Spell of fine October weather—expeditions with
Gerald to Hog's Back, Merrow, East Clandon, to
Selborne, Woolmer Forest, etc.

Tennyson has had very severe attack of gout—a
nurse—confined to his room. We were invited to tea,
and a note from Hallam put us off.

Heard he was better, then—a relapse.

Saturday, October 27.—Mrs. Graham Robertson and
her son appear. They look round ; H. comes in from
fir-wood. They drive round by Brook, return, and take
the place [Sandhills].

Thursday, November 1.—Rain or drizzle all day.
H. drives with Gerald to visit Mrs. Ramsden, Miss
Jekyll, Mrs. Longman ; home after dark. I writing,
sharpening penknives ; dance with children.

Friday, November 2.—Reading *Troilus and Cressida*
to H. Shakespeare's hand in it, but not his play :
poor in some parts, loaded in others : a re-cooking of
familiar matter, with Shakespeare sauce.

Saturday, November 3.—To Haslemere by train,
walked up to Aldworth among the yellowing trees ;
met Mrs. Tennyson driving F. Palgrave to the station.

Up to study, and found T. leaning back on a chair,
his legs on another, thin and pale ; he gave me his
brown hand and said ' I'm glad to see you.'

He had a book in his hand, and the light of two
candles close by fell on the right side of his face, which
showed striking and noble. He wore a black skull-cap,
his long Don Quixote nose was sharply outlined, his
moustache looked dark and full. By general impression
one might have guessed him seventy rather than eighty.
He said, ' I have been in the doctor's hands—been very
ill—never had such a time of it in my life !—gout and
rheumatic fever.'

Zola—his question ' How can a book corrupt ? '

Martial—' Leigh Hunt said a boy found out in vice

might ask "Why did you put such books into my hands?" Are these books necessary for the learning of Latin?'

Tennyson.—'There might be purified editions.'

November 19.—H. and I to London. I to consult Mr. G. Buckston Browne. He finds an enlarged gland, and indigestion. Am I henceforth an invalid? ah me!

November 30 *to December* 8.—H. paying many calls, people all kind and friendly.

A beautiful dream : a garden with a pear-tree and an apple-tree, both in blossom : slope of sward and inexpressible happiness—(reminiscence of early childhood). Glad that I can be thus happy even in a dream.

First year of Old Age, I fear! Has the unwelcome guest really come at last, and to stay? We never realise beforehand what *old* means, or how the old feel.

[It was not old age, for Allingham was not yet sixty-five : the feeling he speaks of was caused by the malady from which he was afterwards found to be suffering.]

Sunday, December 9.—Walk, Evey and I ; Park Lane, Banacle, golden sunset light ; Hindhead a blue jewel ; Venus, evening star ; long band of orange light along south. Feel rather better.

Tuesday, December 11.—Good-bye to Sandhills, after seven and a half peaceful, on the whole happy, years. H. and children at 3 Eldon Road—I to 23 Rudall Crescent, Alick and Mary Carlyle, Tommy and Oliver. All very kind. Much talk about Carlyle— 'a treat (Mary says) to have somebody to talk about him to.'

Wednesday, December 19.—To Eldon House. Sleep there for the first time.

1889

January 3.—In the house since December 31 (bronchitis seized me all at once).

January 12.—Take Gerald to University College
School.

January 20.—I call several times at Miss Eade's, Well Walk, for Henny and Evey about 12.30, we walk on Heath.

February 1.—To U. C. School Concert, 4. Gerald and I sit in front.

March 14.—This book has not been opened since February 3. I have no wish to keep the diary of an invalid. I am sometimes better, often worse ; on the whole going down-hill in strength, and with fresh troubles coming on top of the others. Every day is a weary trial, and every night a worse one.

I had a very curious dream whose floating imagery evades every cast of the net of language. I thought I found myself somehow, by merely looking aside, aware of some of the main secrets of Nature's material workshop. There was no tinge of atheistic feeling. Merely, I saw a little below the superficial appearance of things, and found the methods by which forms are innumerably varied and sent on their courses to be so simple and obvious that I smiled at myself with a sort of impatience at not having seen all this before. A pleasurable satisfaction remained after I had awaked and said to myself ' This is the haschisch.'

[Of another night he writes :—]

The curtain of darkness fell on my brain for perhaps a couple of hours—too, too short ! I have not had a sound night's rest for ever so long.

Prayer

O Great One ! may my dear Wife and Children and myself not forget Thee—ever draw nigher to Thee ! May we keep our hearts pure !

[The illness increased. In April Allingham was told by Mr. Browne that there was serious internal trouble ; and it became so acute, early in June, that immediate operation was necessary.

This saved his life for the moment, and brought some temporary relief : he gradually became able to take short walks around his house in Hampstead.

He had been specially interested in tracing the different localities connected with Keats : and in his note-book is the following little poem.]

POET AND BIRD

Per contra

(IN A HAMPSTEAD GARDEN)

'Thou wert not born for death, immortal Bird !
No hungry generations tread thee down ;'
KEATS : *Ode to a Nightingale.*

A Nightingale, upon a time,
　Here tried his tone :
Here, too, a Poet made a rhyme :
　Bird—Poet—gone !

Trivial at best the Bird's gay song,
　A shapeless trill :
The Poet's rhyme will last as long
　As Hampstead Hill.

July 12, 1889.—The house and garden are still to be seen in John Street, Hampstead, on the left-hand as you go up from Hampstead Heath railway station.

[In August Allingham went with his family to Eastbourne, and here he seemed at first to be a little better. During these weeks he would get up at four, sometimes even at three o'clock, to watch the sunrise, and the following, written at this time, is the last of his poems.]

SUNRISE AT EASTBOURNE

A Photograph

Dim sea, dim sky,—a level streak or two,—
A gradual flush in the chilly atmosphere,—
What flames upon that eastern head ?   The Sun !
A blazing point—a hemisphere—full orb—
Laying a road of gold across the wave,
Gilding wet glossy sands, green-swarded cliffs,
Fresh-flowing tide-streams, far-off sails, tower-clouds.
Till wide-spread heaven, as lifts the Globe of Fire,
Is fill'd with yellow light, and Day rules all,
Two Shrimpers, black amid the radiancy,
Pushing their nets along the ripple's verge,
These are the only life ; our silent Town,
With smokeless chimneys, glittering window-panes,
Still sunk in torpor and fantastic dreams.
Town after Town along this English coast,
And down the shore of France, awakes in turn :
Thousands of ships, unpausing day or night,
Of every country bathed by the salt flood,
Slide smooth between them, each upon its course,
As rolling Earth on hers, and I on mine,
And each on his of all my fellowmen.

Wish Tower Hill, *August* 10, 1889,
4.30-5 a.m.

[The improvement in health was, alas, but for the time.   After his return home on September 5, he slowly grew worse.   Sometimes the trouble seemed almost too great to be borne : but, now and again, there were moments when he could detach himself from the present, as it were, and feel an interest, even write a little, about outside matters.

For some time past he had been revising his poems for a final edition, of six volumes—most of which had, by now, appeared—also preparing his prose writings for press.]

October 23.—I resume writing here after a long interval.

Du Maurier has visited me often in the evening, and given me a pleasant hour's talk. He is better read, I imagine, in French than in English literature.

One night he read to me from *Les Femmes Savantes*. He thinks the scene of the two Poets, Trissotin and Vadius, the funniest thing in Molière.

He has nearly finished a story, one volume size. The hero acquires a power of regulating and continuing his dreams. In Dreamland he often meets a lady whom he has fallen in love with. He discovers that she has similar dreams, and meets him in her Dreamland. At length they find themselves able to communicate with each other in Dreamland. She dies : he dies in a lunatic asylum, leaving behind this narrative, ' Edited by G. du M.' I strongly advise him to intersperse plenty of sketches up and down the pages, and to offer it first, tentatively, to Harper.

I have had visits also from Harvey Orrinsmith : William Herford and his niece, Evelyn Herford : F. G. Stephens and his wife : Mr. Clayton—very agreeable and sympathetic man, lover of poetry and art. He began by recalling the time, nearly forty years ago, when he used to meet me at the P.R.B. evenings. Says he readily recollects my features and voice. Stephens and Mrs. S. came the same Sunday evening, and we had an harmonious tea-table in the dining-room. I read to them ' The Spinster's Sweet'arts,' and when done found that du M. had slipt silently into the room during the reading.

October 25.—Du M. came in about half-past six. We talked of his story. I cannot find that he himself has the least belief in the possibility, even the imaginative possibility, of the ground-motive of it. He regretted he could not now read Shakespeare, the time was past. Much-talked-of poets he looks into, as part of the social life of the day, and greatly admires Tennyson.

He lives in an atmosphere of conventional London

society and comic literature, mingled. Yet there is a deeper stratum in his mind than that which is amused and affected by these ; and he is an honourable fine-natured man, with various accomplishments—not speaking of his art genius—and great charm of manner. His descriptions of character, when it comes within his range, are keen and very neatly put.

[This is the last entry in the diary.

During the year, and especially in these last months, the intimate friendship of Mr. and Mrs. Alexander Carlyle was a constant help and comfort.

Mr. Briton Riviere would often come in for a little quiet talk ; also many other old friends.

The kindness and attention of his doctor, Mr. Buckston Browne, was untiring.

Here a note, taken from among Allingham's memoranda, seems to find a fitting place.

'I care for my old diaries for the sake of the Past, the sad, sacred, happy Past, whose pains, fears, sorrows, have put on the calm of eternity,—mysterious Past, for ever gone, for ever real, whose footsteps I see on every page, invisible to other eyes ! '

In November fresh complications arose in his illness, and, with these, an ever-increasing weakness, although he kept his bed only for about a week.

On Sunday the 17th it was evident that the end was very near.

When asked if he had any requests to make, he said 'No, my mind is at rest' : then to his wife

'"And so, to where I wait, come gently on."

'I thank you (to Mr. Buckston Browne)—I thank every one.'

After this he lay in a kind of trance, and died peacefully about two o'clock in the afternoon of the next day, November the 18th.

Once that morning he said, 'I am seeing things that you know nothing of.'

The cremation, which was by his special wish, took place at Woking.

A few friends and relations only were present.

There was no service : Mr. F. G. Stephens, the oldest of the friends there gathered together, read aloud Allingham's own Poet's Epitaph :—

> 'Body to purifying flame,
>   Soul to the Great Deep whence it came,
>   Leaving a song on earth below,
>   An urn of ashes white as snow.'

The urn was buried in the churchyard at Bally-shannon.

> 'No funeral gloom, my dears, when I am gone,
>   Corpse-gazings, tears, black raiment, grave-yard grimness ;
>   Think of me as withdrawn into the dimness,
>   Yours still, you mine, remember all the best
>   Of our past moments, and forget the rest ;
>   And so, to where I wait, come gently on.']

LIST OF WORKS

Published in

1850.   *Poems.* Dedicated 'To Leigh Hunt, Esq.' (Chapman and Hall.)

1854 and 1855. *The Music Master,* a Love Story, and two series of Day and Night Songs. With nine woodcuts, seven designed by Arthur Hughes, one by D. G. Rossetti, and one by John E. Millais, A.R.A. (Routledge and Co.)

1860.   *Day and Night Songs* ; and *The Music Master.* A Love Poem. With nine woodcuts (as above). 'This little volume comprises, along with the *Day and Night Songs* of the writer, published in 1854, a second series of short poems, and a narrative composition. Some of these appeared in a volume published in 1850, and since withdrawn, some in periodicals ; others are now added, and all have been carefully revised. *The Music Master,* in particular, is perhaps nearly entitled to be considered as a new poem' (from Preface). (Bell and Daldy.)

1860.   *Nightingale Valley.* A collection, including a great number of the choicest lyrics and short poems in the English language Edited by Giraldus. (Bell and Daldy.)

1862.   Reissue of *Nightingale Valley.* A collection of choice lyrics and short poems. From the time of Shakespeare to the present day. Edited by William Allingham. (Bell and Daldy.)

1864.   *Laurence Bloomfield in Ireland.* A modern poem. This poem first appeared in *Fraser's Magazine,* and is now presented much revised and partly rearranged (from Preface). (Macmillan and Co.)

1865.   *Fifty Modern Poems.* 'To A. F.' (Bell and Daldy.)

1869.   A new issue of *Laurence Bloomfield in Ireland* ; or The New Landlord. (Macmillan and Co.)

1872.   *The Ballad Book.* A selection of the choicest British ballads. Edited by William Allingham. (Macmillan and Co.)

1873.   *Rambles* by Patricius Walker. Dedicated 'To Mr. and Mrs. W. H. Forbes.' (Longmans, Green and Co.)

1877.   *Songs, Ballads, and Stories,* including many now first collected, the rest revised and rearranged. (George Bell and Sons.)

1882.   *Ashby Manor.* Dedicated 'To my Wife.' And *Evil May Day.* Dedicated 'To my Children.' (Longmans, Green and Co.)

Published in

1884. *Day and Night Songs.* Dedicated 'To my Friends' (a new edition). And *Blackberries*, picked off many bushes by D. Pollex and others : put in a basket by W. Allingham. (G. Philip and Son.)

1886. *Rhymes for the Young Folk.* Dedicated 'To Gerald, Eva and Little Henry, and others like them.' With pictures by Helen Allingham, Kate Greenaway, Caroline Paterson, and Harry Furniss. (Cassell and Co., Ltd.)

1887. *Irish Songs and Poems*, with nine airs harmonised for voice and pianoforte. (Reeves and Turner.)

1888. *Flower Pieces* and Other Poems. Dedicated 'To Dante Gabriel Rossetti, whose early friendship brightened many days of my life, and whom I never can forget.' With two designs by Dante Gabriel Rossetti. *Laurence Bloomfield.* Dedicated to Samuel Ferguson. (Reeves and Turner.)

1892. New edition of *The Ballad Book*, Golden Treasury Series. Edited by William Allingham. (Macmillan and Co.)

1893. *Varieties in Prose*, including 'Rambles by Patricius Walker,' and Essays, now first collected. A portrait of the Author is in Vol. I. (Longmans, Green and Co.)

1890. *The Works.* In six volumes.
1905. *Sixteen Poems.* Selected by W. B. Yeats.
1907. *A Diary.* Edited by H. Allingham and D. Radford.
1912. *Poems.* Selected and arranged by Helen Allingham.
1912. *By the Way.* Verses, Fragments and Notes arranged by Helen Allingham.
1914. *Letters from William Allingham to Robert and Elizabeth Barrett Browning.*
1945. *A Bibliography of William Allingham.* P. S. O'Hegarty.
1951. *Poetry in Ulster.* J. N. Browne. (In *The Arts in Ulster*, edited S. H. Bell).

INDEX

395

399

THE END

MORE ABOUT PENGUINS, PELICANS, PEREGRINES AND PUFFINS

For further information about books available from Penguins please write to Dept EP, Penguin Books Ltd, Harmondsworth, Middlesex UB7 0DA.

In the U.S.A.: For a complete list of books available from Penguins in the United States write to Dept DG, Penguin Books, 299 Murray Hill Parkway, East Rutherford, New Jersey 07073.

In Canada: For a complete list of books available from Penguins in Canada write to Penguin Books Canada Ltd, 2801 John Street, Markham, Ontario L3R 1B4.

In Australia: For a complete list of books available from Penguins in Australia write to the Marketing Department, Penguin Books Australia Ltd, P.O. Box 257, Ringwood, Victoria 3134.

In New Zealand: For a complete list of books available from Penguins in New Zealand write to the Marketing Department, Penguin Books (N.Z.) Ltd, Private Bag, Takapuna, Auckland 9.

In India: For a complete list of books available from Penguins in India write to Penguin Overseas Ltd, 706 Eros Apartments, 56 Nehru Place, New Delhi 110019.

THE PENGUIN ENGLISH DICTIONARY

The Penguin English Dictionary has been created specially for today's needs. It features:

* More entries than any other popularly priced dictionary
* Exceptionally clear and precise definitions
* For the first time in an equivalent dictionary, the internationally recognised IPA pronunciation system
* Emphasis on contemporary usage
* Extended coverage of both the spoken and the written word
* Scientific tables
* Technical words
* Informal and colloquial expressions
* Vocabulary most widely used *wherever* English is spoken
* Most commonly used abbreviations

It is twenty years since the publication of the last English dictionary by Penguin and the compilation of this entirely new *Penguin English Dictionary* is the result of a special collaboration between Longman, one of the world's leading dictionary publishers, and Penguin Books. The material is based entirely on the database of the acclaimed *Longman Dictionary of the English Language.*

1008 pages   051.139 3   £2.50   ☐

PENGUIN TRAVEL BOOKS

☐ **Arabian Sands** **Wilfred Thesiger** £3.50

'In the tradition of Burton, Doughty, Lawrence, Philby and Thomas, it is, very likely, the book about Arabia to end all books about Arabia' – *Daily Telegraph*

☐ **The Flight of Ikaros** **Kevin Andrews** £3.50

'He also is in love with the country . . . but he sees the other side of that dazzling medal or moon . . . If you want some truth about Greece, here it is' – Louis MacNeice in the *Observer*

☐ **D. H. Lawrence and Italy** £4.95

In *Twilight in Italy, Sea and Sardinia* and *Etruscan Places,* Lawrence recorded his impressions while living, writing and travelling in 'one of the most beautiful countries in the world'.

☐ **Maiden Voyage** **Denton Welch** £3.50

Opening during his last term at public school, from which the author absconded, *Maiden Voyage* turns into a brilliantly idiosyncratic account of China in the 1930s.

☐ **The Grand Irish Tour** **Peter Somerville-Large** £4.95

The account of a year's journey round Ireland. 'Marvellous . . . describes to me afresh a landscape I thought I knew' – Edna O'Brien in the *Observer*

☐ **Slow Boats to China** **Gavin Young** £3.95

On an ancient steamer, a cargo dhow, a Filipino kumpit and twenty more agreeably cranky boats, Gavin Young sailed from Piraeus to Canton in seven crowded and colourful months. 'A pleasure to read' – Paul Theroux

PENGUIN TRAVEL BOOKS

☐ *The Kingdom by the Sea* **Paul Theroux**   £2.50

1982, the year of the Falklands War and the Royal Baby, was the ideal time, Theroux found, to travel round the coast of Britain and surprise the British into talking about themselves. 'He describes it all brilliantly and honestly' – Anthony Burgess

☐ *One's Company* **Peter Fleming**   £2.95

His journey to China as special correspondent to *The Times* in 1933. 'One reads him for literary delight . . . But, he is also an observer of penetrating intellect' – Vita Sackville West

☐ *The Traveller's Tree* **Patrick Leigh Fermor**   £3.95

'A picture of the Indies more penetrating and original than any that has been presented before' – *Observer*

☐ *The Path to Rome* **Hilaire Belloc**   £3.95

'The only book I ever wrote for love,' is how Belloc described the wonderful blend of anecdote, humour and reflection that makes up the story of his pilgrimage to Rome.

☐ *The Light Garden of the Angel King* **Peter Levi**   £2.95

Afghanistan has been a wild rocky highway for nomads and merchants, Alexander the Great, Buddhist monks, great Moghul conquerors and the armies of the Raj. Here, quite brilliantly, Levi writes about their journeys and his own.

☐ *Among the Russians* **Colin Thubron**   £2.95

'The Thubron approach to travelling has an integrity that belongs to another age' – Dervla Murphy in the *Irish Times*. 'A magnificent achievement' – Nikolai Tolstoy

A CHOICE OF PENGUINS

☐ **The Complete Penguin Stereo Record and Cassette Guide**
Greenfield, Layton and March £7.95

A new edition, now including information on compact discs. 'One of the few indispensables on the record collector's bookshelf' – *Gramophone*

☐ **Selected Letters of Malcolm Lowry**
Edited by Harvey Breit and Margerie Bonner Lowry £5.95

'Lowry emerges from these letters not only as an extremely interesting man, but also a lovable one' – Philip Toynbee

☐ **The First Day on the Somme**
Martin Middlebrook £3.95

1 July 1916 was the blackest day of slaughter in the history of the British Army. 'The soldiers receive the best service a historian can provide: their story told in their own words' – *Guardian*

☐ **A Better Class of Person** John Osborne £1.95

The playwright's autobiography, 1929–56. 'Splendidly enjoyable' – John Mortimer. 'One of the best, richest and most bitterly truthful autobiographies that I have ever read' – Melvyn Bragg

☐ **The Winning Streak** Goldsmith and Clutterbuck £2.95

Marks & Spencer, Saatchi & Saatchi, United Biscuits, GEC . . . The UK's top companies reveal their formulas for success, in an important and stimulating book that no British manager can afford to ignore.

☐ **The First World War** A. J. P. Taylor £3.95

'He manages in some 200 illustrated pages to say almost everything that is important . . . A special text . . . a remarkable collection of photographs' – *Observer*

A CHOICE OF PENGUINS

☐ *Man and the Natural World* **Keith Thomas** £4.95

Changing attitudes in England, 1500–1800. 'An encyclopedic study of man's relationship to animals and plants . . . a book to read again and again' – Paul Theroux, *Sunday Times* Books of the Year

☐ *Jean Rhys: Letters 1931–66*
Edited by Francis Wyndham and Diana Melly £3.95

'Eloquent and invaluable . . . her life emerges, and with it a portrait of an unexpectedly indomitable figure' – Marina Warner in the *Sunday Times*

☐ *The French Revolution* **Christopher Hibbert** £4.50

'One of the best accounts of the Revolution that I know . . . Mr Hibbert is outstanding' – J. H. Plumb in the *Sunday Telegraph*

☐ *Isak Dinesen* **Judith Thurman** £4.95

The acclaimed life of Karen Blixen, 'beautiful bride, disappointed wife, radiant lover, bereft and widowed woman, writer, sibyl, Scheherazade, child of Lucifer, Baroness; always a unique human being . . . an assiduously researched and finely narrated biography' – *Books & Bookmen*

☐ *The Amateur Naturalist*
Gerald Durrell with Lee Durrell £4.95

'Delight . . . on every page . . . packed with authoritative writing, learning without pomposity . . . it represents a real bargain' – *The Times Educational Supplement*. 'What treats are in store for the average British household' – *Daily Express*

☐ *When the Wind Blows* **Raymond Briggs** £2.95

'A visual parable against nuclear war: all the more chilling for being in the form of a strip cartoon' – *Sunday Times*. 'The most eloquent anti-Bomb statement you are likely to read' – *Daily Mail*